*Conflict
in the
Southern Cone*

Conflict in the Southern Cone

The Argentine Military and the Boundary Dispute with Chile, 1870–1902

George v. Rauch

PRAEGER

Westport, Connecticut
London

Library of Congress Cataloging-in-Publication Data

Rauch, George v.
    Conflict in the Southern Cone : the Argentine military and the
boundary dispute with Chile, 1870–1902 / George v. Rauch.
      p. cm.
    Includes bibliographical references (p. –) and index.
    ISBN 0–275–96347–0 (alk. paper)
    1. Argentina—Relations—Chile. 2. Chile—Relations—Argentina.
3. Argentina—Boundaries—Chile. 4. Chile—Boundaries—Argentina.
5. Argentina—Armed Forces—History—19th century. 6. Chile—Armed
Forces—History—19th century.
F2833.5.C5R38   1999
303.48'282083—dc21   98–44597

British Library Cataloguing in Publication Data is available.

Library of Congress Catalog Card Number: 98–44597
ISBN: 0–275–96347–0

First published in 1999

Praeger Publishers, 88 Post Road West, Westport, CT 06881
An imprint of Greenwood Publishing Group, Inc.
www.praeger.com

Printed in the United States of America

The paper used in this book complies with the
Permanent Paper Standard issued by the National
Information Standards Organization (Z39.48–1984).

10 9 8 7 6 5 4 3 2 1

Copyright Acknowledgment

English translation of poem on page 7 reprinted from *A History of Argentine Political Thought* by
Jose Luis Romero with the permission of the publishers, Stanford University Press, © 1963, renewed
1991, by the Board of Trustees of the Leland Stanford Junior University.

Contents

Tables

Preface

Early in the twentieth century the most progressive states in South America braced themselves for war over possession of territories situated in the Southern Andes. Although these countries had much in common, their political and economic developments had taken different paths.

This book will discuss the development and growth of the Argentine armed forces in relationship to the boundary dispute with Chile. Although a substantial bibliography on the boundary question exists in English as well as Spanish, no comprehensive study of the role played by the Argentine armed forces and their development in relation to the frontier dispute with Chile has ever been undertaken. This is precisely what prompted me to begin such a study. My own interest in the Argentine armed forces and their institutional development began in 1962, when I first came across the ample Chilean bibliography on the dispute. However, the often told incident about the Chilean "ultimatum" presented to Argentina in 1898 did not seem to be fully documented. According to most Chilean sources, the Platine nation was given a choice between arbitration and war. Confronted with her own military weakness, Argentina complied with Chilean demands. Yet a simple glance at the more commonly available naval annuals of the period negated the Chilean claim that in 1898 her navy was the strongest in South America. An investigation of the arms purchasing process of both countries seemed to point out that the Argentine army had not only more than sufficient guns and powder, but almost three times as much modern artillery as the potential rival.

During the second half of the nineteenth century, the growth and development of the armed forces of the major powers as well as Alfred Mahan's theories on sea power and the development of the English navy highlighted the strategic and geopolitical uses of military power. In the Ibero-American world, these influences were felt during the process of modernization. Most works on the subject save but a few published in Argentina have emphasized the superiority of the Chilean armed forces over their Argentine counterparts. One of the major problems, in order to weigh the opposing views, is the lack of detailed works on the institutions involved and the arms-purchasing process. Few of the European or American studies on the subject appear to be objective. If the Chilean armed forces were indeed superior, as for example most Chilean sources would have us believe, why did Argentina emerge as the victor in the boundary dispute according to these same sources? If the Argentines were so badly equipped and led, why were they feared?

The present study was undertaken in order to answer these questions. Chapter 1 deals with the discovery and settlement of the land that is now Argentina, its development from a forgotten colony of the Spanish Crown to viceroyalty, as well as the coming of independence, which led to the breakup of the old colonial order and the dissolution of the Argentine national state that succeeded the viceroyalty.

Chapter 2 covers the boundary dispute from 1843 to the "Conquest of the Desert." While Argentina was balkanized and ceased to function as a nation-state, Chile emerged as a strong nation in the 1840s and began to project southward. Argentina was torn by the never-ending wars between Unitarians and Federals and could not deal with what she considered the Chilean challenge. A lengthy debate over colonial titles, which were quite often contradicting and overlapping, began during the 1850s. Both nations concluded a treaty of friendship and commerce in 1856 by which they agreed to respect the *utis possidetis* of 1810. Both countries claimed Patagonia as their own, but for Argentina its possession was doubly imperative, for control of Patagonia would in turn render the *pampas*, so vulnerable to Indian attacks, safe for colonization. Offensive sallies against the fierce tribes of the region were planned as early as the eighteenth century but would not materialize until 1833, when Juan Manuel de Rosas led his forces into the "desert," inflicted grievous losses upon the Indians, and afterward concluded a peace treaty with them.

The overthrow of Rosas in 1852 meant an end to the truce and the renewal of large-scale raids on the towns and settlements of the pampas. A war against Paraguay in the 1860s as well as *caudillo* risings in the years that followed delayed a permanent solution to the Indian threat. A series of military outposts stretching from the province of Buenos Aires to the Andes had stood guard against the hostile tribes since the eighteenth century. To meet the needs of the expanding livestock sector for grazing lands, the frontier was pushed further south, until the various tribes, molded into a "Confederation" by the Araucanian chief Calfucurá began to launch massive attacks, and settlement after settlement was destroyed.

The motivating factor behind these raids was of course the wealth in cattle, horses, and booty offered by the plains of Argentina. The drain on Argentine resources was considerable, and by obstructing Argentine control of Patagonia, the Indians were in fact creating a ''no-man's land'' whose northernmost limits coincided with the most extreme of all Chilean claims to Patagonia. After a series of hit and run strikes to debilitate the Indian tribes, the Argentine army began the 1879 ''Conquest of the Desert.''

Chapter 3 examines the Conquest of the Desert and its end results. In 1879 Chile went to war against Bolivia and Peru. Argentina, which was in a stronger bargaining position, began her long-delayed campaign against the so-called pampa Indians. The latter were largely Araucanians who had migrated in large numbers into the Argentine plains throughout the 1830s and 1850s. A vast and meticulously planned operation designed to capture as many Indians as possible was undertaken by General Julio A. Roca with five fast-moving divisions. In little over a month, Patagonia was at last secured. A treaty concluded between Argentina and Chile in 1881 awarded Patagonia to Argentina. An additional campaign undertaken during 1881 to 1883 to complete the occupation of the southern portion of Patagonia led to renewed fighting with the Araucanians and occasional border clashes with Chile. By 1884, Argentina was in full possession of the territories awarded her by the convention of 1881. This treaty established a line drawn between the peaks of the Andes, which affected the water parting. Yet different interpretations of the criteria resulted in tensions which, in turn, brought about an arms race.

Chapter 4 reviews the economic growth of Argentina and Chile. When available, trade surpluses provided much of the revenue that both of the countries required to cover government expenditures. Whereas by the early 1870s the foreign trade and government revenues of both nations were roughly equivalent, by 1900 Argentine foreign trade was almost three times as large as Chile's, and her revenues were on the average 1.5 times as large as those of the Transandine nation; hence she was able to devote greater sums to military spending. Foreign immigration, which was vital to Argentine agriculture as well as overall national development, contributed to population growth. Many in Chile feared that their nation would soon be relegated to a secondary status to Argentina. Whereas both countries had approximately equal populations in 1870, or about 1.6 million people each, thanks to successive waves of immigration, the population of Argentina topped the 4 million mark in 1900, while Chile's barely exceeded 2.6 million. Quite naturally manpower resources available for mobilization in Argentina became considerably larger than Chile's.

Chapter 5 provides the essential background for understanding the institutional development of the Argentine armed forces in the last quarter of the nineteenth century, their arms-purchasing process and mobilization procedures. The central logic addressed in this book is the transition made by the armed forces of Argentina in the latter part of the nineteenth century. The Argentine army in 1862 was little more than a poorly supplied militia backed by hastily trained national guard contingents. Similarly, the Argentine navy did not exist as such, except for a few armed packet steamers. Yet by the late 1890s, in response to the Chilean boundary dispute, both of these services had evolved into formidable deterrents.

Chapter 6 analyzes the Chilean armed forces and compares them with their Argentine counterparts, in terms of capabilities, training, manpower mobilization, and equipment programs. Because military strength played such an important role in the eventual solution of the dispute, the war potential of each nation deserves careful analysis. From a comparative perspective, it becomes clear that the policies pursued by the Argentine government provided the economic base for the development and growth of an export economy resilient enough to withstand defense military expenditures designed to wrest military and naval superiority from Chile.

In Chapter 7, the focus shifts to an analysis of the geographic basis of the dispute along the Southern Andes as well as the diplomatic aspects that brought both nations to the brink of war on several occasions.

Much has been discussed in Argentine and Chilean works about the solution of the long-standing frontier controversy. There is a good deal of evidence to suggest that many of the leading Chilean figures involved in this process compiled their memoirs and reports according to their aspirations and according to the roles they wished to play, or those they wished they had played, rather than on the events as they actually occurred. Chilean works on the boundary dispute, based systematically on these sources, are inherently flawed and should be treated with care. Most of the territory in dispute had already been awarded to Argentina by the Treaty of 1881. What remained for demarcation after the convention was a territory almost as large as Hungary, but what was really involved was a question of South American supremacy and prestige. Who emerged as the victor can be best judged by the events of the succeeding decades.

The author has made use of primary materials from the National Archives of Argentina and the United States, as well as from the Public Records Office facilities at London and Hemel Hempstead and the Museo Roca at Buenos Aires. Research in these facilities has produced documents that have contributed to this study. Most of the extensive bibliography available, whether Argentine or Chilean, is partisan but cannot be ignored.

The author wishes to thank his wife, Helene, who helped to research and copy primary documents in Argentine, British, and U.S. Archives, proofread some of the chapters, and warmly encouraged and supported him in the long gestation period of this work.

Abbreviations

AM	*Archivo del General Mitre*
AOC	*La Argentina desde el ochenta al centenario*
BAPU	*Bulletin of the Pan American Union*
BCN	*Boletín del Centro Naval*, Buenos Aires
CHNCD	*Congreso sobre la historia de la Conquista del Desierto*
CHLA	*Cambridge History of Latin America*
DE	*Desarrollo Económico*, Buenos Aires
EST	*Estrategia*, Buenos Aires
EUDEBA	*Editorial Universitaria de Buenos Aires*
GP	*A Guerra do Paraguai*
HAC	*Historia Argentina Contemporánea*
HAHR	*Hispanic American Historical Review*
IE	*Investigaciones y Ensayos*, Buenos Aires
JEH	*Journal of Economic History*
JISWA	*Journal of Latin American Studies and World Affairs*
JLAS	*Journal of Latin American Studies*
MB	*Monthly Bulletin of the Pan American Union*
RCHG	*Revista Chilena de Historia y Geografía*
RH	*Revista Histórica*, Buenos Aires
2o. CNRHA	*Segundo Congreso Nacional y Regional de Historia Argentina*
3o. CNRHA	*Tercer Congreso Nacional y Regional de Historia Argentina*
4o. CNRHA	*Cuarto Congreso Nacional y Regional de Historia Argentina*
6o. CNRHA	*Sexto Congreso Nacional y Regional de Historia Argentina*
TAM	*The Americas*

1

The Frontier in Argentine History

Spain's conquest and exploration of present-day Argentina began in the early part of the sixteenth century, when Juan Díaz de Solís discovered a wide body of water he named Mar Dulce, or "Sweet Sea." Others would follow in his footsteps. Ferdinand Magellan would explore the shores of Patagonia and discover the Straits that now bear his name, while Sebastian Cabot would venture into the Paraná, Pilcomayo, and Paraguay rivers and eventually found the first Spanish upriver settlement in the region, the fort of Sancti Spiriti, near the present-day city of Rosario. A misguided belief in the area's mineral wealth caused Cabot to rename the broad, chocolate-colored body of water Solís had discovered Río de la Plata, the "River of Silver," or "River Plate," as Englishmen would later call it.[1]

The lure of new world silver also attracted the Portuguese to the Plate area. To safeguard Spain's interest in the region, the crown appointed Pedro de Mendoza as *adelantado*, or royal advance agent. Mendoza sailed from Sanlúcar de Barrameda on August 24, 1535, with an impressive expedition consisting of fourteen ships and 1,500 men. The fleet reached the estuary of the Plate in January. Mendoza reconnoitered the shore, and on February 3 he founded a settlement known as Nuestra Señora Santa María del Buen Aire ("Our Lady Saint Mary of the Fair Wind"), a name that with the passing of time would be shortened to Buenos Aires.[2]

Initially, relations between the Querandí Indians who inhabited the region were cordial, but this state of affairs proved to be short-lived, as the Querandís massacred a Spanish foraging party and laid siege to the palisaded settlement.[3] Short of provisions, the inhabitants of this first Buenos Aires were soon reduced to eating rodents and even leather furnishings. Discouraged and ill, Mendoza decided to abandon the settlement and commissioned his lieutenants to head

upstream with a small flotilla.[4] Juan de Ayolas, one of his subordinates, rees-
tablished an outpost near the ruins of Sancti Spiriti and erected a fort at the
junction of the Paraná and Paraguay rivers at a natural port which he named
Candelarias.[5] While Ayolas, lured by tales of a silver mountain, ventured into
the jungles of the Chaco, his lieutenant governor, Martinez de Irala, outfitted a
small expedition that sailed upriver and established the settlement of Asunción.[6]

By mid-1541, 350 men, strung out on a wide arc between Buenos Aires,
Candelarias, and Asunción, were all that remained of Mendoza's once proud
expedition. Irala decided to concentrate the meager forces at his disposal at one
single strong point, Asunción; thus he evacuated Buenos Aires and burned that
unfortunate settlement. The abandonment and destruction of the first Buenos
Aires resulted in the dispersion of the small herds of cattle and horses that the
Spaniards had brought with them.[7]

Ironically, in their search for gold and silver, the Conquistadores had completely overlooked the vast and seemingly endless plains that surrounded their
settlement and which one day would become more productive than any of the
silver-bearing districts of other Spanish colonial possessions. These plains, or
pampas, include the territories occupied by the current provinces of Buenos
Aires, Santa Fé, Córdoba, and La Pampa. These pampas rest on a base of shat-
tered and worn granite upon which erosion has despited hundreds of feet of
sediments that have created these fertile, temperate zone plains.[8]

Free to roam at will, the horses and cattle that survived the destruction of
Buenos Aires multiplied almost prodigiously. The size of these herds astonished
the members of an expedition led by Juan de Garay, which established the
second Buenos Aires in 1580. These wild herds would continue to grow unimpeded until they came to constitute the lifeblood of the new colony.[9] The
pampas are but one of the regions of Argentina. The other regions include the
Andes, the Argentine Mesopotamia, the Chaco, and Patagonia. Andean Argentina extends from Patagonia in the south to the Bolivian border. On the west it
is bordered by the Chilean frontier, and on the north by the Chaco region.

The northern half of Andean Argentina includes the provinces of Jujuy, la
Rioja, Salta, and Tucumán in the pre-Cordillera, as well as Catamarca and the
southern half of Santiago del Estero. A subdivision of Andean Argentina known
as the Cuyo region comprises the provinces of Mendoza, San Juan and San
Luís. The Andean portion of Argentina is predominantly arid, although rainfall
and streams, seconded in modern times by artificial irrigation, have made the
development of crops possible. Cuyo was famed as a wine-producing area even
during the colonial period.[10]

The Chaco region includes the northern half of the provinces of Santiago del
Estero as well as the provinces of Formosa, Chaco, and the northern portions
of the provinces of Córdoba and Santa Fé. The Chaco is covered by scrub forest
and grassy savannas and is traversed by major rivers, such as the Pilcomayo in
the north and the Salado in the south.[11] The provinces of Entre Ríos, Corrientes,
and Misiones constitute the Argentine Mesopotamia, whose borders are bathed

by tributaries of the Paraná and Uruguay rivers. In modern times, oceangoing vessels sail upstream as far as Concepción del Uruguay, while large river boats make the journey to Asunción.[12]

Patagonia stretches almost 2,000 kilometers from the Río Colorado to Tierra del Fuego and covers the provinces of Chubut, Neuquén, Santa Cruz, Río Negro, the National Territory of Tierra del Fuego as well as the Southern half of the province of Buenos Aires. While eastern Patagonia is a land of arid plateaus, criss-crossed by rivers and streams formed by the melting snows, western Patagonia receives substantial amounts of rainfall and is dotted with fertile valleys and lakes.[13]

After the failure of the first attempt of colonization from the east, Spanish explorers penetrated Argentina from the west and from the north, using old Inca trails. These newcomers from Peru settled in northwestern Argentina, beginning with the foundation of Santiago del Estero in 1553. Spanish explorers based in Chile would found Córdoba del Calchaquí, Cañete and Mendoza (1561), San Juan (1562), Tucumán (1565), Córdoba and Santa Fé (1573).[14]

The land under the jurisdiction of Tucumán and the Cuyo region were initially dependencies of the Spanish authorities in Chile. In 1564, Tucumán was placed under the jurisdiction of Peru and Chilean jurisdiction east of the Andes was confined to Cuyo. In fact, further Chilean expansion to the east was expressly forbidden by royal decrees.[15]

In due course, Tucumán would be established as a large governorship comprising the provinces of Córdoba, Salta, and Santiago del Estero and spanning an area of some 700,000 square kilometers. Following the rise of Potosí as a silver-producing area in Upper Peru, Tucumán became an economic appendage of that region. It would provide the silver-mining town with a vast range of raw materials and processed goods, livestock, textiles, and carriages of various sorts, establishing a relationship that would endure well into the nineteenth century. A dichotomy based on economic grounds that would split Argentina asunder during most of the nineteenth century thus emerged. Buenos Aires, rebuilt in 1580, later became a shipping outlet for Paraguay and Upper Peru. The merchants of the port city smuggled silver in order to defray imports of European goods and African slaves that entered Buenos Aires until that port was closed to the slave trade in 1605. In fact, Buenos Aires emerged as a vital link between Potosí and Brazil.[16]

THE SOUTHWESTERN FRONTIER

In his work about the frontier in Latin American history, Alistair Hennessy describes various types of frontiers, mainly: (1) the silver frontier, (2) the mission frontier, (3) the cattle frontier, (4) the political frontier; and (5) the Indian frontier. All of these frontiers could be found in colonial Argentina. The "silver connection" mentioned earlier developed as it reduced the time needed to convert silver into imported goods. Instead of the four months required by llama trains slowly and laboriously driven over ancient Inca trails to reach coastal Peru, the wagon trains of Tucumán reached it in half that time.[17]

The mission frontier evolved as a result of the activities of the Jesuits along northeastern Argentina and Paraguay during the early 1600s. By the late 1640s, some thirty Indian communities, or *reducciones*, with a population well in excess of 100,000, were under Jesuit control. The order was also active in Patagonia, among the Araucanians.[18]

Under Platine conditions, as mentioned, horses and cattle had multiplied at a prodigious rate. Cattle and hides became the economic staple of the region. In the limitless pampas, devoid of trees and iron deposits, leather would substitute for wood and nails; leather flaps served as door and windows. The wheels of carriages were bound with the same material and leather rather than canvas covered the wagons that plied the overland trails between Buenos Aires and Tucumán. The industrial revolution in Europe and the wars that followed the French revolution increased the demand for leather. Buenos Aires met much of the demand and prospered.[19]

The political frontier in the northeast was born as a result of a territorial dispute between Spain and Portugal. According to the Papal bulls, the 23rd Parallel divided Spanish and Portuguese dominions in the new world. Whereas Spanish claims were based upon legal definitions, the Portuguese applied the principle of *utis possidetis*. Thus, Portuguese Brazil expanded westward over territories that belonged to its Spanish American territories, except at the Rio de la Plata, where the militias of Buenos Aires, supported by peninsular troops and Guaraní Indians from the Jesuit missions, were able to check Portuguese encroachment in the area.[20]

Finally, there were two Indian frontiers in Argentina: one in the southwest and the other in the north. The northern frontier consisted of the scrub forests and arid lands of the Chaco. Various factors discouraged development of the northern frontier. The fierce Chaco Indians raided settlements and wagon trains, but these attacks did not induce government concern because the area offered little economic inducement. Therefore, by 1810 the northern Indian frontier remained basically what it had been two hundred years earlier.[21]

The southwestern frontier, in direct contrast, was economically important. It extended in a sort of semicircle from an area roughly 100 kilometers south of the city of Buenos Aires, curving in a northwesterly direction across the provinces of Santa Fé, Córdoba and the Cuyo region. At this time, hostile Indian tribes occupied vast areas to the south, an underdeveloped domain of nearly 1.2 million square kilometers, larger than the combined areas of France, Italy, and Spain. Large numbers of Araucanian Indians from neighboring Chile had migrated to the Argentine pampas during the first half of the eighteenth century, attracted by the immense herds of cattle and horses that gave them both sustenance and mobility.[22] Simultaneously, the ever-demanding requirements of the merchants of Buenos Aires for cattle and horses pushed them further south, thus sowing the seeds for future discord. Temporary truces were concluded between the Spanish authorities and the so-called pampa Indians during the 1730s, but as white settlers attempted to push their line of colonization further south, the Indians retaliated by raiding the towns of the pampas. A line of defense was not established until 1739, after a large-scale Indian attack (*malón*) wrought havoc to the towns of Luján, Areco, Matanzas, and Magdalena. To counteract these raids, the first *fortin*, or outpost, was established at Arrecifes in 1739. These fortines were crude installations which comprised a few straw-roofed structures with walls of sun-dried mud bricks and were surrounded by a palisade or sometimes a moat and crowned by a watchtower called *mangrullo*.[23]

Financial stringency and the lack of experienced troops prevented further expansion of the line of defense. To remedy the situation, the governor of Buenos Aires sought to raise local militias that would be financed through a new tax levied on the salt merchants. Poor administration of the funds frustrated this project. To fill the gap, the settlers volunteered their services, but neither proper training nor arms were available, and so this experiment also failed.[24]

In their place, in February 1752, the governor of Buenos Aires authorized the creation of several companies of mounted militia, known as Blandengues. Pressed for funds, the cabildo, or town council, of Buenos Aires levied a tax on all iron, steel, wine, and brandies imported through the port city. Furthermore, in order to consolidate the frontier, the cabildo sought to establish military colonies, agricultural settlements in which members of the militia would be granted lands, farm animals, and agricultural implements. Salto, Sanjón, Laguna Brava, and Laguna de los Lobos became the first outposts in what would later become a permanent line of defense to guard the frontier against Indian attacks.[25]

When the Viceroyalty of the Río de la Plata was established in 1776, Pedro de Ceballos, the newly appointed viceroy, sought to establish additional fortines and proposed an *entrada general*, or offensive sally, against the Indians, employing a force of 10,000 to 12,000 men. Before he could implement this far-sighted project, Lieutenant General Juan José de Vertíz had been appointed as his successor. Rather than an expedition Vertíz chose to extend the line of frontier outposts. Accordingly, Lieutenant Francisco Betzebe was entrusted with the task of exploring the frontier and finding suitable locations for the new forts. Six forts were to be erected at Rojas, Salto, Luján, Monte, Ranchos, and Chascomús, and fortines or *guardias* at Melincué, Mercedes, Areco Navarro, and Lobos. Major forts would be garrisoned by a company of Blandengues, and the smaller outposts by detachments of twelve to sixteen men that would be relieved periodically. The southwestern frontier of Buenos Aires would remain basically unchanged until the immediate postindependence period.[26]

Another line of fortines guarded the southern flank of the province of Córdoba. The Cordoban outposts were manned by a 100-man company known as Los partidarios de la Frontera. This defensive line was centered around Fort La Carlota and curved west, toward the San Luís border. There were fortines at Pilar, San Carlos, La Reducción, San Fernando, and La Concepción. East of Fort La Carlota the line extended up to the border with Buenos Aires, with fortines at San Rafael de los Lobos and Loreto as well as forts at Asunción and Tunas. The southern flank of Mendoza was protected by a force of twenty-five volunteer soldiers from Fort San Carlos, while the line at Santa Fé was guarded by a company of 100 Blandengues until the beginning of the nineteenth century.[27]

Buenos Aires was thus a focal point in which the silver, cattle, Indian, political, and mission frontiers met. Furthermore, the cattle frontier provided the Platine area with an exportable item for a growing area. The number of hides exported rose from an annual average of 150,000 during the 1700s to 800,000 by 1763 and to 1,400,000 by the turn of the century. The discovery of large salt deposits at Salinas Grandes, near Buenos Aires, was followed by the establishment of the first large-scale *saladeros*, or beef salting plants. The growth of the shipping industry, coupled with these developments, enabled the export of sizable amounts of *charquí*, or salt beef, to the Caribbean, England, and Spain.[28]

RISE OF THE VICEROYALTY

The establishment of a viceroyalty at Buenos Aires was but one of the many reforms implemented by the Bourbon dynasty to modernize government institutions and further economic development. During the reign of Charles III (1759–1788) some of the most enlightened reforms in this direction were enacted. Buenos Aires became the seat of an administrative unit that encompassed the modern states of Argentina, Bolivia, Paraguay, and Uruguay. Trade between Spain and her colonies had been monopolized by the Casa de Contratación since its inception in 1503. For greater administrative efficiency, the Casa de Contratación, along with the whole administrative machinery of the Carrera de Indias, or convoy system, channeled New World raw materials to Spain. The War of the Austrian Succession (1740–1748) forced Spain to abandon the convoy system. The port of Buenos Aires was opened to ships of Spanish register and thus furthered trade. Finally, in 1778 Buenos Aires and other colonial ports were granted the right of *comercio libre*, or free trade. This "free trade" only meant trade with selected Spanish ports, thus ending the trade monopoly that Cadíz had enjoyed during the eighteenth century.[29] In 1796 Spain entered into an alliance with France against England. As a result, Spain lost control of the sea lanes and could no longer supply her colonies. Consequently she was forced to make concessions.[30]

Trade between Spanish possessions and neutral nations such as Brazil and the newly independent United States was legalized. An emerging liberal faction in Buenos Aires, led by a rising young lawyer named Mariano Moreno, clamored for free trade. Moreno gained notoriety in the spring of 1809, when he published his *Representación de los Hacendados*. In this pamphlet, Moreno charged that the mercantile monopoly imposed by Spain had resulted in economic stagnation. With the demands for free trade inevitably came demands for political power as well. When the *porteños* (port dwellers or inhabitants of Buenos Aires) learned in May

1810 that Napoleon had conquered Spain, popular agitation soon translated into demands for a *cabildo abierto*, an open city council meeting. This was followed by the establishment of a governing body known as the Primera Junta, thus putting a de facto end to Spanish colonial rule. The junta soon experienced an ideological cleavage between liberals and conservatives. Moreno's faction proposed social reform, free trade, and a united Argentina. Cornelio Saavedra, the acknowledged leader of the conservative faction, was a merchant closely tied to the trade in hides. His faction did not want to change the social system, merely a change in the leadership.[31]

Although Moreno's faction initially prevailed, it was elbowed out by December 1810. The new junta reorganized the governmental structure creating several new provinces, including the Banda Oriental, or "eastern bank" of the Plate (the present-day state of Uruguay), Cuyo, and Tucumán. These would be further subdivided in later years. The successor state to the Viceroyalty of the Río de la Plata styled itself "the united provinces of the south." These measures were ephemeral, as many hinterland provinces had long raised the standard of rebellion against Buenos Aires and a rapid dissolution of the newly established state would soon follow.[32]

THE DISSOLUTION OF THE UNITED PROVINCES

The new trade patterns established by Buenos Aires at the turn of the century brought about a dislocation of the old colonial order. The merchants of Paraguay resented the taxes levied by the port city upon their tobacco and *yerba maté*. Their feelings were reciprocated in Corrientes, whose homespun textiles were driven from the market by English products under the free trade system implanted by Buenos Aires, and in Entre Ríos, whose hide producers were in direct competition with their counterparts in the port city. More importantly, there were the mine owners of Upper Peru, who were affronted by the increased taxes necessitated by military spending during the viceroyalty. Finally, the old colonial aristocracy at Charcas was staunchly proroyalist.[33]

Buenos Aires, on the other hand, was a proud and contented city. Its rising wealth and strong military had contributed decisively to the defense of the viceroyalty against Portuguese encroachment in the eighteenth century and repelled British invasions in 1806 and 1807, after the Spanish viceroy fled ignominiously. With genuine pride, one of her poets wrote:

> Let Sparta not speak of her virtues,
> nor Rome her grandeur flaunt;
> Silence! On the world's stage appears
> the mighty capital of the South![34]

The revolutionary junta sent expeditions to the interior in order to maintain control. In view of the deep-rooted resentment against the economic policies of

Buenos Aires in the hinterlands, it should not be too surprising that these expeditions did not meet with overwhelming success. A weak force under General Manuel Belgrano, a lawyer cum soldier, was dispatched to Paraguay in January 1811, only to be overwhelmed by Paraguayan militias that outnumbered it ten to one. Belgrano's ill-fated expedition was to the Paraguayans a replay of the British invasions of Buenos Aires, and it served to discredit the Spanish authorities at Asunción, who played a weak and indecisive role, while the Creoles undertook the defense of their country. Emboldened by their success, the Paraguayans overthrew the intendant of Asunción and appointed a junta that favored independence from Spain as well as from Buenos Aires.[35]

A similar fate befell the Auxiliary Army sent to Upper Peru. Despite initial military successes, the actions of Juan José Castelli, a sort of political commissar attached to the army, angered the Upper Peruvian ruling classes. Castelli, a self-professed Jacobin who abolished the *mitá*, the ancient system of forced labor, and did away with Indian taxes. In a move that was even more threatening to the conservative oligarchs of Upper Peru, Castelli promised to turn the Indian into a soldier and a citizen. When the amateurish and ineptly led militias of Buenos Aires suffered a series of setbacks, the alienation of Upper Peru from Buenos Aires began. The reason seems rather obvious to a contemporary Bolivian historian: "The real cause of the separation of Bolivia from the independent nation was due to the desire of the agricultural and mining elites of Upper Perú to avoid social reforms which would have elevated the Indian from the status of a mere object to that of a human being."[36]

Northwestern Argentina soon became a battlefield, as royalist troops from Peru mounted offensives that were easily repulsed by the Argentines, while Argentine offensives against Upper Peru met with a similar fate. Thus developed a stalemate that was to endure for over a decade. The spirit of Upper Peruvian independence was cemented during these years, and it would culminate with the proclamation of an independent state known as Bolivia in August 1825.[37]

If events in the north were hardly propitious, the situation in the Banda Oriental across the Plata were even more disheartening. Montevideo had repudiated the authority of the viceroy of Buenos Aires in 1808, and in 1810 it also repudiated the junta that replaced him. Late in that year, Francisco Javier de Elío arrived at Montevideo from Spain as the newly appointed viceroy in the Plata, with orders to destroy the rebel junta at Buenos Aires. Elío commanded a small but highly efficient naval squadron that initially swept Argentine ships off the Plata estuary. However, the interior of Uruguay had fallen to the insurgents, and Elío was in an awkward position. His fleet exercised a blockade of Buenos Aires and raided the towns of the Argentine littoral with impunity, but Montevideo was surrounded by patriot forces.[38]

The leader of the combined forces of Entre Ríos and Uruguay was José Gervasio de Artigas, who represented the cattle ranchers of the Banda Oriental. These men nursed strong grievances against the policies of Buenos Aires, which they considered oppressing and centralizing. Artigas and Entre Ríos were supported by Corrientes. Not surprisingly, when Buenos Aires summoned a meeting of deputies for a general assembly, Artigas countered by calling for a congress of his own at Peñarol, near Montevideo. Six deputies were elected to represent the Banda Oriental at Buenos Aires, and these received detailed instructions calling for absolute independence from Spain as well as a republican form of government based upon a loose federation of provinces.[39]

By 1814, the Argentine navy had gained control of the Plata estuary and was blockading Montevideo, paving the way for the capture of that royalist bastion by the armies of Buenos Aires led by General Carlos María de Alvear. The walled fortress surrendered to the Argentines on June 23. In the name of Artigas, Fernando Otorgues, one of his lieutenants, demanded control of the city. Alvear refused and marched against Otorgues, defeating his forces on June 25 at Las Piedras. Alvear and Artigas signed a convention, which was never ratified by Buenos Aires, and hostilities began anew in September. The forces of Buenos Aires were defeated at the battle of Guayabos in January 1815. Preoccupied with other fronts, Buenos Aires took no action.[40]

In the meantime, the Portuguese, who had never reconciled themselves to the loss of "their" Platine border, took profit from this situation, and in 1816 they launched an invasion of the Banda Oriental, and by 1820, after a running fight with Artigas, they were in virtual control.[41]

Meanwhile, across the Plata, Argentina had declared her independence from Spain in July 1816, and Juan Martín de Pueyrredón was elected as director. Opposition to Buenos Aires did not abate and in February 1820 the forces of the newly appointed director were routed at the battle of Cepeda by the combined armies of Francisco Ramírez and Estanislao Lopéz, caudillos of Entre Ríos and Santa Fé, respectively. These caudillos were representatives of the *estanciero*, a class group that had gained status and economic power after independence.

RISE OF THE ESTANCIERO CLASS

The early loss of Upper Peru to the royalists had the effect of displacing the merchants of Buenos Aires from a hitherto privileged position, since they were no longer able to pay for imports in silver bullion. As the port city was flooded with English goods, British merchants were able to gain some advantages, and in some cases the once-wealthy merchants of Buenos Aires became mere appendages of their English counterparts. A rare opportunity created by the law of emphyteusis, passed during the administration of president Bernardino Rivadavia (1825–1827), enabled some merchants to go into ranching. Land was the only tangible asset the embryonic Argentine state had at its disposal. By leasing it according to the emphyteusis law (which granted the right to develop the land), the government retained ownership. But since no limits were placed on the amount of land that could be leased to a single individuals, the cattle ranchers (*estancieros*) were able to subvert the spirit of the law to such an extent that by 1830, 538 individuals had acquired 8.6 million hectares.[42]

When the Araucanian Indians began to filter through Andean passes into the plains of Argentina, the *gaucho*, the Argentine cowboy and national type, became an armed retainer for the estancieros. Unequaled as a horseman and adept at warfare, the gaucho emerged as a figure approximately fifty years after the conquest and gained his apogee during the age of Rosas. The gaucho was a patriot who hated all Europeans, especially Spaniards, and despised them because of their inability to ride a horse. Like most honest patriots, the gaucho was easily deceived by scoundrels. He was:

Half Indian and half Spanish, the *gaucho* nursed hatred of the Indian who stole his horses and women; patient of hardship and starvation, the *gaucho* was savagely careless of his own and other people's lives. Armed with the *bolas*, which he inherited from the Indian, the lasso and a long knife, living on beef and *maté*, the gaucho could cover one hundred, or one hundred and twenty miles (on horseback) a day.[43]

This hardy race of fighters was the raw material from which the Argentine armies of the nineteenth century filled their ranks. The gaucho would also become the unwitting tool of the tyrant Juan Manuel de Rosas.

President Rivadavia, a far-sighted visionary who tried to modernize the nation but failed to secure a strong central government, resigned in 1827. In the chaos and confusion that followed Buenos Aires recovered her autonomy. Manuel Dorrego, a member of the Federal party, was elected governor. Dorrego pacified the interior, concluded an armistice with Brazil in 1828 and brought the army home. This proved to be his undoing. Most of the professional army officers were Unitarians, so called because they wanted a united Argentina, rather than the loose confederation advocated by the Federals. In November 1828, the 1st Army Division, under General Juan Galo de Lavalle, rose against the government. In response, Dorrego mobilized the militias commanded by Juan Manuel de Rosas. The militia and its Indian auxiliaries were easily routed by the army at Navarro. Dorrego was captured and in a senseless act of cruelty summarily executed. This drove Buenos Aires into the arms of Juan Manuel de Rosas, who was elected governor. Rosas also became head of the Argentine Confederation, a loose federation of provinces ruled by caudillos who owed some measure of allegiance to Rosas. The Federal League Pact, enacted in 1831, gave the provinces the right to govern themselves, granting Buenos Aires the power to deal with national defense and foreign affairs.[44]

As head of the Confederation, Rosas won new acclaim when he launched an expedition against the pampa Indians in 1833. Large numbers of Araucanian Indians from neighboring Chile had moved eastward across the Andes, into the fringes of the pampas, giving themselves access to land and sustenance. As the livestock sector boomed and settlers began to occupy lands to the south of the Salado River, conflict was inevitable.[45]

The "Araucanization" of the pampas posed an insurmountable problem of security for frontier settlements and *estancias*. To bring an end to Indian depredations, Rosas submitted a proposal for a punitive expedition to the Buenos Aires legislature. The strategic aims were simple: to drive all hostiles beyond the Río Negro. The Chilean army was expected to drive the Indians east to the Andes while two Argentine divisions would then link up and attack the Indians who would be pouring through the mountain passes at Neuquén.[46]

Although Chilean assistance did not materialize, Rosas began operations in March 1833, and by January of the following year, the expeditionary force returned home in triumph. The frontiers of Buenos Aires, Santa Fé, and Mendoza were consolidated, and the new frontier line now extended west of Bahía Blanca and 2,900 square leagues of territory were now safe for colonization and development. Furthermore, Rosas undertook to supply the Indians with food supplies and other staples, underscoring the facts that such supplies could be obtained peacefully from the Argentines and that if they opted for war, it would be a simple matter to organize and launch another punitive expedition. Rosas's Pampean diplomacy worked rather well, and with the exception of a few minor raids the frontier was comparatively peaceful until his overthrow, in 1852.[47]

INTERNAL STRIFE AND FOREIGN INVOLVEMENT

During the 1830s Argentina faced external and internal enemies. Some of the neighboring states sought to profit from the maelstrom of the Argentine civil wars to intervene, hoping to annex some of her territories. In 1835, Marshall Andrés Santa Cruz, dictator of Bolivia, imposed his rule over Peru, establishing the Peruvian-Bolivian Confederation. Santa Cruz's ambitions made for a hostile attitude toward Argentina and Chile, which entered an alliance against him. The conflict between Argentina and the Andean Confederation stemmed from the unwillingness of Santa Cruz to curb the activities of Argentine Unitarians exiled in Bolivia. There is evidence to suggest that Santa Cruz assisted and encouraged these groups in order to annex Jujuy. Santa Cruz had an army of 6,000 men, of which 2,000 to 2,400 were concentrated along the Argentine border. After initial mobilization, General Alejandro Heredia, the governor of Jujuy, could only field about 400 men, miserably clothed and trained, inadequately armed, and spread along a number of badly situated outposts, far too weak to prevent the numerous border violations that occurred prior to the Bolivian invasion in August 1837. Despite some melodramatic and highly imaginative Bolivian accounts of this short-lived conflict, the "war" between Argentina and Bolivia, or rather, the war between the militias of Jujuy and Bolivia, was but a series of armed clashes between small detachments, in which cavalry had little use. Initially, the Bolivians under General Felipe Braun overwhelmed minute Argentine garrisons at Cochinoca (August 28), Santa Victoria and Iruya (August 29) and Humahuaca

(September 11). When Argentine forces approached Humahuaca on September 12, the Bolivians withdrew in great haste to a fortified position in the heights of Santa Barbara, north of town. On September 13, the Argentines stormed Santa Barbara. After token resistance, the Bolivians withdrew across the border. On January 2, in another encounter between patrols, the Bolivians were routed. Uprisings led by Unitarians as well as the mutiny and defection of the Jujuy militia brought the counteroffensive to an end. By May, the Argentine forces had been reinforced, and 1,000 men were available for an invasion of Bolivia. After initial successes at Acambuco (April 27), Zapatera (May 2) and Pajonal (May 6), the Argentines were repulsed at Montenegro (June 24) and withdrew to Jujuy. In March 1838, Argentina found herself at war with France. Under these conditions, Argentine military operations in the northwest came to an end.[48]

The arrest of a Frenchman who had attempted to sell detailed maps of Argentina to Bolivia and the drafting of French citizens into the Argentine army provided for the pretext for French intervention. On March 28, France declared a blockade on the port of Buenos Aires. In order to secure a base of operations to enforce the blockade, the French turned to Uruguay, which had become a refuge for many Unitarian émigrés. In July 1836 Fructuoso Rivera, leader of the liberal or Colorado party, raised the standard of rebellion against Manuel Oribe, the constitutional president of Uruguay and leader of the Blanco, or conservative party. Assisted by the Argentine Unitarians under General Juan Galo de Lavalle, Rivera gained control of the interior provinces and encircled Oribe, at Montevideo. In October 11, a combined force of French and Uruguayan warships sailed upstream and seized the island of Martín García. Oribe and 150 of his followers sailed to Buenos Aires on October 27. Under pressure from the French on February 24, 1839, Rivera declared war against Buenos Aires, while civil war broke anew in Argentina. Rivera soon concluded a treaty of alliance with Beron de Astrada, governor of Corrientes. Rivera attempted to detach the Mesopotamian provinces from the Argentine Confederation. On March 6, Astrada proclaimed its secession from the Argentine Confederation. This attempt to revive Artigas's "Federal League" greatly offended the Unitarian Commission at Montevideo. By mid-February, Astrada had an estimated 5,000 men of the Army of Corrientes poised at the border with Entre Ríos, where he hoped to link with the forces of Rivera. To prevent such a linkup Pablo Echagüe, governor of Entre Ríos, crossed into Corrientes and at Pago Largo (March 31, 1839) he defeated Astrada in a battle of annihilation. To punish Rivera for the seizure of Martín García and his alliance to the French, Echagüe invaded Uruguay and was defeated at Cagancha (December 29) by the forces of Rivera and by Lavalle at Don Cristobal (April 10, 1840). But when the Unitarian army attacked Echagüe at Sauce Grande (June 16) it was driven pell-mell from the field and withdrew under the protection of the guns of the French fleet. A few days later, the Unitarian army boarded the

French transports and headed downriver for Buenos Aires. The brave but unfortunate Lavalle with the remainder of his army undertook a senseless march toward northwestern Argentina, a tragic journey punctuated by a series of defeats, which would culminate with his death. With the interior largely pacified, Argentina could concentrate her attention on Uruguay. When Rivera, at the head of an army perhaps 8,500 strong, crossed the Paraná and advanced toward the Gualeguay, the federal army under Oribe defeated him at Arroyo Grande (December 5, 1842). This crushing defeat and the destruction of the Uruguayan naval squadron by the Argentine navy in a series of naval engagements fought along the tributaries of the Plata paved the way for a new invasion of Uruguay and a siege of Montevideo (1843–1850), which would trigger an Anglo-French intervention. After four years, France and England signed a peace treaty that gave the honors of war to Rosas.[49]

The regime seemed unassailable until 1851, when Justo José de Urquiza, strongman of Entre Ríos and once a trusted ally, clashed with Rosas over a commercial dispute. Rosas tried to block trade between Urquiza's fief and Montevideo, which was at war with the Confederation, Urquiza broke openly with Rosas, entered into an alliance with Brazil and Uruguay in May 1851 and was subsequently appointed commander in chief of the Allied Army, known as the Ejército Grande. This "Grand Army" clashed with the forces of the Confederation at the battle of Caseros on February 1852 and defeated them, thus bringing the era of Rosas to an end.[50]

TOWARD NATIONAL UNIFICATION: 1852–1862

After the battle of Caseros, Urquiza marched his forces into Buenos Aires and invoked the provisions of the Federal Pact of 1831 in order to maintain control of the Confederation. Urquiza became what Rosas had once been, not only the governor of a province, but the titular head of the Argentine Confederation. An enabling treaty giving Urquiza power to handle the foreign affairs of the Confederation was soon enacted. Once this had been dealt with, an invitation was sent to the governors of the interior provinces, requesting their assistance at a national convention intended to create a national state and draft its constitution. However, the province of Buenos Aires seceded from the Confederation before the Constituent Assembly met, in defense of the prominent political and financial role which the province played.[51]

When the assembly finally met in 1853, it drew up the Constitution of 1853, a document designed to overcome all disagreements by granting the nation a federal system patterned on the American model. The executive power would be exercised by the office of the president; the legislative power would be exercised by a bicameral legislature composed of an upper house, or senate, and a lower house, or chamber of deputies, while a supreme court would exercise the judiciary power. Deputies were elected by popular vote, as in the United States.

Two senators were designated by each of the provinces. Thus the weight of Buenos Aires, which was the most populous of the Argentine provinces, was offset by the representation of the provinces in the Senate.[52]

All provinces subscribed to the new constitution, and Urquiza was elected president according to its clauses. The government of the Confederation moved to the port of Paraná, in Entre Ríos, which Urquiza, in a vain attempt to offset the power and importance of Buenos Aires, attempted to develop. Unable to attract British or French capital, Urquiza turned to an old ally, Brazil. Brazilian gold flowed through the Confederation and a branch of the Mauá bank was inaugurated at Rosario, a sleepy upriver village Urquiza tried to upgrade as an alternative port to Buenos Aires.[53]

During the 1850s, Buenos Aires and the Confederation began to prepare for war. The first confrontation took place at Cepeda in October 1859. The forces of Buenos Aires, led by Bartolomé Mitre, were at a disadvantage. Their cavalry was badly outnumbered by the enemy and easily dispersed. However, Mitre's well-trained infantry formed a front and allowed him the opportunity to retreat while saving the larger portion of his army. Once in Buenos Aires, Mitre regrouped and reorganized his forces.[54]

In the city of Buenos Aires, barricades were going up at strategic points, a sign the porteños were preparing for a house-to-house, street-by-street struggle. Urquiza lacked sufficient artillery and infantry to lay siege to the city. The ministers of Brazil, England, and France offered their good services, which were accepted, and eventually an agreement known as the Pact of November 1 was reached. The pact stipulated how the constituent assembly would be elected, established procedures for the introduction of new amendments to the constitution, and allowed Buenos Aires to retain her administration, with the exception of the customs house. Buenos Aires was further barred from pursuing an independent national policy, as she had done in the past.[55]

Although the battle of Cepeda had given the nation a semblance of peace, the struggle for power continued. In the interior some provinces, including Santiago del Estero, Tucumán, and Salta, sided with Buenos Aires. There remained, particularly, the matter of representation at the national congress and the port city's refusal to surrender her customs revenue. When the representatives of Buenos Aires arrived at the National Convention at Paraná, they were rejected because they had been elected according to provincial rather than national laws. Buenos Aires and the Confederation began to arm feverishly, though the British and French consuls had put out peace feelers. On July 3, 1860, while talks were still under way, the Confederation declared the government of Buenos Aires, now headed by Bartolomé Mitre, to be in sedition.[56]

In August 1861, the Army of the Confederation, 16,000 strong (11,000 cavalry, 5,000 infantry, and 42 pieces of artillery) crossed the Paraná river, and on September 17, it clashed with the forces of Buenos Aires near a brook called Pavón. The Army of Buenos Aires also had approximately 16,000 men (6,000 cavalry, about 9,000 infantry, and 35 cannon). An attack by the

Buenos Airean cavalry was repulsed, but the splendid infantry of the port city stood its ground and advanced by columns, enveloping the enemy's infantry and artillery and breaking the cavalry charges of the Confederates. Urquiza ordered a withdrawal. Some historians have argued that the victory of Buenos Aires was inconclusive; others maintain that Urquiza withdrew after defeating Mitre, who thus turned from vanquished to victor. There is no evidence to substantiate this claim. Mitre's forces smashed the enemy's infantry and captured most of his cannon. Urquiza withdrew to save his cavalry, leaving behind 1,200 prisoners, 37 cannon, 3,000 rifles, and 5,000 horses. The Confederation could not replace the arms park lost at Pavón; thus the military initiative passed to Buenos Aires. Rosario was occupied by Mitre's forces on October 11, and the remnants of the Confederate army were soundly beaten at Cañada de Gómez on November 21. The province of Santa Fé fell to the forces of Buenos Aires; Corrientes soon followed. This pattern was repeated until, by mid-1862, most of the interior was under control of the Buenos Airean forces.[57]

Congressional elections were scheduled at Buenos Aires on May 25. The problem of the national capital remained unsolved until October 1, when Buenos Aires was designated as the seat of the federal government. The electoral college then unanimously acclaimed Mitre as president of the newly united Argentina. Mitre thus initiated the long list of presidents who have uninterruptedly governed the Argentine nation.[58]

NOTES

1. Ernesto Palacio, *Historia de la Argentina, 1515–1943*, 2 vols. Buenos Aires: A. Peña Lillo Editor, 1965), I: 26–27.

2. Vicente F. Lopez, *Historia de la República Argentina; Su orígén, su revolución y su desarrollo político hasta 1852*, 8 vols. (Buenos Aires: Editorial Sopena Argentina, 1949), I: 128–133; Julio Cesar Chaves, *Descubrimiento y Conquista del Río de la Plata y el Paraguay* (Asunción: Ediciones Niza, 1968), pp. 76–90.

3. Palacio, *Historia*, I: 34.

4. Ibid., I: 35.

5. Ibid., I: 36.

6. Lopez, *Historia de la República Argentina*, pp. 135–139.

7. Palacio, *Historia*, I: 38.

8. James Scobie, *Argentina: A City and a Nation* (New York: Oxford University Press, 1974), pp. 23–24.

9. Palacio, *Historia*, I: 74.

10. Scobie, *Argentina*, p. 17.

11. Ibid., p. 20.

12. Ibid., p. 21.

13. Ibid., pp. 21–22.

14. David Rock, ed., *Argentina, 1516–1982: From Spanish Colonization to the Falklands War* (Berkeley and Los Angeles: University of California Press, 1985), pp. 148–149; Palacio, *Historia*, I: 46–50.

15. Palacio, *Historia*, I: 49.

16. Tulio Halperin Donghi, *Politics, Economics and Society in Argentina During the Revolutionary Period* (London and Melbourne: Cambridge University Press, 1975), pp. 12–13. For the mule trade, see Nicolás Sanchez-Albornoz, "La Saca de Mulas de Salta al Peru: 1778–1808" in *América Colonial, Población y economía* (Rosario, Argentina: Universidad del Litoral, 1965), pp. 261–312.

17. Leslie B. Rout, Jr., *The African Experience in Spanish America: 1501 to the Present Day* (London: Cambridge University Press, 1976), p. 42.

18. Alistair Hennessy, *The Frontier in Latin American History* (London: Edward Arnold, 1978), pp. 15–16.

19. Hennessy, *The Frontier*, p. 77.

20. Ibid., p. 65.

21. Rock, *Argentina, 1516–1982*, pp. 34–35; also Gaylord Warren, *Paraguay: An Informal History* (Norman: University of Oklahoma Press, 1949), pp. 90–91.

22. Hennessy, *The Frontier*, pp. 64–65.

23. Ibid., p. 65.

24. Juan Carlos Walther, *La conquista del desierto* (Buenos Aires: Editorial Universitaria de Buenos Aires, 1970), pp. 88–90.

25. Ibid., p. 90.

26. Juan Beverina, *El virreinato de las provincias del Río de la Plata: su organización militar*, Biblioteca del Oficial, Vol. 204–205 (Buenos Aires: Círculo Militar, 1935), pp. 61–62.

27. Ibid., pp. 62–63, 70–72.

28. Horacio C. E. Giberti, *Historia económica de la ganadería argentina* (Buenos Aires: Ediciones Solar, 1981), pp. 84–94.

29. Ibid., p. 75.

30. J. H. Parry, *The Spanish Seaborne Empire* (New York: Alfred A. Knopf, 1966), pp. 134–135, 286–287, 307–308; Palacio, *Historia*, 1: pp. 107, 134.

31. Hubert Herring, *A History of Latin America: From the Beginnings to the Present* (New York: Alfred A. Knopf, 1968), pp. 264–265; Halperín Donghi, *Politics, Economics and Society*, pp. 207–209; and Harold F. Peterson, "Mariano Moreno: The Making of an Insurgent," *HAHR* 14 (1934), pp. 450–476. For details on Saavedra and other *criollo* merchants see Susan Migden Socolow, *The Merchants of Buenos Aires, 1778–1810: Family and Commerce* (London, New York, and Melbourne: Cambridge University Press, 1978), pp. 133–134.

32. Rock, *Argentina, 1516–1982*, pp. 74–75.

33. Ibid., pp. 88–90.

34. José Luís Romero, *A History of Argentine Political Thought* (Stanford, CA: Stanford University Press, 1963), p. 76.

35. John Lynch, *The Spanish American Revolutions: 1808–1825* (New York: W. W. Norton, 1973) pp. 95–101; see also John Lynch, *Spanish Colonial Administration, 1782–1810: The Intendant System in the Viceroyalty of the Río de la Plata* (London: Athlone Press, 1958), pp. 142–143; Rock, *Argentina, 1516–1982*, pp. 81–83, Warren, *Paraguay*, pp. 143–147, Félix Best, *Historia de las guerras argentinas: De la independencia, internacionales, civiles y con el indio*, 2 vols. (Buenos Aires: Ediciones Peuser, 1960), I: 173–174.

36. Luis C. Peñaloza, *Historia del movimiento nacionalista revolucionario, 1943–1952* (La Paz: Editorial Juventud, 1965), p. 14.

37. Best, *Historia de las guerras argentinas*, I: 178–189, 191–195, 200–203; Emilio A. Bidondo, *La guerra de la independencia en el Norte Argentino* (Buenos Aires: Editorial Universitaria de Buenos Aires, 1976), pp. 78–85, 91–103; Charles W. Arnade, *The Emergence of the Republic of Bolivia* (Gainesville: University of Florida Press, 1957), pp. 77–80.

38. Gabriel A. Puentes, *Don Francisco Javier de Elío en el Río de la Plata* (Buenos Aires: Ediciones Esnaola, 1959), pp. 235–240, 242–255; John Street, *Artigas and the Emancipation of Uruguay* (Cambridge: Cambridge University Press, 1959), pp. 92–99. The naval aspects of the independence campaigns in the Plata area are treated in Felipe Bosch, *Historia naval argentina* (Buenos Aires: Editorial Alborada, 1962), pp. 50–65; Lopez, *Historia*, II: 593–599.

39. Street, *Artigas*, pp. 190–191; Percy Alvin Martin, "Artigas, the Founder of Uruguayan Nationality," *HAHR* 19, 1 (February 1939), pp. 2–15. An account of Artigas's relationship with the caudillo of Santa Fé is contained in Gianello Leoncio, *Estanislao López, vida y obra del patriarca de la federación* (Santa Fé: El Litoral, 1958), pp. 80–85.

40. Best, *Historia de las guerras argentinas*, 1: 228–230.

41. Street, *Artigas and the Emancipation of Uruguay*, pp. 302–304.

42. Best, *Historia de las guerras argentinas*, I: 131–151. An account from the Brazilian side, seen through the eyes of a German soldier of fortune, can be found in *Contribuçoes para a historia da guerra entre o Brasil e Buenos Aires: una testemunha ocular* (Belo Horizonte: Livraria Itabatia, 1976). For details on the emphytheusis law, see Rock, *Argentina, 1516–1982*, pp. 107–108; Lynch, *The Spanish American Revolutions*, pp. 80–83; Giberti, *Historia económica*, pp. 112–122.

43. John Walker, *The South American Sketches of R. B. Cunningham Graham* (Norman: University of Oklahoma Press, 1978), pp. 40–41, 88–89. The story of the gaucho is also treated in Richard Slatta, *Gauchos and the Vanishing Frontier* (Lincoln: University of Nebraska Press, 1983); and in Ricardo Rodríguez Mola, *Historia social del gaucho* (Buenos Aires: Ediciones Maru, 1968).

44. Best, *Historia de las guerras argentinas*, I: 368–371, for details of the overthrow and execution of Dorrego. See Domingo F. Sarmiento, *Civilización y barbarie; Trilogía de Quiroga, Aldao, El Chaco, Mi Defensa, Recuerdos de Provincia* (Buenos Aires: El Ateneó, 1957), p. 271. Sarmiento summarized the organization of the Confederation as follows: Andean region (under Quiroga); provinces of Jujuy, Salta, Tucumán, La Rioja, San Juan, Mendoza, and San Luis; Littoral region (federation under the Pact of the Federal League); Entre Ríos, Santa Fé and Córdoba (under López); Buenos Aires (under Rosas). Santiago del Estero (which Sarmiento calls "the feudal area") was under the rule of Ibarra.

45. John Lynch, *Argentine Dictator: Juan Manuel de Rosas, 1829–1852* (Oxford: Oxford University Press, 1981), pp. 15–17.

46. Ibid., pp. 18–19; Alfred Hasbrouck, "The Conquest of the Desert," *HAHR* 14 (1935), pp. 195–197, 218–220.

47. Walther, *La conquista del desierto*, pp. 220–224.

48. Best, *Historia de las guerras argentinas*, II: 165–178; Emilio A. Bidondo, "Un episodio de la guerra contra el Mariscal Santa Cruz: El combate de Santa Barbara (Hu-

mahuaca, Provincia de Jujuy, 13 de Septiembre de 1837)," *IE* 33 (Julio–diciembre 1982), pp. 277–312.

49. José Fausto Rieffollo, *Urquiza: Padre de la Constitución* (Rosario: Tipografía Llordén, 1951), pp. 36–52; Ysabel F. Rennie, *The Argentine Republic* (New York: Macmillan 1945), pp. 55–62.

50. Horacio Rube, *Hacia Caseros, 1850–1852* (Buenos Aires: Ediciones La Bastilla, 1973). Urquiza employed a flotilla of whaling boats and lighters to smuggle European goods purchased at Montevideo and then shipped them to Buenos Aires, disguised as *productos de procedencia interior*. When Rosas banned the exports of gold bullion, Urquiza bought gold in Buenos Aires at low prices and made a profit selling it in Montevideo, where gold was scarce and fetched substantially higher prices.

51. James R. Scobie, *La Lucha por la consolidación de la Nacionalidad Argentina, 1852–1862* (Buenos Aires: Libreria Hachette, 1964), pp. 85–88, 90–92.

52. Ibid., pp. 101–105.

53. Ibid., pp. 105–106.

54. Ibid., pp. 250–256.

55. Ibid., pp. 277–285, 300–307.

56. Ibid., pp. 354–355, 387–390; Best, *Historia de las guerras argentinas*, 1: 29–31, López, *Historia*, II: 573–577. Buenos Aires placed great confidence in her fleet of armed steamers and in the fortifications at Martín Garcia. The Confederation hurriedly purchased ships in Montevideo and Rio de Janeiro and organized a squadron under Admiral Mariano Cordero. On October 14, Cordero gave orders to force the narrows at Martín Garcia. After a furious cannonade, the Confederate ships destroyed two of the batteries, damaged two of the Buenos Aires vessels, and headed upstream. The engagement was inconclusive, since Buenos Aires still held the key to the estuary, and the Confederate fleet was trapped upstream.

57. Best, *Historia de las guerras argentinas*, II: 20–31; Mariano Pelliza, *Historia Argentina: desde su origén hasta la organización nacional*, 2 vols. (Buenos Aires: J. Lajouane Editores, 1910), II: 594–604.

58. Scobie, *La Lucha*, pp. 344–346, 387–390.

2

The Frontier Dispute

During the colonial period, the border between the present-day states of Argentina and Chile had been determined by the mountain range of the Andes. Due in part to an imperfect knowledge of its extensive dominions, but more importantly because it was primarily concerned with the effective colonization of these, the Spanish Crown issued confusing and quite often contradictory decrees to its colonial officials. There were *cédulas* and *capitulaciones*, or contracts, under which the Crown selected an individual to conquer and colonize a determined area and appointed him governor once these tasks were accomplished. Often the Crown modified the boundaries of these governorships.

In 1537, Francisco Pizarro, conqueror of Peru, entrusted Pedro de Valdivia with the conquest of Chile. Valdivia landed at Copiapó, took possession in the name of the Crown, and named the newly acquired territory Nuevo Extremo, or Nueva Extremadura.[1] When colonization from the Atlantic coast of South America was frustrated by the destruction of the first Buenos Aires, the Spanish authorities in Chile began settlement of Andean Argentina. Because of the distances involved, the exploration and colonization of northwestern Argentina were rendered more feasible from the Pacific seaboard of the continent rather than from the Atlantic. An incursion of the English corsair Francis Drake in the Straits of Magellan drove the Spanish Crown to promote the establishment of military colonies in the threatened area. One such settlement, near the present-day Brunswick peninsula, was called Fort San Felipe, later baptized Puerto Hambre, or Port Hunger. Further raids by Drake in 1580 led Francisco de Toledo, Viceroy of Peru, to organize a fleet to pursue the interlopers. Pedro de Sarmiento, chief sergeant of that expedition, was ordered to explore the Straits of Magellan and to take possession in the name of the king. It should be noted that Chile was a dependency of the Viceroyalty of Peru and as such subject to the same.[2]

The borders of the modern-day states of Argentina and Chile were generally established in 1776, by the creation of the Viceroyalty of the Rio de la Plata, which included the Cuyo region, formerly under the captaincy general of Chile. In the immediate postindependence period, no border controversy existed between the two newly established republics. The long-smoldering border dispute began in 1843, when Chile planted the colony of Fort Bulnes, formerly Puerto Hambre, in the Straits of Magellan, a territory Argentina considered hers by right. At the time, Argentina was far immersed with her endless civil wars and the Anglo-French intervention in the Plate to effectively challenge this move. It was only in December 1847 that the Argentine government lodged a protest denouncing the establishment of a settlement at Punta Arenas, situated east of the Andes, a clear violation of the Treaty of Friendship, an alliance concluded between both nations in 1826. Rosas instructed Felipe Arana, his foreign minister, to begin negotiations with Chile by stipulating that the borders between both nations should be the same as those which separated them in colonial times.[3]

To assert Argentine claims to the disputed area, Rosas commissioned Pedro de Angelis, an Italian researcher and historian. De Angelis published the results of his research in 1852, in a book called *Memoria Histórica*, in which he stated that Chile had no rights to the Straits and cited forty-five royal cédulas and 164 other documents as proof of Argentine jurisdiction.[4]

THE ARGENTINE CLAIM

The Argentine Confederation and Chile claimed the Straits on the basis of maps, colonial explorations, and the *utis possidetis* (a diplomatic term regarding the actual possession of territories) of 1810. Argentina could assert that Pedro de Mendoza, the first Adelantado (leader of an expedition and governor of all the territories; a discoverer or conquerer) sent to the Plata was empowered to take under his jurisdiction 200 leagues of sea frontage (approximately 1,200 kilometers) from the Plata to the Straits.[5]

This policy of colonization and conquest was reaffirmed in a series of cédulas and pemits over the next two centuries. In the year 1671, the governor of Buenos Aires began a Southward expansion, towards the pampas. A royal cédula dated January 13, 1681 empowered him to undertake the conversion of the Indians of the pampas, while confining them to reservations. On January 2, 1683, Joseph de Herrera y Sotomayor, governor of Buenos Aires, sought consent of the crown to undertake the conversion of the Indian tribes who inhabited the vast expanses of territory between the port of Buenos Aires and the Straits of Magellan. His request was granted on May 24, 1684. A similar permit was issued on November 5, 1741, which further authorized a sally against the Patagonians and "other nations inhabiting said territories up to the Straits of Magellan."[6]

Further cédulas empowering Buenos Aires to evangelize and explore the southern regions all the way to the Straits were issued by the Crown on November 24, 1743, and July 23, 1745. In addition, a letter from the Spanish minister, the Marquis of Ensenada, dated January 1745, reaffirmed the powers granted to the governor of Buenos Aires by the Crown to undertake the exploration and pacification of Patagonia. Again, on December 29, 1766, Francisco de Buccarelli, the governor of Buenos Aires who had evicted the English from the Malvinas archipelago, was ordered by the Crown to explore Patagonia up to the Straits in order to determine whether the English had planted settlements along the Patagonian coast. The governor of Malvinas was further ordered to assist Buccarelli in this enterprise.[7]

Voluminous correspondence of the period between 1776 and 1778 that further reaffirmed the Argentine claim to Patagonia exists in the Royal Archives. As we have seen, when the Viceroyalty of the Río de la Plata was established, the Cuyo region, hitherto administered by Chile, became subordinate to Buenos Aires. The city of Mendoza in Cuyo was to have jurisdiction over all lands between the Atlantic and the Mar del Norte, as the Atlantic Ocean was then known.[8]

In 1778, concerned over the possibility of an English invasion, Manuel Gálvez, Minister of Indies, ordered the governor of Buenos Aires to develop outposts along the Atlantic coast of Patagonia in order to occupy the area more effectively. These outposts would serve as links in a defensive line that would stretch all the way down to the Straits. Commissioners were ordered to explore the interior of Patagonia and to establish new settlements to forestall the seizure of these lands by the English.[9]

An expedition outfitted at Montevideo sailed on December 15, 1778, carrying Juan de la Piedra and Francisco de Biedma, who were to act as commissioner-superintendents of the new settlements. On January 1779, de la Piedra founded San José, at Sin Fondo Bay, the Atlantic outlet of the Río Negro. In June, Biedma established a settlement and fort at Carmen de Patagones, on an area previously explored by Basilio Villarino, a pilot of he Royal Spanish Navy. Of these settlements, only Carmen de Patagones would endure until the nineteenth century.[10]

Nevertheless, the Argentine republic could claim rights to Patagonia not only as the successor state of the Viceroyalty of the Río de la Plata and the *utis possidetis* of 1810, but by right of continuous possession since the beginnings of Spanish rule. Legal rights, the Argentines maintained, were theirs, as the flag of Spain had been borne by expeditions dispatched by Buenos Aires; and that flag had continuously waved over Patagonia, Tierra del Fuego, and the islands in the Straits of Magellan from 1776 to 1810.[11]

THE CHILEAN CLAIM

Chilean claims to the Straits and Patagonia stem from a royal cédula of April 18, 1548, which gave Pedro de Valdivia the governorship of Nueva Extremadura and the provinces of Chile, granting him jurisdiction between the 27th parallel in the north and the 41st parallel in the south, thus giving Valdivia control of 100 leagues of littoral along the Mar del Sur, or Pacific Ocean, and to a width of 100 leagues from the coast. Valdivia was further empowered to act as captain general and governor of any settlement he might establish beyond the limits imposed by the Spanish Crown until further notice.[12] Valdivia petitioned the Crown and Spanish authorities in Peru to extend his jurisdiction south of the 41st parallel down to the Straits and reaffirmed his authority east of the Andes by the foundation of Villarica. The Crown granted Valdivia his request, but he would not live to see this. Jerónimo de Alderete, his successor, presided over an expanded Chile, which had jurisdiction down to the Straits as well as the right to "discover, conquer and populate lands on the other side of the Straits of Magellan," that is to say, Tierra del Fuego and other islands to the South.[13]

The task of consolidating Chilean control in lands east of the Andes fell to Francisco de Villagra, who founded the cities of Mendoza and San Luis de Punta and conquered an area south of Mendoza designated as the province of Conlara. The boundaries of Chile were further defined in 1688, when King Carlos II compiled and approved a statue of laws known as the *Recopilación de Leyes de Indias*. Law no. 12 of this statute described the boundaries of the kingdom of Chile as "all towns and villages in the provinces already inhabited as well as other lands to be conquered and pacified in the future, inwards or outwards of the Straits of Magellan, and to the province of Cuyo, in the interior." A royal official at Santiago compiled a description of the Chilean boundaries as follows: "From Cape Horn at 56 degrees latitude to San Benito hill at 24 degrees of latitude, it includes the whole of the pampa up to the Atlantic Ocean from Sin Fondo to Río de los Leones."[14]

According to such interpretations, the territory of Chile extended up to the Gulf of San Matías on the Atlantic, near the present-day port of San Antonio Oeste.[15]

The government of Chile availed itself of the services of a researcher who would gather evidence to support its contentions. The task fell to a "relatively inexperienced historian" Miguel de Amunátegui, who published his findings in a book titled *Títulos de la República de Chile* in the year 1853. In his rebuttal of Argentine claims, Amunátegui charged that De Angelis had deliberately overlooked documents that obviously decided the dispute in Chile's favor. The documents which emerged from Amunátegui's research included Law no. 12, Title no. 12 of the Recopilación de Las Indias; a royal cédula of May 1566; and a map by Juan de la Cruz Cano y Olmedilla dated 1775, reportedly sent to Pedro de Ceballos, future Viceroy of the Plata. The map placed Cuyo under the jurisdiction of Buenos Aires but assigned Patagonia to Chile.[16]

Amunátegui's research was capricious at best. He cited, for example, the presence of Jesuit missionaries from Chile in the Nahuel Huapi region, east of the Andes, as evidence of his nation's right to possession, but dismissed the activities of Jesuit missionaries from Paraguay as proof of Argentine claims.[17]

After studying royal dispatches sent to Francisco de Bucarelli in the matter of Patagonia, the Chilean argued:

It was natural for a suspicious and watchful court as Madrid to dispatch two or three vessels to protect the Malvinas. Since it would not make any sense at all to station those vessels (in the area) merely to protect the islands, the king's ministers determined that the coasts of Patagonia belonged to the governor of Chile, while the Malvinas belonged to the governor of Buenos Aires.[18]

Amunátegui asked the reader whether in fact orders that merely entrusted Buenos Aires with the protection of the Patagonian coast did, in fact, place that territory under the jurisdiction of Platine authorities, adding that the government of Chile, "under whose jurisdiction Patagonia really belonged," was distantly removed from the area, and that the Spanish authorities at Buenos Aires were far more closely situated. Therefore, he surmised, Buenos Aires was entrusted with the task of patrolling and colonizing the area. In the royal orders, Amunátegui saw nothing that countervened Chilean rights to the disputed regions, but his research came under closer scrutiny in his native country in the 1870s, when other historians, including Benjamin Vicuña Mackenna and José Lastarria, examined the evidence at length. Recent authorship on the subject has deemed Amunátegui's work suspect and considers that in the end, it proved worthless.[19]

An initial exchange of notes between Buenos Aires and Santiago led to the Treaty of Friendship, Peace and Navigation of 1856, under which both parties agreed to recognize the *utis possidetis* of 1810 and pledged to solve the boundary dispute by peaceful means and to submit to arbitration if direct negotiations failed. The dispute, however, would transcend the polemical phase between historians and researchers on both sides of the Andes and enter into another phase, that of the diplomatic missions.[20]

ARGENTINE-CHILEAN RELATIONS: 1865–1873

The first diplomatic mission entrusted with the solution of the frontier dispute was Chilean. José V. Lastarria, appointed minister plenipotentiary to Argentina, Brazil, and Uruguay, arrived in Buenos Aires in February 1865. Lastarria was firmly convinced that Chile had no valid claims to Patagonia and stated it on a letter to Amunátegui: "I am sorry to learn by your letter of the 14th that you are trying to convince me that we are (the) owners of the continent. This is a useless task and will serve no purpose, but to demonstrate your creative abilities, however, the studies which I have made have given me the irrefutable conviction that we are not the owners of Patagonia."[21]

Prior to his departure from Chile, Lastarria received detailed instructions from the foreign minister, under which he was to promote an Argentine-Chilean alliance against Spain. At this time, Spain was involved in a dispute with Peru that would ultimately lead to Spanish military intervention in the Pacific coast of South America. Chile allied itself to Peru and declared war on Spain in September 1865. Bolivia and Ecuador joined their neighbor republics in the struggle against the former mother country.[22]

In his efforts to draw Argentina into the alliance, and perhaps of his own initiative, Lastarria offered President Mitre a solution to the border dispute. The boundary was to be determined by a line drawn parallel to the eastern foothills of the Andes. Well aware that this arrangement weakened its own claims, Santiago disavowed Lastarria's initiative. Moreover, the Argentine government was more concerned about the deteriorating political situation in Uruguay, the fuse that would detonate the powder keg of the Paraguayan war. Wary of Chilean intentions, Mitre paid little heed to Lastarria, while his foreign minister, Rufino de Elizalde, reminded him that Chile had previously refused Argentine mediation with Spain and that nothing short of an alliance would satisfy the Transandine nation.[23]

Argentina went to war in April 1865, after Paraguayan forces had invaded her territory. Argentina, Brazil, and Uruguay made common cause against Paraguay and a Treaty of the Triple Alliance was signed on May 1. The war would drag for five years, and by necessity the Chilean boundary dispute was laid aside.

As we have seen, the reunification of Argentina had only been completed in 1862; thus at the outbreak of the Paraguayan conflict, the central government's control over the interior was precarious at best. The war against Paraguay was viewed by many caudillos in the interior as Buenos Aires's war rather than as a national conflict. Fanned by Federalists who had never reconciled themselves to the peace arranged between Mitre and Urquiza, revolts broke out in the Andean provinces. Uprisings against the central government began at La Rioja in September 1865 and soon spread to San Juan, Mendoza, Catamarca, and Córdoba. The government was forced to withdraw a significant portion of its forces from the Paraguayan front to quell the rebellion. At the battle of Pozo de Vargas on April 10, 1867, the forces of the rebel caudillo Felipe Varela were utterly defeated by the national army. Noteworthy of this episode was the fact that the governments of Chile and Bolivia did nothing to curb the activities of Argentine rebels who had sought shelter in their territories but in fact assisted them. The Chilean government, for example, did not prevent Varela, who resided in Chile, from recruiting men and purchasing arms; nor did it impede Varela's invasion of Argentina. According to a reliable source, a battalion of Chilean regulars outfitted with modern weapons fought alongside Varela at La Rioja. If this information is correct, it would appear that the government of Chile, motivated by the boundary dispute, sought to destabilize Argentina, as it would again in the 1870s, when the Platine nation faced repeated Indian invasions and the prospect of a war with Brazil. Chile could then take advantage of her rival's other commitments and begin exploration and settlement of the Atlantic coast of Patagonia.[24]

During the Paraguayan war (1865–1870), Argentina and Brazil bore the brunt of the military effort against Paraguay. However, these age-old adversaries found it hard to cooperate with one another. Therefore it was not too surprising that at war's end, Argentina and Brazil reverted to their traditional antagonism and struggle over spheres of influence in the Plata region. As both powers continued to spar over Paraguay in the early 1870s and engaged in plots and counterplots in that country, war seemed a real possibility. To close the rift with Brazil, President Sarmiento of Argentina appointed his predecessor, Bartolomé Mitre, as envoy to Rio de Janeiro. Mitre enjoyed some successes in his mission, but during the next two years both Argentina and Brazil armed, as war appeared imminent.[25]

During May 1873 it was learned that Bolivia and Peru had concluded an anti-Chilean alliance into which they hoped to enlist Argentina. Buenos Aires, however, maintained a border dispute with Bolivia and would not make any commitments until that issue was resolved. On the other hand, an alliance between Argentina's main rivals, Brazil and Chile, appeared probable at this time. Chile was certainly eager to conclude a pact with Brazil. Brazil was less anxious to enter into such an agreement. The Brazilian minister in Santiago considered Chile a poor nation devoid of a proper army and navy, unable to bear the expenses of a war in such a remote theater, and felt that Chilean assistance in the event of war against Argentina would be as negligible as that rendered by the tiny republic of Uruguay to Argentina and Brazil during the Paraguayan conflict.[26]

Buenos Aires, on the other hand, appeared closer to an understanding with Bolivia and Peru in the second half of 1873. A treaty of alliance was submitted to the Argentine congress in a special secret session on September 25. Approval at the Chamber of Deputies was quickly obtained, but the Senate delayed further action until its members reconvened from vacation. The chamber, nevertheless, approved a motion by Dardo Rocha granting the executive a credit of 3 million pesos for arms. It was well known that Chile had let out important arms contracts in Europe, including one for two very powerful seagoing ironclads.[27]

In September 1871 the Chilean government established the Foreign Ministry as an independent branch of the cabinet, on an equal footing with other departments, and appointed Adolfo Ibañez to head the new office. Ibañez attached great importance to the Patagonian issue. The Argentine envoy, Félix Frías, had been dispatched to Chile in 1869 to improve relations, strained by Chilean denunciations of the Triple Alliance Treaty, and to induce the Chileans to take steps to circumscribe the activities of Argentine revolutionaries, who in the safety of their refuge organized and equipped military expeditions to invade Argentina and recruited Chilean citizens. These instructions notwithstanding, Frías, a scholar well versed in the boundary question who felt that Chile had no rights to Patagonia, zealously served the interests of his nation. On January 1, 1872, General Domingo Urrutia, of the Chilean army, concluded a peace treaty with the Pehuelche Indians, under which the latter recognized the government of Chile as their "faithful friend" and agreed to come to its aid whenever required. Since the lands inhabited by the Pehuelche were located east of the Andes, Frías protested. In an attempt to dismiss the incident, the Chilean government replied that Urrutia had acted of his own initiative and lacked authority to sign such an agreement. On February 7, Ibañez held a meeting with the Argentine envoy and offered a "transitory" boundary treaty, under which Chile would retain control of the Straits, Tierra del Fuego, and adjacent islands as well as the Atlantic coast of Patagonia up to Río Deseado. Above the Deseado, a line would be drawn across the Andes, leaving Argentina in control of the rest of Patagonia. Ibañez spoke at length about the financial sacrifices incurred by Chile to sustain the colony at Punta Arenas, adding that if the proposal was not accepted by Frías or his government, alternative solutions, such as monetary compensation, could be found. Frías, although angered by the suggestion since he felt Chile had no rights at all over Patagonia, replied that he was not authorized to make such concessions.[28]

Frías met with Ibañez on May 1 to protest an item published by Guillermo Blest Gana, Chilean envoy to Buenos Aires, in *The Times* of London and a Chilean claim to the islets of Magdalena and Quartermaster, located in the Straits, just east of Punta Arenas. The advertisement in the *Times* served vessels of all flags notice that the Chilean government had declared a ban against the gathering of *guano*, bird droppings used for fertilizer, in the islands adjacent to the Strait, Tierra del Fuego, and near the Patagonian coast. Offending vessels would be confiscated. Ibañez attempted to dismiss this incident, adding that his government had never intended to extend the ban to the eastern coast of Patagonia but merely wished to prevent foreign ships from exploiting the guano deposits in the Straits. Unconvinced, Frías registered a protest and reaffirmed his nation's rights to the two islands now claimed by Chile.[29]

In a note dated May 2, Ibañez reasserted the Chilean claim over the islands, arguing that this did not constitute a violation of the status quo, since Chile exercised sovereignty over Punta Arenas, which was Patagonian territory, after all. Frías refused to be taken in by the Chilean's sophisms and on a note dated May 31 replied that Patagonia, the Straits, and Tierra del Fuego were separate territories, adding that for the sake of clarity in future negotiations, these geographic expressions should not be confused. Further correspondence ensued, but Frías upheld his position with the tenacity that often accompanies profound knowledge of the subject at hand. In a note dated December 12, he invited the Chilean government to bring forth its titles to the disputed territories and listed in detail the legal, geographical, and historical antecedents that endorsed the Argentine claim. Ibañez acknowledged receipt of the note on February 8, apologizing for not replying in length, as he was required on behalf of his government to undertake a journey through the Chilean south. Further notes, in which each country fully asserted its claims, were exchanged. On June 25, Blest Gana, alarmed by the announcement that the Argentine government planned to colonize Río Negro and that a naval training ship had sailed for Patagonia, addressed a note to Carlos Tejedor, complaining that the status quo had been violated and warning him that Chile would not allow any act whatsoever that would affect its sovereignty or tolerate any act whatsoever that might affect its sovereignty over the territories under its possession, which extended up to the Santa Cruz river. Frías replied, tersely refuting the Chilean claim, reminding him that

The Chilean government promised my government that it would not exploit the guano deposits in the islands of the Straits, near Punta Arenas, and that guano has been sold. It promised not go ahead with [its plans] for a colony in the Straits and it has extended its possession to the Eastern shore. In Tierra del Fuego it has lent support to aggression, placing a warship at the disposal of Mr. E. Pertuisset. It promised to respect our jurisdiction over Eastern Patagonia, and had visited these shores bringing homes and then settlers; first at Río Gallegos, and later on to Santa Cruz, and today it has stated to us, in the note to which I am replying, that it has decided to impede Argentine jurisdiction from the Santa Cruz river to Cape Horn.[30]

While the search for solutions continued, Chile sought to occupy the Atlantic coast of Patagonia, thus violating the treaty of 1856 under which both nations had agreed to respect the status quo of 1810. Argentina countered Chilean moves by exercising acts of sovereignty in the disputed area. These moves would bring both litigants to the brink of war.

ARGENTINE AND CHILEAN EXPANSION ALONG THE ATLANTIC COAST

In spite of the treaty of 1856, Chile began to actively explore the Atlantic coast of Patagonia, establishing outposts and exercising acts of sovereignty, something she would accuse Argentina of doing. Oscar Viel, governor of the Chilean settlement at the Straits designated as the Territory of Magallanes, with its capital at Punta Arenas, sought to improve the conditions of the colony under his charge. Viel fostered the development of coal deposits and the establishment of a sawmill to provide planking for the small craft constructed at Punta Arenas. In 1873, Viel wrote to Santiago asking for a new interpretation of the 1848 charter which governed the territory of Magallanes. Viel felt that Chilean jurisdiction on the Atlantic should be extended beyond the 48th parallel, over the Patagonian mainland, and north of the Deseado River.[31]

In 1859, Captain Luís Piedrabuena, a veteran Argentine mariner and explorer, erected trading posts at Santa Cruz and Staten Island. The Argentine government also issued permits to gather the guano used as fertilizer and began planting colonies in Patagonia. A contingent of Welsh immigrants was granted lands in the present-day province of Chubut. The settlers arrived at their new home in July 1865.[32]

On July 25, 1871, a concession of land was granted to Ernest Rouquad, a French citizen, who would operate a fish-oil factory at Los Misioneros Glenn in Santa Cruz established earlier by Luis Piedra. Rouquad, his family, and a number of journeymen for the factory arrived at Santa Cruz in October 1872. To protect the colonists, the Argentine government ordered the commander of the *Chubut* to proceed to Santa Cruz and establish a port captaincy. The *Chubut* was a decrepit sailing cutter of 120 tons, armed with a single 9-pound muzzle-loading cannon, which was not even mounted, but stowed in the hold. When Rouquad's venture failed, the crew of the *Chubut* took over its installations and began to explore the Santa Cruz River, reaching its source on November 26, 1873. The arrival of the *Abtao*, a Chilean 650-ton steam corvette armed with three 150-pound rifled cannon, caused the *Chubut*, which was in a lamentable state of repair, to withdraw upriver. Nevertheless, a tiny Argentine settlement under Piedrabuena remained active at the island of Pavon. Viel tried to make things difficult for the sailor, as he had done with Rouquad, but the Argentine was made of much sterner material, and the outpost remained.[33]

In 1875 Viel was replaced by Major Duble Almeida. The new governor of Magallanes established close contacts with the Tehuelche Indians, who kept him apprised of developments along the Argentine pampas, acting as auxiliaries and coast watchers, reporting the movements of Argentine ships. Punta Arenas had grown considerably by this time. A railway linked the colony with nearby coal deposits, while steamers maintained a lively trade with Montevideo. Roads had been built, connecting the Straits with Río Gallegos.[34]

Tensions mounted when the Argentine government issued licenses to foreign vessels, enabling them to extract guano off the coast of Santa Cruz. The first of these was the French barque *Jeanne Amelie*, which was operating in the area during February 1876. A party of Tehuelches who had spotted the vessel relayed the news to the governor of Magallanes, who in turn ordered the gunboat *Magallanes* to Santa Cruz to uphold the Chilean claim. The commander of the *Magallanes*, Captain Juan J. Latorre, captured the French barque and took the crew off the vessel, intending to tow it to Punta Arenas. The attempt failed and the *Jeanne Amelie* foundered. The entire episode greatly angered Argentina.[35]

In 1875, José Alfonso had succeeded Ibañez in the Chilean foreign ministry. Alfonso considered the Patagonian issue far less important than his predecessor, perhaps reflecting a new trend in the Chilean government, which now seemed determined to relinquish some of its more extreme claims. Alfonso entrusted the delicate task of reaching a settlement with Argentina to Diego Barros Arana, a renowned scholar with many contacts among the aristocracy of Buenos Aires.[36]

Barros Arana was instructed to inform the Argentine president, Nicolás Ave-llaneda, that Chile was prepared to recognize Argentine sovereignty to all of Patagonia as far as Río Gallegos. The detailed instructions of the Chilean foreign minister were contained in a folio dated May 1876, which stipulated that the territories of Patagonia, Tierra del Fuego, and the Straits would be submitted to arbitration. This notwithstanding, Barros Arana was to insure that the matter of the Straits was handled separately, offering the Argentine government a strip of Patagonian territory, ample enough to offset whatever advantages Chile had derived from the control of the Straits. The instructions further stipulated that the mediator's decision should be arrived on the basis of article no. 39 of the treaty of 1856, which defined the boundaries between both countries as those existing in 1810. Alfonso further emphasized that Chile was willing to cede all rights to Patagonia in return for Argentine recognition of Chilean sovereignty to all the lands below the southern bank of the Santa Cruz river along its entire length; from its point of origin in the Andes to its outlet, in the Atlantic Ocean, following a parallel line to the corresponding meridian. All territories south of this line were to be recognized as integral parts of Chile. If the Argentine government rejected this proposal, Chile was prepared to relinquish all claims to Río Gallegos, since it was most anxious to reach an accord.[37]

Barros Arana greatly exceeded his instructions and signed a protocol that granted Chile only partial control of the Straits, as well as an agreement to settle the *Jeanne Amelie* affair. The Chilean government promptly disavowed the actions of its envoy and recalled him in May of 1878.[38]

Tempers on both sides of the Andes were running high when the capture of another vessel by a Chilean warship added fuel to the fire. The ship affected this time was the U.S. barque *Devonshire*, which was seized by the gunboat *Magallanes*, of *Jeanne Amelie* incident fame. To protect their nation's rights in the area, President Avellaneda and his minister of war and marine, General Julio A. Roca, decided to occupy the Santa Cruz river and dispatched a flotilla of ships to that region. Commodore Luís Py of the Argentine navy was ordered to organize and lead the naval division, which would sail for Santa Cruz. The vessels that composed it were largely those ordered during the Sarmiento administration (1868–1874) and intended for operations in the tranquil waters of the Plata tributaries. They included the gunboat *Constitución*, the monitor *Los Andes*, and the corvette *Uruguay*. The latter carried a complement of "floating torpedoes," or mines, with which the Argentines sought to protect the Santa Cruz river from further Chilean incursions. The squadron, which would be later reinforced by the gunboat *República*, the torpedo boat *Monte León*, and the cutter *Los Estados*, departed from Buenos Aires on November 8, and after encountering heavy seas near Bahía Blanca, arrived at Carmen de Patagones on November 15 and dropped anchor at Los Misioneros three days later.[39]

The departure of the Argentine fleet was duly noted by Thomas Osborne, the American consul at Buenos Aires, in his report of November 18: "Two of the Argentine vessels have already sailed for the Santa Cruz river under secret orders, and three other war vessels will follow as soon as they can be put in condition. Chile is believed to have sent two or three gunboats to Patagonia with engineers to fortify the Straits."[40]

Osborne felt that since the barque *Devonshire* had been returned, the Argentine government would not be disposed to press the issue with Chile to a final settlement by war, particularly if it could be avoided with honor. The report also indicated that there was a large war party in Argentina, led by the president of the lower house and former minister to Santiago, who had apparently been badly treated by Chilean officials. Osborne met with the Argentine foreign minister, Bernardo de Yrigoyen, who assured him that Argentina did not desire war and had done everything possible to avoid it. Chile had offered arbitration and then rejected it, adding that "Argentina was still willing to arbitrate, that Chile had been and was aggressive, had planted colonies on Argentine territories and assumed jurisdiction by the capture of vessels of other nationalities in Argentine waters."[41]

Osborne reported on December 5 that the Chilean gunboat *Chacabuco* had been ordered to proceed with guns and war materials to the Straits, that orders would be received to seize and fortify the narrows, and that the entire Chilean naval squadron would follow afterward. The ironclad *Blanco Encalada* had been spotted fifty miles south of Valparaiso. Argentina, however, was appeased by the return of the *Devonshire*, which was seen as a conciliatory move made by Santiago. In return for this major concession, Chile asked that the press of Buenos Aires should refrain from publishing details of the agreement.[42] The inference was clear: the Chilean government wanted to withhold information from its people in order to not appear weak vis-à-vis Argentina. It would not be the last time that Chile made such a request.

Neither side was prepared to go to war, and negotiations between Mariano de Sarratea, the Argentine consul general in Santiago, and Alejandro Fierro, the Chilean foreign minister, were initiated. Sarratea was married to a Chilean woman, well connected with the Chilean aristocracy. Through his contacts, he soon learned that the president of Chile and the "peace-party" were willing to negotiate. After patient deliberations, a convention known as the Fierro-Sarratea Treaty was concluded on December 6, 1878. The document stipulated that both governments would appoint representatives who would constitute a tribunal. Pending arbitration, Chile would exercise jurisdiction over the waters and shores of the Straits of Magellan while Argentina exercised similar rights over the waters and shores of the Atlantic as well as adjacent islands. The Fierro-Sarratea Treaty was ratified by both houses of the Chilean legislature on January 14, 1879. Chile notified Argentina with its conformity with the new agreement.[43]

Chile, in fact, was most desirous of settling the Patagonian issues as news of another crisis reached Santiago. Chilean labor and capital had been largely responsible for the development of the nitrate deposits in the Bolivian province of Antofagasta. When Hilarión Daza, head of the Bolivian government, decided to levy a tax of ten cents on each *quintal*, or hundredweight, from the Antofogasta mines, the Chilean-owned *Compañía de Salitre y Ferrocarril de Antofogasta*, the largest employer in the nitrate fields, refused to pay. Consequently, the Bolivian government imprisoned the company's manager and shut down operations, throwing 2,000 men off their jobs. The Chilean fleet, which had been ordered south to Lota, where it was to stock coal "in case of war with Argentina," was now ordered north. On February 7, the *Blanco Encalada* reached Antofogasta, where on February 14 it was joined by its sistership, the

Cochrane, and the corvette *O'Higgins*. That day, Chilean forces seized Antofogasta, and the War of the Pacific had began.[44]

Chile's attention was therefore concentrated on its northern borders, as Argentina's had been drawn earlier by the Paraguayan war and the cold war with Brazil a few years before. The question of Patagonia had been resolved, at least on paper, to Argentina's satisfaction. Nevertheless, the Indian tribes who inhabited the region were retarding effective colonization of the pampas as well as control of Patagonia. Free from entanglements in the north, and having successfully stamped out the last remaining caudillos in Entre Ríos during the 1870s, the Argentine government had at its command a well-equipped army and a nation exhibiting a greater degree of cohesion than ever before. There were many in Argentina who counseled the termination of the Indian threat, which had long impeded Argentine colonization in the pampas, in order to make the frontier safe for the new settlers which the Argentine government hoped to establish there. The conquest of the desert was about to begin.

NOTES

1. Carlos Segretti, *Límites con Chile bajo Austrias y Borbones* (Buenos Aires: Editorial E.R.A., 1981), pp. 2–4. For details of English and Dutch exploration of Patagonia, see Eric Shipton, *Tierra del Fuego: The Fatal Loadstone* (London: Charles Knight, 1973).

2. Hubert Herring, *A History of Latin America: From the Beginnings to the Present* (New York: Alfred A. Knopf, 1968), pp. 143–144; Ricardo Caillet-Bois, *Cuestiones Internacionales, 1852–1966* (Buenos Aires: *EUDEBA*, 1970), pp. 30–31.

3. Aquiles D. Ygobone, *Soberanía argentina en las islas Malvinas, Antartida Argentina: cuestiones fronterizas entre Argentina y Chile* (Buenos Aires: Editorial Plus Ultra, 1970), pp. 140–142.

4. Ricardo A. Paz, *El Conflicto pendiente* (Buenos Aires: *EUDEBA*, 1980, 2 vols.), 1: 1–3.

5. Pedro De Angelis, *Memoria histórica sobre los derechos de soberanía y dominis de la Confederación Argentina a la parte austral del continente* (Buenos Aires: 1852), pp. vi–ix.

6. Mariano Pelliza, *La Cuestión del Estrecho* (Buenos Aires: *EUDEBA*, 1969), pp. 9–15.

7. De Angelis, *Memoria histórica*, pp. xii–xiv, xiv–xvi.

8. Ibid., pp. xviii–xxi, xxvii; Segretti, *Límites con Chile*, p. 12.

9. De Angelis, *Memoria histórica*, pp. xxvii–xxxii.

10. Pelliza, *La cuestión*, pp. 53–55; Laurio H. Destéfani, ''Buenos Aires, exploradora y colonizadora de la Patagonia: 1745–1810.'' *6o. CNRHA* (Buenos Aires: 1982, 4 vols.), III: pp. 452–454.

11. Pelliza, *La Cuestión*, pp. 54–55.

12. Mateos Martinic Beros, *Presencia de Chile en la Patagonia Austral* (Santiago de Chile: Editorial Andres Bello, 1963) pp. 16–17.

13. Ibid., p. 18.

14. Ibid., p. 20.

15. Ibid., pp. 21–22.

16. Exequiel Gonzalez Madariaga, *Nuestras relaciones con Argentina: Una historia deprimente*, 3 vols. (Santiago: Editorial Andres Bello and Neupert, 1972–74), 1: 57–58; Miguel Luís Amunátegui, *Títulos de la República de Chile a la soberanía y domínio de la extremidad austral del continente* (Santiago: Imprenta de Julio Belin, 1853), pp. 87–89; Allen Woll, *A Functional Past: The Uses of History in Nineteenth Century Chile* (Baton Rouge and London: Lousiana State University Press, 1982), pp. 106–107.

17. Woll, *A Functional Past*, pp. 88–91.

18. Amunátegui, *Títulos de la República*, pp. 88–89.

19. Woll, *A Functional Past*, pp. 120–124. Vicuña Mackena was a detractor of Amunátegui and his theories. Woll describes him as an ardent Pan-Americanist whose vision of a Pan-American union caused him to view the possibility of a war with Argentina with horror.

20. Pelliza, *La cuestión del Estrecho*, pp. 112–116; Mario Barros, *Historia diplomática de Chile* (Barcelona: Ediciones Ariel, 1971), pp. 176–177.

21. Solar Domingo Amunátegui, *Archivo Espistolar de Don Miguel Luís Amunátegui* (Santiago: 1942), pp. 166–167. The actual words of Lastarria were "Siento saber por tu carta del 14 que te ocupas en probarme que somos dueños de la Patagonia. Semejante tarea es inutil y *no servirá más que para probar to ingenio.*" The word *ingenio* in Spanish describes a person's ability to argue or to invent things rapidly and opportunely, as well as a poetic and creative ability. According to Pelliza, *La cuestión del estrecho*, p. 101, Amunátegui was a literary critic and aficionado whose knowledge of the law, particularly international law, was dubious.

22. Barros, *Historia diplomática*, p. 253; Luís Galdames, *A History of Chile* (Chapel Hill: University of North Carolina Press, 1941), pp. 306–307. For a detailed account of the Spanish expedition see Robert Ryal Miller, *For Science and National Glory: The Spanish Expedition to America, 1862–1866* (Norman: University of Oklahoma Press, 1968).

23. Jaime Eyzaguirre, *Chile durante el gobierno de Errázuriz Echaurren, 1896–1901* (Santiago: Empresa Editora Zig-Zag, 1957). Eyzaguirre states that Lastarria's lack of faith in his country's titles accounted for the "high-handed way" in which he was willing to "surrender" Patagonia to Argentina. Barros, *Historia diplomática*, p. 252, offers a rather more fanciful version: "Aside from the picturesque, the Lastarria mission had its positive side: the Argentines formed such a low opinion of Chile and her diplomacy that in the end, this was beneficial to us." Bartolomé Mitre, *AM*, 26 vols. (Buenos Aires: 1911–1912) 13, 100–101; Robert N. Burr, *By Reason or by Force: Chile and the Balancing of Power in South America, 1830–1905* (Berkeley and Los Angeles: University of California Press, 1967), pp. 102–103. According to Burr, the Chilean government was irritated at Argentina's failure to come to its aid against Spain because it failed to see that the Paraguayan campaign was proving a problem for Argentina and Brazil.

24. Charles Kolinski, *Independence or Death! The Story of the Paraguayan War* (Gainesville: University of Florida Press, 1965), pp. 143–145; Félix Best, *Historia de las guerras argentinas*, 2 vols. (Buenos Aires: Ediciones Peuser, 1960), pp. 2: 60–66, for details of the provincial uprising and the campaigns directed against Varela; Ricardo Caillet-Bois, *Cuestiones internacionales, 1852–1966*, pp. 52–53.

25. Gaylord H. Warren, *Paraguay and the Triple Alliance: The Post-war Decade,*

1869–1878 (Austin: University of Texas Press, 1978), pp. 189–200, 201–203. As a result of strained relations with Brazil, Argentina increased her armaments. Caillet-Bois, *Cuestiones internacionales*, pp. 24–25. At the time of the Brazilian crisis, the Argentine forces in Paraguay numbered less than 300 men without artillery or cavalry, and her naval forces were represented by the *Espora* and the *Gualeguay*, mere armed steamers, the latter out of commission.

26. Caillet-Bois, *Cuestiones internacionales* pp. 45–47; Juan José Fernández, *La República de Chile y el Imperio del Brasil: Historia de sus relacciones diplomáticas* (Santiago: Editorial Andres Bello, 1959), pp. 68–69.

27. Caillet-Bois, *Cuestiones internacionales*, pp. 40–41. Perú was most anxious to enlist Argentina into the anti-Chilean alliance, as Lima was aware that Chile would soon take delivery of the ironclads. See also Ximena Rojás Valdéz, *Don Adolfo Ibañez: su gestión con el Perú y Bolivia, 1870–1879* (Santiago: Editorial Andres Bello, 1970), pp. 74–75. Ibañez was appointed as the Chilean envoy to Peru in 1870. From his post in Lima he advised the president of Chile to purchase new warships. In 1871, the Chilean congress appropriated funds for the construction of two ironclads, which became the *Blanco Encalada* and *Cochrane*.

28. Pelliza, *La cuestión del Estrecho*, pp. 119–137. Frías was appointed special envoy and minister plenipotentiary to Chile on January 8, 1869, and presented his credentials to the president of Chile in March. The Chilean foreign minister at this time was Miguel Luís Amunátegui (Barros, *Historia diplomática*, pp. 265–266).

29. Pelliza, *La cuestión del Estrecho*, pp. 131–136; Horacio E. Molina, "La crisis argentino-chilena de 1878–1879: Algunos entretelones del pacto Fierro-Sarratea" *Revista Histórica* no. 12, (1983), pp. 66–71.

30. Martinic Beros, *Presencia de Chile*, pp. 136–137.

31. Alfredo Marcelo Serres Güiraldes, "Usurpación del Puerto de Santa Cruz," *Investigaciones y Ensayos* 22 (enero-junio 1977), pp. 420–425. Details of the *Chubut* can be found in Pablo E. Arguindeguy, *Apuntes sobre los buques de la armada argentina, 1810–1970*, 7 vols. (Buenos Aires: Comando en Jefe de la Armada, Secretaria General Naval, Departamento de Estudios Históricos Navales 1972) 3: 1447–1449; Humberto F. Burzio, *Armada nacional: Reseña histórica de su origen y desarrollo orgánico* (Buenos Aires: Secretaria de Estado de Marina, Subsecretaria, Departamento de Estudios Históricos Navales, ser. B., no. 1, Historia Naval Argentina, 1960), pp. 92–93; Rodrigo Fuenzalida Bade, *La armada de Chile: Desde la alborada al sesquicentenario, 1813–1968*, 4 vols. (Santiago: 1978), III: pp. 681–699, 721–722. In 1873 the Chilean navy possessed a pair of steam corvettes of 1,650 tons displacement, capable of eleven knots. Their armament consisted of three seven-inch 150-lb. rifled cannon, 2 × 70 lb., and 2 × 40 lb. In addition there were two gunboats, the *Magallanes* (742 tons, 11 knots, 1 × 150-lb. cannon, 1 × 64 lb., 1 × 20 lb.) and *Covadonga* (412 tons, 2 × 70-lb. cannon, 3 × 40 lb., 2 × 9-lb.); corvettes *Abtao* (1,057 tons, 3 × 150-lb. cannon, 4 × 40-lb.) *Esmeralda* (850 tons, an armament of 20 × 32 lb. cannon), and assorted auxiliaries. By comparison, the Argentine navy, which had still not taken delivery of the warships ordered in 1872, comprised thirteen small steamers, all of them converted packet boats armed with smoothbore guns ranging from 9 to 32 pounders, a sail brig, several cutters, one hulk, and three pontoons.

32. Martinic Beros, *Presencia de Chile*, pp. 118–120. Dora Noemí Martínez de Gorla, "Antecedentes de la colonización y explotación económica de la Patagonia y su relación

con la cuestión de límites con Chile, 1870–1881," *Revista de Historia de America*, no. 115 (enero-junio 1993): pp. 99–104.

33. Paz, *El Conflicto*, 1: pp. 10–11; Martínez de Gorla, "Antecedentes de la colonización y explotación económica de la Patagonia y su relación con la cuestión de límites con Chile, 1870–1881," pp. 99–104; Rosario Güenaga, *Santa Cruz y Magallanes: Historia socioeconómica de los territorios de la Patagonia austral argentina y chilena* (Mexico D.F.: Instituto Panamericano de Geografía e Historia, Pub. No. 475, 1994).

34. Martinic Beros, *Presencia de Chile*, pp. 166–167, 170–177.

35. Burr, *By Reason or by Force*, p. 133; Pelliza, *La cuestión del Estrecho*, pp. 208–215.

36. Burr, *By Reason or by Force*, pp. 133–134; Barros, *Historia diplomática* pp. 300–302. Diego Barros Arana was in fact the nephew of Felipe Arana, Argentine foreign minister under Rosas.

37. Barros, *Historia diplomática*, pp. 311–316.

38. Oscar Espinosa Moraga, *El precio de la paz chileno-argentina*, 3 vols. (Santiago: Editorial Nascimento, 1969): I: pp. 140–141. Burr, *By Reason or by Force*, p. 134, states that Barros Arana was transferred to Rio de Janeiro because the Chilean government disapproved of his actions. Pelliza, *La cuestión del Estrecho*, pp. 250–254, gives the same reason, adding that the Argentine envoy was recalled as well. Barros, *Historia Diplomática*, pp. 317–318, gives an imaginative but rather dubious version according to which Barros Arana, "sick of it all, asked for his passport and left for Rio."

39. Humberto F. Burzio, *Historia de la Escuela Naval Militar*, 3 vols. (Buenos Aires: Departamento de Estudios Históricos Navales, ser. B. Historia Naval Argentina no. 16, 1972), I: 263–266.

40. Osborne to Ewarts, telegram No. 207, November 18, 1878.

41. Ibid.

42. D. Warren Lowe to General T. O. Osborne, December 5, 1878.

43. Burr, *By Reason or by Force*, pp. 134–135.

44. Barros, *Historia diplomático*, pp. 318–324.

3

The Conquest of the Desert

By the early 1870s, Argentina's southwestern frontier remained open for a variety of reasons. As in the United States, the Indians were contained by treaties, subsidies in cash and kind, and a system of forts. The subsidy or "tribute" in the form of food staples, cattle, and horses was looked upon as an inexpensive alternative to punitive expeditions and as something that would deter the Indians from raiding settlements and ranches. The subsidies were particularly offensive to many Argentine statesmen. By the late 1870s, the Argentine Republic no longer found this sort of arrangement tolerable and decided effectively to occupy Patagonia.

FRONTIERS AND INDIANS

The area the Argentines called "the desert" included vast sectors of fertile lands, from the Río Negro to the provinces of Buenos Aires, Córdoba, Mendoza, and Santa Fé. After the campaign of 1879, these lands would be transformed into some of the richest and most productive in the world. This "desert" or wilderness also comprised the present-day provinces of La Pampa, Neuquén, Santa Cruz, and Río Negro, an area of more than 321,000 square kilometers stretching from the Andes to the Atlantic Ocean.[1]

As we have seen in chapter 1, Indians from neighboring Chile filtered into the plains of Argentina. Since time immemorial, the Indians raided settlements and ranches in the pampas, driving the stolen herds across the Andes along a trail significantly known as El camino de los chilenos, or "the road of the Chileans." The tribes who had invaded the desert included the Voroganos, who took their name from their place of origin, a place called Voroa, near the Cantín River, in Chile; the Huiliches also came from across the Andes, as did the

Ranqueles, Pehuenches, and Tehuelches. The Spanish conquistadores had contained the Araucanian but never subdued them. The reputation of the Araucanians as proud and tenacious defenders of the lands they occupied was already established by the sixteenth century. The southern frontier bore witness to 300 years of savage warfare between the Araucanians, first against the Spaniards and later on against the Argentines. The last effective Indian campaign was that undertaken by Juan Manuel de Rosas in 1833. Rosas's strategic plan would presage the 1879 campaign in many respects. Three fast-moving divisions would proceed south in a parallel course along a 400-league front stretching from the Andes to the Atlantic in a vast pincer operation in order to trap the Indians and seal off the Andean passes, thus preventing their escape into Chile. The Right Division (800 troopers and 26 Indian scouts) under General Félix Aldao would advance through the south of Mendoza along the Andes. The Left Division (2,010 men, 5 pieces of horse artillery), led personally by Juan Manuel de Rosas, would advance to the Colorado River and then turn west, while the Central Division (1,000 men) under General José Huidobro would push through the central pampas. These columns were to link up at the junction of the Limay and Neuquén rivers. The operation was well planned and conceived. Astronomers and surveyors as well as the well-known Italian cartographer Nicolá Descalzi were attached to the expedition. A map-making section provided charts of the zone of operations. To ensure the greatest possible mobility, the infantry was mounted. Special attention was given to the arms and equipment issued to the soldiers. The cavalry troopers carried sabers, lances, and short carbines, or *tercerolas*. Artillery, considered an impediment, was reduced to a minimum. The expedition included a small naval detachment that would explore the Colorado and Neuquén rivers aboard flat-bottomed boats. Sufficient horses were requisitioned to ensure there were at least three mounts per man. General depots were established at Bahía Blanca and Carmen de Patagones. Operations got underway in February, and within a year, all of the objectives had been reached. In several major encounters 3,200 braves were killed, 1,000 Indians of both sexes were captured, and 1,000 captives rescued. The frontier line had been pushed West of Bahía Blanca, Médano Redondo, and Carmen de Patagones, and 2,900 square leagues of territory were made safe for development. Rosas planned to extend the campaign for another year, but the legislature in Buenos Aires ordered the troops home.[2]

Although the Indians were severely chastised in this campaign, once the Argentine forces had withdrawn, they returned from their Chilean havens. Their progress across the Andes was unimpeded, largely because Chile had not yet completed the pacification of her own Indian frontier, which in the 1830s stood exactly where it had been since colonial times, South of the Bío-Bío River.[3] Late in 1834 a new invasion of Chilean Indians occurred. Among the newcomers was a chief known as Calfucurá, who conquered the Voroganos after murdering their chiefs, who had once sheltered him. Calfucurá incorporated them into a vast Indian confederation that also included the Mapuches, Huiliches, and Tehuelches. This confederation embraced 15,000 people, including 2,600 warriors.[4] Calfucurá's legions were further augmented when Sayhueque, chief of the Manzanero tribe and once a bitter enemy, concluded a pact with the Araucanian and became his vassal. Thus Calfucurá gained control over an additional 15,000 subjects, including 1,500 warriors. He was quick to realize the importance of the rich pastures of the province of Buenos Aires. This source of cattle and booty was vital to the Indian confederation. Without them, it would wither and perish.[5]

In 1835 Calfucurá observed a truce with the Argentine government. In return, Rosas decreed that the Indians should receive a yearly subsidy of 8,000 steers, as well as determined quantities of such staples as sugar, yerba maté, tobacco, and flour. Despite the peace sworn to Rosas, the Indians continued to raid settlements and ranches. In retaliation, minor punitive raids were undertaken by the Argentines in February and November 1835. In 1836, a chief called Cañuquir emerged as the new leader of the Voroganos. Cañuquir refused to parley with Rosas. In response, Rosas issued orders to Colonels Sosa and Zelarrayán at Fort Argentino, in Bahía Blanca, to lead an expedition against Cañuquir. On March 22, government troops had their first glimpse of the Indians at Guaminí near the Pescado brook. The soldiers took the Indians by surprise and engaged them in a ferocious hand-to-hand battle that lasted for three hours. Though Cañuquir and about 300 of his warriors managed to escape, 400 others were killed, and over 500 prisoners were taken. On April 19, an army detachment departed from Fort 25 de Mayo. On the next morning, the troopers surrounded the Indian camp. In the ensuing battle, Cañuquir and 250 braves were killed, and another 300 were taken.[6]

The army conducted punitive strikes in 1839, 1844, 1845, and 1849, with positive results. After each strike, the frontier line was pushed further south, and new outposts were established. Unable to withstand the determined assaults of the cavalry, the Indians retreated, suffering heavy casualties. Except for minor raids, the frontier would remain comparatively peaceful until the fall of Rosas in 1852.[7]

The frequency as well as the intensity of the Indian attacks increased during the struggles between Buenos Aires and the Confederation, when the frontier was denuded of its best units and officers. Ever alert to changes in the Argentine political scenario, the Indians became bolder. With greater freedom of movement and less fear of retaliation, they engaged in widespread depredations. To protect the frontier, small contingents of national guards were mobilized; they, however, were few in numbers and led by inexperienced officers with poor knowledge of the terrain. Despite some military successes, the Indians' power remained unbroken, and during the campaigns of 1855–1858, the army suffered 2,500 casualties. Under the renewed fury of the Indian raids, the province of Buenos Aires alone lost almost 64,000 square kilometers of territory, as the hostiles devastated areas such as Saladillo in the west, Pergamino in the north, and Tandil in the south.[8]

On May 19, 1859, Fort Argentino, which defended Bahía Blanca, was attacked by a wave of 1,500 warriors led by Calfucurá. The Indians surrounded the settlement, which contained 1,200 inhabitants and was protected by a garrison of 400 men, and at three in the morning, they broke into town without awakening the garrison. Then the alarm was given and the soldiers, armed with old Tower muskets and sabers, rushed to the streets. A hand-to-hand battle in which quarter was neither given nor asked took place until dawn, when the Indians retired, leaving sixty dead on the square and on the streets.[9]

WARFARE ON THE SOUTHWESTERN FRONTIER

Hand-to-hand combat between the gaucho soldiers and the Indians was common, as the muskets issued to the frontier forces were ancient and required an inordinate amount of time to reload. Morever, these weapons were often unrepaired and useless. In April 1854, the garrison at Fortín Esperanza, which consisted of a second lieutenant and twenty troopers, was armed with two unserviceable carbines and two rifles for which there were neither flints nor cartridges. In addition, there were three cavalry sabers and a four-pounder cannon with ten shrapnel and twenty solid shot shells.[10]

The Indians normally charged on horseback, wielding their long *tacuará* lances, much as a medieval knight would, until they were on top of the skirmish line. Then they would dismount and engage in combat at close quarter. Knives and *bolas* were used by both gauchos and Indians in toe-to-toe fighting. The bolas were stone or lead balls wrapped in leather and attached to thongs of the same material. They were used to entangle the adversary or his horse or wielded as a maze. When used in this fashion, the bolas could break a man's ribs or crush a skull with ease. The soldiers were equipped with curved cavalry sabers and their own, private-issue *facón*, a long triangularly bladed knife. Attacks upon frontier settlements would generally involve war parties of three to five hundred warriors, although in the 1870s these numbers increased considerably. The men would be killed immediately, and the women and children would be taken captives. The buildings were burned, and cattle and horses were rounded up. While one Indian party was fighting the men, another would secure the captives and round up the stock.[11]

The ranks of the frontier forces were filled by *levas*, or forcible drafts. In theory, individuals were required to serve for one year, but in practice were forced to serve for ten or twenty.[12] There were the *destinados*, men convicted of vagrancy or other offenses. A number of immigrants, largely Italian, but with a sprinkling of other nationalities as well, joined the army as *enganchados*, or volunteers. Some achieved senior officer status and fought with distinction in the struggles for national unification as well as in the Indian and Paraguayan wars.[13] The *gringo*, or foreigner, was most often ridiculed for notorious inability to ride a horse. Thus the artillery and infantry in the post-Rosas period contained a high proportion of immigrants, particularly Italian.[14]

Table 3.1
Argentine Military Expenditures for 1874 (in gold pesos of 48 d.)

Army	4 ,046,453
Navy	270,339
Indians	220, 033
War Ministry	33,434
Grand Total	4, 574,259

Source: M. G. Mulhall and E. T. Mulhall, *Manual de las Repúblicas del Plata* (Buenos Aires: 1876), 348.

Among the gaucho levies, desertion was high, discipline marginal; hence draconian measures were often used to instill these virtues into them. As for the fighting qualities of the Argentine soldier, Martin De Moussy found him

docile, indefatigable, insensitive to either privations or exposure. He is the man of the desert, accustomed to a frugal and adventurous life, who does not recoil from the harshest of campaigns. As far as his courage is concerned, the fifty years of warfare which have so deeply troubled this republic, with their never ending battles without quarter well testify of his energy and tenacity. With adequate military training, he will be one of the finest soldiers in the world, because he possesses (the qualities) of the valiant: coolness, physical strength and a taste for adventure.[15]

The frontier forces, which seldom exceeded 3,000 men, were denuded of their best units when Argentina went to war with Paraguay in 1865. In the years that followed, the nation had to uproot the last remaining caudillos. Once these threats were dispelled, the government turned its attention to the Indian frontier.[16]

The livestock owners of Buenos Aires were demanding protection against Indian attacks and at the same time wanted to expand their holdings south of the Río Negro, into an area hitherto occupied by Indians. The frontier dispute with Chile further impressed upon the Argentine ruling class the need to effectively occupy Patagonia.[17] The upkeep of the frontier forces was high. Included in these expenses was the "tribute" paid to the Indians, which in 1876 included 43,294 horses and mares. Government revenues averaged around 18.1 million pesos per year during 1872 and 1874. Military expenditures, as shown in table 3.1, were 4.5 million pesos, or 28 percent of the total income. The share of the budget allotted to "Indians," 220,033 pesos, was almost as large as that assigned to the Argentine navy, and greater than the 148,375 pesos destined for railway subsidies.[18]

The Argentine army at this time comprised about 6,000 men, half of whom were deployed along the southwestern frontier. In a book titled *Indios, fronteras y seguridad interior*, originally published in the 1870s, Álvaro Barros, former commander of the frontier forces, gave a detailed account of the period between 1857 and 1872, noting that 48 million pesos had been spent on the defense of the frontier and tributes or subsidies.[19] In addition to military expenditures, and excluding tribute, in the fifty-year period between 1820 and 1870 the Indians had stolen 11 million head of cattle and 2 million horses, destroyed over 3,000 houses, killed or captured 50,000 people, and carried off 20 million gold pesos of property.[20]

Aside from the devastation they wrought upon the lands, the Indians created a sort of no-man's land in a vast area from the Andes to the Atlantic. Moreover, the Indians assiduously rendezvoused with Chilean traders and squatters, and soon, settlements grew along the eastern slopes of the Andes from Mendoza to Neuquén. Such was the case of Malbarco, a hamlet of 600 inhabitants south of Mendoza. The Chilean squatters not only maintained close relations with the Indians but also participated in their raids; thus they gained possession of herds numbering 15,000 head of cattle, 4,000 horses, and 1,000 sheep and goats. The Chilean government conferred military titles and civilian offices upon both Indians and rustlers, and practically all major chiefs heeded the call of Chilean authorities. Some chiefs acted as foremen of Chilean cattlemen, who wintered their stocks in lands east of the Andes. An Argentine historian recalled that the infamous Pincheira brothers, scourges of the pampas, had received commissions in the Chilean army. The notorious Indian chief Juan Agustín was known in Chile as Juan Agustín Terrado, a Chilean government official and judge of Barranca. Chief Caepe of Neuquén was married to a niece of General Manuel Bulnes, once in charge of the Chilean frontier forces. The administrator of his ranch was a certain chieftain called Ailal, of notorious reputation as a clever thief, known in Chile as Francisco Palacios, while a former police official known as Manuel Palacios realized huge profits from Indian attacks.[21]

The establishment of Chilean colonies in Patagonia, its explorations along the Atlantic seaboard—in short, its very presence in the contested area—in spite of the agreement signed in 1856 were serious factors to be reckoned with. The conquest of the desert was doubly imperative to the Argentines. The drain of resources occasioned by the maintenance of the frontier forces and the system of forts, the devastation visited upon frontier settlements as well as the siphoning of livestock that would eventually find its way to the Chilean market, were no longer tolerable to a nation which at last was tapping long-dormant energies and beginning to modernize its infrastructure and populate its empty spaces with agricultural colonies. In 1870 the frontier was still uncomfortably close to Buenos Aires. The border dispute with Chile must be added to all of these considerations. Not unexpectedly, the Argentine government decided to end this state of affairs by ordering a punitive strike against the Indians. However, the modernization of the army's equipment would have to precede any operation of that magnitude.

MODERNIZATION OF THE ARMY IN THE 1870s

Prior to 1870, the Argentine army was equipped with a variety of muzzle-loading muskets and a small number of breechloaders of dubious reliability and accuracy. The best of the lot, the Spencers and Sharps, suffered from a common defect among early breechloaders; gas escaped at the breech, parts were fouled, and as a result the projectiles lost velocity and accuracy. A former British officer who served with the Argentine army remarked that the weapons of those days were so inadequate, their rate of fire so low that it was not implausible to state that the long lances and bolas of the Indian were far more effective. Then came the Remington, and the Indians were finished. However, the officer noted in his memoirs, the Remington was an effective weapon only in the hands of brave and disciplined soldiers, such as the Argentines. The Remington was a breech-loading rifle, 11 mm. caliber, with an effective range of 1,000 meters. The infantry was equipped with the Model 1870 rifle and the cavalry with the Model 1879 carbine. Officers and gunners carried 12-mm. Leffecheux revolvers, models 1859 and 1870. These would be replaced by the Forehand and Wadsworth model 1873 and the Smith & Wesson model 1878.[22]

Steps were also taken to reorganize the remount and supply branches. On paper, the soldiers' rations were quite adequate; in practice they often went hungry and were forced to subsist on a diet of horse meat. Traditionally, army mounts were obtained from civilian purveyors of doubtful honesty who provided wretched specimens. Furthermore, under indifferent care, many of these animals died, until in 1873, when steps were taken to correct this situation. Frontier garrison commanders were ordered to grow forage for their mounts. Large grazing fields were developed next to the forts, so that the animals could be properly rested and fed.[23]

As late as 1870, army uniforms were purchased in Europe, but the Comisaria de Guerra, or supply branch, began to produce these items at its workshops in Buenos Aires. The communications branch had been established during the ministry of Adolfo Alsina, when the five major frontier detachments were linked to Buenos Aires by telegraph. In addition, a course in military telegraphy was added to the curriculum of the military academy founded by Sarmiento in 1869.[24]

EARLY RETALIATORY STRIKES

Better armed, led, and equipped than ever before, the frontier forces began to defeat the Indians in a series of pitched battles, fought literally toe-to-toe. To be sure, the Indians had been repulsed on numerous occasions, but in pursuit, the soldiers soon fell behind. Their wretched mounts simply could not compare with the superb horses of the Indians, who simply melted into the limitless plains.

One of the most significant encounters of the Indian wars took place at San

Carlos, on March 5, 1872. At the head of 6,000 warriors, Calfucurá invaded the province of Buenos Aires. The districts of Alvear, 25 de Mayo and 9 de Julio, were devastated in rapid succession. The Indians carried off 2,000 steers and 500 captives after killing another 300 settlers and setting their houses on fire. General Ignacio Rivas, commander of the frontier forces, gathered a force of 500 men and marched toward Fort San Carlos, near the town of Azul, where he linked up with a detachment of 500 men under Colonel Juan Boer. In addition, there were 800 Pampa Indian auxiliaries, led by Chiefs Catriel and Coliqueo. Rivas rested his troops and awaited the return of Calfucurá. On the morning of March 8, patrols riding point sighted the Indians, and the army attacked. The Indians regrouped and charged. The Argentines dismounted and fought on foot. At first, the Indian allies were reluctant to fight their brethren, but urged by Catriel, who swore to shoot all shirkers, the Pampas defeated a band of 1,000 warriors led by Reuque Curá, brother of Calfucurá. The encounter was a bloody one indeed. Wielding their carbines as clubs, using bayonets, sabers, and knives, the soldiers fought like wild beasts. Overwhelmed, the Indians withdrew in haste, leaving behind 200 dead and 500 wounded. The army, which suffered minimal losses, recovered part of the enormous booty and freed many captives. Exhaustion and poor knowledge of terrain prevented an effective pursuit. Calfucurá's prestige suffered a serious blow. Once again the Argentine trooper had shown himself to be a formidable adversary.[25]

Calfucurá died in December 1873 and was succeeded by his son and heir, Namuncurá. The threat remained. The Indians could be defeated in battle, but the raids would not stop. In pursuit they would simply disperse over the vast ranges or flee to the safety of their native Chile. The task of finally securing the Indian frontier would fall to the government of President Nicolás Avellaneda (1874–1880). Avellaneda's war minister, Adolfo Alsina, suggested a plan to hold back the Indians. Two parallel lines of outposts, 100 kilometers apart, would be constructed along the frontier. The outer network of forts would be protected by a long trench, mockingly dubbed Alsina's ditch by detractors of this plan. From time to time, the lines would be pushed forward so that new territories could be gained, as the line advanced.[26]

The line, a pampean precursor of the Maginot Line, was erected at great expense, but the new commander of the frontier forces, General Julio A. Roca, thought this plan ineffective, as small military detachments isolated in forts were soon demoralized and discipline suffered as a result. Furthermore, the Indians were still capable of mounting massive attacks.[27]

One such raid, recorded in Argentine history as the great invasion, took place in November 1875. In a furious attack, 3,500 warriors, including 1,000 Araucanians newly arrived from Chile, fell upon the settlements like a tidal wave. The villages of Olavarría, Tandil, Azul, Tres Arroyos, and Tapalque were devastated. In an orgy of destruction, pillage, and murder, more than 400 settlers were killed, another 300 taken captive, and 300,000 head of cattle carried off. The Argentine army retaliated with a series of punitive strikes, inflicting heavy losses upon the Indians. Fifteen hundred hostiles were defeated by the forces under Lieutenant Colonel Leopoldo Vinttner at Laguna de la Tigra, near Olavarría, on January 1, while other detachments prevailed in the engagements at San Carlos (January 2) and Horqueta del Sauce (March 10). On March 18, the colorful, Italian-born Colonel Nicolás Levalle led 1,700 men of the Puan and Guamini divisions to Paragüil, where Indian war parties had been sighted. Advancing under heavy fog, the Argentines were blocked by more than 3,000 warriors. A furious hand-to-hand battle ensued until the first cavalry regiment, under Colonel Salvador Maldonado, charged and the Indians withdrew in complete disarray.[28]

This retaliatory strike presaged the shape of things to come. General Roca advocated precisely the sort of tactics successfully proven in the battles of 1872–1875. Roca had the quintessential requirement of any gifted commander or successful executive: he had demonstrated his ability to innovate. The static defense advocated by Alsina, Roca maintained, was destined to fail. Hit-and-run raids by mobile forces, he argued, would bring an end to the Indian menace, noting that the best system of overcoming the Indians was to drive them beyond the Río Negro, in an offensive like that undertaken by Rosas in 1833.[29]

In a letter published in the newspaper *La República*, Roca maintained that such an operation would greatly benefit the nation, not only because of the well-irrigated, fertile lands that would be added to the national patrimony but also because it would allow Argentina to secure her borders and end the illicit cattle trade that had existed between Indians and the Chilean provinces of Talca, Maule, Linares, Nuble, Concepción, Arauco, and Valdivia. Estimating the number of cattle driven off to Chile by the Pehuenches alone at 40,000 head per year, Roca added, "Persons who have lived near the Chilean border have assured me that some of the leading statesmen of that nation, who possess or have possessed ranches in those provinces are not strangers to this illicit trade, from which they derive large profits, and even their entire fortunes."[30]

The trade in stolen cattle conducted between Indians and Chileans was the motivating factor behind the savage warfare that ravaged the frontier. In addition, the Indians occupied lands east of the Andes and thus delayed effective control by Argentina. Argentine strategists believed that a war against Chile would not be fought in Patagonia nor in adjacent waters, but rather on the northern and eastern fringes of the pampas. Was this not, after all, the extent of the most extreme Chilean claims to Patagonia?[31]

Numerous requests for Chilean cooperation in efforts to put an end to the cattle trade between Indians and Chilean merchants and persistent notes of protests were met with equally persistent Chilean refusals. Fears that the Araucanians might constitute the advanced spearhead in a contemplated invasion of Patagonia by the Chileans were not unfounded. Chilean officials, as we have seen, had concluded treaties with the Indians in order to secure recognition of sovereignty to lands east of the Andes. The frontier dispute that festered during the 1870s was seen as a stratagem on the part of the Chileans to divert the attention of the Argentine government and force postponement of the campaign long advocated by Mitre and Roca. By manipulating the Indians and refusing to cooperate with the Argentine government in its punitive campaigns while at the same time engaging in active exploration of southern Patagonia, Chile played a delaying game in the expectation that, as in the past, internal or external factors would prevent Argentina from occupying the disputed territory. In order to secure Patagonia, Roca had planned and would conduct an exceptionally simple but smooth operation that called for an offensive sweep by light forces. The campaign began on April 1879, after meticulous preparations. In a space of a month and a half, the desert would be secured at last.[32]

ROCA'S MILITARY STRATEGY

In March 1878 Roca was appointed to the War Ministry. He surrounded himself with a group of very capable staff officers that included men like Colonels Conrado Villegas, Lorenzo Vintter, Camilo García, and Manuel Olascoaga, forged in the harsh school of frontier service. Manuel J. Olascoaga was an expert cartographer who shared Roca's outlook on the Patagonian questions. In 1864, for political reasons, Olascoaga went into exile in Chile, where he worked as a journalist and explored Araucania, the Chilean Indian frontier. In 1867 he published a map of that region that was adopted by the Chilean government. Upon returning to Argentina, he published a series of articles that attracted the attention of Roca, who reinstated Olascoaga to his former military rank and appointed him chief of the army's cartography department.[33]

Roca's strategy called for a prolonged series of hit-and-run raids by small, mobile forces of cavalry and mounted infantry to carry the war into the heart of Indian territory, depriving them of their stolen herds, their sole means of sustenance. The daily lives of the Indians as well as their offensive strikes were closely linked to the availability of water sources. Recognizing the factor of water in the desert, vital to the Indians while conducting and returning from their raids, Roca sought to drive them away from the rivers and streams, thus forcing them to either submit or to offer the army the sort of battle that the Indians had sought to avoid. The primary objective, however, was to break their spirit by fear and terror, to soften them up before the final blow fell. Long neglected, the frontier forces were now better equipped and supplied. The Remington rifles, previously issued on a limited scale, were now available in large quantities; ammunition was plentiful, as were remounts for the expeditionaries. The harassing raids foreseen by Roca were greatly facilitated by the introduction of two major innovations, the telegraph and the railways. By the end of 1878, the Argentine army was ready for the long-awaited drive.[34]

PRELIMINARY OPERATIONS

With the passing of Calfucurá in 1873, the crown of his once-feared confederation passed to his son and heir, Namuncurá. Though the hostiles were still numerous, they were demoralized by recent defeats. In January 1878, shortly before Roca was appointed to the War Ministry, elements of the Argentine army raided the once secure and remote Araucanian camp at Chiloe, or Salinas Grandes, in the southwestern sector of the province of Buenos Aires. The Indians were so utterly demoralized by the fury of this unexpected attack that they broke and fled, retreating further into the desert, leaving their camp littered with the bodies of 200 dead and wounded. On October 16, Lieutenant Colonel Vintter led a raid against Catriel's tribe. An advance party led by Major Lucero broke into the Indian camp on October 31, but Catriel, who had been alerted, fled. With the army close at his heels and fearing total annihilation, he surrendered the remnants of his tribe to the authorities at Fort Argentino.[35]

On November 2, Colonel Conrado Villegas, commander of the northern frontier forces, left his encampment at Trenque Lauquen at the head of a contingent of 300 men from the third cavalry regiment and the second infantry battalion. After a brief skirmish. Chief Pincen and the war parties led by his lieutenants, Epumer and Melidéo, were captured. When intelligence reports indicating that Namuncurá was gathering a force of 2,000 braves at Salinas Grandes reached Roca, he ordered General Levalle to lead the Western, Carhue, and Puan divisions in a punitive expedition. Levalle reached Salinas Grandes on November 27, and although the reports of a large-scale invasion proved unfounded, numerous war parties were sighted in the vicinity. On December 6, elements of the Puan division under Colonel García clashed with a war party at the Lihue-Calel heights. In a brief but hotly contested engagement, 50 braves were killed, 270 captured, and 33 captives freed. Between December 11 and January 24, a detachment led by Colonel Eduardo Racedo, composed of the fourth cavalry regiment, the tenth infantry battalion, and 100 Indian auxiliaries, swept an area of 60,000 square kilometers south of Córdoba and broke the power of the once-powerful Ranquel tribe. On the morning of January 2, Lieutenant Colonel Rufino Ortega's detachment left Fort General San Martín on a southerly direction and reached the river Neuquén. Numerous encounters of this sort would follow, until by December 1878 over 4,000 Indians had been captured, 400 braves killed, 150 captives freed, and 15,000 head of cattle recovered. The army suffered only eighteen casualties in the course of these operations; thus at a small cost, it gained knowledge of a terrain hitherto unexplored, knowledge that would prove of the utmost value in the campaign that was about to begin. It would be what the Argentines would term the conquest of the desert.[36]

To implement Roca's strategy, the executive power requested 1.6 million pesos, and Congress sanctioned a law on October 4, 1878, allocating funds. According to the plan formulated by Roca, the expeditionary army would consist of five divisions, a total of 6,000 men who would cross the desert between the Río Negro and the Andes and capture as many Indians as possible in a giant pincer movement. The five divisions, which in reality were regimental-size units, were assigned the following objectives: the first division, led personally by Roca, would advance towards the island of Choele-Choel, in the Río Negro. The second division would march from Carhué to Chadi Levú and send detachments to link up with units under Colonels Godoy and Racedo in the north and the Colorado river in the south. The third division, under Colonel Racedo, was to begin deployment on April 10, reconnoiter the area occupied by the Ranquel tribe, and sweep it clear of Indians. The fourth division, under Colonel Uriburú, was to depart from San Rafael, in Mendoza, on March 15–20, skirting the Andes as far as Chos Malal; scout for a suitable location to establish a permanent settlement; and later effect a linkup with units sent by Roca from Río Negro. The fifth division, established on April 15 under Colonel Hilario Lagos, received marching orders on May 1, instructing the commander to scout the area between Trenque Lauqen and Tobay, link up with fourth division, and trap any stragglers who had avoided capture by other army units. The five divisions were to sweep the territories open and act as a gigantic net to catch as many Indians as possible. The fourth division would seal off mountain passes that led into Chile and then advance to the junction of the Limay and Neuquén rivers, where it would link with the first division. When the jaws of the pincers were closed, all Indians trapped inside would have to surrender.[37]

THE CONQUEST OF THE DESERT

The plan conceived by Roca worked perfectly, thanks to meticulous planning and the fact that the Indians had been weakened by previous military operations. Facing the army were 8,000 Indian warriors. The hardest task of all fell to the fourth division, which was to skirt the Andean foothills and seal off mountain passes through which the Indians might escape into Chile. This unit had begun operations rather late in the season, and the men suffered from the intense cold. The country they had to traverse was heavily wooded and impassable for horses. The division established two forts; one at San Martín, near the Atuel River, and the other, known as the fourth division on the Neuquén. On June 7, the division linked up with the vanguard of the first division under Lieutenant Colonel Fotheringham. A detachment of the fourth division under Sergeant Major Saturnino Torres rode into the encampment of Chief Baigorrita and captured over 100 Indians, who were taken into a detention center established at Fourth Division Fort. Unfortunately, the Indians contracted smallpox from the soldiers and the disease spread rapidly, decimating them.[38] As the end of the campaign neared, the fourth division had fulfilled all its assigned objectives: it had swept the hostiles from a large area stretching from the southern part of Mendoza to the Neuquén River and traversed 500 kilometers of mountainous terrain under freezing temperatures.[39]

The first division, under Roca, had linked up with elements of the fourth in June and returned to Choele-Choel soon afterward, leaving a small detachment as a permanent garrison. With understandable pride, Roca cabled the acting minister of war and marine: "Occupation of the military line along the Negro and Neuquén rivers, and search operations through those vast territories completed. I am pleased to inform your excellency that the portion of the desert once used by those thieving Indians as a base of operations for their raids against our settlement has been completely and effectively conquered by our arms.''[40]

The conquest of the desert was completed two months and twenty days after it had begun. Over 15,000 Indians had been taken prisoner, 1,313 warriors killed, and 15,000 square leagues of territory effectively added to the national patrimony.[41] Roca returned to Buenos Aires in July, leaving small detachments along the new frontier. However, the Indian problem had not been completely resolved, and further operations would be required throughout the years 1881–1883, until the last marauding bands were killed or captured.

The frontier dispute with Chile also remained unsolved. In March 1879, at a time when Roca was about to launch his Patagonian campaign, Chile sent José M. Balmaceda as envoy to Argentina to expedite a boundary settlement. Chilean spies in Montevideo reported to Santiago that Roca's expedition served as a pretext to organize the army, create a corps of engineers, secure loans and study the pampas: in other words, to prepare for war against Chile. Marcos Avellaneda, the president of Argentina, however, viewed the prospect of a war with Chile with horror and vowed he would resign if hostilities broke out.[42]

Unofficially, Manuel Montes de Oca, Avellaneda's foreign minister, told Balmaceda that Argentina would not take advantage of the difficulties with Chile and would observe the strictest neutrality in the War of the Pacific, which had broken out nine months earlier. United States mediation was accepted by both parties and a convention known as the Treaty of 1881 was concluded on July 23. In return for Argentine recognition of Chilean sovereignty over the Straits of Magellan, Chile gave up her claim to Patagonia. Tierra del Fuego would be divided and provisions for arbitration of the treaty were made. Diplomatic tensions between both countries abated. However, differences of interpretations of the treaty as well as border incidents would serve to reawaken old suspicions. The border incidents occurred as a result of mop-up operations conducted by the Argentine army during 1881–1883, designed to bring the last remaining Indian war parties to submission.[43]

THE ANDEAN CAMPAIGNS OF 1881–1883

Driven from the Río Negro during the 1879 operations, large numbers of Indians found refuge West of the Andes. Once the army withdrew, the Indians emerged from their sanctuaries in Chile to attack small outposts and settlements in Neuquén, Mendoza, and Buenos Aires throughout 1880. Determined to put an end to their depredations, in January 1881, the War Minister ordered General Conrado Villegas's third division, now composed of three brigades, to police the provinces of Buenos Aires and Córdoba and the territories between the Colorado and Challeo rivers. The operational plan called for the three brigades to converge upon Lake Nahuel Huapi, while engaging hostile bands along the route. Naval transports ferried troops, supplies, and equipment from Carmen de Patagones to Choele-Choel. Logistical problems delayed the start of operations until March 15. Forewarned, the Indians fled to their Chilean havens. After minor skirmishes, the First Brigade, under Colonel Ortega, reached Nahuel Huapi on April 5. The Second Brigade arrived four days later, and the Third Brigade on April 10. In May, as the cold season set in with full vigor, Villegas ordered the forces under his command to return to their bases. Chief Reuque Curá ordered an attack against the Second Brigade, at Fort Roca. If the attack were successful, it would be followed by separate strikes against the Third Brigade at Choele-Choel and the First Brigade at Chos-Malal, on the gamble that the destruction of the frontier forces would turn public opinion in Buenos Aires against further military expeditions to Patagonia. Fort Roca, on the Río Negro Valley, constituted a major obstacle for the Araucanians, since it blocked the trails normally used in their raids. The path to Fort Roca was protected by First Division Fort, a newly established outpost that guarded the junction of the Limay and Neuquén rivers. On the dawn of January 16, 1882, 1,000 warriors attacked the tiny garrison, composed of fifteen troopers of the seventh cavalry and fifteen civilians. The defenders fought with fierce determination, throwing rocks at the attackers after their ammunition was exhausted. The Indians were repulsed with heavy losses.[44]

On March 22, a government decree established the second Army division under General Villegas on the basis of the forces deployed along the Limay and Neuquén, and the third division under Colonel Eduardo Racedo. The second division would police Río Negro while the third would be responsible for the central pampas, a stretch of territory between the borders of the provinces of Buenos Aires, Córdoba, and San Luis and the rivers Colorado and Chalileo. Once this was accomplished, the War Ministry ordered Villegas to draw up a plan for a new expedition scheduled for the spring of 1882, designed to subdue the last remaining Indian war parties. Villegas laid out a plan that embodied the experiences gained in previous campaigns. Fully elaborated, it called for the deployment of small detachments and patrols in a sweep of the region between Ñorquín, Catan-lil and Nahuel Huapi. Across the Andes, the Chilean government, whose attitude had been equivocal at best, at long last decided to occupy Araucania, the Chilean Indian frontier that had long sheltered the Araucanians and their allies after their raids against the pampas. By mid-November 1882, in various engagements the second division had killed 363 warriors, taken 1,721 prisoners, recovered large herds, and established a series of new forts and mountain trails to safeguard the frontier.[45]

On January 16, 1883, while a forty-man detachment under Captain Emilio Crouzeilles was in pursuit of a large Indian war party, it chanced upon another detachment of uniformed soldiers, led by an officer who brandished a sword. The newcomers, who were identified as Chileans, raised the white flag of truce, but as Crouzeilles and Lieutenant Nicanos Lazcano ventured forward to with a platoon of fifteen soldiers to parley, they were cut down by a volley of rifle fire. The troopers fought with their cavalry sabers at close quarters. Crouzeilles, Lazcano, and trooper Carranza died in the engagement, but the Indians, who experienced heavier losses, fled at the approach of the rest of the detachment. On February 17, Lieutenant Colonel Juan Díaz, at the head of a sixteen-man detachment, was trailing a war party of 100 to 150 braves. Upon reaching Pulmarí, they were surrounded by the hostiles. Heavily outnumbered, Díaz skillfully deployed his men along the small rises of the terrain. While the Indians charged his rear, Díaz spotted a Chilean army detachment of forty to fifty men approaching on his left flank, bearing a flag of truce. This flag notwithstanding, the Chileans formed a line of skirmish, and Díaz gave the order to fire. In a report to Colonel Enrique Godoy, commanding officer of the Second Brigade, Díaz noted:

When I noticed the Indians were about to charge our rear, I took positions along a dry creek bed. At that moment, a Chilean infantry soldier appeared in my left flank, under a flag of truce, but as I saw that an infantry company advanced in a line of skirmish, while the Indians attacked us from the rear, and bearing in mind the fate of other detachments, I gave the order open fire, being the first to do so. From that moment on, a furious battle took place, the enemy charged with the bayonet until they got within 40 paces of our position, where they left seven dead and some wounded which were picked up by the Indians, which withdrew promptly. We have captured from the enemy six Martin [*sic*] Henry rifles, ammunition pouches, a kepi and a cartridge belt with the inscription "Guardia Nacional."[46]

In the report, Díaz also noted that from Indian prisoners taken after this incident, he had learned the Chileans were about to establish an outpost near the Lien-Curá. Lieutenant Rodríguez, the officer in charge of the defeated Chilean unit, for his part, stated in a report that his intentions were honorable, that the Argentines probably suspected the Chileans were setting a trap and opened fire. Since his men could not properly operate their rifles, Rodríguez ordered a bayonet charge, but unable to dislodge the Argentines from their positions, gave the order to retreat. Godoy reacted by dispatching a scouting party to Lien-Curá with orders to disarm and apprehend any Chilean army unit found in Argentine territory and warmly congratulated Díaz.[47]

No further incidents involving Chilean troops were recorded. Namuncurá surrendered the remnants of his once proud and feared tribe in 1884. Chiefs Inacayal and Sayhueque remained at large, raiding ranches in what in reality were but pinprick attacks, until Inacayal, fearing the total destruction of his tribe, surrendered in 1885. Patagonia was now free of the Indian threat and more effectively under Argentine control than ever before.[48]

THE OCCUPATION OF SOUTHERN PATAGONIA

In 1878, the Argentine congress enacted a law that created the governorship of Patagonia, which encompassed all of that territory as well as Tierra del Fuego. A temporary capital was established at Mercedes de Patagones, the present-day

Table 3.2
Territorial Expansion of Argentine Pampean Provinces, 1855–1890 (in square kilometers)

Province	1855	1867	1876	1890
Buenos Aires	88,667	116,667	236,628	311,196
Santa Fé	55,000	57,000	82,585	131,582
Entre Ríos	77,079	77,079	77,079	75,137
Córdoba	150,000	150,000	150,000	174,768
La Pampa	----------	---------	-- --------	149,919

Source: Roberto Cortés Conde, *El Progreso Argentino* (Buenos Aires: Editorial Sudamericana, 1983), 56.

city of Viedma. The conquest of the desert enabled the provinces of Mendoza, San Juan, Córdoba, Buenos Aires, and Santa Fé to increase their geographical span (see table 3.2). As far as Patagonia, which had been awarded to Argentina by the Treaty of 1881, Roca, elected to the presidency in 1880, felt the need for legislation that would divide the large tract of land now firmly incorporated to Argentina into smaller, more manageable units. A territorial law approved in October 1883 established five territories under federal control: Chubut, Neuquén, Río Negro, Santa Cruz, and Tierra del Fuego.[49]

To encourage colonization of Patagonia, army garrisons and naval prefectures were established as nuclei for villages and townships. Thus were born the population centers at Acha and Victoria in La Pampa; Pringles, Conesa, Choele-Choel, and Junin de los Andes in Neuquén; Trelew and Madryn in Chubut; Río Gallegos, Santa Cruz, and Deseado in Santa Cruz; and Ushuaia in Tierra del Fuego.[50]

To assist in the occupation and exploration of Patagonia, the Argentine navy maintained a flotilla of cutters operating off the coasts of the region and in the Straits of Magellan. In July 1880, the recently acquired transport *Villarino* inaugurated the Servicio de la Costa Sur, a monthly run between Bahía Blanca and Patagones and predecessor of the Naval Transport Command of our time, fostering Patagonian development by carrying passengers and cargo to coastal settlements not served by commercial shipping. The naval budget of 1883 called for the creation of subprefectures at Isla de los Estados and Tierra del Fuego and allocated funds for the construction of lighthouses and other permanent aids to navigation. In addition, a flotilla of small steamers, specially designed to operate in shallow waters, began operations in the Río Negro.[51]

The South Atlantic Expeditionary Division was organized in 1884 under Commodore Augusto Laserre to assist with the development and exploration of the Patagonian shores. It included the gunboat *Paraná*, the transport *Villarino*, and other auxiliaries. The division reached Isla de Los Estados on April 18 and Ushuaia on September 28. In both cases, lighthouses and buildings to house the subprefectures were erected, thus completing Argentina's de facto occupation of Patagonia, which she had obtained de jure under the Treaty of 1881.[52]

Obviously playing party politics, former President Domingo Sarmiento, a passionate critic of Roca, would write in the columns of the newspaper *El Nacional*: "General Roca saw it, and it is to him that we owe the discovery of the truth, that there were no such Indians as the imaginary hordes of popular legend. Thinking it over, one is ashamed that we needed a powerful military establishment and sometimes eight thousand men to finish off two thousand lances."[53]

Sarmiento extracted the figure of 2,000 lances from a preliminary estimate submitted by Olascoaga. A simple addition of the number of warriors killed and captured would reveal that the number of lances eliminated by the Argentine army during the years 1876–1878 alone was probably closer to the 6,000 mark and that even larger numbers were known to have retreated across the Andes into their native Chile. The campaign of the desert was a climactic chapter in the long history of warfare between the Patagonian Indians and the Argentines.

The Argentine soldier proved to be a formidable fighter, well adept at the hit-and-run tactics that the Indians had once applied against white settlements. The campaign of the desert revealed the talent of Roca's subaltern officers, who were given ample freedom of action. Their audacity and fearless courage earned them the devotion of their men and were major factors determining the successful outcome. Few major battles such as Chiquilof, Parahüil, and San Carlos mark the conquest of the desert, but there were hundreds of toe-to-toe encounters where the Argentine army defeated a most valiant foe.

With the elimination of the Indian threat, Patagonia was effectively incorporated into Argentina, and the pampas were at last safe for colonization, a process that would totally change the aspect of the nation in a few short years. From 1876 onward, more than 400,000 square kilometers were added to provinces of the pampa region—that is to say, 40 million hectares of land in the richest part of Argentina. This land would be covered by thousands of kilometers of railway tracks and would witness the expansion of areas under cultivation as well as the establishment of numerous population centers.[54]

NOTES

1. Alfred Hasbrouck, "The Conquest of the Desert," *HAHR* 15 (1935): pp. 195–197.

2. Juan C. Walther, *La conquista del desierto* (Buenos Aires: Editorial Universitaria

de Buenos Aires, 1970) pp. 188–206; Enrique Gonzalez Lonsieme, *La armada en la conquista del desierto* (Buenos Aires: Instituto de Publicaciones Navales, Centro Naval, 1973), pp. 43–50.

3. Andrea Merrill, ed., *Chile: A Country Study* (Washington, DC: American University Press, 1982) pp. 7–8. Ricardo Fernando Brun, *Y así nació la frontera: Conquista, guerra, ocupación y pacificación: 1550–1900* (Santiago: Editorial Antartida, 1986), pp. 95–102; Diego Barros Arana, *Historia General de Chile* (Santiago: Editorial Nascimento, 1932, 7 vols.) 6: 44–47. The governor of Chile decided to abandon all forts south of the Bío-Bío River, as the forces under his command were small and ill equipped.

4. Salvador Canals Frau, "Expansion of the Araucanians in Argentina," in *Handbook of South American Indians*, 4 vols. (New York: Cooper Square Publishers, 1963) 2: 762–776; Emiliano Endrek, "La conquista del desierto durante el segundo gobierno de Rosas, 1835–1852," *Historia* 1, no. 4 (diciembre-noviembre 1981): pp. 44–57; Walther, *La conquista*, pp. 45–46. The Voroganos and Ranqueles had migrated to the pampas during the first decades of the nineteenth century.

5. Walther, *La conquista*, pp. 249–250. The Transandean origin of these tribes is something readily acknowledged by their descendants even today. According to *Mapuche World: English Supplement of Mundo Mapuche* (Livingston, NJ, 1, no. 2, 1998), "As we have said before, the Mapuche nation, originally from Central Chile, spread out from the Cordilleran valleys towards the pampas, to the East. Their culture and strength dominated the native people of Río Negro and Neuquén, in Patagonia." We can only surmise that this "domination" was not achieved through peaceful means, but rather the opposite. History shows us that in the cycle of migrations, people conquer and are conquered. The Araucanians and Proto-Araucanians who filtered into Argentina in the 1830s ruthlessly conquered the inhabitants of the region until they in turn were conquered by the Argentine criollos native to the soil.

6. Ibid., pp. 222–223, Curuhuinca-Roux, *Las matanzas del Neuquén: Crónicas mapuches* (Buenos Aires: Editorial Plus Ultra, 1984), pp. 112–113. This book, written by a member of the Mapuche tribe, offers a unique perspective, as it is one of the few known Indian accounts of the frontier wars in Argentina.

7. Endrek, "La conquista," pp. 56–57; Walther, *La Conquista del desierte*, pp. 267–269; Eduardo E. Ramayón, *Ejército guerrero, poblador y civilizador* (Buenos Aires: EUDEBA, 1978), pp. 153–164; Juan C. Vedoya, *La campaña del desierto y la tecnificación ganadera* (Buenos Aires: EUDEBA, 1981), pp. 63–64.

8. Félix Best, *Historia de las guerras argentinas: De la independencia, internacionales, civiles y con el indio*, 2 vols. (Buenos Aires: Ediciones Pueser, 1960), 2: 361–362.

9. George Earl Church, *Aborigines of South America* (London: Chapman and Hill, 1912), pp. 280–283.

10. Bartolomé Mitre, *AM* (Buenos Aires: 1911–1912), 14: 160.

11. Hasbrouck, *Conquest of the Desert*, p. 203; Ricardo Rodriguéz Molas, *Historia social del gaucho* (Buenos Aires: Ediciones Maru, 1968), pp. 447–448; Alfred J. Tapson, "Indian Warfare on the Pampa during the Colonial Period," *HAHR* 42, no. 1 (February 1969).

12. Church, *Aborigines of South America*, pp. 282, Ramoyón, *Ejército Guerrero, poblador y civilizador*, pp. 80–83; Rodriguéz Mola, *Historia social del gaucho*, pp. 445–447; Richard Slatta, *Gauchos and the Vanishing Frontier* (Lincoln and London: University of Nebraska Press, 1983), p. 129; Alfred Ébélot, *Relatos de la frontera* (Buenos Aires: Editorial Solar/Hachette, 1968), pp. 88–91.

13. Jorge F. Sergi, *Historia de los italianos en la Argentina* (Buenos Aires: Editorial Italo Argentina, 1940). Among the Italian officers were Colonel Juan Bautista Charlone; Mayors Pedro Sagari and Rosetti of the Legión Militar, which fought with distinction in the Paraguayan campaign; and Nicolás Levalle, who served at Cepeda, Pavón, in the Paraguayan front and the Indian campaigns and became war minister in the 1890s. See also Héctor Juan Piccinali, *Vida del Teniente General Nicolás Levalle* (Buenos Aires: Círculo Militar, 1982), pp. 15–16. For the reminiscences of a former British officer who served with the Argentine army, see Ignacio H. Fotheringham, *La vida de un soldado o reminescencias de las fronteras*, 2 vols. (Buenos Aires: Círculo Militar, 1970).

14. Slatta, *Gauchos and the Vanishing Frontier* p. 130; A. J. Walford, "General Urquiza and the Battle of Pavón," *HAHR* 19, no. 4, (November 1939), pp. 464–493. At Pavón, in the army of General Mitre, the artillery was excellent and manned principally by Italians.

15. Hasbrouck, *Conquest of the Desert*, pp. 213–214; V. Martin De Moussy, *Description géographique et statistique de la Confédération Argentine*, 2 vols. (Paris: Firmin Didot, 1960) 2:642.

16. Walther, *La Conquista del desierta*, p. 306; Best, *Historia de las guerras*, II: 364.

17. Enrique Barba, "Estudio Preliminar," in *La conquista de 15,000 leguas*, ed. Estanislao S. Zevallos (Buenos Aires: Libreria Hachette, 1975), pp. 161–163.

18. M. G. Mullhall and E. T. Mulhall, *Manual de las Repúblicas del Plata* (Buenos Aires: 1876), pp. 347–348.

19. Álvaros Barros, *Indios, fronteras y seguridad nacional* (Buenos Aires: Editorial Solar/Hachette, 1975), pp. 161–163.

20. H. S. Ferns, *Britain and Argentina in the Nineteenth Century* (London: Oxford University Press, 1960), p. 387.

21. Caillet-Bois, *Cuestiones internacionales*, pp. 74–75; Manuel J. Olascoaga, *Estudio topográfico de la pampa y Río Negro* (Buenos Aires: EUDEBA, 1974), pp. 78–79.

22. Augusto C. Rodríguez, "Ejército Nacional," in *Historia argentina contemporánea, 1862–1930*, 7 vols. (Buenos Aires: El Ateneo, 1966), II: 311–316, 331–332; hereafter referred to as *Ejército Nacional*. While visiting the *Museo de Armas de La Nación* at Buenos Aires in November 1987, the author noted a Remington Model 1868 11 mm. single-shot pistol. Apparently this weapon was only issued in very limited numbers. Joseph E. Smith, *Small Arms of the World* (Harrisburg, PA: Stackpole Books, 1973), pp. 51–53, Letter of Alberto Landini, (Weapons and Ballistics Correspondent of *La Prensa*, Buenos Aires to the author, August 24, 1969). The Smith & Wesson Model 1878 was in fact manufactured under license by the firm Deutsche Waffenfabrik of Berlin. Smith & Wesson did in fact deliver a few samples of the original model to the Argentine army, but their facilities were taken up by a very large order from tsarist Russia. A Wadsworth & Forehand .44 revolver designated Model 1873 was issued in limited quantities but proved unsatisfactory. The Model 1878 was supplemented by the Belgiant Nagan in the 1880s, and these were replaced by the Colt .30 Model 1895, 5,000 of which were procured. For details of these weapons, see Pedro E. Marti Garró, *Historia de la artillería argentina* (Buenos Aires: Comisión del Arma de Artillería "Santa Barbara," 1984), p. 474.

23. Alfred Ébélot, *Relatos de la Frontera* (Buenos Aires: Solar/Hachette, 1968), p. 51, Eduardo E. Ramayón, *Las caballadas en la guerra del indio: Adhesión de remonta y veterinaria del ejército argentino en el centenario de la conquista del desierto* (Buenos Aires: EUDEBA, 1975), pp. 78–86.

24. John E. Hodge, "The Role of the Telegraph in the Consolidation and Expansion of the Argentine Republic," *TAM* 21, no. 1 (July 1964): pp. 59–80.

25. Walther, *La Conquista del desierto*, pp. 364–365.

26. Ibid., pp. 363–367; Vedoya, *La Campaña del desierto*, pp. 65–66; Best, *Historia de las guerras argentinas* II: 373–374.

27. Hasbrouck, "Conquest of the Desert" p. 212; Adolfo Alsina, *La nueva linea de fronteras: Memoria especial del Ministerio de Guerra y Marina, año 1877* (Buenos Aires: *EUDEBA*, 1977), pp. 30–32. Assorted materials as well as sufficient wire to install 1,000 kilometers of telegraph lines were obtained in Europe. In addition, the Southern Railway was given a subsidy to install an additional line to its existing network and to extend existing lines to Azul by February 1876.

28. Best, *Historia de las guerras argentinas*, II: 377–378; Walther, *La conquista del desierto*, pp. 357–361.

29. Richard D. Perry, "Argentina and Chile: The Struggle for Patagonia, 1843–1881," *TAM* 26, no. 3 (January 1980), pp. 346–364.

30. Letter of General Roca to the Editor of *La República*, April 24, 1874, in Olascoaga, *Estudio topográfico*, pp. 76–80.

31. Alfredo M. Serres Güiraldes, *La estrategia del General Roca* (Buenos Aires: Editorial Pleamar, 1979), pp. 62–67.

32. Olascoaga, *Estudio topográfico* pp. 242–243. The Chilean government refused to curb the rustlers, arguing that these individuals were "empowered to contract and sell." Perry, "Argentina and Chile," pp. 363–364; Caillet-Bois, *Cuestiones internacionales*, pp. 73–74; Ministerio de Guerra y Marina, *Campaña de Los Andes al sur de La Patagonia año 1883: Partes detallados y diario de la expedición* (Buenos Aires: *EUDEBA*, 1978). A report to the army inspector general, Colonel Ortega, Commander of the Second Division, noted: "If the Chilean troops guarding the Andean passes only gave us the slightest cooperation and prevented the crossing of their borders by the Indians, that rich and vast region encompassed by the triangle formed by the Limay and Neuquén would be forever safe and secure."

33. Nicolás Bustos Dávila, "Coronel Manuel José Olascoaga, precursor de la Patagonia," *2o. CNHRA*, 4 vols. (Buenos Aires: 1980), pp. 63–77.

34. Juan Carlos Vedoya and Ana María Mauco, "Antecedentes de la Campaña del Desierto: Alsina y Roca," *CNHCD*, 4 vols. (Buenos Aires: 1980), III: 237–250.

35. Walther, *La conquista del desierto*, pp. 413–414; Best, *Historia de las guerras argentinas*, II: pp. 385–386.

36. Hasbrouck, "The Conquest of the Desert," pp. 213–214; Walther, *La conquista del desierto*, pp. 415–426, Best, *Historia de las guerras argentinas*, II: 386–387.

37. Hasbrouck, "The Conquest of the Desert," p. 215. The emphasis in these operations was not the extermination of the Indians, but rather their submission to the national authorities.

38. Lobodón Garra, *A sangre y lanza* (Buenos Aires: Ediciones Anaconda, 1969), pp. 452–453; Rómulo Félix Menéndez, *Las conquistas territoriales argentinas* (Buenos Aires: Círculo Militar: 1982), pp. 302–303. Numuncurá had 2,300 warriors at Salinas Grandes; Chief Catriel, 760; Chief Reuque-Curá, 2,200; Pincen, 1,800; the Rannqueles under Chiefs Ramón, Baigorrita, and Mariano Rosas, 600; and there were smaller war parties in Mendoza.

39. Menéndez, *Las conquistas territoriales argentinas*; Garra, *A Sangre y lanza*, pp. 466–468.

40. Walther, *La conquista del desierto*, p. 467.

41. Serres Güiraldes, *La Estrategia del General Roca*, pp. 81–82.

42. Geoffrey S. Smith, "The Role of José M. Balmaceda in Preserving Argentine neutrality during the War of the Pacific," *HAHR* 18, no. 2 (May 1969), pp. 253–267.

43. Walther, *La conquista del desierto*, pp. 479–480; Best, *Historia de las guerras argentinas*, II: 396–398.

44. Garra, *A sangre y lanza*; Currunhuica-Roux, *Las matanzas del Neuquén*. The small detachment, led by Captain Juan José Gómez, was equipped with Remingtons, which somewhat compensated for the overwhelming superiority in numbers of the combined war parties of Namuncurá, Reuque-Curá and Ñancucheo. The moat was soon filled with the bodies of the dead and wounded. The Indians tried to scale the palisade several times, but when Captain Gómez killed one of the chieftains, they lost heart and retreated.

45. Best, *Historia de las guerras argentinas*, II: 398–401; Walther, *La conquista del desierto*, pp. 514–517.

46. Ibid., pp. 511–512; Manuel Prado, *La conquista de la Pampa* (Buenos Aires: Libreria Hachette, 1960), pp. 152–153. According to Mayor Prado, a veteran of the Indian war, the Indian war party numbered between 150 and 200, *Campaña de Los Andes*, pp. 240–241. Telegram No. 377, Mr. T. O. Osborne to Frelinghusen, May 29, 1883, refers to both of the incidents at Pulmarí as follows: "On 21 February, the Argentine vanguard was attacked by a large body of Indians, most of which were armed with Winchesters and Martini-Henry rifles. For four hours the battle was arm [sic] and when the main body of the troops came forward and put an end to the struggle. The loss on the part of the Indian warriors, as reported was 100, and on the side of the Argentines, killed and wounded 22." The telegram also mentions a brush between Argentine and Chilean army companies in the Andes in which several lives were lost. Osborne added that it was not believed that deplorable consequences would result, as both sides believed they were in their own territory. The casualty figures quoted by Osborne are much higher than those given by Argentina and open to question.

47. *Campaña*, pp. 224–243. On a communiqué dated February 21 addressed to Lieutenant Colonel Díaz, Colonel Godoy noted, "The lesson given to the Chileans who have made common cause with the savages was harsh and deserved . . . It is well that our perfidious neighbors get accustomed to (the idea) of showing their backs to our soldiers (even when they outnumber ours) in the proportion of ten-to-one, as was in the case in the brilliant action (with the troops) under your command which speaks so highly of your valor and your skill." Oscar Espinosa Moraga, *El precio de la paz chileno-argentina*, 3 vols. (Santiago: Editorial Nacimento, 1969), II: 224–230. This author views the effect of the clash as follows: "As soon as details of the incident became public knowledge, a wave of indignation shook all of Chile; awakening that instinctive anti-Argentine hatred which all Chileans bring to the world the minute they are born," p. 230.

48. Walther, *La conquista del desierto*, pp. 534–535; Curruhuinca-Roux, *Las matanzas del Neuquén*, 174–183.

49. César A. Vapñarsky, *Los Pueblos del Norte de la Patagonia, 1779–1957* (Fuerte General Roca: Editorial de la Patagonia, 1979) pp. 33–34, 66–67; Armando Braun Menéndez, "Primera Presidencia de Roca," *Historia Argentina Contemporanéa* (1966), I: 296–297.

50. Humberto F. Burzio, *Armada nacional: Reseña histórica de su origen y desarrollo orgánico* (Buenos Aires: 1960), pp. 216–217.

Conflict in the Southern Cone

51. Enrique Gonzalez Lozieme, *La armada en la conquista del desierto* (Buenos Aires: Institutó de Publicaciones Navales, 1973), pp. 150–159.

52. Burzio, *Armada nacional*, pp. 218–219.

53. Ysabel F. Rennie, *The Argentine Republic* (New York: Macmillan, 1945), p. 127. The figure of 2,000 lances which Sarmiento quoted comes from President Avellaneda's message to Congress on August 14, 1876, requesting an appropriation for the Indian wars. In his letter to *La República*, Roca stated that Purran had between 5,000 and 6,000 lances under his command, while chieftains Millaln and Tranaman could call on an additional 300 to 400 lances. Héctor Juan Piccinali, *Vida del teniente general Nicolás Lavalle* (Buenos Aires: Círculo Militar, 1981), pp. 150–151. On a report dated March 20, 1877, Levalle noted the strength of the hostile chiefs along the southwestern frontier as follows: Namuncurá, 2,370 warriors; Catriel, 805; Requencurá, 2,260, a total of 5,435. However, these figures do not reflect the numbers of Chilean Indians on the western slopes of the Andes who were quite ready to assist their brethren in their raids against the pampas. See Edouard Séve, *La patria chilena: Le Chile tel qui'il est* (Valparaíso: Imprimerie du Mercurio, 1876), I: 85–86. In 1876, the Huiliches south of Cautin and Tolten had a combined strength of 10,683 warriors.

54. Roberto Cortés-Conde, *El progreso argentino, 1880–1914, la formación del mercado nacional* (Buenos Aires: Editorial Sudamericana, 1979) pp. 55–56.

4

The Economic Progress of Argentina and Chile

In the nineteenth century, the economies of Argentina and Chile, though completely dissimilar, were entirely dependent on their foreign trade: Argentina's on the export of livestock products and grain, Chile's on the export of minerals. Trade surpluses, when available, were used to defray the growing expenses of the national state and the costly arms race in which both countries engaged throughout the 1890s. In both nations customs receipts were the principal source of government revenues. During the early 1870s, both countries were approximately equal in terms of population and revenues, but the situation changed radically in Argentina's favor in the last quarter of the century.

ARGENTINE ECONOMIC PROGRESS: GROWTH OF THE LIVESTOCK SECTOR

From the colonial period until the middle of the nineteenth century, cattle ranching had been the principal economic activity in Argentina. Hides and jerked beef were exported while the meat was consumed locally. In the first half of the nineteenth century, the Mesopotamian provinces and Buenos Aires developed as cattle-ranching areas. The affluents of the Plate were used as outlets for their products. Tallow, fats, and unwashed wool were added to the list of exportables by the 1840s, while the expansion of sheep grazing pushed cattle herds further to the south and was a prime factor in the expansion of the frontier in the years after 1852. Sheep, in fact, became more important than cattle until a disastrous flood in 1902 destroyed approximately 14 million head. The sheep population and wool exports grew progressively, from 2.5 million head and 1,812 metric tons in 1830 to 41 million and 65,704 tons on 1870, 61 million and 92,112 in 1880 to 75 million head and 228,358 tons in 1901.[1]

The competition for grazing lands between sheepherders and cattle ranchers in turn triggered an expansion of the southwestern frontier, the first advance since Rosas's expedition to the desert in 1833–1834. However, the addition of new grazing lands per se would not have been significant without the incorporation of technological improvements that allowed the preparation and transportation of meat over long distances. The oldest and for a long period the only form of reserved meat exported by Argentina was jerked beef, known locally as *charquí* or *tasajo*. Since it was hard and rather unappealing to European palates, British ships plying the Plate refused to handle it. In November 1815, a young Juan Manuel de Rosas formed a partnership with Juan Nepomuceno Terrero and Manuel Dorrego to run a beef-salting plant known as Las Higueritas, which began to ferry salt cargoes from Patagones to Buenos Aires aboard its first ship. Soon afterward, the firm had a small fleet of brigs and schooners, aboard which charquí was exported to Brazil, Cuba and the United States, where it was used to feed slave populations.[2]

Charles Tellier, a French engineer, was responsible for the introduction of mechanically produced refrigeration that was to change both output and markets. The first ship equipped with this system, *Le Frigorifique*, arrived in Buenos Aires in December 1876. On October 7, 1877, the *Paraguay*, fitted with an improved refrigeration system devised by Ferdinand Carré, sailed from Buenos Aires to Le Havre with a cargo of 5,500 frozen sheep carcasses. Despite unavoidable teething problems, the cargo arrived at Marseille in perfect order. French investors did not show further interest in this new field, but the British did. In 1882, the River Plate Fresh Meat Company established the first packinghouse in Argentina. Local combines and North American firms would follow. As a result of the technological advances introduced, meat exports soared from 64,578 tons in 1890 to 172,396 in 1900.[3]

Argentine mutton and beef were claimed inferior to the Australian and New Zealand products; therefore, they fetched lower prices and a smaller share of the English market. The introduction of improved breeds such as Lincolns, Rambouillet, and Shorkshire among the sheep, and the Shorthorns and Herefords in the cattle herd were followed by a larger share of English imports. The appearance of new and better breeds was followed by the widespread use of fencing, which made it possible to control the herds. Wire fencing in Argentina had been introduced in 1844, and Tarquino, the first Durham bull, arrived in 1846, but most ranchers lacked either the money or the economic incentive to improve the breed of their herds or fence their properties.[4]

The successful Indian campaigns of Alsina in 1876 and Roca in 1879 pushed the frontier to the Río Negro and opened up the central pampas, giving the *estancieros* greater security and cheaper lands. The imports of wire fencing grew accordingly. The long-horned cattle of Argentina has existed on the tough grass, or *pastos fuertes* of the pampas. Cattle thus fed were lean, and the small sheep were jokingly called ''mice'' in the London markets. By the 1880s, pastos tiernos, such as clover, thistles, barley, and foxtail, had replaced the older grasses. Alfalfa would follow.[5]

The estancieros of Argentina had at last realized that improvements of the stocks was achieved through the introduction of better breeds as well as improved fodder. Hence the need for wire to insure adequate breeding and increased grazing areas. The amount of wire imported multiplied from 3,367 tons in the mid-1860s to 30,000 in the 1880s and 50,000 by 1903.[6]

All of these technological improvements made the export of Argentine fresh meat possible. However, frozen beef, which is carried at temperatures of 10 to 15 degrees Fahrenheit, arrived hard and required thawing. Furthermore, its taste suffered somewhat, hence Argentine *frigoríficos*, or packinghouses, were unable to compete with American beef, which was exported alive or chilled. The latter was carried at temperatures between 29 and 30 degrees Fahrenheit and arrived soft, ready for consumption. Argentine chilled beef, however, did not become a major export item until 1901. Nevertheless, the Argentine export sector continued to grow, thanks to an agricultural revolution that had also taken place.[7]

THE EXPANSION OF THE AGRICULTURAL SECTOR

The expansion of agriculture in Argentina was related to immigrant settlements combined with the development of the railway network and a steady rise of the world demand for grain. In the late 1870s wheat production began to exceed local demands, and small quantities were available for export to Belgium, Britain, and Paraguay. Wheat could be grown by lightly skilled farmers, it could be stored easily, and because of its compactness the freight costs involved were relatively low, even in the days when wagon trains were the only means of overland transportation. The most remarkable expansion of the area sown to wheat took place in Santa Fé, where immigrant agricultural colonists had settled in large numbers. Whereas only 1,600 hectares had been sown to wheat in that province in 1860, the total had risen to 35,00 in 1875, 275,000 in 1884, 764,000 in 1890 and 1,058,00 by 1895. By the early 1890s, the wheat-growing belt of Argentina lay in a broad sector of the pampas about 320 kilometers wide, stretching from the city of Santa Fé (capital of the homonymous province) in the north to Bahía Blanca in the southern part of the province of Buenos Aires.[8]

The expansion of the areas sown to wheat was accompanied by technological improvements in the flour mills. Steam power was first introduced to the flour mills of Buenos Aires during the 1840s, but would not see widespread use until the following decade. The development of flour mills brought about the construction of storage facilities along the harbors of the wheat belt, most particularly in Buenos Aires. By the turn of the century, a giant conglomerate had emerged in this field by a merger of Argentine, Belgian, and German capital, which through their subsidiaries, Molinos Harineros del Río de la Plata and Molinos y Elevadores de Granos, absorbed the smaller and less economical flour

Table 4.1
Argentine Grain Exports, 1875–1900 (in hundreds of tons)

Year	Corn	Flax	Wheat	Bran	Flour
1875	2	----	----	1	----
1880	150	9	11	22	-----
1885	1979	694	785	57	----
1890	9072	307	3278	28	----
1895	7723	2264	10102	297	539
1900	7123	2232	19297	733	512

Source: Simon G. Hanson, *The Argentine Meat Trade and the British Market: Chapters in the History of the Argentine Meat Industry* (Stanford, CA: Stanford University Press, 1938), p. 1.

mills. This enabled Argentine flour mills to compete with American companies in the Brazilian market.[9]

The areas sown to alfalfa, linseed, and corn also experienced great expansion. Alfalfa emerged as an export item as a result of the land rental system applied by cattle and sheep producers. Under this arrangement, tenant farmers would have to sow the land to alfalfa at the end of their lease. The introduction of linseed as a commercial crop followed decades after the cultivation of wheat. Corn, however, accounted for the bulk of grain exported from Argentina until the turn of the century. The expansion of the agricultural sector created an export boom, best illustrated in tables 4.1 and 4.2.

Sugar cane was cultivated as early as the sixteenth century, albeit on a reduced scale. It would only enter into a net stage of development when a line of the Central Argentine Railway connected the sugar-producing regions of the province of Tucumán, on the northwest, with Rosario, a port in the Paraná. Sugar production in Tucumán barely reached 3,000 tons in 1876, but with the completion of the railway, modern machinery could be transported with ease from the littoral. Production therefore increased until it averaged 131,000 tons by 1902–1904.[10]

The development of such industries had in the past been handicapped by transportation costs and the reduced home market available by a low population density. Colonization and immigration, which had been pursued since the 1820s, though with little success until the 1870s, enabled the population of Argentina to achieve a significant increase.

THE POPULATION OF ARGENTINA

Argentina suffered from a persistent manpower shortage during the nineteenth century. Colonization attempts made prior to the 1870s had met with little suc-

Table 4.2
Composition of Argentine Exports, 1893–1900 (in million gold pesos)

Year	Total Exports	Livestock	Agriculture
1893	94. 0	53. 0	25. 7
1895	120. 0	74. 6	41. 4
1896	116. 8	70. 5	43. 4
1898	133. 8	87. 3	42. 6
1899	184. 9	115. 5	65. 1
1900	154. 0	71.2	77. 4

Source: Noemí Girbal de Blacha, "Comercio exterior y producción agrícola de la República Argentina," *Investigaciones y Ensayos* 21 (julio-diciembre 1976), p. 343.

cess because of the high transportation costs and the lack of interests among the local landowners. As the Argentine economy became more integrated with the global economy, the population shift to the littoral areas became more pronounced. In 1810, for example, 50 percent of the population lived in the northwestern areas and 35 percent in the littoral, but as the provinces of Corrientes, Entre Ríos, and Buenos Aires began to export hides in greater quantities, the population center of gravity changed, until by the 1850s the interior accounted for 49 percent of the total number of inhabitants and the littoral, 51 percent.[11]

The Argentine population increased fourfold between 1810 and 1869, as the First National Census of 1869 would show. Only 12.1 percent of this total were foreigners. The second national census, taken in 1895, revealed that there were 3,954,922 inhabitants, of whom 2,950,383 (74.6 percent) were native born and 1,004,527 (or 25.4 percent) were foreign born. Between 1869 and 1895 the population of Argentina grew at the rate of 30.4 per thousand annually, of which immigration accounted for 17.2 percent and natural growth for 13.2 percent. Net immigration to Argentina reached a high figure of 220,260 in 1889, then dropped to 30,375 in the crisis year of 1890 and registered a negative result in 1891, when as a result of the economic depression the number of emigrants exceeded immigrants by 29,835. The number of newcomers would increase again between 1892 and 1902, when net immigration averaged around 38,000 per annum, or a total of 680,000 for the period 1899–1902.[12]

Immigrants were more prone to settle in urban areas; hence immigration affected regional distribution. Whereas in 1869, 71 percent of the population lived in rural areas and 29 percent in urban groupings, the proportions had changed to 65 and 37 percent, respectively, in 1895, and by about 1900 the proportion of urban to rural population was about equal. This period also coincided with the growth of the railway system, which further accentuated the population shift from the interior to the littoral and from rural regions to population centers.[13]

Immigrants provided much of the muscle power and the skills required by the expanding Argentine economy. In the province of Santa Fé and Entre Ríos, where colonization by small farmers was fomented, rather as in the United States, immigrants played an important role in the cultivation of wheat. In Santa Fé, for example, the number of colonies rose from 30 with 481,000 hectares in 1872 to 180 and 2,024,206 hectares in 1887 and again to 339 and 3.8 million hectares in 1899.[14]

Two-thirds of the immigrants who entered Argentina during 1875–1895 described themselves as farmers; the rest were masons and artisans in general. Their employment in the new land appears to have been motivated by a desire for upward mobility. Most immigrants preferred to remain in Buenos Aires, where wages were sometimes two or three times those of their native lands. Italian masons erected the buildings and much of the infrastructure of the urban areas of the Argentine littoral. Italians also predominated in the artisans' craft in general and in the embryonic metallurgical sector. This was particularly true in Buenos Aires, where most of the industrial establishments were located.[15]

The death rate in the capital city experienced a sharp drop between 1890, when it reached a total of 30 per thousand inhabitants, and 1899, when it barely reached 17 per thousand. The decline in the death rate was largely the result of an improved drainage system, begun in 1890. This, coupled with the process of protoindustrialization that was taking place in the city, accounted for an increase in the population, from 547,144 in 1890 to 795,000 in 1899. Developments in the transportation system, most notably the railways, would further national development and the creation of a national market.[16]

DEVELOPMENT OF THE RAILWAY SYSTEM

A railway map of Argentina at the end of the nineteenth century would reveal that the network resembled a fan with its center at Buenos Aires and other important nuclei at various ports in the littoral area. The first railway line was established in 1857. This was the Ferrocarril Oeste, or Western Railway, which served the province of Buenos Aires. The shareholders were for the most part merchants and ranchers of Buenos Aires; financial backing was provided by the provincial government. By 1860 the Oeste had 39 kilometers of track serving the outskirts of Buenos Aires. The completion of the line to Chivilvoy in 1868 brought the total track length to 168 kilometers. The railway concentrated its attention on the western part of the province of Buenos Aires, and by the 1880s spurs connecting San Antonio de Areco, Pergamino, and Luján had been completed, as well as a line to the town of San Nicolás, on the Paraná River. By the 1890s, when the Oeste's network exceeded 1,000 kilometers of track, and its infrastructure included shops where locomotives and railway cars were built as well as training schools for personnel, the provincial government took a fateful step and sold the railway to British investors.[17]

British capital was attracted to the Argentine by generous inducements. The British were granted tax exemptions, free lands, a guarantee that the government would not interfere in rate fixing, and a guaranteed return of 7 percent on their investment. A direct line would connect Tucumán with Rosario in 1891; that port city, which was already a terminus for overland traffic from Córdoba and fluvial traffic, became an important railway terminus as well.[18]

A subsidiary of the Central Argentine, the Andino Railway Company, was formed in 1867 to build a line that would connect the Villa María station of the parent company with the provinces of Mendoza and San Juan and another that would link the city of Córdoba with the Andean provinces of Salta and Tucumán. The concession gave the Central a league of land on either side of the tracks for colonization. The company sent an agent to Europe in 1869 to attract agricultural immigrants who would form colonies along the line. By the end of 1870, sixty agricultural colonies had been established. The Central began to attract trade from the northwestern provinces to the littoral, rather than Chile, where some Argentine products were marketed, thus giving the Argentine economy an eastern or Atlantic orientation. This railway was also credited with the rapid expansion of the sugar industry in the provinces of Tucumán, Salta, and Jujuy in the 1890s. A Transandine Railway, designed to link Argentina and Chile, was begun in 1895, but for political as well as financial considerations, it would not be completed until 1910.[19]

The Southern Railway, a British company, like the Central, received a concession to build lines connecting the city of Buenos Aires with points along the southwestern portion of the province. The line to Chascomus, 114 kilometers in length, was completed in December 1865. From that locality, the line branched out; one spur reached Las Flores in 1872, and the other arrived at Dolores in 1874. These spurs would reach Azul and Ayacucho by the end of the decade. By 1880, the Southern had a network of 563 kilometers. A line connecting Olavarría and La Madrid was inaugurated in 1883, and extended to Tandil and Juárez by 1885, and to Bahía Blanca by 1886. In that year a spur between Maipú and Mar del Plata was completed.[20]

The country had by this time entered into a railroad-building frenzy, and the number of railway companies reached thirty in 1891, when 2,446 kilometers of track had been added to the growing network. The rail network had developed from a mere 39 kilometers worth 741,000 gold pesos in 1857 to 17,737 kilometers with an aggregate capital of 560.3 million gold pesos by 1902. Passenger and railway traffic had grown enormously, as can be observed in table 4.3. Railways enabled products such as hides, wool, meat, and grains to be dispatched more efficiently than had been possible by other means of overland transportation, such as the oxcart. The nation's grain belt for the most part lay within a radius of 100 kilometers of the littoral, a decisive advantage when the

Table 4.3
Argentine Railway Traffic

Year	Passengers	Tons of cargo
1857	56, 190	2, 257
1867	1, 648, 404	128, 818
1877	2, 353, 406	760, 818
1887	8, 199, 051	3, 844, 045
1897	16, 410, 945	8, 891,129
1902	19, 815, 439	14, 030, 340

Source: Ernesto Tornquist and Co., *The Economic Development of the Argentine Republic in the Last Fifty Years* (Buenos Aires: 1919), p. 118.

fact that Argentina exported as much as 70 percent of her grain production is taken into consideration. Furthermore, lands once considered too distant from the urban centers for economic development became readily accessible thanks to the railways. The railways also allowed displacement of the labor force when the country was rocked by a serious economic crisis in the early 1890s. Surplus labor from the urban centers went into the rural areas, thus helping to increase the amount of land sown. In short, the railway enabled the territories it served to be incorporated into the productive structure, with epicenters at Buenos Aires and Rosario. These centers would in turn become markets for local products and focal links to overseas markets. When the Argentine system was in its embryonic stage, a market for capital, goods and services in a strictly national sense had failed to develop. By the turn of the century the railways had played a fundamental role in the formation of a national market and in the creation of needs, demands, and opportunities while it encouraged the growth of agriculture and fostered the development of the sugar- and beef-packing industries.[21]

The railways of Argentina attracted considerable amounts of foreign capital, which in the period discussed was synonymous with British capital. A certain amount of Belgian, French, and German capital flowed into utilities and railways, but this did not affect the dominant position of British capital in Argentina.

FOREIGN INVESTMENT

In the years 1862–1902, Britain had surplus capital that she was willing to invest, while Argentina offered an opportunity for high returns. The South American nation was favorably located on the Atlantic coast and enjoyed the advantages of a well-integrated river system, served by twenty foreign and fifty-five river ports. British investments in Argentina went primarily into railway companies, tramways, public utilities, and land development companies. During these years, financial institutions in Argentina were few, and the need for infrastructure development was critical. Ports and warehouses, urban sanitation facilities and public utilities were required. The state, which had given the initial impetus, was unable to supply the required capital. Private Argentine capital was based upon fixed assets, such as lands or urban houses. Government revenues, which depended largely upon customs revenues, were insufficient to provide for national development; hence loans had to be secured in Europe. Under these circumstances, the flow of British capital to Argentina increased dramatically, as will be seen in table 4.4. In order to attract further investments, mainly in the railway sector, the Argentine government offered substantial guarantees.[22]

The attraction that Argentina offered foreign capital varied as did conditions in the British economy and the direction of British capital exports. The conquest of the desert, which made the pampas safe for cultivation, was needed before significant railway investments by British capital could take place. In 1884, Argentina adopted the gold standard. Between 1885 and 1890, the country experienced a flow of capital estimated at 140 million pounds sterling, or 710 million gold pesos. Government programs calling for the construction of dams, bridges, ports, government buildings, and parks became more ambitious and costly every year, while the value of imports began to exceed exports by a considerable margin. To cover unfavorable balances, the government used its gold reserves. As these shrank, however, the peso began to depreciate. The gold premium, which was at a par in January 1884, when 100 paper pesos equaled 100 gold pesos, rose to 137 in 1885, 139 in 1886, 148 in 1888, 191 in 1889, and 251 in 1890. Instead of reducing the amount of money in circulation, the government resorted to new issues of inconvertible paper. This policy suited the embryonic industrial sector, which paid its workers in inflated paper currency, the landed aristocracy, as well as political favorites who received enormous loans without adequate backing. The amount of paper money in circulation rose from 50 million pesos in 1884 to 251 million in 1891. The price of Argentine exportables declined in the world market, and the government repudiated the foreign debt.[23]

During the years 1895–1897 Argentine exports rose, despite the fact that the terms of trade were unfavorable until 1896. The Argentine economy demonstrated once again its resilient capacity to expand production despite falling world prices. From 1896 onward, world prices as well as the demand for the Argentine exportables increased. The peso therefore appreciated in value, and in 1899 Argentina returned to the gold standard, attracting new waves of foreign capital and immigration, both of which had been severely curtailed by the economic crisis of the early 1890s.[24]

Table 4.4
British Direct and Portfolio Investments in Argentina (in millions of pounds)

Type	1865	1875	1885	1895	1905
Total Investment	2, 7	22, 6	46, 0	190, 9	253, 6
Direct Investment	0, 5	6, 1	19, 3	97, 9	150, 4
Portfolio Investments	2, 2	16, 5	26, 7	93, 9	103, 4
Government loans	2, 2	16, 5	26,7	90, 6	101, 4
Corporate Securities				3, 4	2, 2

Source: Irving Stone, "British Direct and Portfolio Investment in Latin America Before 1914," *Journal of Economic History* (1977), p. 706.

ARGENTINE FOREIGN TRADE

Trade was one of the keys to Argentine prosperity. As the expansion of the livestock and agricultural sectors gained momentum, world improvements in shipping resulted in lower freight rates, and the shift to iron-hulled, steam-powered vessels, coupled with Argentina's abandonment of the world standard in the 1880s, made Argentine products cheaper against competition from the United States and Canada. The incorporation of virgin lands along the former southwestern frontier also contributed to the growth of the Argentine foreign trade sector.[25]

Throughout this period Argentina's main trading partner was England, which provided 30 percent of all Argentine imports and took 20 percent of her exports. There was a brisk commerce with Belgium, France, Germany, Italy, and the United States, but the value of trade with Germany or the United States, for example, was equivalent to two thirds of the trade realized with Britain. In most of the years between 1870 and 1890 Argentina experienced heavy trade imbalances, as will be seen in table 4.5. The years between 1893 and 1902 were characterized by restrictive import and a substantial amount of import substitution. Home-grown tobacco, alcoholic beverages, and consumer goods replaced products formerly imported. The export sector continued to grow, thus allowing for a favorable balance of trade. As the Argentine economy diversified and the national state evolved, its sources of revenue grew more varied and sophisticated.[26]

ARGENTINE GOVERNMENT REVENUES AND MONETARY POLICIES

Throughout most of the nineteenth century, customs receipts accounted for virtually all Argentine government revenues. As late as 1873, for example, when revenues were 20.2 million pesos, import duties provided 16.5 million (or 80 percent) and export duties 2.4 million (12 percent) while the remainder came from railway shares, storage and postal fees, and sundry items. Alternative sources of revenue were developed in the years between 1875 and 1902. There were slingage or harbor crane charges on sanitary inspections of incoming vessels, but most of all there was a wide range of excise taxes, which considerably reduced the dependency on customs receipts, as will be seen in table 4.6. By 1889 only 66 percent of all Argentine government revenues came from customs duties. By 1902 the proportion had fallen to 44 percent, while excise taxes and miscellaneous duties accounted for 20 percent of the total. However, neither these new sources of taxation nor an overall increase in government revenues resulted in a balanced budget. To finance government spending, funds were borrowed abroad, and this in turn led to a mounting foreign debt, whose service consumed a substantial amount of government revenues. During the five-year period between 1886 and 1890 Argentina borrowed 710 million gold pesos

Table 4.5
Argentine International Trade (in thousand gold pesos of 48 d)

Year	Exports	Imports	Balance
1870	23, 000	28, 200	- 5, 200
1880	58, 700	45, 900	+ 12, 800
1885	83, 879	92, 222	- 8, 343
1890	100, 800	142, 000	- 41, 000
1891	103, 400	62, 207	+ 36, 011
1892	113, 370	91, 481	+ 21, 889
1893	94, 090	96, 223	- 2, 133
1894	101, 687	92, 888	+ 8, 899
1895	120, 067	95, 096	+ 24, 971
1896	116, 169	112, 163	+ 4, 638
1897	101, 169	98, 288	+ 2, 880
1898	133, 829	107, 428	+ 26, 400
1899	184, 197	116, 850	+ 68, 066
1900	154, 600	113, 485	+ 41, 115
1901	167, 716	113, 959	+ 53, 756
1902	179, 486	103, 039	+ 76, 447

Source: Ernesto Tornquist and Co., *The Economic Development of the Argentine Republic in the Last Fifty Years* (Buenos Aires: 1919), p. 140.

to finance her development, but when the country entered into an economic depression in 1890, known as the Baring Panic, attempts to raise new loans failed. A funding loan agreement with foreign creditors was reached in 1891, freeing Argentina from the necessity of remitting loan payments to Europe for three years. For five years the interest on certain Argentine securities was reduced.[27]

The country began to recover from the economic crisis by 1895. Foreign investments and loans showed moderate recoveries, but the boundary dispute

Table 4.6
Percentage Distribution of Argentine Government Income (selected years)

Source	1893	1895	1897	1898	1899	1902
Imports	69,3	59,7	49,0	52,3	44,6	39,8
Exports	7,5	5,1	5,0	4,6	4,8	4,2
Alcoholic Beverages	4,3	5,5	7,4	7,4	11,8	10,9
Matches	1,1	1,2	1,3	1,3	1,3	1,4
Stamped Paper and Patents	6,7	6,1	5,2	6,0	6,1	5,7

Source: Laura Randall, *A Comparative Economic History of Latin America. Volume 2: Argentina* (New York: Columbia University Press, 1971), pp. 237–238.

with Chile, as we shall see further on, created new government deficits. The country enjoyed a favorable balance of payment, nevertheless, and met her liabilities through her exports (see table 4.7). Furthermore, as shown in table 4.8, the combined balance of borrowings and trade was favorable to Argentina except in 1897. Thus, there was an inflow of gold into the country throughout most of the peak years of the dispute with Chile, and the government had access to both internal and external loans. The Argentine public debt, external and internal, had risen from 80 million gold pesos in 1875 to 392 million by 1900. Then, in a brilliant stroke, the administration consolidated these debts and floated bonds abroad known as Consolidados Argentinos for the amount of 435 million gold pesos. The value of the bonds floated exceeded the actual debt by 49.2 million. This sum was to be used for arms purchases in the period of "armed peace" with Chile.[28]

In the last three decades of the nineteenth century Argentina had undergone a considerable transformation from a backward and divided society into a promising nation-state. Generous infusions of capital were responsible for the development of the railways, grain elevators, port facilities, and public utilities.[29]

The nation's public debt had increased, to be sure, but so had its wealth and its infrastructure, which from its school system to its railways was the largest in South America. The Argentine economy was expanding in all sectors, and the country appeared to many as one of the lands of opportunity. There was great demand abroad for horses, grains, hides, and beef. The Argentine population had more than doubled in forty years, and her sound currency attracted both immigrants and investors.[30]

CHILEAN ECONOMIC GROWTH UNTIL 1902

At the present time, Chile covers an area of approximately 741,167 square kilometers, but during the early part of the nineteenth century, it exercised control over only one third of this territory. The territories taken from Bolivia and Peru during the War of the Pacific, that is, the provinces of Antofagasta and Tarapacá, constitute Chile's Great North, or *Norte Grande*. The Little North, or *Norte Chico*, is an area composed of short valleys that render transportation difficult. The provinces of Atacama, Coquimbo, and part of the province of Aconcagua form this region, which possesses large mineral deposits and considerable agriculture. Wheat, temperate-zone fruits, and other crops are grown here for both local consumption and export.[31]

The Central Valley is an area formed by the basin of the Aconcagua River north and east of Valparaíso. This extraordinarily fertile region not only constitutes the nation's heartland as well as its historical locale, but it also contains about 70 percent of the population and 40 percent of the nation's arable land and produces 80 percent of its beans and potatoes, 75 percent of all its garden vegetables, 87 percent of all its wines, and most of its corn, henequen, sunflower seed, and tobacco.[32]

Table 4.7
Argentine Government Revenues and Expenditures (in million pesos of 48 d)

	1	2	3 Cols. 1-2	4	5	6 Cols. 1-6
Date	Borrowing	Interest	Balance	Exports	Imports	Balance
1895	17.1	38.1	- 20. 0	120.0	95. 0	+ 4. 0
1896	37.1	39.8	- 2.7	116.8	112.1	+ 1. 9
1897	38.2	43.9	- 5.6	101.1	98.2	+ 2. 8
1898	46.0	50.3	- 4.4	133.8	107.4	+ 21.9
1899	24.9	54.6	- 29.7	184.1	116.8	+ 38. 3
1900	27.5	58.5	- 31.0	154.6	113.4	+ 9.0

Source: J. H. Williams, *Argentine International Trade under Incovertible Paper Money* (Cambridge, MA: Harvard University Press, 1920), p. 152.

Table 4.8
Argentina's International Balance (in million gold pesos of 48 d)

Year	Revenues	Expenditures	Balance
1875	15. 9	28. 5	- 12. 6
1880	19. 5	26. 9	- 7. 4
1885	26. 5	40. 5	- 14. 0
1890	29. 1	38. 1	- 9. 0
1895	38. 2	48. 5	- 10. 3
1896	42. 0	78. 2	- 36. 2
1897	51. 4	61. 0	- 9. 2
1898	53. 1	121. 3	- 68. 2
1899	72. 8	76. 3	- 3. 8
1900	64. 8	68. 5	- 3. 7
1901	64. 5	69. 3	- 5. 4
1902	65. 4	85. 3	- 19. 4

Source: Vicente Vázquez Presedo, *Estadisticas históricas argentinos compraradas* (Buenos Aires: Ediciones Machi, 1975), 1: 93.

South central Chile, or the lake region, is a mountainous region which begins south of the Bío-Bío River. Its coastline is jagged but contains some excellent natural harbors in the north. The lake region comprises the provinces of Valdivia, Osorno, and Llanquihue and produces about 40 percent of the nation's grain; it is famous for its timber resources and dairy farms.[33]

Southern Chile, or the Channel Region, includes the provinces of Chiloé, Aysén, and Magallanes. The coastline is broken by numerous islands, canals, and fjords that render navigation hazardous. The scarcity of arable land has traditionally forced the population of Chiloé to emigrate to Argentina in search of economic opportunities.[34]

THE POPULATION OF CHILE

In 1865 the population of Chile was estimated at 1.8 million people, while in 1869 Argentina had approximately the same number of inhabitants. However, by 1895 the population of Chile had increased by 1 million, while that of Argentina, largely thanks to massive waves of immigration, exceeded 3.9 million. Net immigration to Chile accounted for 3 percent of this increase and natural growth for 97 percent. Yet, the birth rate, estimated at 37.4 percent, was slightly higher than Argentina's. A high mortality rate negated the higher birth rate.[35]

In his *Raza Chilena*, Nicolás Palacios blamed the high mortality rate on the Chilean laborer's low standard of living. His rate of pay was merely one-fourth that of his Argentine counterpart and one-eighth of that received by a North American worker. Whereas food was sufficiently abundant and cheap in Argentina, many Chileans went to bed hungry. Malnutrition ranked high among the causes of infant mortality. Furthermore, poor sanitation practices ranked high among infant mortality, and inadequate housing among the urban masses resulted in an alarming death rate in the principal Chilean cities.[36]

Though its population was experiencing a modest boom that enabled it to populate the Norte Grande and Patagonia, the rather limited labor market in Chile failed to absorb it, and excess population does not favor immigration. Unlike Argentina, Chile never appeared to immigrants a land of opportunity. In fact, just the opposite occurred; throughout the nineteenth century great numbers of Chilean laborers left to seek their fortunes elsewhere. About 70,000 migrated to California during the gold rush in 1848, and perhaps as many as 20,000 left for the nitrate fields in the 1860s. The anomaly between the obvious lack of employment and opportunities and the government's attempts to encourage European immigration was due to the outlook of the local elites, who considered the *roto*, or Chilean national type, racially inferior and too shiftless to become a good colonist.[37]

The Chilean government, which had always considered immigration essential for the country's modernization, expected to attract immigrants for the skills they imparted rather than for their manpower, which was not needed in Chile. Immigration was encouraged, but except for about 6,000 Germans who migrated between 1846 and 1875, most immigrants shunned Chile and opted for Argentina, Brazil, and Uruguay. (Chile's occupation of its Indian frontier, which involved an area of 40,000 square kilometers and comprised about 5.5 percent of the nation's territory, was seen by many as an opportunity to attract more foreign settlers. However, wealthy investors were able to purchase large tracts of lands and implanted the institution of latifundium in the frontier.[38]

By 1895 the population of Chile included 79,506 foreigners. Among these were 6,507 Argentines, 8,669 Bolivians, 15,999 Peruvians, and smaller numbers of other Latin American nationalities, but only 7,797 Italians 1,550 Austro-Hungarians, 7,560 Germans, and 8,494 Spaniards. The awareness that Chile was falling behind its Eastern neighbor in wealth and power as well as in population was disquieting to many Chileans. Journalists advised the government to sponsor massive immigration in which to base Chile's industrial and military might unless they were willing to see Chile relegated to the status of a poor backwater. This was indeed disturbing to an elite and to a public accustomed to the belief that theirs was the leading nation of South America in all endeavors. Argentina

was simply growing much faster, not only in terms of its population, but economically as well. The two main Chilean economic sectors, agriculture and
mining, were stagnating in the latter part of the nineteenth century, while the
economy of Argentina, as we have seen, was booming.[39]

CHILEAN AGRICULTURE

Chilean wheat exports to Peru, which began during the late colonial period,
were expanded after the wars of independence. The discovery of gold in California would provide Chile with an additional market. When news of the Cal-
ifornian gold rush reached Chile during August 1848, a sizable exodus of
Chilean labor and ships began. In their wake came an increased demand for
Chilean wheat, flour, jerked beef, hides, fruits, and wine, primarily because at
that stage it was easier to supply San Francisco from Valparaíso than overland,
from the East Coast of the United States, or by ships sent around Cape Horn.
The inauguration of the Panama railway in 1855 would deflect trade away from
Valparaíso.[40]

Rumors of a gold rush in Australia in 1851 prompted some Valparaíso merchants to dispatch sailing ships to that continent. Soon Chilean wheat and other
agricultural products were sold in Australia as well as New Zealand and Tahiti.
However, by the mid-1850s Australia and New Zealand were producing their
own wheat, and the demand for the Chilean product fell; the inauguration of
the Panama railway in 1855 would also deflect a large segment of the California
trade away from Valparaíso. Nevertheless, Argentina and Britain had begun to
import Chilean wheat as well. Wheat exports from central Chile averaged 50,000
metric quintals during the 1840s (a metric quintal equals 45.45 kilograms, or
100 pounds), 200,000 quintals in the 1860s, 500,000 quintals in the 1860s, and
1,690,000 by 1874.[41]

When new wheat-exporting nations such as Argentina, Canada, Russia, and
the United States entered the global market, wheat prices began to drop. Wheat
production in the Chilean Central Valley was labor intensive and encompassed
a rather limited area when compared to the vast wheat-growing areas of the
other producers; hence it could no longer complete. Through mechanization and
lower production costs, the new wheat-exporting countries soon drove Chilean
wheat from the world market. Nevertheless, the incorporation of the former
Indian territories in the 1880s brought about a regional distribution of Chilean
agriculture and an increase in the area sown to wheat, largely to meet local
needs, particularly in growing urban centers and the Norte Grande. Nevertheless,
the agricultural share of exports fell from 30 percent in 1864 to 21.5 in 1881.[42]

THE MINING SECTOR: COPPER, SILVER, AND NITRATES

Mining, the other traditional activity, had correspondingly increased in importance. The expansion of this sector would provide the Chilean economy with

resources to effect major changes in the infrastructure and motivate its foreign policy. Copper deposits are found almost throughout the entire territory of Chile. During the colonial period, mining was centered around the Copiapó area, which in addition produced silver and gold. In 1825, Chilean merchants, sometimes in partnership with British and German capital, began to develop the Copiapó deposits. Smelters, however, were crude and few in number; hence Chilean copper exports were in the form of raw ore or copper ingots. Between 1817 and 1825, 75 percent of all Chilean copper exports went to Asiatic ports, particularly Calcutta. The Asiatic trade was interrupted because of a war in Burma that effectively closed the Gulf of Bengal to navigation. During the conflict, India began to import Scandinavian zinc, a metal that became a substitute for copper and displaced the Chilean product. A downward turn in the British economy and export taxes levied on copper by the Chilean government brought an end to this trade.[43]

British capitalists invested significantly in Chilean copper mines during the 1830s and 1840s, but native capital continued to play an important role. Production increased from an annual average of 620 tons in the eighteenth century to 1,500 tons by the first two decades of the nineteenth century. It almost tripled to 4,000 tons during 1821–1843 and climbed prodigiously to an average of 22,000 by the 1850s (see table 4.9), when Chile emerged as the world's largest copper producer.[44]

The world demand for copper increased during the 1870s because of new techniques and inventions. Copper became a sort of wonder metal and was used in the manufacture of shells and cartridges, for electrical implements and boiler tube. This growing demand brought new producers into the arena, including the United States. Consequently, prices in the world market fell, and Chilean production declined in response.[45]

Similar declines were observed in other traditional Chilean mining areas, such as silver. During the colonial period, silver was so abundant that domestic utensils were made from this metal instead of iron. The largest deposits, however, were exploited after independence. The Arqueros mine, for example, was discovered in 1825, and by 1900 it was estimated that it had produced more than 600 tons of pure silver. Another silver strike at Chañarcillo occurred in 1832. These deposits were responsible for the mining boom Chile experienced in the 1830s and actually yielded 450 million of the 891 million pesos' worth of silver produced in the country during the nineteenth century. The shift made by the leading European nation in 1870 from a silver to a gold standard, followed by a 50 percent decline in the price of copper as well as the loss of small but highly lucrative agricultural markets overseas, signaled the end of a Chilean economic cycle.[46]

Chile was to find a substitute for silver and copper in nitrates and thus entered into one of the most radical cycles in its economic history. The nitrate era would lift Chile from its economic depression and would have long-lasting effects on its foreign relations as well. The nitrate deposits at Antofagasta in Bolivia and at

Table 4.9
Chilean Copper Production, 1844–1902 (in tons)

Period	Average production
1844-1848	9, 608
1849-1853	12, 546
1854-1858	22, 164
1859-1863	32, 004
1864-1868	40, 459
1869-1873	45, 283
1874-1878	49, 073
1879-1883	42, 139
1884-1888	37, 203
1889-1893	23, 377
1894-1898	22, 777
1899-1902	26, 287

Source: Adolfo Ortúzar, *Chile of Today* (New York: 1907), p. 96.

Tarapacá in Peru were discovered in the 1500s. However, exploitation of this mineral would not begin until the 1850s, when Europe began to use nitrate as a fertilizer. Chilean and English capitalists invested in the Tarapacá fields in the early 1820s and 1840s. Further deposits were discovered in the southern half of Tarapacá during 1850, and by the following year ten nitrate-processing plants, known as *oficinas*, were in operation. Attempts to develop these new deposits failed, largely because of the low productivity of these processing plants, which even working twenty-four hours a day, could barely average 900 tons per annum. However, the introduction of narrow-gauge railroads in the 1860s and the incorporation of steam engines in which ore was boiled to extract nitrate improved productivity.[47]

Chilean and British capital joined to create Melbourne Clark and Company. Clark, an Anglo-Chilean, appointed George Hicks as the manager in Antofogasta, and Hicks proceeded to fill positions in the company with British personnel, although at this stage the British played a secondary role, and development of the nitrate fields was essentially still a Chilean enterprise. The drop in copper and silver prices had created serious unemployment in Chile, and perhaps as many as 30,000 laborers migrated to the nitrate fields, where they constituted the bulk of the work force.[48]

During the period 1873–1875, the Peruvian government enacted legislation designed to monopolize the sale of nitrate, while in 1879, cash-hungry Bolivia levied new taxes on nitrate. This triggered the War of the Pacific and the eventual seizure of the nitrate-bearing districts by Chile. Nitrates saved Chile from economic decline and gave it the revenues that would spur Chilean economic development for the next fifty years. With nitrates came an era of easy money and corruption as well as the beginnings of economic dependency.[49]

Like most other Latin American countries, Chile depended on customs receipts for its revenues. Thus, in order to foster trade, the Chilean government began to enact legislation regarding credit, transportation, and altered tariffs. Customs revenues collected from nitrate grew from 2 million gold pesos in 1880 to 50 million by 1895.[50]

In order to legitimize the seizure of the nitrate deposits, the Chilean government decided to honor bonds and certificates issued by the government of Peru to investors when it had created a nitrate monopoly. Numerous speculators bought bonds and certificates held by the Peruvian government when a Chilean victory seemed imminent. The most notorious were two Englishmen, Robert Harvey and John Thomas North. Thus, the Chilean nitrate industry was denationalized at a time when virgin lands had been opened for cultivation in Argentina, Canada, Ukraine, and the United States, and when European producers, in order to compete in price and quantity, were forced to undergo major technological innovations, including the use of inorganic fertilizers. Chilean products therefore found newer and larger markets. Production grew accordingly to meet the demand, as can be seen in table 4.10.[51]

CHILEAN FOREIGN TRADE

Even at the peak of the agricultural cycle at mid-nineteenth century, minerals ruled the export sector—first copper and silver, gold to a much lesser extent, and finally nitrate. Coal would not become a major export until the turn of the century. By 1902, the export of agrarian products barely exceeded 12 million pesos, while mineral exports accounted for 158.9 million pesos. England was Chile's main trading partner, as befitted the nation with the largest capital investments there, absorbing approximately 81 percent of her exports and providing 43 percent of her imports by the late 1890s. Chile had trade deficits with virtually all her other trading partners, a situation that forced her to sign treaties with some of them, lifting tariffs from each other's products.[52]

A growing demand for nitrate in the late 1890s resulted in an export boom (see table 4.11), and although some Chilean trade statistics tend to show a favorable balance of trade, the Chilean economist Daniel Martner indicates that the service of the Chilean foreign debt actually caused a negative gold flow.[53]

A recent article in the field of Chilean government finance after the fall of

Table 4.10
Chilean Nitrate Production and Exports, 1880–1890 (in thousands of metric tons)

Year	Production	Exports
1880	224	224
1881	356	360
1882	492	492
1883	590	590
1884	559	559
1886	451	451
1887	713	704
1888	767	767
1889	951	948
1890	1,075	1,098

Source: Carmen Cariola Sutter and Osvaldo Sunkel, *Un siglo de historia económica de Chile, 1830–1930* (Madrid: 1982), p. 126.

Balmaceda points out the difficulty of assessing Chilean statistics, for there are several contradicting sets of figures. Some of these show considerably larger amounts of government revenues, but they were obtained by including foreign loans and even issues of paper money as "extraordinary revenues." Since the smaller set of figures given in this article correspond closely to those presented by other Chilean economists and reflect government revenues obtained from customs fees and internal taxes, the author has selected these and incorporated them into table 4.12.[54]

According to these statistics, Chile had an aggregate surplus of $12.4 million during the years 1895–1902, and government revenues experienced an increase of 4.62 percent since 1890; the Chilean economy was also undergoing a serious crisis at this time. The seizure of the nitrate deposits presented the Chilean government with an economic windfall that enabled it to reduce excise duties. The taxes on alcohol, tobacco, and real estate as well as the lighthouse and tonnage fees and export duties on copper and silver were progressively abolished after 1881. The contribution made by internal taxes to government revenues fell from 26 percent in 1878 to below 1 percent by 1893, while the share represented by nitrate taxes rose steadily from 4.7 percent in 1880 to 28.2 percent in 1885 and 48.9 percent by 1900.[55]

The altered income structures exposed the Chilean government to the fluc-

Table 4.11
Chilean Foreign Trade, 1875–1900 (in million pesos of 18 d)

Year	Exports	Imports
1875	87.5	87.4
1880	88.0	63.0
1885	108.2	84.4
1890	144.3	143.4
1895	153.9	146.1
1896	156.9	156.3
1897	138.7	136.2
1898	168.0	102.2
1899	163.1	106.0
1900	167.6	128.5
1901	171.8	139.3
1902	185.9	132.4

Source: Guillermo Subercaseaux, *Monetary and Banking Policy of Chile* (Oxford: Clarendon Press, 1922), pp. 214.

tuations of the global market for nitrates. The War of the Pacific also marked the beginning of long-term inflation. The government abandoned the gold standard and issued paper currency to finance the war, an anti-cyclical measure that served to activate the depressed Chilean economy and to encourage investment. The practice continued throughout the 1890s. Successive issues of paper not only brought severe hardship to the population at large but affected the international value of the Chilean gold peso, which depreciated from 24 1/16 pence in 1890 to 18 13/16 in 1891 and to a low of 12 9/16 in 1894. A mild recovery took place in 1900, when the gold peso stood at 15 7/8 pence.[56]

In order to return to the gold standard, in 1892 the Jorge Montt administration withdrew 10 million pesos from circulation, but the plan misfired when the value of Chilean bonds and the peso dropped. Foreign investors began to withdraw their deposits, and fear of a general collapse forced the government to abandon its plans for conversion. A second attempt was made in 1895, when the government borrowed 2 million pounds sterling to buy up paper pesos. Unfortunately, the government failed to exercise any control credit, which often went into the importation of luxury goods rather than sound investments. In addition,

Table 4.12

Chilean Government Expenditures and Revenues (in million U.S. dollars)

Year	Expenditures	Revenues
1870	12.0	12.8
1875	17.8	27.1
1880	17.8	27.0
1885	21.6	18.6
1890	32.5	32.4
1895	32.5	36.3
1896	43.2	42.3
1897	37.1	32.0
1898	37.2	37.9
1899	35.0	41.1
1900	40.2	46.3
1901	45.0	39.9
1902	44.1	37.7

Source: John R. Bowman and Michael Wallerstein, ''The Fall of Balmaceda and Public Finance in Chile: New Data for an Old Debate,'' *IISWA* (November 1982), pp. 449–450.

like their counterparts in Argentina, the landowning gentry, who had contracted debts in paper currency, benefitted by currency depreciation. The government promised to redeem the paper currency at 18d, but the boundary dispute with Argentina forced postponement of the redemption date to January 1902 and later on to October 1903. In fact, the era of paper money would not reach its high water mark until 1907. The Chilean foreign debt in 1900 stood at 234.2 million pesos, or approximately 17.7 million pounds sterling, and at 301.6 million, or 23 million pounds in 1901.[57]

Thus, at the turn of the century, the most Chileans recognized that Argentina had surged well ahead in wealth, power, and population. The growing disparity between the economies of Chile and its eastern neighbor evoked mixed emotions—from disbelief to envy to apprehension. To be sure, Chile had continue to grow, albeit at a slower rate than her Transandine neighbor. Argentina's population exceeded Chile's by more than 1 million, but more importantly, Argentina's foreign trade was 2.3 times that of Chile, and both nations depended heavily on such trade for the bulk of their revenues. Therefore, Chile, whose economy grew at a slower rate, could not match Argentine military expenditures. As will be demonstrated in chapter 6, in these nations' competition for naval supremacy, each new Chilean acquisition was immediately followed by new Argentine naval constructions that were inevitably larger and more powerful.

NOTES

1. Roberto Cortés Conde, "The Growth of the Argentine Economy, 1870–1914," *CHLA* (London: Cambridge University Press, 1985), V: 328; Alistair Hennnesy, *The Frontier in Latin American History* (London: Edward Arnold, 1978), p. 84.

2. Ibid., pp. 83–85; David Rock, ed., *Argentina in the Twentieth Century* (London: Duckworth, 1977), pp. 95–96, 133–134. For details of the trade in jerked beef, see Aurelio González Climent and Anselmo González Climent, *Historia de la marina mercante argentina* (Buenos Aires: 1972–1977, 19 vols.), II: 133–135; Roberto Cortés Conde, "La frontera ganadera: Aspectos económicos sobre la conquista del desierto," in *CHNCD* 3: 343; Simon G. Hanson, *The Argentine Meat Supply and the British Market: Chapters in the History of the Argentine Meat Industry* (Stanford, CA: Stanford University Press, 1938), pp. 29–32, 44–46.

3. Vicente Vázquez-Presedo, *El caso argentino: Migración de factores, comercio exterior y desarrollo, 1875–1914* (Buenos Aires: Editorial Universitaria de Buenos Aires, 1975), pp. 175–178.

4. Richard Perren, *The Meat Trade in Britain, 1840–1914* (London: Routledge and Kegan Paul, 1978), pp. 212–213.

5. Juan C. Vedoya, *La campaña del desierto y la tecnificación ganadera* (Buenos Aires: *EUDEBA*, 1981), pp. 122–123; Hanson, *Argentine Meat Supply and the British Market*, pp. 10–11; Ysabel Rennie, *The Argentine Republic* (New York: Macmillan, 1945), p. 147.

6. Vedoya, *La campaña del desierto*, pp. 203–204, 205–207.

7. Hanson, *Argentine Meat Supply and the British Market*, pp. 48–49.

8. Ibid., p. 17; James R. Scobie, *Revolution in the Pampas: A Social History of Argentine Wheat, 1860–1910* (Austin: University of Texas Press, 1964), p. 38; also Ezequiel Gallo, *La Pampa Gringa: La colonización agrícola en Santa Fé; 1875–1895* (Buenos Aires: Editorial Sudamericana, 1984), pp. 198–210, 298–299; Romain Gaignard, *La Pampa Argentina: Ocupación, poblamiento, explotación de la conquista a la crísis mundial, 1550–1930* (Buenos Aires: Ediciones Solar, 1989), pp. 139–150, 160–164.

9. Scobie, *Revolution in the Pampas*, pp. 14–22, 111–113.

10. Roger Gravil, *The Anglo-Argentine Connection, 1900–1939* (Boulder: Westview Press, 1985), pp. 183–185; Rolf Sternberger, "Occupance of the Humid Pampa, 1865–1914," *Revista Geográfica* (junio 1972), pp. 75–78; Ernesto Tornquist and Co., *El desarrollo económico de la República Argentina en los ultimos cincuenta años* (Buenos Aires: 1919), pp. 55–56.

11. Cortés Conde, "The Growth of the Argentine Economy," p. 337.

12. Ibid., pp. 335–336.

13. Ricardo M. Ortíz, *Historia económica de la Argentina, 1830–1930* (Buenos Aires: Editorial Plus Ultra, 1987), pp. 221–237.

14. José Panettieri, *Immigración en la Argentina* (Buenos Aires: Ediciones Macchi, 1970), pp. 115–118.

15. Vázquez-Presedo, *El caso argentino*, pp. 101–103.

16. *Monthly Bulletin of the Bureau of American Republics*, no. 3 (1900), pp. 393–394.

17. Eduardo A. Zalduendo, *Libras y rieles: Las inversiones británicas para el desarrollo de los ferrocarriles en la Argentina, Brasil, Canada e India durante el siglo XIX* (Buenos Aires: Editorial El Coloquio, 1979), pp. 256–257; Raul Scalabrini Ortíz, *Historia de los ferrocarriles Argentinos* (Buenos Aires: Editorial Devenir, 1958), pp. 27–49, 51–76. For details of the Oeste workshops, see Zalduendo, *Libras y rieles*, p. 273; also *National Car and Locomotive Builder* (New York: January 1885). The latter includes an excellent description of the locomotives and railway cars manufactured in the shops at Tolosa, as well as details of the railway shops and their equipment.

18. George S. Brady, *Railways of South America, Part I: Argentina* (Washington, DC: U.S. Government Printing Office, 1926), pp. 38–43; Ricardo Ortíz, *Historia de los ferrocarriles argentinos*, pp. 40–41, 50–58, 148–149.

19. Zalduendo, *Libras y rieles*, pp. 286–298; Winthrop Wright, *British-owned Railways in Argentina: Their Effects on Economic Nationalism, 1854–1948* (Austin: University of Texas Press, 1974), pp. 51–56; Ricardo Ortíz, *Historia económica de la Argentina*, pp. 258–259, 270–272, 277–279, 312–314.

20. Zalduendo, *Libras y rieles*, pp. 302–308, 330–334.

21. Tornquist, *El desarrollo*, pp. 116–118; Zalduendo, *Libras y rieles*, pp. 354–355.

22. A. G. Ford, "British Investments in Argentina and Long Term Swings," *Journal of Economic History* 31, no. 3 (September 1971), pp. 652–658; H. S. Ferns, *Britain and Argentina in the Nineteenth Century* (London: Oxford University Press, 1960), pp. 432–433, 492–494, Cortés Conde, "The Growth of the Argentine Economy," pp. 341–342; Scalabrini Ortíz, *Historia de los ferrocarriles*, pp. 144–146, for details of the guarantees given to British-owned railways.

23. A. G. Ford, *El patron oro: 1880–1914, Inglaterra y la Argentina* (Buenos Aires: Editorial del Instituto, 1968), pp. 150–152, 318–332; Ford, "British Investments," p. 652, Rennie, *The Argentine Republic*, pp. 176–180.

24. Ford, *El patron oro*, pp. 257–258.

25. Ford, "British Investments," p. 652; H. S. Ferns, *The Argentine Republic: 1516–1971* (Newton Abbott: David & Charles, 1973) pp. 87–90.

26. Ortíz, *Historia económica de la Argentina* pp. 226–229; Adolfo Dorfman, *Historia de la industria argentina* (Buenos Aires: Solar/Hachette, 1970), pp. 202–205; Noemí Girbal de Blacha, "Comercio exterior y producción agrícola en la Argentina," in *Investigaciones y ensayos* 21 (julio-diciembre 1976), pp. 343–346.

27. Ferns, *Britain and Argentina in the Nineteenth Century*, pp. 472–479; Horacio Juan Cuccorese, *Historia económica de la Argentina, 1826–1930* (Buenos Aires: Editorial El Ateneo, 1962), pp. 72–73.

28. Horacio Juan Cuccorese, *En tiempo histórico de Carlos Pellegrini*, 2 vols. (Buenos Aires: Fundación para la Educación, la Ciencia y la Cultura, 1985), II: 168–171; Albert B. Martínez, and Maurice Lewandoski, *The Argentine in the Twentieth Century* (London: T. Fisher Unwin, 1911), pp. 325–327.

29. Cuccorese, *Historia económica de la Argentina*, pp. 82–83.

30. Martínez and Lewandoski, *The Argentine in the Twentieth Century*, pp. 300–303, 326–327; Jonathan C. Brown, *A Socioeconomic History of Argentina, 1776–1960* (London, New York, Melbourne: Cambridge University Press, 1979), pp. 226–229. Prior to the First World War, 40 percent of British capital investments in Latin America went to Argentina. Although foreign companies operated the railways, hydroelectric plants, gas-

works, tramways, and telephone systems, Argentines retained control of the agricultural and pastoral sectors, thus retaining control of the means of production.

31. David Rock, *Argentina: 1516–1982: From Spanish Colony to the Falklands War* (Berkeley: University of California Press, 1985), pp. 164, 166; John E. Hodge, "The Formation of the Argentine Primary and Secondary School System," TAM 44, no. 1 (July 1987), pp. 45–63; Alberto Palcos, "Presidencia de Sarmiento," in *HAC*, 1: 137; Carlos Heras, "Presidencia de Avellaneda," in *HAC*, 1: 217; International Bureau of the American Republics, *Argentine Republic: A Geographical Sketch* (Washington, DC: Government Printing Office, 1903); Allen Woll, *A Functional Past: The Uses of History in Nineteenth Century Chile* (Baton Rouge and London: Louisiana State University Press, 1982), p. 153; Harold Blakemore, *British Nitrates and Chilean Politics, 1885–1896: Balmaceda and North* (London: Athlone Press, 1974), p. 72. In 1868, there were 30,000 students in the Argentine school system. Under the Sarmiento administration, 800 schools were established and the number of students had risen to 100,000. It would continue to rise dramatically in the years that followed, to 120,812 in 1876, 150,188 in 1885, 242,736 in 1890, 326,752 in 1899, and 460,229 two years later. By contrast, the Chilean school system had 61,000 students in 1861, 79,000 by 1886, and 150,000 by 1890. Tornquist, *El desarrollo*; E. Bradford Burns, *The Unwritten Alliance: Rio Branco and Brazilian-American Relations* (New York and London: Columbia University Press, 1966), p. 182, Carmen Cariola Sutter and Osvaldo Sunkel, *Un siglo de historia económica de Chile: 1830–1930, dos ensayos y una biografía* (Madrid: Ediciones Cultura Hispánica del Instituto de Cooperación Iberoamericana, 1982), 142. In 1902, the Argentine railways, with 17,377 kilometers of track, were the most extensive in South America. Brazil, with 14,614 kilometers, came second; Chile lagged far behind with a total of 4,352 kilometers in 1900. Ford, *El patron oro*, pp. 257–258.

32. Brian Loveman, *Chile: The Legacy of Spanish Capitalism* (New York: Oxford University Press, 1979), pp. 20–26.

33. Corporación de Fomento de la Producción Agrícola, *Geografía económica de Chile* (Santiago: 1968), pp. 61–62; Thomas A. Weil, ed. *Chile: A Country Study* (Washington, DC, American University Press, 1982), pp. 53–54.

34. Corporación de Fomento, *Geografía Económica*, pp. 11–12.

35. Ibid., pp. 12–14.

36. Carl E. Solberg, *Immigration and Nationalism: Argentina and Chile, 1890–1914* (Austin and London: University of Texas Press, 1970), pp. 2–5; Nicolás Palacios, *Raza chilena: Un libro escrito por un chileno y para chilenos*, 2 vols. (Santiago: Editorial Chilena, 1918), II: 32–33.

37. Solberg, *Immigration and Nationalism*, pp. 6–8.

38. Ibid.

39. Nicolás Sánchez-Albornoz, *The Population of Latin America: A History* (Berkeley and Los Angeles: University of California Press, 1974), pp. 71–75); Pierre Blancpain, *Les Allemands aux Chilli: 1816–1945* (Köln and Wien: Bölau Verlag, 1974), pp. 478–479. The opportunities offered by Argentina tempted many immigrants, originally bound for Chile, who opted to remain in the Platine nation. The 1901 report of the Chilean General Inspectorate of Land and Colonization lamented the flight of the best foreign colonists toward Argentina. María R. Stabili, "Las políticas immigratorias latinoamericanas de los gobiernos chilenos desde la segunda mitad del siglo pasado hasta la decada de 1920," in *Estudios Migratorios Latinoamericanos* 1, no. 2 (Abril 1986), pp. 181–202. Conversely, a number of Italians who failed to make a life for themselves in Ar-

gentina crossed the Andes into Chile. Carl E. Solberg, "A Discriminatory Frontier Land Policy: Chile, 1870–1914" *TAM* 26, no. 2 (October 1969), pp. 115–133.

40. Solberg, *Immigration and Nationalism*, p. 22.

41. Mario Barros, *Historia Diplomática de Chile* (Barcelona: Ediciones Ariel, 1971), pp. 191–193.

42. Cariola Sutter and Sunkel, "Un siglo de historia ecónomica de Chile," pp. 75–76.

43. Thomas C. Wright, "Agriculture and Protectionism in Chile," *JLAS* 7, Part 1 (May 1975), pp. 45–48.

44. Claudio Velíz, *Historia de la marina mercante de Chile* (Santiago: Ediciones de la Universidad de Chile, 1961), pp. 29–31.

45. Adolfo Ortúzar, *Chile of Today* (New York: Tribune Association, 1907), pp. 95–97; Maurice Zeitlin, *The Civil Wars in Chile* (Princeton, NJ: Princeton University Press, 1984), pp. 24–25.

46. Ibid., pp. 145–146.

47. Ortúzar, *Chile of Today*, pp. 139–140.

48. Loveman, *Chile*, p. 168; Oscar Bermúdez Miral, *Historia del Salitre: Desde sus orígenes hasta la Guerra del Pacífico* (Ediciones de la Universidad de Chile, 1983), pp. 42–43, pp. 136–138; Michael Monteón, "The British in the Atacama Desert: The Cultural Bases of Economic Imperialism," *JEH* 25, no. 1, (March 1975), pp. 119–120.

49. Barros, *Historia diplomática de Chile* p. 326; Edulia Silvia Salas, "Biografía de don Adolfo Ibáñez," *RCHG* 34, no. 38 (1920), pp. 342–388.

50. Loveman, *The Legacy of Spanish Capitalism*, p. 185; Michael Monteón, *Chile in the Nitrate Era: The Evolution of Economic Dependence* (Madison: University of Wisconsin Press, 1983), pp. 20–21.

51. Cariola Sutter and Sunkel, "Un siglo de historia económica de Chile," p. 136.

52. Ibid., pp. 86–87; Loveman, *The Legacy of Spanish Capitalism*, pp. 199–201.

53. Blakemore, *British Nitrates and Chilean Politics*, pp. 26–27.

54. John R. Bowman and Michael Wallenstein, "The Fall of Balmaceda and Public Finance in Chile: New Data for an Old Debate," *JISWA* 24, no. 4 (November 1982), pp. 421–460. Mamalakis's figures are given in pounds. For purposes of this work, they have been converted into U.S. dollars at the rate of five to one. Other Chilean historians who disagree with the higher revenue figures, since they contain issues of paper and money as well as foreign loans, include Francisco Encina. See, for example, *Nuestra inferioridad ecónomica* (Santiago: Editorial Universitaria, 1986), pp. 14–135; Subercaseaux Guillermo, *Monetary and Banking Policy of Chile* (Oxford: Clarendon Press, 1922), p. 214; Daniel Martner, *Estudio de la política comercial chilena e historia ecónomica nacional*, 2 vols. (Santiago: Imprenta Universitaria, 1923), I:512–513.

55. Daniel Martner, *Historia de Chile: Historia Económica* (Santiago: 1929, 2 vols.), I: 504–506; Martner, *Estudio de la política comercial chilena e historia económica nacional*, I: 512–513.

56. Bowman and Wallenstein, "The Fall of Balmaceda and Public Finance in Chile," pp. 421–460.

57. Frank Whitson Fetter, *Monetary Inflation in Chile* (Princeton, NJ: Princeton University Press, 1931), pp. 13–14; Guillermo Subercaseaux, *Monetary Inflation in Chile* (Princeton, NJ: Princeton University Press, 1931), pp. 13–14, 113–119.

5 ———————————————————————————

The Armed Forces of Argentina

The Argentine army can trace its origins to the militias established during the late colonial period. As mentioned in Chapter 1, several companies of mounted frontier militia were organized in the mid-eighteenth century to protect settlements from Indian attacks. A major military reorganization took place during 1778, when Buenos Aires became the capital of the newly established viceroyalty of the Río de la Plata. A series of undeclared wars with Portugal over possession of Uruguay, the Tupac Amarú Indian risings, which spread into Upper Peru as well, and invasions of Salta by Mataco Indians forced the viceroy to expand the army and militias. Successive reorganizations of the latter took place in 1780 and 1791, until these formations had a strength of 14,141 men.[1]

Army officers were drawn from regular units either in the peninsula or the viceroyalty. Enlisted men were recruited by a lottery, a voluntary system known as *enganche*, or meted out as punishment to peninsular troops with poor service records, and later on to *criollos* classified as vagrants. The regular army units were primarily composed of peninsular Spaniards. They were badly trained and seldom bothered with mandatory formations, while the criollos met regularly on Sundays for musket training and close order drill. The equipment included smoothbore flintlock muskets, Spanish model 1777 in 17.5 mm. caliber for the infantry, and carbines, saddle pistols, sabers, and lances for the cavalry. The artillery consisted of horse-drawn models ranging from 4 to 32 pounders, as well as a few 6- and 12-inch mortars in fixed batteries. To economize, colonial authorities reduced military emoluments by 50 percent. This, coupled with a shortage of arms and uniforms, led to a high rate of desertion. Nevertheless, the colonial militia fought with distinction against the Portuguese during the Cisplatine War of 1762–1763 and made the Indian frontier secure.[2]

The poor showing of Spanish troops during the English invasions of 1806–

1807 contrasted with the aggressiveness of the local militia, which defeated the British forces in an episode that has entered Argentine history as the reconquest. After the first British invasion in 1806, a number of volunteer militia units were organized in Buenos Aires. These units were reorganized in 1809, by which time they comprised nine infantry battalions, a battery of horse artillery, and a troop of cavalry. After the overthrow of Spanish colonial rule in Buenos Aires occurred in May 1810, the revolutionary junta reclassified these militias as regular army units, or *tropas veteranas*, and they became the cadre of the Argentine army.[3]

The state that succeeded the viceroyalty, known as the United Provinces of the Río de la Plata, virtually disintegrated. The army of the United Provinces was little more than a collection of poorly trained militias led by badly or totally untrained officers. These deficiencies notwithstanding, it managed to check the royalist forces from Upper Peru in the northwest but failed in its invasions of Upper Peru and Paraguay, while the royalists at Montevideo maintained control of the sea lanes as well as of the Plata estuary.[4]

The independence movement in the Plata was foundering by 1812, a year that marked the arrival of José de San Martín to Buenos Aires. Born in the northeastern province of Corrientes, San Martín was a graduate of the Spanish School of Nobles and a veteran of the Napoleonic Wars. In March 1812, he was appointed commander of a new squadron of mounted grenadiers that he was to establish according to French regulations. By December 7, the squadron had been expanded into a full regiment that would become the first truly professional training center in the Argentine army. Its personnel were carefully selected, and from its officers' ranks arose 100 generals who played crucial roles in the wars of independence and national reorganization. The grenadier regiment later became a principal part of the Army of the Andes, which freed Chile and Peru from royalist control. A division of this Army of the Andes was sent to the aid of Simón Bolívar, the liberator of Northern South America.[5]

During 1820, the United Provinces fell into a period of anarchy. With the sole exception of the units guarding the Indian frontier, the army and navy were disbanded. The well-seasoned units that fought in the independence wars were replaced by a small volunteer force. This small standing force was reorganized on May 31, 1825, seven months before the Empire of Brazil declared war on the United Provinces. Under the army reorganization plan, a general staff was established, standardized uniforms were issued to all branches of the service, new legislation regarding enrollment in the militia was enacted, and the Maestranza de Artillería, or Artillery Arsenal and Repair Shops, was established. The new army consisted of five infantry battalions and one infantry regiment, nineteen regiments of cavalry and one of artillery, as well as an engineer battalion.[6]

The officer corps was still made up of veterans of the independence wars, the most proficient of whom were those formed by San Martín in the Mounted

Grenadier regiment. A decree dated May 1, 1823, provided for twenty scholarships for officer candidates, who were to undergo a Course of Military Studies administered in civilian institutions. An artillery school for officers, or Academia Teórico Práctica de Artillería, was founded in 1828.[7]

The reconstituted Argentine army, led by an experienced group of officers who had fought with distinction in the wars of independence, was destined to see action in another foreign war in which it would acquit itself brilliantly. A long-standing controversy between Spain and Portugal over control of the Banda Oriental was pursued by their successor states. The dispute climaxed in December 1825, when the Empire of Brazil declared war on the United Provinces. Though the Brazilian army enjoyed superior numbers and armaments, the Argentine army possessed the indisputable advantages of better training, organization, and leadership. Consequently, the Argentine forces inflicted a series of defeats upon their adversaries. Minor encounters at Bagé, Bacacay, and Ombú were followed by the war's major land engagement, the battle of Ituzaingó, on February 20, 1827, which was won by Argentina. By September of that year, the Argentine army in operations numbered 12,805 men and was articulated into one artillery regiment with 28 pieces and 500 men, 8 cavalry regiments with a total of 5,370 men, 5 infantry battalions with 3,765 men, plus 3,200 Uruguayan militiamen.[8]

Despite external threats, the political struggle in Argentina continued unabated. Internal dissensions negated a final victory and eventually forced the president of the United Provinces to resign in 1827. Juan Manuel de Rosas became head of state in 1829. Under his rule, the national army of the United Provinces was disbanded and replaced by militias controlled by caudillos allied to Rosas, their two principal formations the armies of Buenos Aires and Entre Ríos. The general staff, artillery academy and officer school were dissolved. Officers were politically appointed and had little, if any, formal training. Many of the professional officers trained by San Martín had been murdered or forced into exile. Most of them joined the *Unitarios* in their war against Rosas.[9]

Recruitment procedures were unchanged since the colonial period. Forced levies were conducted by the provincial warlords, and in the course of the civil wars, those prisoners who did not have their throats cut were forced to serve their former enemies. The gauchos were quite ready to listen to whatever firebrand attracted their attention. In a country where practically every man knew how to ride a horse and horses were abundant, cavalry formations were easily raised. There was little to choose between the equipment, tactics, and leadership of either side; thus quite often superior numbers prevailed. Although during the wars of independence local arsenals had produced serviceable muskets and sabers as well as excellent cannon, production was sporadic, and most of these facilities ceased to exist by the early 1820s. In this industrially backward land there were no arsenals that could turn out small arms, artillery, or even cloth for uniforms in sufficient quantities. Infantry and artillery were harder to train and equip than cavalry, which became the dominant branch of the service. The weapons used by the warring factions were essentially those inherited from the viceroyalty and trophies taken during the English invasions.[10]

The fall of Rosas in 1852 did not mark the end of the internal struggles. Both Argentinian states established national guards as "ready reserves." Buenos Aires did so in 1852 and the Confederation two years later. All males of military age could be summoned for military duty if required. In 1852 Buenos Aires displayed a standing army of 3,500 men and a national guard of 70,000, while the Confederation could field an army of 2,500 men and, theoretically, count on a national guard of 83,000. During the two most crucial battles for national unification, Cepeda (1859) and Pavón (1861), each side deployed around 16,000 men. As we have seen, Buenos Aires defeated the Confederation and proceeded to unify Argentina. The national guard was unified as well. Nominally, the national guard was under presidential control, but each province was responsible for the training and equipment of its own contingents and thus retained a measure of military strength. A Ministry of War and Marine was established in 1864. It included an inspectorate general, the Comisaría de Guerra, or supply branch, which would provide for the everyday needs of the troops, such as uniforms and rations, and the Parque de Artillería, which would be responsible for the acquisition, maintenance, and storage of ordnance. Despite these improvements, the army of Argentina at the outbreak of the Paraguayan war was best described by one of the characters in a novel by Manuel Galvez: *una montonera con música!*, a guerrilla force with a military band.[11]

GENESIS OF THE PARAGUAYAN WAR

In June 1811, Paraguay declared her independence from both Spain and Buenos Aires. Congress elected a five-man junta, presided over by Lieutenant Colonel Fulgencio Yegros. Among his associates was a lawyer named José Gaspar Rodríguez de Francia. In 1814, Congress voted to give one man absolute power for three years. That man was Francia, who had outmaneuvered and outwitted the other members of the junta. Two years later, he became dictator for life, and styled himself El Supremo. Fearing invasion from Argentina and Brazil, Francia banned foreign trade and enforced a policy of strict isolation. The dictator died in October. In March 1841, Congress established a dual consulate made up of Carlos Antonio López and Colonel Mariano Roque for a three-year period. In 1844, a newly promulgated constitution ended the consulate and established López as president. Carlos Antonio ended the isolation enforced by Francia. Foreign trade was restored and immigration encouraged.[12]

Relations with Argentina were tense at best. Both nations claimed the territories of Misiones and the Central Chaco. While Argentina was in the throes of civil war, Paraguayan forces occupied the disputed territory. Paraguay was also engaged in a serious border dispute with Brazil, which had began to encroach in southern Matto Grosso, on the northern border of Paraguay. Under the terms of a treaty concluded on October 7, 1844, Brazil and Paraguay agreed to appoint commissioners to settle the boundary dispute, but the convention was not ratified by Brazil, which established two military outposts in the disputed area. Carlos Antonio López dispatched a force to evict the intruders. Hoping to enlist Paraguay into an alliance against Rosas, Brazil swallowed the insult. After the fall of Rosas in 1852, the Argentine Confederation recognized Paraguay as an independent state and opened the Paraná River to international trade. Brazil was anxious to obtain free and unimpeded navigation to the Paraná and Paraguay rivers in order to foster development of the province Matto Grosso. In 1855, in a fit of anger, López expelled the Brazilian minister. Enraged, the Brazilian government dispatched a naval squadron under Admiral Pedro Ferreira de Oliveira up the Paraná to exact an apology. Oliveira dropped anchor below Humaitá on February 20. The elder López ordered his son to concentrate 6,000 men at Humaitá, which was hastily fortified with a battery. Negotiations concerning navigation in the Paraguay River began new in 1856, and after protracted bargaining López signed a convention granting the Brazilians free navigation in the Paraguay River. Convinced, however, that war with Brazil was inevitable, he increased his army and fortified Humaitá.[13]

When Carlos Antonio died in 1862, the thirty-five-year-old Francisco Solano López was unanimously elected to the presidency. While touring Europe in the 1850s, Francisco Solano developed a profound admiration for Napoleon Bonaparte. In 1859, the younger López successfully mediated between Buenos Aires and the Confederation. This limited experience fanned his ambitions and his vanity, which knew no bounds. In 1863, the American minister in Asunción reported to the secretary of state that Francisco Solano intended to declare himself emperor and that recognition by France and Brazil would soon follow. The desire for grandeur led to a more ominous switch in the foreign policy of Paraguay. Whereas Francia and the elder López had been concerned with preserving the territorial integrity and independence of Paraguay, in the eyes of Solano López, the very existence of his country depended upon the maintenance of the balance of power in the Plata basin. To ensure this aim, the demands of Paraguay must be heard in the councils of her powerful neighbors. López had been in power for merely six months when events in Uruguay provided him with a pretext to put his theories to the test. Venancio Flores, leader of the Uruguayan Colorado exiles in Argentina, had fought for Mitre during the struggles for Argentine reunification. By mid-1862, Flores began to prepare an expedition to overthrow the Blanco government of Bernardo Berro. In April 1863, Flores and 500 of his followers landed in Uruguay and then headed toward the Brazilian border. In June, Uruguay seized an Argentine merchant vessel carrying contraband of war. Argentina demanded reparations, blockaded the Uruguay River, and threatened war. However, tensions relaxed by the end of June. Berro had sent an envoy to Asunción, promising to accept Solano López as a mediator. On September 6, Solano López wrote to Mitre, requesting an ''amicable and ample explanation of charges made by the Uruguayan government regarding

Argentine intervention.'' Mitre replied on October 2, reminding López that the Argentine Republic had observed strict neutrality and firmly denying allegations to the contrary. In December, in another impudent note, López demanded an explanation about the new fortifications at Martín Garcia and the deployment of army units along the littoral area. In a letter dated February 29, 1864, addressed to López, Mitre noted that the Argentine government was within its rights when it ordered Martín García fortified, most particularly since the island was Argentine territory. Paraguay mobilized. By March, 30,000 men were being drilled at Cerro León, 17,000 at Encarnación, 10,000 at Humaitá, 4,000 at Asunción, and 3,000 at Concepción. Paraguay's effective manpower was 150,000 out of a total population variously estimated at 500,000 to 800,000. There were sufficient weapons and equipment to outfit over 200,000 men. By comparison, on the eve of war, Brazil had a population of 8 million, Argentina 1.2 million, and Uruguay barely 350,000. Paraguay hurriedly let out additional contracts for arms abroad, including one for a pair of ironclad monitors, and the production of arms and munitions at the arsenal was stepped up. The fortress of Humaitá mounted 110 cannon on the eve of war, and 195 by 1868, of which 160 were really effective weapons. López postulated that the Paraguayan soldier had no equals and dogmatically proclaimed his troops more than a match for the Brazilians, Argentines, Uruguayans, and even the Bolivians, if they were foolish enough to get involved.[14]

In an attempt to mediate between the Blancos and Colorados, the Brazilian government sent José Antonio Saraiva, one of its ablest and most personable diplomats, to Montevideo. The Argentine foreign minister, Rufino de Elizalde, Edgar Thornton, the British minister at Buenos Aires, and Saraiva soon managed to arrange a truce between the warring factions. The peace initiative collapsed, and on August 4, Saraiva presented the Blanco government with an ultimatum. On October 16, the Brazilian army invaded Uruguay, and soon the town of Paysandú was under siege. On November 12 Solano López ordered the seizure of the *Marquez de Olinda*, one of the Brazilian steamers in the Matto Grosso run bearing the governor of that province and a cargo of 2,000 muskets. The Paraguayan war had began. To strike at vital areas of Brazil, in January 1865, López demanded permission to cross the Argentine province of Corrientes. When Mitre refused, López called for a special session of Congress and declared war on Argentina on March 29. On April 13, before the declaration of war had reached the Argentine authorities, Paraguayan forces invaded Argentina and captured Corrientes, an undefended port on the Paraná.[15]

The attack against Corrientes was a major blunder. Argentine neutrality might have better served Paraguayan interests in the long run, particularly, since there was every indication that Urquiza was ready to assist Paraguay in her struggle against Brazil. A neutral Argentina would have allowed free passage of arms and supplies through her territory, but the unprovoked Paraguayan invasion drove her into an alliance with Brazil. Such an alliance would eventually spell the doom of this would-be Napoleon and the ruination of Paraguay. With the defeat of the Blancos, Flores became president of Uruguay, and on May 1, Argentina, Brazil, and Uruguay united in a common cause against Paraguay under the terms of the Treaty of the Triple Alliance.[16]

THE ARMY OF PARAGUAY

Convinced that war with Brazil was imminent, the elder López contracted British engineers to erect a fortress at Humaitá. British technicians developed the bast furnaces at Ybycuí, the shipyard at Asuncíon, and expanded the state armory into an arsenal that produced artillery and shells and built a railway connecting Asunción and Villarica. The foundations of the arsenal were laid down in August 1856, and construction of the foundry began in the following years. By 1860, the foundry was producing machinery of various types, including steam engines. Under the guidance of William Keld Whytehead, the arsenal turned out increasing quantities of 12, 24, and 32-pounder cannon, fixed and mobile gun carriages, and shells of all calibers. Weapons were also imported from abroad. Steamers for the fledgling Paraguayan navy were acquired abroad, and others were built locally. By the outbreak of the Paraguayan War, a telegraph line 270 miles long connected Asunción with Paso de la Patria, while a leather manufactory at Asunción turned out saddles, belts, and ammunition pouches for the army. The Paraguayan war has been described as ''a battle of Brown Bess and poor old flint muskets against the Spencer and the Enfield, of honey-combed carronades, long and short against Whitworths and Lahittes, of punts and canoes against ironclads.''[17] This comparison probably applies to the equipment of Brazil and Paraguay in the latter stages of the war, but certainly not to Argentina. Paraguay, in fact, had many initial advantages. Although the Argentine army was battle hardened in civil wars, it was smaller and not as well equipped as its Paraguayan counterpart. It has been commonly alleged that Paraguay was armed with decrepit, smoothbore guns. But more recent authorship proves that Paraguay had a certain number of rifled cannon acquired in Europe and produced others in its arsenal. These guns varied in caliber from 12 to 68 pounders. In fact, the number of cannons manufactured at the arsenal and the foundry at Ybycuí amounted to more than 250. Prior to the war, Paraguay received a consignment of 250 Turner-breech-loading carbines for the presidential escort detachment, 2,000 to 3,000 Witton-type Minié rifles, as well as a number of 68 and 80 pounder rifled cannon. To counteract these weapons, in 1865 the Argentine army acquired 300 Sharps carbines, rather similar to the Paraguayan breechloaders. The conflict soon became a war of positions, for which the Paraguayans, with their sizable artillery park, estimated at over 400 pieces, and their Congréve rocket launchers were admirably equipped. Not the least of Paraguay's assets was Colonel George Thompson, a former British officer and a former engineer on railways who built fortifications, entrenchments, and ordnance for López.[18]

THE ARGENTINE ARMY IN THE PARAGUAYAN WAR

When hostilities with Paraguay began in April 1865, the Argentine army had a strength of 6,840 men, including national guards, organized into seven infantry battalions, nine cavalry regiments, and light artillery regiments. A decree enacted on April 2 provided for the establishment of a company of engineers, later expanded into a full battalion. The Argentine army was ill prepared for the Paraguayan campaign. There was no military academy or training institutions for enlisted men. At the beginning of the war, the Argentine army employed a bewildering variety of muzzle-loading muskets and a small number of breech-loaders that made them a veritable nightmare for the supply branch. The cavalry was armed with ancient Tower carbines, so called because they bore the inspection seal of the Tower of London arsenal. These were the Brown Bess Model 1777 muskets, 11,000 of which had been captured from the British during the invasions of 1806–1807. In addition, there were 17.5 mm French Model 1840 rifles cut down as carbines, 18 mm French Model 1855 percussion carbines, and several hundred Sharps rifles and Spencer repeaters purchased during the Paraguayan war. The infantry was equipped with Tower muskets, 18 mm French rifles models 1849 and 1853, and the 12 mm Norwegian Model 1842, a percussion breechloader. In December 1865, six Enfield rifles were dispatched to the front for evaluation. In the event, few battalions were equipped with Enfields, Sharps, or Spencers. There were 285 pieces of artillery at various depots and garrisons throughout the republic, but most of these were pitted, ancient tubes with a range of 400–600 meters, less than half the range of rifled guns in service with the Brazilian, Paraguayan, and Uruguayan armies. Prior to the war, a limited number of these smoothbores had been converted into rifled artillery by the firm of Antonio Massa, in Buenos Aires.[19]

A Krupp 12-pounder was purchased for evaluation purposes in July 1866, and nine others followed in 1867. Mitre requested twelve pieces of heavy artillery "of the latest models," in either 68, 120, or 150 pounder models and to include at least a pair of 300 pounders to strengthen the defenses of Martín García, adding that Argentina was "probably the only nation in the globe without such weapons." Financial stringency forced the abandonment of this scheme. Aside from the Krupp 12 pounders, during 1865–1866, the Argentine army took delivery of a battery of six rifled 6-pounders, and six 20-pounder rifled steel guns. From his post in Washington, Domingo F. Sarmiento, the Argentine minister, urged his government to procure arms and equipment declared surplus after the conclusion of the U.S. Civil War. In his correspondence, he noted that all sorts of vessels, wagons, harnesses, tents, and saddles were available at a fraction of their original price. Under instructions from Mitre, Sarmiento purchased 8,000 Springfield rifles, machinery to manufacture cartridges for these weapons, several hundred Spencer repeating carbines and Sharps rifles, and, in April 1867, a Gatling gun.[20]

Argentine field artillery units at the front were equipped for the most part with six-pounder guns, insufficient in quantity or power to demolish Paraguayan fortifications. However, this branch of the service performed brilliantly. At the onset of the war, line units were adequately clothed in uniforms closely patterned after French models. Imported shoes were preferred, as those made locally did not stand up under the conditions of the Paraguayan front. The infantry carried a knapsack, a canteen, blanket, and a waterproof sack for their rations. The medical branch was practically nonexistent until the Cuerpo Médico del Ejército de Operaciones was organized in May 1865. As in the United States, an all-volunteer civilian Comisión Sanitaria, or Sanitary Commission, was established to check the spread of diseases and to ensure hospitals had the prerequisite instruments and drugs. Ambulances similar to American models used during the Civil War were ordered from coach makers in Buenos Aires at no cost to the government. Hospitals were established at Buenos Aires, Concordia, and Corrientes. Women ran bazaars and rolled bandages. Bandages, tents to house the sick, and drugs and surgical equipment were acquired in quantity. The army required over 300 head of cattle a day to feed its front-line soldiers. The supply branch issued contracts to private purveyors for the provision of cattle on the hoof for the troops at the front. At first deliveries were irregular; furthermore, the herds were driven over long distances; hence the animals were weak and lean and their meat less than palatable. By December 1865, the supply system functioned quite well. Large depots were erected at Corrientes, while ships docked at the harbor served as floating deposits for flour, hard tack and corn-meal, stored uniforms, tents, ammunition and spare parts for small arms and artillery weapons. The troops received a daily ration of two and a half pounds of fresh beef or a pound and a half of either jerked beef or preserved meat, four ounces of flour, rice, or beans, half a pound of hard tack, and half an ounce of salt. In addition, troops received a monthly ration that included a pound of Paraguayan tea, two bars of soap, and a pound of tobacco, and during the winter months, an extra issue of coffee, sugar, and spirits.[21]

The mobilization of the national guard units from Buenos Aires and the littoral provinces proceeded fairly smoothly. At Buenos Aires, these troops boarded transports that ferried them to the front. However, poor communications and the great distances delayed the arrival of units from the provinces in the interior. In 1865, there was only one railway line in service, the Oeste, which connected the city of Buenos Aires with various towns in the southern portion of the province. The first spur line of the Central Railway connecting Rosario with Cañada de Gómez had been completed only in 1867. Troops from the northwestern provinces and the Cuyo region traveled on foot, on horseback, or aboard wagons to ports in the province of Santa Fé, where they were outfitted with uniforms and arms and sent to the front by steamer.[22]

When news of the Paraguayan invasion reached the Argentine government on April 16, it reacted vigorously, imposing a state of siege, instituting a blockade of Paraguayan ports, and mobilizing the national guard. Large numbers of volunteers gathered at Plaza de Mayo. On the following day, the provinces of

Entre Ríos and Corrientes were ordered to mobilize 5,000 national guardsmen each as a preliminary measure. However, these were irregular formations of raw country boys, without experienced leadership, training, or armament. Regular forces were needed to defeat the well-disciplined and trained Paraguayans. On June 5, Congress sanctioned legislation that authorized the executive to raise an army of 25,000 men, with a significant infantry component. A decree enacted four days later called for the organization of twelve battalions, of which eight would be contributed by Buenos Aires, the rest by the interior provinces. Though volunteers were plentiful in Buenos Aires, recruitment proved a difficult task in the interior provinces, which had only been subjected to the authority of the central government since 1862. Many of these provinces were controlled by men who still remained hostile to Buenos Aires and who seized every opportunity to strike against her while refusing to get involved in what they considered "Buenos Aires's war." In Entre Ríos, Urquiza raised over 8,000 men, outfitted with arms and equipment sent by the national government, only to watch as they deserted en masse, since they refused to fight for Mitre. Nevertheless, by November, 14,000 men were at the front. The Paraguayan war marks, then, a departure point in Argentine military history. The central government was able to equip and maintain an army of more than 25,000 men while it successfully pacified the interior, guarded the Indian frontier, and fought Paraguay.[23]

OPERATIONS IN ARGENTINE TERRITORY

On April 13, without warning, five Paraguayan steamers sailed into the port of Corrientes. After a brief skirmish, landing parties seized two small Argentine vessels undergoing repairs and towed them away. On the following day, the Paraguayan fleet returned, and disembarked a force of 3,000 men under General Wenceslao Robles. This was the vanguard of the Ejército del Sur, which would soon total 25,000 men. Paraguayan strategy called for the two columns to proceed on a parallel course, while the Paraguayan fleet cleared the rivers. Robles would advance through Argentine territory, along the Paraná with 25,000 men, while Colonel Antonio de la Cruz Estigarribia would march through Brazilian territory with 12,500 men. These forces would then converge on the Uruguayan border. On June 10, the Paraguayan fleet of eight gunboats and six flat-bottomed barges, each mounting an 8-inch, 68-pounder gun, sailed from Humaitá under Captain Pedro Meza. One of the Paraguayan steamers lost its propeller and was unable to continue. On the morning of June 11, Meza's fleet clashed with the Brazilian squadron at a bend of the river below Corrientes known as Riachuelo. Superior numbers and firepower prevailed. The Paraguayans lost four steamers and the rest, badly damaged, limped back to Asunción. The battle of Riachuelo dealt the Paraguayan fleet a blow from which it never recovered and gave the allies control of the rivers.[24]

By this time, the allies (Argentina, Brazil, and Uruguay) had concentrated an army of 10,700 men and 32 guns under General Flores near the town of Paso de los Libres. Estigarribia advanced toward Sao Borja, with a vanguard of 3,200 under Major Duarte. On August 6 Estigarribia entered the town of Uruguayana, which the Brazilians had fortified, but later abandoned without a fight. Duarte encamped at Yatay. On August 17, the allied Vanguard Army attacked. The battle was over at 1430 hours. Duarte's column, which lost 1,700 dead, 300 wounded, and 1,200 prisoners, was totally annihilated. When he received news of the defeat at Yatay, Estigarribia attempted to retreat, but found himself encircled by Brazilian forces. On August 19 and 31 the allied commanders sent separate notes to Estigarribia, inviting him to surrender. The Paraguayan refused. On September 18 the allies began to march on Uruguayana, but the attack was delayed to enable the Brazilian war minister to deliver an intimation to surrender, which Estigarribia accepted. In all, 5,545 men and five cannon were captured. López still had 27,000 in the east bank of the Paraná, under General Francisco I. Resquín, who had replaced Robles late in July. When news of Estigarribia's capitulation reached López, he ordered the evacuation of Corrientes. The allies reentered the city in November, but even then the Brazilian fleet hesitated before a town defended only by dummy guns. Resquín was allowed to withdraw his entire army and over 100,000 head of cattle without interference.[25]

THE INVASION OF PARAGUAY

Comparative strength on the eve of the invasion of Paraguay showed a manpower superiority of 2 to 1 in favor of the allies, which had 60,950 troops, of whom 25,000 were Argentines, 2,850 Uruguayans, and 33,100 Brazilians. In addition, the Brazilians had a reserve army of 14,900 men poised at Sao Carlos, in Rio Grande do Sul, north of Corrientes. Although López had lost 21,000 men in his frustrated drive to the Plata and no less than 40,000 since the war began, he could still field an army of 27,000–30,000. As the front got closer, Paraguay had a logistical advantage that negated the preponderance in number of the allies, who had to ferry replacements, supplies, and equipment from Buenos Aires up the Paraná, a distance of 687 miles.[26]

The allied operational plan for the invasion, as devised by Mitre, called for an initial landing in force that would secure and protect the beachhead from possible counterattack until the rest of the invasion would be landed. Shipyards in Corrientes began building boats and ferry-rafts. Merchant steamers were leased to transport supplies and tow the fleet of lighters. The plan also called for a feint at Paso de la Patria, while the real landing would take place upstream, in the Paraguayan River. Allied troops began to embark on the boats before dawn on April 16. The fleet steamed toward Itapirú and silenced its batteries, while the invasion fleet headed upriver. Ten thousand Brazilians landed and secured a beachhead. Another 5,000 men under General Flores followed suit. On April 17 a force of 3,000 Paraguayans staged a counterattack but, outnumbered and outmaneuvered, withdrew toward Estero Bellaco. (Estero denotes a creek or inlet.) Estero Bellaco consisted of two parallel streams separated by a thick forest of palms, which the Paraguayans began to fortify. On May 2, López ordered the recently promoted Colonel Díaz with a force of 5,000 men (4,000 foot, 1,000 horse, 400 artillery) to scout allied positions and fall upon them by surprise. The Paraguayans broke through the Sidra and Caretta passes before the allied forces were aware of their presence. Taken by surprise, Brazilian infantry units broke, abandoning four guns that were captured by the Paraguayans. The three Uruguayan battalions gave way to avoid being enveloped and fought bravely under their commanders. Elements of the sixth Brazilian division, supported by four Argentine infantry battalions and a cavalry regiment counterattacked and captured the Paraguayan colors and four cannon. Altogether, the Paraguayans lost 2,300 killed and wounded, and the allies about 1561 (1,000 Brazilians, 400 Uruguayans, 61 Argentines).[27]

The allied advance continued unhindered. Light forces forded the Bellaco swamps. Once across, the allies set up camp at Tuyutí, about a mile and a half from Paraguayan lines. At Tuyutí, the allies had 35,000 men and ninety-three guns, most of which were rifles, except for a few smoothbores belonging to the Argentines. New recruitment brought the Paraguayan army once again to a strength of 25,000 men. López hastily conceived a plan designed to finish off the allies. The operation would be undertaken by four columns attacking simultaneously along a broad front. The center column, under Mayor Hilario Marco (four infantry battalions, two cavalry regiments with 4,200 men) would pour through the Gómez Pass and fall upon the allied center, composed of Brazilians and Uruguayans. The right column, under Colonel Cesar Díaz, had 5,000 men. Four howitzers would strike at the allied left flank. The extreme right column, under General Barrios (ten infantry battalions, two cavalry regiments), with 8,700 men, would envelop the allied flank and link up with General Francisco Resquín. The left column, under Resquín (two infantry battalions, eight cavalry regiments), with 6,300 men, would attack the Argentines, which manned the allied right—in all, 24,200 men. Though outnumbered, the Paraguayans had a tremendous advantage in terms of cavalry, since they had 8,500 men versus 2,400 for the Allies. Allied sentries were on the alert, and when Paraguayan troops were spotted, they sounded the alarm gun at 1130 hours. Díaz's cavalry fell upon two Uruguayan infantry battalions, overwhelmed them, and cut them up, then charged the Brazilian artillery positions, twenty-eight Whitworth and La Hitte guns under General Emilio Mallet, protected by a ditch soon filled with mounds of dead and wounded Paraguayans.[28]

Resquín's cavalry fell upon and scattered regiments like a tidal wave. Part of the column then turned right and fell upon the Argentine artillery and took twenty guns. The Paraguayans were about to swing these around to take them away, when the second Argentine Division led by Captain Nicolás Levalle formed a line of skirmish and fired two volleys in rapid succession, cutting swaths through the enemy squadrons, which fell back to the woods. The fighting was desperate, but the Argentines recaptured their guns and turned them against the Paraguayan cavalry, which charged repeatedly, until it was virtually annihilated at point-blank range by a shower of musket balls and canister shot. The column led by Barrios was repulsed by Brazilian infantry and decimated by heavy artillery. Despite heavy losses, Díaz ordered a charge, but when fresh Brazilian strength advanced, he abandoned his guns and retreated. On the allied right, after the destruction of Resquín's cavalry, the Argentine troops mounted a bayonet charge, dislodged the Paraguayan foot soldiers from the tall grass, and drove them to edge of the woods. Marco's surviving cavalry squadrons charged once again but were badly mauled by the Argentines. The remnants of Resquín's forces were chased by the Argentines to the edge of the inlet. At 1630 hours the battle was over. The Paraguayans were totally defeated, their army destroyed. A lack of horses prevented the allies from pursuing the remnants of the defeated enemy. Tuyutí was truly a battle of annihilation, which cost the Paraguayans over 6,000 dead, 7,000 wounded. In addition, the allies took 370 prisoners, 5,000 muskets, 4 howitzers, and a rocket launcher. The allies lost over 4,000 killed and wounded, of whom 3,000 were Brazilian, 800 Argentine, and about 400 Uruguayan.[29]

On July 10, two Paraguayan infantry battalions attempted to break through the Argentine lines, but when the Argentine reinforcements were rushed to the sector, the Paraguayans retreated to the islet of Yataity-Corá, with the Argentines in close pursuit. On the following morning, determined to stop the Argentines at Paso Leguizamón, López summoned a force of 2,250 and two rocket launchers, which he hurled against the Argentine vanguard at Yataity-Corá. The Corrientes battalion, heavily outnumbered, put up a stubborn fight but suffered heavy casualties and fell back to Leguizamón Pass. The Paraguayans dashed forward, only to run into two infantry battalions that had formed a line of skirmish. The Argentines launched a furious counterattack and were soon joined by elements of the second Division. After a great deal of firing on both sides, the Paraguayans retreated, leaving many killed and wounded. Although the Congrève rockets of the Paraguayans failed to inflict any casualties among the allied troops, they set the tall grass on fire, and the action was suspended. When the fire was extinguished, Mitre ordered Paunero to occupy Yataity-Corá. The Paraguayans regrouped and tried to outflank the Argentines but withdrew, having lost 400 killed and wounded, and the Argentines some 256.[30]

To force the allies to launch a major attack, López sent a detachment under Colonel George Thompson to dig trenches between Potrero Piris and Potrero Sauce in order to threaten the allied rear. The trench was completed on July 14 and manned by several battalions with artillery. Although in the battles of Boquerón (July 16) and Sauce (July 18) the allies suffered heavier casualties than the Paraguayans (4,500 versus 2,500), they secured the woods on the left flank of Tuyutí, hitherto threatened by the enemy.[31]

To protect his right flank, threatened by the Allied advance, López ordered the fortifications extended as far as the Chichí Lagoon. And the redoubts at Curuzú and Curupaity were reinforced. On September 2, after a preliminary bombardment, the Brazilians landed below Curuzú. On the next day, after a furious bombardment, Porto Alegre ordered an assault on the trenches. Despite heavy losses, the Brazilians fought with gallantry and the Paraguayans were driven out, leaving behind 700 dead, 13 guns, and 30 prisoners, although they succeeded in carrying away their 1,700 wounded. After the fall of Curuzú, López reinforced General Díaz at Curupaytí, bringing this command to about 5,000, and sent more artillery. Thirty feet above river level, Díaz began a trench that was 2,000 yards long, eleven feet wide, and six feet deep. On the inner wall of this trench, a pit for riflemen was constructed, protected by a dirt revetment. In front of this position the Paraguayans laid down a line of abatis, defensive obstacles formed by felled trees with sharpened branches facing the enemy. Forty-nine pieces of artillery were available, including several 32-pounders, five 12-pounders, four rifled 9-pounders and eight 68-pounders, four of which faced the Paraguayans; the others pointed toward Curuzú. The 68-pounders were capable of firing canister shot with iron balls almost two inches in diameter, capable of destroying an entire platoon with a single round.[32]

On September 6, an allied council of war drew up plans for the capture of Curupaytí. A preliminary bombardment designed to smash enemy positions and drive troops away from trenches would precede an infantry attack. The assault force would proceed in four columns, with units of the II Brazilian Army Corps at the left, and troops of the Argentine I and II Army Corps on the right, 18,000 men in all.

On the morning of September 22, at 0700 hours the fleet moved into position. Three ironclads began the bombardment of the redoubt at Curupaytí, while the remaining vessels, well out of range of enemy fire, readied to bombard the landward side of the fortifications. The bombardment went on until noon, without appreciable results; nevertheless Admiral Tamandaré hoisted a signal that the bombardment had achieved its objectives. The assault at Curupaytí brings to mind Pickett's charge at Gettysburg. The troops were given an impossible task. The charge was an incredible mistake and should not have been made. The two center columns advanced as planned, shoulder to shoulder, gleaming bayonets at the ready. They swept forward under terrible artillery through the swamps and the river, with water up to their knees, loaded with their full packs, scaling ladders and fascines. When they reached the center of the trench, the pit and the parapet blocked their path. The second column was stopped by a lagoon and the line of abatis, then swung left under terrible fire. The Argentine infantry swept forward, cool and deliberate, at a steady pace, as though on parade. The canister shot and musketry mowed down the already-thinned ranks, yet the suicidally heroic charge continued. The Argentine officers, riding with great bravery and élan through the hail of lead, reached the trench, urging their men onward. Mayor Ayala, commander of the twelfth infantry, was wounded. Lucio V. Mansilla, second in command, took charge but was wounded as well. Colonels Juan Bautista Charlone and Manuel Rosetti fell mortally wounded. Corporal Gómez was hit on the kneecap by a musket ball but disobeyed an order to withdraw. Another ball hit his right knee, and he could no longer stand; he kept firing from a prone position. The cannonade redoubled in volume; battalions melted into companies; companies were reduced to platoons. The exploding shells threw up fountains of water and mud; arms, legs, torsos flew in every direction. One in ten reached the trench. From the safety of their parapet, Paraguayan infantry shot them at point-blank range. At 1700 hours, Mitre ordered the troops to fall back. The crack Argentine sixth infantry battalion marched backward in order not to show their backs to the enemy. Mayor Julio A. Roca rode back to the edge of the trench, to encourage his troops, then picked up another wounded officer and slung him across his saddle, trotting his horse slowly, as enemy shells whistled over his head. The allies suffered 4,045 killed and wounded (2,095 Argentines, 1,950 Brazilians), while Paraguayan losses are given as only 92.[33]

In the seven months that followed the allied reversal at Curupaytí, no major action took place. There were important changes in the allied command structure. The Baron of Porto Alegre was replaced by General Alves de Lima e Silva, Marquis of Caxias. On November 9, 1866, rebellion broke out in the Andean province of Mendoza. The uprising soon spread to Salta, Jujuy La Rioja, and Córdoba. As the Argentine government lacked sufficient forces, Mitre was forced to detach Argentine front-line troops to restore order. On January 25, General Arredondo departed Tuyutí with five infantry battalions to quell the rebellion. As the internal situation in Argentina took a turn for the worse, Mitre dispatched additional troops to Rosario, and Mitre delegated command of the Allied Forces in an interim basis to Caxias. To further aggravate matters, cholera, a disease propagated by infected water, spread to the armies first, and eventually to the civilian population. By late March, 4,000 men at Curuzú were affected, of whom 2,400 died. By the beginning of May, at Tuyutí alone over 13,000 Brazilians were hospitalized. The outbreak soon spread to Paraguay, where it was reported that deaths in the army averaged fifty a day. By late October, Argentine military authorities managed the control the outbreak of the diseased among front-line troops. The epidemic, however, reached Rosario and eventually Buenos Aires with devastating effects. Vice President Marcos Paz, who contracted the disease on December 28, died on January 2, 1868, and Mitre turned over command of the Argentine forces to General Juan Gelly y Obes and overall command of the Allied army to General Caxias (Luíz Alves de Lima e Silva, Marquis of Caxias).[34]

López took advantage of the lull to extend and improve his fortifications. Curupaytí was reinforced with guns taken from Humaitá, and to improve communications, a trail was cut between Curupaytí and Sauce, and it extended the system of trenches and strong points to cover all the openings and passes through Estero Bellaco. This line of defense appeared on military maps as a trapezoid; hence allied commanders referred to it as the Cuadrilátero, or Quadrilateral. Under the guiding hand of Colonel Thompson, a new trench was excavated at Potrero Sauce, and the Bellaco swamp was dammed up, causing the water level to rise by six feet. Work commenced on a new battery at Yataity-Corá. Many guns were cast at the arsenal, including a 10-inch rifle known as El Cristiano, cast from the bells from all the churches in Paraguay. Some 24-pounders were bored and rifled to fire 56-pounds shells, 4 pounders rifled into 9-pounders, while five smoothbore 9-pounders were modified to fit 32-pound Lahitte ammunition. Old iron-guns were cut down into mortars, including two 10-inch and a pair of 8-inch. Three batteries of rifled howitzers capable of firing either 12-pounder shot or 32-pounder Lahitte shells were made according to Thompson's own design. They had a range of 5,500 yards, greater than any gun in the allied camp. In addition, a 10-ton gun was cast and rifled to fit Whitworth 150-pounder shot, thousands of which were fired by the Brazilian fleet but recovered intact by the Paraguayans.[35]

On June 22, 1867, the Brazilian fleet forced the pass at Curupaytí, and the allied army, 30,500 strong, advanced to Tuyu-Cué. In a series of battles fought between October 3 and 21, the Paraguayans were driven off after suffering over 2,500 casualties. The allies lost less than 1,000 killed and wounded. To avoid total encirclement, López ordered the evacuation of Curupaytí, though not before he attempted an offensive against the main allied camp at Tuyutí. When a force of 8,000 men, consisting of four infantry brigades and two cavalry regiments, was assembled, he directed General Juan Caballero to approach the allied camp during the night. The attack would begin at dawn. While the infantry stormed the trenches, the cavalry would charge the Brazilian redoubts on the right of the camp and send any captured guns, particularly the 32-pounder Whitworths that López craved, back to the Paraguayan lines. On November 3, at daybreak, the Paraguayans took the first line of trenches by surprise. The second line of trenches fell rapidly when four Brazilian battalions manning them broke and fled toward Itapirú. Paraguayan cavalry under General Caballero captured 250 Brazilians, until allied cavalry launched a successful counterattack. At this point Argentine and Brazilian infantrymen emerged from the redoubt and fell upon the Paraguayans, who had stopped to loot allied stores. The Paraguayans retreated, leaving 1,200 dead on the field and about the same number of wounded returned. Allied casualties numbered 1,250.[36]

In February 1868, the Brazilian fleet forced Humaitá. Asunción was evacuated and the town of Luqué, fifteen kilometers away, was proclaimed as the provisional capital. Humaitá surrendered to the allies on August 5, 1868, and López began a long retreat through the Chaco. A defensive line, protected by large-caliber guns evacuated from the Cuadrilátero, was established at Angostura. In order to flank these defenses Caxias ordered a road built through the Chaco, parallel to the Paraguay River. On December 6, the Brazilian force of 18,500 under Caxias reached a narrow bridge that crossed a stream known as Ytororó, defended by 5,000 Paraguayans and twelve guns under General Caballero. In a bitterly contested action, the outnumbered Paraguayans were dislodged, leaving six of their guns behind and 1,200 dead and wounded. But at 2,400, including several senior officers, Brazilian losses were far higher. On December 11, under torrential rains, 18,000 Brazilians under General Andrade Neves slowly began their advance toward the Avahy creek. General Caballero with about 5,000 men and twelve guns faced them. The Paraguayans were quickly surrounded, and although they held their ground desperately, they were cut to pieces. Paraguayan losses exceeded 4,500—3,500 dead, 1,000 prisoners, including 600 wounded abandoned on the field of battle; the Brazilians lost 770 killed and wounded. To delay the allied steamroller, the Paraguayans began to construct new trenches linking López's headquarters at Angostura with the gradient of Itabaité. The positions were defended by about 3,000 Paraguayans with guns, including a Whitworth 32-pounder. At 1500 hours, on December 21, the Brazilians reached the outer defense perimeter. The Paraguayans put up a fierce resistance but were overwhelmed. The Brazilians managed to break through the enemy lines, but the attack was beaten back by López's personal escort. Repulsed, the Brazilians broke off the action. In the first battle of Itabaité (also known as the battle of Lomas Valentinas) Brazilians suffered casualties of 4,250 dead and wounded, which exceeded allied losses at Curupaytí. It is worth noting that Caxias, who had shown hostility and jealousy toward the Argentines, refused to allow their troops to participate in this phase of the operations. However, the heavy losses forced him to reverse his position.[37]

Determined to deny victory to the enemy, López concentrated another 1,600 men from Caacupé and Cerro León and Itabaité, bringing the total to 4,000. The guns were manned from the surviving warships of the Paraguayan navy, which lay hidden in rivers to the north. On December 24, Caxias sent López an intimation to surrender, which the Paraguayan rejected. On the following day, forty-six allied guns began a methodical bombardment of Paraguayan positions. On the morning of December 27, after a furious bombardment, the allied army (16,000 Brazilians, 7,000 Argentines, 1,000 Uruguayans) spearheaded by Argentine contingents under Generals Rivas and Gelly Obes began the final assault. The Córdoba battalion swung right and, supported by the Santa Fé battalion, charged a Paraguayan redoubt protected by four guns. Though the Santa Fé troops suffered heavy losses, the assault succeeded and the redoubt was taken. The Paraguayans counterattacked in superior numbers but, reinforced by elements of the first Buenos Aires division and the Rosario regiment, the Argentines outflanked the enemy and forced him to retreat, leaving many prisoners behind. The Paraguayans withdrew to their fortified positions. The Argentines took the trenches by a frontal assault and repulsed several counterattacks. Only a few dozen Paraguayans escaped from the battlefield. At the second battle of Itabaité, the Paraguayans lost over 1,500 dead and wounded, 1,500 prisoners (mostly wounded), and 14 guns. The Argentines lost 347 dead and wounded and the Uruguayans 120.[38]

López and a handful of survivors arrived at Cerro León. They found the capital city virtually deserted. The government and much of the arsenal and machinery had been shipped to Caacupé. Luis Felipe María Gastâo de Orleans, Comte d'Eu, son of the emperor of Brazil, assumed command of the allied army. The Comte d'Eu arrived at Asunción on April 14, 1869, and began a major reorganization of the Brazilian army. By June when the reorganization was completed and the allied army was ready to resume operation, it comprised 25,000 battle-hardened veterans (18,500 Brazilians, 4,100 Argentines under General Emilio Mitre, and 700 Uruguayans). At Cerro León, López had been reinforced by about 2,500 men who had fled Asunción. They were followed by soldiers who had escaped capture at various battlefields, the very young, the very old, and several thousand convalescent wounded from the military hospitals, until López had a new army of 13,000 at his disposal. With the equipment salvaged from the arsenal, 13 field guns were cast under the guidance of General Resquín. However, the allies were on the move. On August 11 the Brazilians captured Pirebebuy and within two more days Caacupé. López managed to elude them, moving ever westward, but on March 1 he was surprised by a Brazilian detachment on the banks of the Aquidaban River and was killed, and the long, dreadful war came to an end.[39]

THE PARAGUAYAN WAR: AN EVALUATION

As a result of the war, Paraguay lost about 88,000 square kilometers of territory, was saddled with huge reparations, and sank to the bottom rank of the South American republics. For Argentina, the Paraguayan war marked a major turning point in the process of national unification begun by Mitre in 1862. Before 1865 there were many Argentines beyond the boundaries of Buenos Aires for whom a war against Paraguay was unthinkable. This was primarily due to the lack of that essential mystique which acts as the cohesive bond in the formation and consolidation of a nationality. The Paraguayan war was the catalyst that provided that mystique and strengthened the process of national unification. To revisionist historians, the Paraguayan war came as a result of sinister machinations between Mitre, the Empire of Brazil, and British imperialism. These rather simplistic views overlook Argentine military unpreparedness in April 1865, as well as the policies and aims of Solano López. The unprovoked Paraguayan attack on Corrientes left the nation but one choice: to declare war against a foreign aggressor led by a man who sought to carve out an empire in the Plata at the expense of Argentina and Brazil. The war was an unwelcome distraction at a time when the Argentine economy had begun to develop a material base that would permit it to embark upon the reform and development programs long advocated by men like Rivadavia, Mitre, and Sarmiento. Such programs were perforce delayed by the war, which cost the Argentine nation 30 million pesos, 18,000 battle casualties, 5,000 killed as a result of the disturbances and uprisings in the interior provinces, averse to the war, and 12,000 additional casualties, civilian and military due to the cholera epidemic. On the positive side, an aggressive and dangerous rival who wanted to dictate terms in the Plata had been removed.

It has also been asserted that "as a result of the bitter lessons of Argentina's one and only excursion into external warfare, Argentina was never tempted to send her armies beyond her national boundaries again."[40] This statement clearly overlooks wars with Brazil, Bolivia, and Uruguay and the fact that these conflicts were not brought about by Argentina but thrust upon her by force. Brazil had declared war against Argentina in 1825; Bolivia had invaded Argentina in 1837 and constantly violated Argentine territory. Allied to the Unitarians, Uruguay declared war on Argentina and seized the island of Martín García. Artigas tried to incorporate the Mesopotamian provinces into a league under Uruguayan control, a scheme Rivera tried to resuscitate in the 1830s. Paraguay seized disputed territories by force and attacked Argentina in 1865. These are actions taken against a politically divided and militarily weak nation. After 1870, as the Argentine armed forces grew steadily stronger, despite tensions, neighboring countries weighed the theoretical advantages and possibilities of a war against Argentina and found it a hazardous proposition. In the anvil of the Paraguayan war the Argentine army evolved from a dilettante force of brave amateurs into an army that was at last beginning to be professional and destined to become more so in the decades that followed. From the swamps and jungles of Paraguay emerged a battle-hardened, professional national army, whose battalions were true elite units, accustomed to following orders with blind obedience, an army that would further temper its mettle in the Indian campaigns and in the campaigns against the last caudillos. The Argentine soldier fought savagely, asking no quarter and using the old weapon of the Argentine infantry, the bayonet, a vital element demanded by the *offensive à outrance*. Time and time again, a bayonet charge by the Argentine soldiers would turn back a Paraguayan assault and wrest victory from defeat. Their valor and determination amazed Brazilians and Uruguayans, normally wont to praise anything Argentine. Their commanders were always glad to have the Argentines in their sector. The army was imbued with a cult of valor, not unlike that prevailing in the French army in 1914. Officers and troops scarcely took cover and flouted death. When Paraguayan musketry and shrapnel cut jagged chunks through their ranks, they continued to advance, as though on a parade ground. Such a spirit permeated all ranks, from Mitre and his generals to the lowest ranks. The war impressed upon the officer corps the fact that the only way to wage a successful campaign was with an efficient and modern army.[41]

THE ARGENTINE NAVY FROM 1814 TO THE PARAGUAYAN WAR

Although colonial rule in Buenos Aires came to an end in May 1810, Montevideo across the Plata remained in royalist hands. From this anchorage, a powerful and well-trained naval squadron, led by Capitán de Fragata Jacinto de Romarate, soon instituted a blockade of Buenos Aires and threatened to disrupt communications along the littoral. Patriot authorities stirred to action, and by August, three merchant vessels, suitable for conversion into warships had been acquired. These were the brig *25 de Mayo*, the schooner *Invencible*, and the sloop *Americana*. Francisco de Gurruchaga, an Argentine veteran of Trafalgar and a former lieutenant in the Spanish Royal Navy, was of great value in fitting out the little squadron. The scarcity of funds, properly trained personnel, and naval stores greatly complicated his assignment. Overall command was entrusted to Juan Bautista Azopardo, a Maltese corsair, who was seconded by two French privateers, Hipólito Bouchard and Angel Hubac. On February 10, 1811, the three vessels sailed from Buenos Aires and headed up the Paraná. On March 2, they were overtaken by a powerful royalist force. Training and numbers soon prevailed.[42] Aboard the *25 de Mayo*, forty-one men out of a crew of fifty had been wounded or killed. To the chagrin of the patriots, their first squadron was captured and towed to Montevideo, where it served to augment the forces of the new Viceroy of the Plata.[43]

On July 7, a Spanish squadron bombarded Buenos Aires. Aboard a gunboat equipped with a single 18-pounder, Bouchard inflicted serious damage on an enemy ship, and the royalist squadron withdrew. As a result of this raid, the patriots hurriedly fitted out a second squadron consisting of the ketch *Hiena*, the schooners *Nuestra Señora del Carmen* and *Santo Domingo*, and four smaller units. The royalists returned on August 19, but when Bouchard led his force against them, the enemy withdrew and conducted an ineffectual bombardment from a safe distance. On October 20, 1811, a peace treaty concluded between the authorities at Buenos Aires and Montevideo called for cessation of hostilities and an end to the blockade of rivers and shores. The patriot squadron was disarmed. The royalists soon broke the agreement and shelled Argentine towns with impunity, raiding commerce at will. This led to the creation of a third squadron, which was organized in 1814 by an Irish merchant captain, William Brown, rightly considered as the father of the Argentine Navy. The squadron was composed of one frigate, four corvettes, a brigantine, five schooners, and other smaller vessels. The officers and crews were mostly foreign born, but there soon was a growing number of criollos in the fleet.[44]

In May 1814 Brown defeated the royalist squadron, which had once dominated the Plata. Thus he paved the way for the blockade and capture of Montevideo a month later. This brilliant success deprived Spain of her only South Atlantic base of operations and gave control of the local waters to the United Provinces. Furthermore, to harass and destroy Spanish commercial shipping, in September 1814 the government of Buenos Aires began issuing letters of marque to privateers, most of them North American. The exact number of vessels employed by the corsairs has not been recorded. A single vessel was active in 1815, four in 1816, fourteen in 1817, twenty-three in 1819, ten in 1820, and two in 1821. During 1816, Brown led an Argentine naval squadron into the Pacific, blockaded Lima and Guayaquil, captured Spanish California and made a shambles of Spanish shipping. The frigate *La Argentina*, under Hipólito Bouchard, which formed part of this squadron, separated from the main body and became the first Argentine ship to circumnavigate the world.[45]

By 1815, Argentina was the only former colony in the New World that had not been reconquered by Spanish forces. An expedition under General Pablo Morillo was organized to reconquer the Plata, but the loss of Montevideo forced Spain to revise her strategy and send Morillo to New Granada, present-day Colombia, as originally planned. After the War of Independence, the Argentine navy was reduced to a bare minimum. Most of its vessels were auctioned off to private owners.[46]

At the outbreak of the war with Brazil in 1825, the fleet consisted of four frigates, two corvettes, and twelve gunboats. Command was entrusted to Brown, hero of the independence wars. In a quick series of actions, the Argentines defeated the much larger Brazilian navy, and although the latter maintained a blockade of Buenos Aires, the army's supply lines to Uruguay were never cut. By 1827, over fifty Brazilian warships had been either captured or sunk. Furthermore, Argentine warships and privateers captured 445 Brazilian merchant vessels as prizes.[47]

During the Rosas era, the navy became essentially a riverine force, strong enough to prevail over its Uruguayan counterpart in a series of encounters during the year 1841 but not powerful or sufficiently modern enough to prevail against the Anglo-French naval squadrons sent to the Plata. Until the 1830s, officers were formed at a maritime academy. Later, cadets were attached to units of the fleet.[48]

The Argentine navy would not enter the era of steam until 1851. After the fall of Rosas both Argentinian states outfitted naval squadrons with hastily armed commercial steamers. By 1865, there remained only a few vessels in service; the rest were either hulks or pontoons. The navy had no on-shore organization or training schools, infrastructure of any consequence, or proper warships. It was painfully obvious that both the Argentine armed services had failed to develop effectively, not only in relation to the major powers but also in comparison with such neighboring countries as Brazil, Chile, and Paraguay. It was only in 1869 that the first steps to redress this situation were taken.

THE MODERNIZATION OF THE ARMY, 1870–1902: TRAINING ESTABLISHMENTS FOR OFFICERS AND ENLISTED MEN

The most conspicuous shortcoming of the Argentine army was the lack of a military academy where future members of the officer corps could be formed. It was not until 1870 that such an academy, the Colegio Militar, was established. The military academy, housed on the former estate of Rosas at Palermo, was placed under the direction of Janos F. Czetz, a former Austro-Hungarian officer. During Czetz's four-year term, the institution produced forty officer candidates. The initial results were most satisfactory. By 1875, the school had a roster of seventy-five students, and its curriculum included courses in ordnance, tactics, artillery, fortifications, mathematics, and topography. The classrooms were provided with modern materials, such as theodolites, Remington and Enfield rifles, Krupp cannon, and Gatling guns.[49]

Despite the existence of the academy, the army offered an alternative through which enlisted men could achieve commissioned status. Through the 1880s, enlisted men with outstanding efficiency ratings were posted to line units as cadets. Following the successful completion of the fourth year examination at the Colegio Militar, these men would be breveted as lieutenants in the infantry or *alféreces* in the cavalry. An outstanding group of men rose through the ranks through this system, widely respected by the troops who shared with them the dangers and privations of the Indian wars. The Argentine army of the 1880s was disciplined through personalism. By their example, these officers would not only inspire their men to greater achievements but would also instill a sense of loyalty to their commanding officer, and by extension, to the war minister and the federal government.[50]

The Argentine army of the period 1869–1890 was disorganized but aggressive. Its officers and men were forged in the hard schools of the Paraguayan and Indian wars. To upgrade the professional training of officers who had risen from the ranks and bring them up to par with graduates of the Colegio Militar, the War Ministry instituted a special course to impart theoretical as well as practical instruction. Growing tensions with Chile in the 1890s highlighted the need for additional sources of officer procurement. The Colegio Militar offered abbreviated courses in 1897, and in addition an officers' candidate school, or Escuela de Aspirantes a Oficiales, was inaugurated in April 1902. This institution was extremely successful, and graduated 183 fully trained officers by November of that year. Academy graduates, however, were resented by officers formed by the old school, who felt that the new army being developed was neither as well trained nor as disciplined as the old frontier force. But by the 1890s, even these hardened war veterans were willing to admit that the graduates of the Colegio Militar were worthy and capable. Army regulations were largely based on ancient ordinances that dated to the colonial period, while the officer corps was not homogeneous in its composition. Academy graduates served alongside men who had risen through the ranks or had been trained in various European nations. In fact, the officer corps would not become completely homogeneous until 1904, when all of its members were graduates of the Colegio Militar.[51]

To remedy this situation and provide for unity of doctrine, a war academy (Escuela Superior de Guerra, or ESG) was established by War Minister General Luis María Campos. A German mission contracted during 1899 and headed by Lieutenant Colonel Alfred Arendt took charge of the ESG. In fact, five out of the ten instructors at the ESG were German. Courses lasted for two years and were subdivided into two parts. The first was a course of theoretical instruction that covered military history, artillery, fortifications, and other subjects. The second course, applied tactics, stressed tactics and general staff procedures. The number of candidates to the ESG was limited to fifty by army regulations enacted in February 1902. Applicants were selected from the first lieutenant and captain ranks. Candidates were required to have at least two years of active service and to have successfully passed the entrance examination. Outstanding graduates were posted to the general staff.[52]

To provide cadre for all combat branches of the army, most particularly the artillery, a school for noncommissioned officers, or Escuela de Cabos y Sargentos, was created on March 26, 1881. From its inception, the school was attached to the first artillery regiment at Palermo. Candidates were required to have successfully completed an entrance examination and to be Argentine citizens between the ages of seventeen and twenty-one. Ranks conferred upon graduation depended strictly on scores received.[53]

The expansion of the artillery arm, which began in the 1870s, increased the demand for qualified instructors. Thus, on May 27, 1881, a ballistics school, or Escuela de Tiro, was established under the aegis of the Inspectorate of Artillery. The new establishment offered two separate courses, one for noncommissioned officers (NCOs) and the other for officers. As the weapons introduced during this period required more elaborate maintenance facilities, the Parque de Artillería was expanded to meet service needs. Skilled personnel was provided by the School of Mechanical Apprentices, or Escuela de Aprendices Mecánicos, which began operations in 1881. The Artillery Park had about 100 skilled specialists and 90 machine tools in 1880 with another 90 in the process of delivery. The machinery was modern and employed in the manufacture of the 11 mm metallic cartridge employed by the Remington rifles and carbines; it even produced small numbers of a breech-loading artillery piece, designated Modelo Viejobueno in two calibers, 75 and 80 mm for the army and the navy. Gunpowder for army requirements was produced at the newly established Fábrica Nacional de Polvora, at Río Cuarto, Córdoba. The Ministry of War was also fully aware that in the more complex and increasingly technical world of the 1880s, illiterate soldiers would no longer suffice. It therefore established a number of primary schools where servicemen were taught to read and write.[54]

In every army there has been a need to link field units with the upper echelons, thus furthering the chain of command from above. This was essentially the function of the general staff, an institution that had existed, albeit embryonically, since 1862. It was only in 1881 that a permanent general staff, or Estado Mayor Permanente, was established. The general staff was composed of seven "divisions" or departments. One of the functions of a general staff is the provision of maps of the territories they are to defend as well as the study of the territories and armies of prospective adversaries. The Oficina Topográfica Militar, or mapping bureau, was established in December 1879 to study and survey the lands acquired during the conquest of the desert. This mapping office became the fourth department of the general staff and officers assigned to it were required to undergo training in rectilinear trigonometry, astronomy, differential calculus, field and permanent fortifications, geodesy as well as in the constructions of railway lines. This training was supplemented by courses taken at the School of

Engineering of the University of Buenos Aires, upon completion of which applicants received a degree in military engineering.[55]

Once the command structures of the army had been streamlined and established in a permanent basis, it was felt that the combat branches of the service should undergo organic changes that would provide for greater efficiency. The cavalry branch had been predominant in Argentina because of the ready availability of horses and men who knew how to ride them. Geography had been a fundamental factor as well, as the vast plains of Argentina had provided the ideal theater of operations, with fluid conditions in which cavalry could operate unimpeded. Cavalry and mounted infantry had played a preponderant role in the civil wars of the nineteenth century as in the Indians campaigns that followed. However, the introduction of newer and more efficient weapons changed all this. While infantry was still equipped with muskets that required an inordinate amount of time to fire and reload and with a range of a few hundred meters and the artillery limited to a score of outdated and awkward muzzle-loaders, a well-led cavalry charge would carry the field. Infantry began to play a larger role in the civil wars of the 1830s, most particularly in the struggles for national unification of the late 1850s, while the Paraguayan war, which was essentially a war of fixed positions, highlighted the need for a larger artillery component. During the last caudillo uprisings, in the 1870s, cavalry charges that years before would have decided the outcome of battle were broken up by the combined firepower of breech-loading rifles, modern artillery, and Gatling guns.[56]

The composition of the army accordingly began to change. Whereas at the outbreak of the Paraguayan war there was only one artillery regiment in existence, as opposed to seven infantry battalions and nine cavalry regiments, the proportions had changed somewhat by the 1880s. There were twelve infantry battalions with 3,500 men, ten cavalry regiments with an equal complement, and two artillery regiments with 800 gunners. The infantry was restructured in 1881, when six regiments were created. The cavalry was reorganized into ten regiments by virtue of a decree dated January 7, 1886. A third field artillery regiment was operational by 1890, and three entirely new formations were called into being in 1896. Mountain artillery, considered of prime importance in the event of a war with Chile, greatly expanded. The first mountain artillery regiment was established in 1892, the second in 1897, and the third in 1898. A sapper battalion, created in August 1888, was expanded into a full-sized regiment in August 2, 1898, and then subdivided into four battalion-sized units of the sapper, railway, telegraph, and bridging specialties.[57]

The practice of grouping combat units into divisions was not a new one. Ad hoc formations rated as such had existed in the past, but these were composed of elements of the different branches as dictated by tactical needs. The first step toward a permanent organization of a modern tactical unit took place on October 29, 1880, when the first Army Division was constituted at Buenos Aires under General Nicolás Levalle, and three others, numbered consecutively, were organized during 1882. Organically, the Argentine army had progressed. Its manpower and mobilization schemes were altered accordingly.[58]

MANPOWER AND MOBILIZATION SCHEMES

We have seen in the previous chapters how the pacification of the interior was necessary for the political unification of Argentina and how national unification had been followed by unification of the national guard. The process of pacification of the rebellious interior culminated in 1876 with the defeat of Ricardo López Jordán, the last of the traditional caudillos. By this time the central government had gained further control of its reserves. Whereas in 1865 three months had been required to raise an army of 25,000 men, only twenty days were required in 1874 to mobilize, outfit, and equip a force of 60,000, which was used to quell an insurrection led by former President Mitre.[59]

The growing loyalty of the army of the line to the national government was further tested during the Tejedor uprising of June 1880. In 1862, a law that federalized the city of Buenos Aires for a period of five years was enacted. The capital question remained unresolved when Avellaneda's term came to a close in 1880. Carlos Tejedor, governor of the province of Buenos Aires and standard bearer for those who opposed the federalization of Buenos Aires, and General Julio A. Roca, hero of the conquest of the desert, emerged as candidates for the presidency. Roca was immensely popular in the provinces, which saw in him the logical candidate to make available the resources of Buenos Aires for the development of the entire nation. In the elections held in the Chamber of Deputies, the representatives of all the provinces except Buenos Aires and Corrientes supported Roca. Tejedor and his followers, for their part, were reluctant to turn over power to a government elected by the provinces.[60]

Tejedor organized the Buenos Aires National Guard. Rifle training was actively pursued at the newly created firing range headed by Colonel Julio Campos. Twelve volunteer battalions were raised, later reinforced by two battalions of Italian volunteers and one of engineers. Aside from these formations, Tejedor had at his disposal 2,600 policemen and prison guards, all veteran soldiers. The provincial government ordered Colonel José I. Arias to raise 10,000 gaucho militiamen in the province of Buenos Aires. To equip these forces, arms were purchased abroad. On June 2, the national forces drew back when the police of Buenos Aires mobilized to protect the landing of 5,000 Snider rifles. President Avellaneda ordered the national army and all government offices to withdraw to the town of Belgrano, in the province of Buenos Aires. On June 7, a squadron of the Argentine navy blockaded the harbors of Buenos Aires and Rosario. Although the *porteños* fought with their traditional élan and determination, the national forces, fresh from the Indian wars and well equipped, overcame them in a series of fierce engagements that took place during June 17–21 in the outskirts of Buenos Aires.[61]

As a result of the Tejedor affair, the army was federalized. This gave the president, in his role as commander in chief, a greater concentration of power than any of his predecessors. Hence the executive was able to introduce military reforms that would have met with serious opposition in the past. The recruitment statutes enacted on September 21, 1872, still made the Argentine army a volunteer force. Article no. 18 of this recruiting code called for the enrollment of all male citizens between the ages of eighteen and forty-five into the national guard. The army of the line, or Ejército de Línea, would be composed of individuals who would serve two to four years without any enlistment bonus, and *enganchados*, or volunteers who received a bonus of 240 gold pesos in four quotas throughout their term of enlistment.[62]

The first step toward compulsory military service was enacted on June 5, 1888. The new recruitment law stipulated that the national guard would integrate the army by age groups. For mobilization purposes three armies were created: active, passive, and reserve. Existing military units throughout the republic would serve as cadre for the active duty army, which when fully mobilized would consist of three army corps of 33,000 men each under the command of Lieutenant Generals Julio A. Roca, Luis María Campos and Juan Gelly y Obes. Each of these armies would be composed of two divisions of two brigades each. The active duty army included all males between the ages of seventeen and thirty-five. The active reserve army would be constituted by national guardsmen throughout the country between the ages of thirty-five and forty, while the passive reserve army would include men in the forty–five to fifty age group. The Achilles heel of this particular reform lay in the fact that the bulk of the men called into service, except for those mobilized under the provisions of the recruitment law of 1872, would lack military training.[63]

This problem would be solved by a supplementary law approved in 1895. The new legislation, sanctioned on November 22 as Law no. 3318 and incorporated on January 26, 1896, called for the mandatory enlistment of all Argentines who had reached the age of twenty in the previous year. These men would serve for two months and after this brief period of mandatory service would pass on to the national guard, where they would serve for three months a year until the age of thirty. Furthermore, to facilitate mobilization, the country was divided into six military districts, each of which grouped several provinces or territories.[64]

During the last decades of the nineteenth century Argentina had experienced a boom in railway construction. The railway would greatly contribute to the rapid mobilization of men and supplies. During the mobilization decreed for March 12, 1896, known as The Maneuvers at Curá-Malal, 22,242 men and all their equipment were concentrated at Curá-Malal, and Pigüe, in the southern part of the province of Buenos Aires. In the maneuvers of 1898, 20,000 active national guardsmen and 60,000 soldiers were called up. In his yearly message to Congress in May of that year, President Uriburu could take pride in the fact that in forty-eight hours 22,000 men, all their equipment, baggage trains, horses, and mules as well as 252 pieces of artillery had been dispatched to the areas of initial concentration without even altering the schedules or services of the railways.[65]

Recruitment law no. 3318, however, would be modified in 1898, as the Second National Census of 1895 revealed that there were 972,532 men between the ages of eighteen and thirty who would form the national guard, 260,000 between the ages of thirty-one and thirty-five who would be reserve guards, and 326,213 between the ages of thirty-six and forty who would be available for military service if required. With such an abundance of manpower, the government ruled that the citizenry could be called for military service for a period of sixty days, or one year, in case the executive power deemed it necessary, with either the army or the navy.[66]

This system worked out well generally, but deficiencies had to be ironed out. Among them was the fact that this mobilization scheme only produced troops that had been subject to military training for a short period, usually sixty days. Opponents of military reforms argued that the volunteer army had served Argentina quite well in the past. This system *had* worked generally well, although a volunteer force did not always attract the best social elements, but rather those in the lowest social strata. The Argentine army was no exception. The rigorous and often brutal life associated with military service did not make recruiting easy. More often than not these men came from the most backward and the poorest regions of the country, where unemployment was high and opportunities scarce. There were also abuses on the national guard. The wealthy could easily claim exception or obtain a substitute, or personero.[67]

Admiration for the Prussian war machine, which had easily vanquished the French army in 1870, was prevalent among the most progressive Argentine officers. While willing to adopt certain features of the Prussian military system, they were also aware that the larger territorial area and smaller population of Argentina precluded the adoption of the Prussian model in its entirety. Farsighted officers argued that Argentina ought to effect a major reform of her military system that would enable her to train more men for longer periods of time and at the same time place them under national control. While deprived since 1880 of the power to raise armies, many provinces treated their national guard units as such. Reform-minded officers argued that the reserves should be placed under control of the federal government and their training and indoctrination entrusted to professional officers.[68]

The most progressive of these officers was Colonel Pablo Riccheri, a graduate of the Belgian War School who headed the Argentine Arms Purchasing Commission during the 1890s. General Julio A. Roca, who had been elected to the presidency for a second term in 1898, recalled Riccheri from Europe and appointed him as his war minister in July 1900. Riccheri began working on a draft of a project for mandatory universal conscription. The project was presented to Congress on September 4.[69]

Riccheri confronted arduous debates in parliament. His opponents advocated the volunteer service for an army of just 10,000 men, divided into four brigades that would be deployed at strategic passes along the Argentine-Chilean border. They argued that neither Argentina nor Chile could mobilize her reserves as fast as Germany. In the event of a war, they noted, Chile would require two to three months to organize her reserves and mount a serious offensive. By that time, they reasoned, the Argentine national guard would have completed additional training and been dispatched to the front.[70]

Riccheri easily defeated these arguments by pointing out to the chamber that by stationing an army of 10,000 men along a few of the many mountain passes along the 3,000 kilometer-long Andean border with Chile, the initiative would go to the enemy. Riccheri then proceeded to read aloud a list of the most progressive and respected officers in the Argentine army who were in complete agreement with the system he proposed. The mobilization of 1896 and 1899 had produced excellent results because the troops had been kept under colors for five to six months rather than the sixty days prescribed by the statues of 1895. The noncommissioned officers were, as in Germany, considered of foremost importance. As long-term professionals, they were the indispensable element that would train inexperienced conscripts and turn them into veterans. Riccheri also pointed out to the congressional committee the need to decentralize the War Arsenal, hitherto at Buenos Aires. Regional arsenals, he added, would facilitate mobilization and spare the government the unnecessary expense of shipping ordnance across the country, as in the past.[71]

Congress sanctioned Riccheri's project on December 5 and implemented it as Law no. 4031, more commonly referred to as La Ley Riccheri, or Riccheri's law. The new legislation provided for the enrollment of every able-bodied male at age eighteen. For enrollment and mobilization purposes, ten military regions encompassing sixty-eight military districts were created. Two years after enrollment, candidates would report to their local military district, where a *sorteo*, or national lottery, would be effected. Draftees obtaining the highest number were assigned to the navy, whose conscript quota was fixed at 2,000, while 18,000 would enter the army.[72]

The national army would consist of

1. The *Ejército Nacional*, which would include 5,000 professional soldiers as well as 18,000 conscripts who would serve for a one-year period. When reinforced by eight contingents or conscripts (classes of 1874 through 1881), the army would have a strength of 121,211 men.

2. The national guard, which would comprise all males between the ages of twenty-eight and forty. This age group would provide an estimated 10,000 individuals, based on an average of the classes of 1865 through 1878. Thus in case of war, the army would have a strength of 201,230 men.

3. The territorial guard, which would include all males between the ages of forty and forty-five of national classes 1859 through 1874, a total of 35,797 men.[73]

Riccheri spent the next year reorganizing the army. The infantry branch would consist of twelve infantry battalions of four companies each, plus two battalions of mountain infantry troops, or Cazadores de los Andes, 7,000 men in all. Infantry battalions would vary in strength from 450 to 500 men. The cavalry branch would comprise five regiments of field artillery of 450 men each and three regiments of mountain artillery of 350 men each. There were four engineer and one transport battalions as well as independent ambulance and courier companies. As in Germany, the noncommissioned officers were considered the backbone of the army. Therefore, they would comprise one-fifth of the total strength of the army, or 3,265 men.[74]

The war ministry was also reorganized and subdivided into three major departments. First was a military bureau, which in turn would be subdivided in eight sections and whose functions would include the inspectorates of artillery, infantry, cavalry, and engineers, as well as the transmission of military orders, recruitment and mobilization, the remount, military constructions, military publications, military justice, chaplain services, and promotions. Second, the central administration bureau was responsible for accounting and supply, the overall administration of army funds and properties. Finally the general staff, more in line with contemporary German developments and shorn of many other duties which were now the function of the military bureau and the central administration, was subdivided into three sections: (1) war operations, (2) intelligence and (3) transportation.[75] The reorganization of the Argentine army, which brought it to a peak of operational efficiency, was accompanied by a major reequipment process in the 1890s, partly forced by the rapid development of small arms and artillery among the major manufacturing countries, which had rendered existing ordnance obsolete, but largely because of the border dispute with Chile.

THE ARMS PURCHASING PROCESS

We have seen in the preceding chapter how the Argentine army's equipment was a veritable sampler, a heterogeneous collection of doubtful efficiency until the adoption of the Remington rifle in the 1870s. The first ten Krupp artillery pieces were purchased in 1865, along with a few crank-operated Gatling machine guns, after the outbreak of the Paraguayan war. The most commonly used side arms were the 12 mm Leffecheux revolvers, in models 1859 and 1870. These were replaced by the Smith & Wesson model 1878, which was supplemented by Belgian Nagants in the 1880s, and finally by the Colt .38 caliber Model 1895.[76]

By the late 1880s, a major revolution had taken place in the field of shoulder arms. Repeating rifles, which fired projectiles of smaller caliber and greater ballistic efficiency, propelled by smokeless powder, had been adopted by the major European powers. These weapons were characterized by a greater cyclic capacity and lighter overall weights, which allowed the individual soldier to carry a larger quantity of ammunition. In Chile, the Manlicher rifle model 1888, which had been purchased by the congressionalist faction during the civil war of 1891, was generally acknowledged to have been crucial in its victory over the forces of President José M. Balmaceda, which were armed with older, single-shot rifles. In that same year, ever alert to military developments in Chile, the Argentine army had appointed the then Lieutenant Pablo Riccheri as head of its arms purchasing commission in Europe. After careful consideration, he proceeded to select the weapon destined to equip the armed forces of Argentina for the next two decades: the Mauser model 1891.[77]

After the Paraguayan war, the artillery branch received numbers of Krupp model 1871 field and mountain pieces, all in 75 mm caliber and a range of 3,500 meters. Small quantities of French 65 mm mountain guns and Belgian 80 mm howitzers were purchased and tested during the 1870s, but despite their modern features as well as their steel construction, the Krupp product was always preferred, continuing a tradition that would only be interrupted by the First World War and the Treaty of Versailles: Krupp had become the sole supplier of artillery to the Argentine army.[78]

The arms race with Chile dictated the need for greater quantities of artillery. During 1896–1898 contracts worth 12 million marks were placed in Germany for 351 pieces. By 1898 the Argentine army had a sizable artillery component that could count on 180 Krupp Model 1895 75 mm field guns, 26 Krupp Model 1886 105 mm guns, 180 Krupp Model 1896 75 mm mountain guns, and a similar quantity of Krupp Model 1898 75 mm field guns on order. In addition, the war arsenal had over 300 Krupps of older patterns (models 1889, 1891, 1893) that had been modernized in Argentine arsenals and adapted to fire the 75 mm monobloc metallic cartridge introduced by the Krupp Model 1893. On the other hand, one hundred Maxim machine guns Model 1892/1898 had replaced the older Gatling and Nordenfelts. These older weapons were kept in reserve, as were 100,000 Remingtons, most of which had been modified in the war arsenal to accept the 7.65 mm Mauser round. In fact, Argentina had such an abundance of weapons that she could afford to transfer some of these to Bolivia, England, Peru, and Spain. An additional 180 Krupp Model 1898 75 mm mountain guns, 36 Krupp Model 1898 105 mm field howitzers, and 12 Krupp Model 1902 130 mm siege guns were delivered during 1898 and 1902.[79]

Riccheri proved to be a man of remarkable probity, who insisted in personally testing each and every rifle before shipping them to Argentina, and a shrewd purchasing agent, who saved the treasury over 8 million gold pesos. His zeal enabled him to devote the money thus economized to the purchase of eighteen more batteries (108 guns) than authorized by the budget, 600 ammunition wagons as well as locomotives, rolling stock and 400 kilometers of track for a narrow-gauge mountain railway for the territory of Neuquén. The railcars and locomotives could be broken down into pieces small enough to be carried by mules, if necessary. In 1915, Riccheri could recall with pride that in 1902 the artillery branch of the Argentine army was perfectly equipped with standardized materials, since all pieces fired the same metallic cartridge, and that the mobility and efficiency of this branch was unsurpassed by any of its European counterparts. There were 120 artillery batteries with a total of 720 guns, he recalled, manned by 15,000 superbly trained artillerymen, led by officers who by virtue of their training and fighting spirit could have brilliantly fulfilled their roles in any European army of the First World War.[80]

The Argentine army at the turn of the century was no longer a guerrilla force with a military band, as it had once been described. The days of the *destinados*, or forced levies, were memories of the past. The national army had acquired considerable expertise in the Paraguayan conflict, the Indians campaigns, and the various insurrections of the 1870s. It had gained an efficiency and discipline that allowed it to mobilize greater numbers of troops with each passing year. The economic growth experienced by Argentina during the second half of the nineteenth century enabled the government to erect training establishments, provide an adequate supply service, and keep abreast of technological developments. The army had progressively incorporated telegraph and railway battalions, and it had been among the first to adopt the Maxim machine gun and the modern light field howitzers, which Germany would employ to her advantage in the First World War. Moreover, it had become a deterrent in a war that threatened to engulf the Southern Cone on several occasions.

THE MODERNIZATION OF THE ARGENTINE NAVY, 1870–1902

At the outbreak of the Paraguayan war, the Argentine navy was reduced to a handful of armed steamers that doubled as warships, sailing cutters, and hulks that served as storage depots. There was no infrastructure of any kind nor training centers for the formation of personnel. Occasionally, eligible youths were posted as cadets aboard one of the vessels of the fleet. There was no other form of officer procurement. During the Paraguayan war, the command of allied forces was entrusted to President Mitre of Argentina, but since Brazil had the only navy worthy of the name in the allied camp, the viscount of Tamandare was given command of naval operations. Argentine naval participation during the war was largely confined to logistical and support tasks.[81]

The Argentine navy would only begin to develop as a combat organization in the presidency of Sarmiento (1868–1874). A chief exponent of the policy of national modernization who developed the fleet and created training schools for officers as well as enlisted men, Sarmiento had devoted considerable thought to the importance of naval power for communications as well as defense. Therefore, when Major Clodomiro Uturbey, a graduate of the Spanish Naval Academy, suggested the creation of a similar institution in Argentina, Sarmiento readily agreed. Corresponding legislation was enacted on October 2, 1872, and three days later the Escuela Naval Militar (ENM) was formally established aboard the steamer *General Brown*. The ENM would continue aboard the *Brown* until the so-called "peacoat mutiny" occurred. On June 21, 1876, while the *Brown* was berthed at Zárate, the company of cadets was ordered on deck for drill. Since it was rather cold, the cadets donned naval peacoats. When ordered to remove these garments, the cadets refused. When notified, the war minister ordered the school closed. The ringleaders were mustered out of the navy. The "mutiny" did not interfere with the curriculum, as the remaining cadets were transferred to other units of the fleet in order to continue their training. The ENM was based aboard a variety of vessels until it was transferred to its new campus in the heart of Buenos Aires. The number of cadets grew from thirty-five in 1872 to fifty in 1883 and would exceed seventy by 1887. True growth of the ENM would not occur until 1893, when it was moved to the former estate of Juan Manuel de Rosas at Palermo, formerly occupied by the Colegio Militar. The cadet body began to increase once again: 77 in 1895, 88 in 1896, 110 in 1897, and 140 in 1898.[82]

Initially, the ENM's course of studies was divided into six semesters. The first included geometry, rectilinear trigonometry, drafting, foreign languages, ballistics, and basic training. Spatial geometry, physics, nautical astronomy, and other academic subjects were taught in succeeding semesters, while practical instruction progressed similarly, from the duties of an able-bodied seaman to that of a helmsman, from piloting and commanding small craft to the duties and responsibilities of an officer. The last semesters stressed naval construction, steam propulsion, international law, naval ordnance, and history. Cadets were also attached to warships in Patagonian service, and recently graduated midshipmen were assigned to a flotilla of sailing cutters that patrolled the waters off that region, thus gaining valuable experience. Long ocean voyages became standard practice in the early 1880s, when the ENM took delivery of the training corvette, *La Argentina*. This unit would be replaced by a much larger vessel in 1898, the 2,800-ton frigate *Presidente Sarmiento*, which in turn inaugurated periodic around-the-world cruises. By the turn of the century, the prestige and efficiency of the ENM had become acknowledged abroad, and students from other South American countries were vying to be included in its rosters.[83]

In 1875, the barque *Vanguardia* became a floating school for apprentice seaman, and in the following year a reformatory for youthful offenders of the penal code was established aboard the pontoon *Colonel Paz*, which was renamed *Correcional de Menores*. By 1877, there were 200 seamen aboard these vessels and a pair of dispatch boats. But the practice of sentencing juvenile delinquents to naval service was discontinued. Instead, a sea-going school for boys, or Escuela de Grumetes, was established aboard the barque *Cabo de Hornos*. This unit spent the years 1879–1884 patrolling the coast of Patagonia until she was hulked, and her crew transferred to the training ship *La Argentina*. The artillery school, or Escuela de Artillería, was based aboard the ironclad *El Plata* during 1877, while the school for apprentice gunners, or Escuela de Aprendices Artilleros, where gunners's mates were formed, was based aboard several vessels from its inception in 1881. Stokers, engineers, and electricians were trained at the naval school of mechanics, or Escuela de Mecánica de La Armada, which had existed under various denominations since 1880. Finally, a torpedo school was created in 1883 aboard the newly delivered torpedo ram *Maipú*.[84]

A hydrographic bureau, or Oficina Central de Hidrografía (OCH), was created in January 1879. The OCH was responsible for mapping and exploration surveys of the Argentine coasts as well as for the construction of lighthouses and other navigational aids. In January 1881, the OCH and the newly established naval observatory were attached to the ENM. The Argentine navy thus obtained a great deal of valuable information about the inland waterways of Argentina and the Patagonian coasts.[85]

As can be seen, the formation of commissioned as well as subaltern personnel was given special consideration, particularly when the boundary dispute with Chile grew in intensity. In 1883, the Argentine navy had about 2,000 personnel of all ranks, including 1,503 seamen, 320 officers (of which 48 were cadets in the engineering branch), and 133 sublieutenants and cadets. During the struggles for national unification in the 1850s and later on, during the Paraguayan conflict, the Argentine navy had contracted local as well as foreign-born seamen to round off the crews of her vessels. In some cases, Argentine merchant ships complete with crews were chartered for quarantine duties as well as for missions of logistic support. During the decade between 1880 and 1890, the navy experienced a shortage of specialists and engineering officers, so a substantial number of foreign specialists were contracted. The naval roster of 1891 showed that there were eighty-three officers in the engineering branch, of which thirty-two were foreign-born. By 1897, the number of engineering officers had risen to 155, of whom ninety-seven were Argentine, and the remainder foreign born.[86]

As the fleet expanded and its vessels in turn became increasingly larger and more sophisticated, bigger crews were required to man them. The four *Garibaldi*-class cruisers purchased in the late 1890s, for example, needed 25 officers and 440 other ranks per ship, or a grand total of 109 officers and 1,636 seamen. By 1902, the Argentine navy had 8,336 personnel of all ranks, including 327 executive officers, 295 engineering officers, 34 officers in other technical branches, including torpedoes, 7,760 seamen, and 450 marines. The importance of the navy as an institution was tacitly recognized by the government on March 15, 1898, when it was granted independent status. Moreover, it would no longer be a dependency of the ministry of war. Instead, it would be regulated by a ministry of the navy.[87]

As the navy expanded and its vessels increased in tonnage, it was forced to develop a network of bases and anchorages throughout the republic. Fleet expansion will be covered under a separate heading, but it should be mentioned that the first modern units were shallow-draft vessels that could be harbored in the Río de la Plata, or at the naval base at Zárate, in the Paraná River. As larger vessels were incorporated to the fleet, the need for a deep-water port was felt. A site near the town of Punta Alta, in the southern portion of the province of Buenos Aires, was chosen. A renowned Italian engineer, Luigi Luiggi, was entrusted with the plans during 1896. Work commenced in 1898. By July of that year, the first three coastal artillery batteries intended to protect the base were emplaced. When completed in 1902, the strategic port, known as Puerto Militar, would be the largest naval base in South America, with a basin large enough to accommodate twenty *Garibaldi*-class cruisers. Its shore installations spanned an area of 3,000 hectares. A strategic railway connected it with the city of Bahía Blanca, while batteries of naval guns and howitzers protected it against naval attack.[88]

The coast artillery had not received any special attention until the 1870s. Until 1879, coastal defense had been the responsibility of the army, whose Batallón de Artíllería de Plaza, or Heavy Artillery Battalion, garrisoned the island of Martín García. A naval artillery corps was created on November 15, 1879, under Lieutenant Colonel Emilio Sellstrom, a former professor of ballistics and engineering at the ENM and a gifted engineer. The coast artillery also doubled as marine infantry and security forces, but the only fortifications that existed were those at Martín García, a strategic island that controlled access to the interior rivers of Argentina. During the Paraguayan war, the war ministry had ordered the construction of five batteries mounting thirty-six guns. By 1866 the barbettes and entrenchments were constructed, but only seventeen cannon had been emplaced, and these were ancient tubes inherited from the Spanish colonial authorities. Under Sarmiento, the first modern guns, six 10-inch Parrots and four 15-inch Rodmans, were installed. In 1877, these were reinforced by a battery of Armstrong 7-inch rifles, firing 150-pound armor-piercing shells, thus giving Martín García true strategic value. By the 1880s, the guns at Martín García were outdated, as weapons with greater armor-piercing and longer-range capabilities were available. The Argentine navy selected the Krupp 240 mm Model 1887 cannon as standard equipment for its coastal batteries, and these were emplaced at Martín García, at the Naval Arsenal in Zárate and at Puerto Militar.[89] The constant frictions with Chile also led to an expansion of the fleet, which by 1898 would be the largest and best equipped in the Southern Cone.

THE ARGENTINE FLEET

In the years between 1859 and 1862, the navies of the major powers had begun to incorporate armor-clad vessels, while at the same time, naval guns had become progressively larger in order to pierce the wrought-iron plates that protected the vitals of these armored ships. At the outbreak of the Paraguayan war, the Argentine navy had nineteen vessels, few of which were steamers, the largest and best of which was the *Guardia Nacional*, a 520-ton paddle wheeler formerly employed as a passenger ship. In fact there were no true warships available, simply mail packets or river boats armed with a few obsolete cannon and devoid of any armor. The only acquisitions made during this period were the paddle-wheel steamers *Coronel Espora* (552 tons) and the *Coronel Rosetti* (772 tons). These were followed by the *General Brown* in mid-1867, but all of them were, like the other ships in the fleet, merely converted commercial steamers, lightly armed and totally unprotected.[90]

By comparison, the Brazilian navy, which at this time was the largest in Latin America, had forty-five vessels, of which thirty-five were steamers, and had taken delivery of fourteen ironclads of various designs, including several *Monitor* types. The Argentine navy did not possess true warships built from the keel up as such until the 1870s. Congress appropriated 2.6 million pesos in 1872 for a modest naval rearmament program. The ships provided for were the monitors *El Plata* and *Los Andes*, four gunboats, two steam corvettes of 550 tons each, the *Uruguay* and *Paraná*, as well as a pair of dispatch boats. These ships, known collectively as La escuadra de Sarmiento (Sarmiento's fleet), were delivered during 1874–1875 and were intended for service along the Plata tributaries in the event of a war with Brazil. While serving as the Argentine minister in Washington, shortly after the end of the American Civil War, Sarmiento followed military developments, particularly in the field of armaments. His keen intellect was attracted by the use of "floating torpedoes," as mines were then known, by the confederacy in its efforts to counteract the powerful Union navy, which was strangling its commerce and hindering its war effort. Not surprisingly, when he assumed the presidency, Sarmiento contracted several former Confederate naval officers for the Torpedo Division of the Argentine navy, established in 1874 at the Luján River, in the Paraná River delta.[91]

The Torpedo Division consisted of the torpedo-depot ship *Fulminante*, as well as several steam launches armed with spar-torpedoes. Argentine naval strategy at this time was primarily concerned with the defense of the Plata estuary from a possible Brazilian attack. The shallow-draft monitors and gunboats received during 1874–1875 could easily negotiate the approach channels to Buenos Aires, while a system of "floating torpedoes" guarded the waterways which were further protected by the guns at Martín García.[92]

By the late 1870s, relations with Brazil improved somewhat, but the seizure of foreign vessels bearing Argentine permits by Chilean naval units off the Patagonian coast almost led to war. Cooler heads prevailed. War was averted and a convention known as the Fierro-Sarratea pact was concluded. As no permanent solution of the boundary issue with Chile had been reached, Argentina began to develop an ocean-going navy to match the Chilean fleet, which was articulated around two 3,500-ton ocean-going frigates. At this time, most Argentine naval personnel, both commissioned and enlisted, had been formed in the tributaries of the Plata system. These were the *marinos de agua dulce*, or fresh water sailors, which manned the fleet. However, in the early 1860s exploration surveys of the Patagonian coasts were carried out by cutters and brigs. These activities increased by the 1870s, when a cutter escadrille, composed of units displacing between 45 and 100 tons, was deployed in that region. The harsh Patagonian waters, where winter gales reach hurricane proportions and often speeds of above 100 miles per hour and where mountainous waves sometimes fifty feet in height are common, provided the best possible school for the officers, cadets, and crews of the Argentine navy. During the 1879 conquest of the desert, the navy gained valuable experience by providing logistic support to army units engaged in operations against the Patagonian Indians and by exploring the lakes and rivers of the region. In fact, these activities were part of Argentine naval planning in the late 1870s: to train as many officers and crewmen as possible in the South Atlantic, where an armed clash with Chile would probably occur, and to develop an ocean-going navy. A second-class ironclad, the *Almirante Brown*, the protected cruiser *Patagonia*, the torpedo-ram *Maipú*, the training ship *La Argentina*, two second-class torpedo-boats, as well as assorted transports and auxiliaries joined the fleet by the early 1880s. The spar torpedoes were replaced by the newly developed Whitehead automobile torpedo, and the Torpedo Division was reorganized, with the *Maipú* as its flagship.[93]

During the late 1880s Chile instituted a program of naval construction, which included a battleship, two protected cruisers, and a pair of ocean-going torpedo boats. Argentina retorted by ordering a fast and well-protected cruiser, the *Veinticinco de Mayo*, two coastal defense battleships named *Libertad* and *Independencia*, a pair of torpedo-boat destroyers, and fifteen torpedo boats. A most dangerous naval arms race developed in the 1890s, as each country retaliated to the other's purchases by ordering new construction. The Argentine navy soon received two more protected cruisers, the *9 de Julio* and the *Buenos Aires*, the torpedo-cruiser *Patria*, and four destroyers as well as a number of transports and auxiliaries.[94]

A severe economic depression had afflicted Argentina during 1890. Following an unsuccessful rebellion against him, President Juárez Celman resigned. The new government undertook a policy of economic austerity, which somehow did not apply to the armed forces; for despite national economic stringency, by balancing the budget as well as by foreign loans obtained in the most favorable of conditions, Argentina was able to devote 8 million gold pesos to pay for the new construction. The incorporation of these new vessels enabled the creation of three homogeneous combat divisions in 1894; the first (or armored) division, the second (or cruiser) division, and the third (or torpedo) division, which was subdivided into two squadrons: the first, with the large, sea-going torpedo vessels, and the second. With twenty-one smaller craft, the number of torpedo vessels had grown considerably by this time, and the old torpedo base at the Luján River was no longer adequate. A new naval station designed to accommodate the larger units incorporated was built at Río Santiago, near the provincial capital of La Plata, during 1895–1896.[95]

The most important addition to the Argentine navy during 1895 was the first of the *Garibaldi*-class armored cruisers. During the preceding years both Argentina and Chile had replied to each other's acquisitions of protected cruisers simply by ordering larger vessels, each slightly more powerful than the other, built by obliging English yards. The term *protected* implies that the ships designated by this category carried a narrow armor belt below the water line, leaving the superstructure and all vital parts unprotected. Armored cruisers, on the other hand, were considerably better protected. During the 1890s, the Ansaldo shipyards in Italy had laid down a class of armored cruisers designed by engineer inspector Edoardo Masdea. These ships were an intermediate design between the battleship and the armored cruiser, with a powerful armament as well as a high turn of speed that enabled them to outdistance heavier ships. Despite their relatively low displacement, they were well protected and armed. In 1895 the Italian government relinquished the *Garibaldi*, under construction for its own navy. The Ansaldo yard then entered into negotiations with the Argentine minister in London, and a contract stipulating payment of 752,000 pounds was concluded on July 14.[96]

The *San Martín*, a sistership of the *Garibaldi*, was purchased on April 24, 1896, and it was followed by two additional units of this class in 1898 which were renamed *Pueyrredón* and *Belgrano*. With the acquisition of these four powerful and homogeneous ships, the Argentine navy surged ahead of its Chilean counterpart. In order to regain naval supremacy, in 1901 Chile purchased another armored cruiser and six destroyers. Argentina quickly retaliated by ordering two armored cruisers of an improved *Garibaldi* class, slightly larger and faster than the previous four. The Chilean reply came in the form of two 11,000-ton light battleships, but Argentina would have the last word when she formalized a contract with the Ansaldo shipyards, under which the latter would deliver a pair of 14,800-ton battleships. For good measure, six Italian destroyers of the *Nembo* class were ordered as well. Thus, all Chilean attempts to regain their lost naval supremacy came to naught.[97]

The rebirth of the Argentine navy in the 1870s was a by-product of the disputes with Brazil and later on with Chile. By the late 1890s, the Argentine navy had evolved from a purely fluvial defensive force into an ocean-going fleet, capable of meeting the Chilean navy on more than equal terms. When Commodore Martín Rivadavia was appointed chief of the naval general staff in May 1897, training programs were intensified, particularly in the gunnery branch. Argentine naval gunners were put through a severe course of training and attained a high standard of speed and precision. Large quantities of ammunition, spare gun barrels, engine components, and propellers were stockpiled at the arsenal. The fleet worked feverishly day and night in exercises and maneuvers, and when Congress objected that the navy lacked sufficient gunners' mates, Rivadavia could point with pride to 500 well-drilled gun-layers. The stockpiling of supplies, equipment, and crew training for the *Garibaldi*-class cruisers was accomplished under a cloak of secrecy. The balance of power shifted dramatically, as will be seen in the tables of strength. By 1898, the Argentine navy had surged ahead in every respect. For three years it enjoyed complete superiority over its rival. The Argentine navy had developed institutionally as well as professionally. A naval academy and a plethora of service schools were established, along with repair yards, naval bases, anchorages, and a hydrographic service that gave Argentina detailed charts of the Patagonian coasts. As Argentina began to project herself along the South Atlantic, her officers and crews gained considerable experience. The voyage of Commodore Luis Py's squadron in 1878 was undertaken despite certain handicaps. Relatively inexperienced crews, which included cadets from the ENM, embarked upon vessels designed for nothing more serious than river navigation. In 1899, when the presidents of Argentina and Chile met at the Straits of Magellan in order to dispel tensions between both countries, ocean-going vessels of the Argentine navy, expertly handled by officers who were totally familiar with the Patagonian coasts and adjacent waters, appeared through the western approach of the Beagle Channel, a mode which caused both admiration and apprehension in Chile.[98] There was no better way of announcing to the world that at last Argentina had developed a professional navy; in the quality of its crews it was second to none in South America, and in the strength and quality of its ships, it outstripped all others.

NOTES

1. Ejército Argentino, Dirección de Estudios Históricos, *Reseña histórica y orgánica del Ejército Argentino*, 3 vols. (Buenos Aires: Círculo Militar, 1972), I: 70–75 (hereafter referred to as *Reseña histórica*).

2. *Reseña histórica*, I: 78–80, 111–117; Armada Argentina, *Infantería de Marina: Tres siglos de historia y cien años de vida orgánica* (Buenos Aires: 1979), pp. 13–17; Tulio Halperin Donghi, *Guerra y finanzas en los orígenes del estado argentino, 1791–1850* (Buenos Aires: Editorial de Belgrano, 1982), pp. 40–42, 84–85; Comando General del Ejército, Dirección de Estudios Históricos, *Política seguida con el aborígen*, 3 vols. (hereafter referred to as *Política seguida*) (Buenos Aires: Círculo Militar, 1973) I: 94–101; Alfred J. Tapson, "Indian Warfare on the Pampa during the Colonial Period," *HAHR* 42, no. 1 (February 1969), p. 27. This author is critical of the fighting qualities of the Blandengues during the British invasion of 1806, who fled at "the sight of a disciplined army." This was not an uncommon occurrence whenever colonial militia faced well-trained regulars. See Ernest R. Dupuy and Trevor N. Dupuy, *The Compact History of the Revolutionary War: The Story of the American Revolution* (New York: Harper & Row, 1966), pp. 269–270, 274–275. The following statement could well have been written about any of the colonial militias in the Americas: "The American troops lacked the qualities of discipline and regularity which made the British invincible in pitched battles. The American officers, capable men, knew no more of discipline, drill or of other military routine than did their men. The blind were leading the blind." In 1778, to turn these troops into a well-trained, cohesive force, the Americans availed themselves of the services of Lieutenant General Friedrich Willhem von Steuben (Christopher Ward, *The War of the Revolution*, 2 vols. (New York: Macmillan: 1952) I: 242–244, II: 726–728). The Continental army broke and fled before the British on numerous occasions. At the battle of Camden (South Carolina), on August 16, 1780, regulars and militiamen faced the British. The militia panicked and ran, while the regulars stood their ground but were captured almost to a man: "An overpowering fear seized them, they turned and ran, threw away and ran for their lives. North Carolina in the center saw Virginia in full flight and was panic struck. Without pulling a single trigger, nearly 2,000 Carolinians, almost as many men as the whole British force cast away their arms, turned and fled. More than 2,500 fear-stricken Virginians and North Carolinians, like an undammed torrent, burst into the 1st Maryland

brigade, threw it into complete confusion and ran, raving along the roads and bypaths towards the North.'' See Christopher Ward, *The War of the Revolution* (New York: Macmillan, 1952), II: 727–728.

3. *Reseña histórica*, I: 111–117.

4. Félix Best, *Historia de las guerras argentinas: De la independencia, internacionales, civiles y con el indio*, 2 vols. (Buenos Aires: 1 Ediciones Peuser, 1960), I: 163–180, 182–195. For a detailed study of military operations in the northwestern theater of war, see Emilio A. Bidondo, *La guerra de la independencia en el Norte Argentino* (Buenos Aires: *EUDEBA*, 1978).

5. Bartolomé Mitre, *Historia de San Martín y de la emancipación sudamericana*, 3 vols. (Buenos Aires: Editorial El Ateneo, 1950) I: 76–77, 80–82; Secretaría General del Ejército, *Semblanza histórica del ejército argentino* (Buenos Aires: 1981; hereafter referred to as *Semblanza*), pp. 32–33; Francisco O. Farinaccio, "San Martín at Chacabuco," *Military Review* 47, no. 2 (February 1967), pp. 15–21.

6. René Orsi, "1822: Disolución del ejército y marina nacionales," *EST* 3, no. 18 (septiembre-octubre 1972), pp. 112–121; *Reseña histórica*, I: 315–319, 322–323.

7. *Reseña Histórica*, I: 342–344.

8. Amadeo J. Baldrich, *Historia de la Guerra del Brasil: Contribución al estudio razonado de la historia militar argentina* (Buenos Aires: Imprenta La Harlem, 1905), pp. 338–339; Carlos H. Oberacker, "O Marechal de Campo Gustavo Henrique von Braun, Chefe de Primeiro estado-maior do Exercito Brasilero," *JAL* 21 (1984), pp. 211–263.

9. *Reseña Histórica*, I: 322–323.

10. Ibid., I: 223–231; "Fusil Tower," *Autoclub: Revista del Automovil Club Argentino* 12, no. 68 (enero-febrero 1973), p. 6; Best, *Historia de las guerras argentinas*, I: 125–127.

11. *Semblanza*, pp. 57–58; *Reseña Histórica*, I: 541–542; Manuel Gálvez, *Humaitá* (Buenos Aires: Editorial Losada S. A., 1959), p. 20.

12. Harris Gaylord Warren, *Paraguay: An Informal History* (Norman: University of Oklahoma Press, 1949), pp. 157–177, 182–187.

13. Josefina Plá, *The British in Paraguay* (Richmond, Surrey: Richmond Publishing Co. 1976), pp. i–vii.

14. Ibid., pp. ix–x; Warren, *Paraguay*, pp. 208, 215; Efraím Cardozo, *El Imperio del Brasil y el Río de la Plata: Antecedentes y estallido de la guerra de Paraguay* (Buenos Aires: Librería del Plata, 1961), pp. 88–89; George Thompson, *The War in Paraguay* (London: Longmans, Green, 1869), pp. 18–20. Thompson claims the Paraguayan government sent a note asking explanations about the arming of Martín García and that the Argentine government promised explanations, but in ten weeks they had not sent them. Paraguay then wrote again, he says, and Buenos Aires evaded the question. That was not the case, as can be seen in Juan Beverina, *La guerra del Paraguay, 1865–1870, resumén histórico* (Buenos Aires: Círculo Militar, 1973), pp. 54–63. While Thompson is to be considered accurate on his descriptions of fortifications, entrenchments, and ordnance, the validity of many of his statements on other matters, particularly allied casualties, is open to question. His work has been widely accepted and quoted in English-speaking countries, mainly because it is one of the few narratives of the Paraguayan war written in English. The reader should bear in mind that Thompson, who was hired by López and well rewarded for his services, can hardly be considered an impartial observer. Jürg Meister, *Francisco Solano Lopez: Nationalheld oder Kriegsverbrecher?;*

Der Krieg Paraguays gegen die Triple Allianz, 1864–1870 (Osnabrück: Biblio Verlag, 1987), pp. 140–153, dismisses the figures for allied losses often cited by Thompson and the Paraguayans as mere propaganda. Vera Blinn Reber, "The Demographics of Paraguay: A Reinterpretation of the Great War, 1864–1870," *HAHR* 68, no. 2 (May 1988), pp. 289–319.

15. Diego Abad de Santillan, "La Guerra del Paraguay, 1865–1870," in *Historia Argentina*, 5 vols. (Buenos Aires: Tipográfica Editora Argentina, 1965–1971) III: 129–178; R. B. Cunninghame Graham, *Portrait of a Dictator: Francisco Solano López, Paraguay, 1865–1870* (London: William Heineman, 1933), pp. 152–153.

16. Warren, *Paraguay*, p. 22; Charles J. Kolinski, *Independence or Death! The Story of the Paraguayan War* (Gainesville: University Presses of Florida, 1965), pp. 91–92.

17. Gilbert Phelps, *The Tragedy of Paraguay* (New York: St. Martin's Press, 1975), p. 112; Augusto Rodríguez, "Ejercito Nacional," In *Historia Argentina contemparánea: 1862–1930*, 7 vols. (Buenos Aires: El Ateneo, 1966), 2: 287.

18. Plá, *The British in Paraguay*, pp. 99–100; Arturo Bray, *Solano López: Soldado de la gloria y del infortunio* (Buenos Aires: Guillermo Kraft, 1945) gives details of some of the arms purchased and delivered through 1864 and notes that López had ordered Cándido Barreiro, his Paraguayan agent in Europe, to purchase 10,000 modern rifles. Paraguay had also concluded a deal with the Krupp firm involving 36 rifled 24-pounders and 3,600 shells and was about to conclude a contract in France for a battery of rifled 4-pounders. As a result of the war, these weapons were detained in Europe. López had also selected a *Monitor*-type ironclad armed with heavy caliber Krupp rifles, but was unable to pay for these, and they were eventually delivered to the Brazilian navy. Paraguayan historian Cardozo (*El Imperio del Brasil*) remarks that Paraguay's military potential was far more effective than Argentina's, whose weapons and ships were even more outdated than Paraguay's (AM, 23: 223–244). A letter from the Consulate of the Argentine Republic in Liverpool to the Argentine Foreign Minister dated July 23, 1863, noted the departure of the bark *City of Kandy* with a cargo that included a battery of six-pounder guns, ammunition wagons and 62 other boxes from the firm of Fawcett and Preston of Liverpool for the Paraguayan government. León de Palleja, *Diario de la campaña de las fuerzas aliadas contra el Paraguay* 2 vols. (Montevideo: Ministerio de Instrucción Pública y Previsión Social, 1960), I: 228. The Argentine army was desperately short of weapons of all types. When two Uruguayan infantry battalions at Corrientes were issued percussion muskets to replace their old flintlocks, General Flores offered these to the governor of Corrientes in exchange for oxen and horses.

19. Rodriguez, "Ejército Nacional," 2: 287; *Reseña Histórica*, II: 116–118.

20. AM, VI: 98–101, 102–104, 110–111, 167, 274, 294–295; Miguel Angel De Marco, *La Guerra del Paraguay* (Buenos Aires: Editorial Planeta, 1995), pp. 124–130; Liliana María Brezzo, "Armas norteamericanas para la Guerra del Paraguay," *Todo Es Historia* 394 (septiembre 1994): pp. 28–41.

21. De Marco, *La guerra del Paraguay*, pp. 140–147; AM, VI: 10–12.

22. Beverina, *La guerra del Paraguay*, p. 129. The Salta contingent, for example, required fifty-nine days to reach its embarkation point. It had to traverse a distance of 1,450 kilometers at an average speed of 25 kilometers per day. Raúl Scalabrini Ortíz, *Historia de los ferrocarriles Argentinos* (Buenos Aires: Editorial Devenir, 1958), pp. 39–41, 116–117; De Marco, *La guerra de Paraguay*, 150–154.

23. *Ejército Nacional*, pp. 290–295.

24. Warren, *Paraguay*, pp. 226–227; Beverina, *La guerra del Paraguay*, p. 150; Best, *Historia de las guerras argentinas*, II: 238–239.

25. Thompson, *The War in Paraguay*, pp. 87–89, 94–100; Phelps, *The Tragedy of Paraguay*, 170–177; Best, *Historia de las guerras argentinas*, II: 242–244; Palleja, *Diario de la campaña*, pp. 80–92.

26. Best, *Historia de las guerras argentinas*, II: 250–251; Max Justo Guedes, "A Guerra uma análise," in Maria Eduardo Castro Magalhâes, ed., *A Guerra do Paraguai: 130 Anos Depois* (Rio de Janeiro: Reume Dumará, 1995; hereafter referred to as GP), pp. 53–65; Kolinski, *Independence or Death!* pp. 110–113. For Brazil, the most feasible strategy to bring the war to Paraguay was up the Paraná River, through Argentine territory. The distance between Rio de Janeiro and Buenos Aires is approximately 2,020 nautical miles (3,741 kilometers), plus an additional 687 miles up the Paraná. Poor communications and enormous distances prevented major strikes into Paraguay from Matto Grosso. However, in 1865, an expedition under Colonel Manoel Pedro Drago started from Rio de Janeiro on April 1865 with about 3,000 men. It required two years before it reached Matto Grosso. Disease and desertion thinned its ranks to about 1,600 men and reached Paraguayan territory in February 1867. Under constant attacks from Paraguayan cavalry and nearing starvation, only about 700 survivors returned to Brazil.

27. Beverina, *La guerra del Paraguay*, pp. 193–203; Best, *Historia de las guerras argentinas*, II: 252–253; Thompson, *The War in Paraguay*, pp. 121–126.

28. Best, *Historia de las guerras argentinas*, II: 256–258; Thompson, *The War in Paraguay*, pp. 134–146; Palleja, *Diario de la Campaña*, II: 259–279. Resquín's cavalry was utterly destroyed, and horsemen died saber in hand in front of the Argentine guns. Kolinski, *Independence or Death!*, pp. 117–122.

29. Beverina, *La guerra del Paraguay*, pp. 204–210; Kolinski, *Independence or Death!*, p. 130; Best, *Historia de las guerras argentinas*, II: 260–265; Phelps, *The Tragedy of Paraguay*, pp. 149–153. Kolinski and Phelps seem to have accepted Thompson's rather inflated figures on allied casualties without question.

30. Best, *Historia de las guerras argentinas*, II:266–267; Phelps, *The Tragedy of Paraguay*, p. 157.

31. Best, *Historia de las guerras argentinas*, II: 267–269; Thompson, *The War in Paraguay*, pp. 134–146, 155–156; Beverina, *La guerra del Paraguay*, pp. 210–211.

32. Kolinski, *Independence or Death!*, pp. 127–130; Beverina, *La guerra del Paraguay*, pp. 231–232.

33. Phelps, *The Tragedy of Paraguay*, pp. 167–170; Beverina, *La guerra del Paraguay*, pp. 233–239; De Marco, *La guerra del Paraguay*, pp. 314–318; Best, *Historia de las guerras argentinas*, II: 275–278; Thompson, *The War in Paraguay*, pp. 173–183. Thompson gives total allied casualties as 9,000 killed and wounded. This simply does not coincide with Argentine and Brazilian statistics, which Thompson dismisses far too lightly. Alberto Rangel, *Gastâo de Orleáns: O ultimo Conde d'Eu* (Sao Paulo: Companhia Editora Nacional 1935). This source cites a letter from the Comte d'Eu to the Duke of Nemours dated October 8, 1866, in which the former gives total losses at Curupaytí as 4,000, of whom 2,000 were Argentines.

34. AM, 1: 172–175, 305–310; Kolinski, *Independence or Death!*, pp. 143–145.

35. Thompson, *The War in Paraguay*, pp. 191–197.

36. Beverina, *La guerra del Paraguay*, pp. 255–256; Best, *Historia de las guerras argentinas*, II: 282–283.

37. Ibid., II: 290–293; Beverina, *La guerra del Paraguay*, pp. 263–265; Phelps, *The Tragedy of Paraguay*, pp. 236–238; Thompson, *The War in Paraguay*, pp. 293–313.

38. Phelps, *The Tragedy of Paraguay*, pp. 240–242; Best, *Historia de las guerras argentinas*, II: 298–305.

39. Warren, *Paraguay*, pp. 240–241.

40. F. J. Mc Lynn, "Consequences for Argentina of the War of Triple Alliance: 1865–1870," *TAM* 41, no. 1 (July 1984), pp. 81–98.

41. Ibid., p. 242; AM, III: 301; León Pomer, "A guerra do Paraguai e a formaçao do Estado na Argentina," GP, pp. 115–120; Leslie Bethell, "A guerra do Paraguai: Historia e historiografía," GP, pp. 11–26.

42. De Marco, *La guerra del Paraguay*, pp. 298–320; Ignacio H. Fotheringham, *La vida de un soldado o reminiscencias de las fronteras*, 2 vols. (Buenos Aires: Círculo Militar, 1970) I: 132. By the mid 1870s, parity with Brazil in terms of weapons and warships was attained. By the 1880s, the balance of power favored Argentina, as the Baron de Rio Branco would ruefully note, "We have no squadron, no torpedoes, no army, and the Argentines have all this." See Bradford E. Burns, *The Unwritten Alliance: Rio Branco and Brazilian American Relations* (New York: Columbia University Press, 1966), p. 183.

43. Héctor E. Ratto, *Historia de Brown*, 2 vols. (Buenos Aires: Biblioteca de La Sociedad de Historia Argentina VII, Librería y Editorial La Facultad, 1939), I: 22–32; Laurio H. Destefani, *Famosos veleros argentinos* (Buenos Aires: Centro Naval, Instituto de Publicaciones Navales, 1967), pp. 72–77; Lewis Winkler Bealer, *Los corsarios de Buenos Aires: Sus actividades en las guerras hispano-americanas de la independencia, 1815–1821* (Buenos Aires: Facultad de Filosofía y Letras, Publicaciones del Instituto de Investigaciones Históricas, Numero LXXII, 1937), pp. 41–44.

44. Ratto, *Historia de Brown*, pp. 46–47; Destefani, *Famosos veleros*, p. 79.

45. Robert L. Scheina, *Latin America: A Naval History, 1810–1987* (Annapolis, MD: Naval Institute Press, 1987), pp. 2–3.

46. John Lynch, *The Spanish American Revolutions*, pp. 206–209; Arguindeguy, *Apuntes sobre los buques de la armada argentina*, 7 vols. (Buenos Aires: Departamento de Estudios Hístóricos Navales, 1972), I: 68.

47. Baldrich, *Historia de la guerra del Brasil*, pp. 268–270. At the outbreak of the war the Brazilian navy was composed of 108 warships, half of which were major combat units (frigates, brigantines, corvettes) and the rest gunboats and armed schooners of various types and sizes (Ratto, *Historia de Brown*, I: 333–334).

48. Humberto F. Burzio, *Historia de la Escuela Naval Militar*, (Buenos Aires: Departamento de Estudios Históricas Navales, Serie B, No. 16, 1972), 3 vols., I: 132–134.

49. J. García Enciso, *Historia del colegio militar de la nación* (Buenos Aires: Círculo Militar, 1970), pp. 26–27, 78–79, 88–92, 99–100.

50. Fotheringham, *La vida de un soldadó*, I: 131–132, García Enciso, *Historia del Colegio Militar*, pp. 131–133; Alan Rouquié, *Poder y sociedad política en la Argentina*, 2 vols. (Buenos Aires: Emecé Editores, 1978), I: 111.

51. Manuel Prado, *Guerra al Malón* (Buenos Aires: Editorial Universitaria de Buenos Aires, 1960), pp. 56–57.

52. Rodriguez, "Ejército Nacional," 2: 338–339.

53. Frederick Nunn, *Yesterday's Soldiers: European Military Professionalism in South America, 1898–1940* (Lincoln and London: University of Nebraska Press, 1983), pp. 123–129.

54. Rodriguez, "Ejército Nacional," 2: 324–325; *Reseña Histórica*, II: 104–105.

55. Gabriel Nellar Fuad, "Aspectos salientes de la institución ejército durante la primera presidencia del General Roca," *4o. CNRHA*, IV: 71–75; Jacinto R. Yaben, *Biografías argentinas y sudamericanas*, 5 vols. (Buenos Aires: Editorial Metropolis, 1938), II: 1157. Under the direction of General Joaquín Viejobueno a number of compressed bronze, breech-loading rifled field guns, based on the Krupp model, were produced at the Parque de Artillería; Arguindeguy, *Apuntes sobre los buques*, IV: 195.

56. Best, *Historia de las guerras argentinas*, II: 82–83; Rodriguez, "Ejército Nacional," 2: 331–332. This source cites the battle of Don Gonzalo, fought on December 8, 1873, as a prime example in which the trilogy of the Remington rifle, Krupp artillery, and Gatling guns enabled the national forces under Colonel Gainza to defeat the rebels under López Jordan.

57. Nellar Fuad, "Aspectos Salientes," pp. 71–72; Rodriguez, "Ejército Nacional" 2: 327–328.

58. M. G. Mulhall and E. T. Mulhall, *Handbook of the River Plate* (London: Trubner, 1883) p. 69, *Reseña Histórica*, II: 311–312, 353–366.

59. Héctor J. Piccinali, *Vida del Teniente General Nicolás Lavalle* (Buenos Aires: Círculo Militar, 1981), p. 187; Alberto D. H. Scunio, *La conquista del Chaco* (Buenos Aires: Círculo Militar, 1972), pp. 220–221; Rodriguez, "Ejército Nacional," 2: 326–327.

60. Oscar Ozlak, *La Conquista del orden político y la formación del estado argentino* (Buenos Aires: Centro de Estudios de Estado y Sociedad, 1982), p. 22; Rodriguez, "Ejército Nacional," 2: 339–340; Best, *Historia de las guerras argentinas*, II: 90–94.

61. Isidoro Ruiz Moreno, *La Federalización de Buenos Aires* (Buenos Aires: Hyspamerica, 1980), pp. 10–21, 44–5, 128–131; H. S. Ferns, *Britain and Argentina in the Nineteenth Century* (London: Oxford University Press, 1960), pp. 386–390; Best, *Historia de las guerras argentinas*, I: 98–108; Natalio R. Botana, *El orden conservador: La política argentina entre 1880 y 1916* (Buenos Aires: Editorial Sudamericana, 1994), pp. 34–37. In 1865, Jacob Snider, a New York gun maker, developed a hinged block by which it was possible to convert obsolete muzzle-loading rifles into breech-loaders. In England, the large supply of Enfield rifles was subjected to this conversion. See W. Y. Carman, *A History of Firearms: From Earliest Times to 1914* (London: Routledge & Kegan Paul, 1955), pp. 116–118.

62. Rodriguez, "Ejército Nacional," 2: 325–326.

63. Ibid., pp. 338–339.

64. José Ferrer, "The Armed Forces in Argentine Politics, 1862–1930," (Ph.D. diss., University of New Mexico, 1966), pp. 53–55; Rodriguez, "Ejército Nacional," 2: p. 339.

65. Ibid., p. 340, *Reseña Histórica*, pp. 377–388; Roberto Levillier, "Presidencia del Doctor José Evaristo Uriburu (22 enero 1895–12 octubre 1898)," *HAC* I: 463–464.

66. Argentine Republic, *Segundo Censo de la República Argentina*, 3 vols. (Buenos Aires: 1895), III: 44–45; Levillier, "Presidencia del Doctor José Evaristo Uriburu," p. 464.

67. Rodolfo Martínez Pita, *Riccheri* (Buenos Aires: Círculo Militar, 1952), pp. 88–90, Ferrer, "The Armed Forces in Argentine Politics," pp. 51–53.

68. Martínez Pita, *Riccheri*, pp. 90–100.

69. Ferrer, "The Armed Forces in Argentine Politics," pp. 54–55.

70. Martínez Pita, *Riccheri*, pp. 129–131.

71. Plácido Grela, *Fuerzas armadas y soberanía nacional: Vida y obra del teniente*

general Pablo Riccheri, forjador del moderno ejército argentino (Rosario: Litoral Edi-ciones, 1973), pp. 114–117.

72. Martínez Pita, *Riccheri*, pp. 144–145.

73. Ibid., pp. 138–141.

74. Ibid., pp. 157–161. Details of the parliamentary debate can be found in Argentine Republic, *Camara de Diputados, Diario de Sesiones* (Buenos Aires, 1902), Sessions of September 13, 1901, pp. 722–758. For the complete text of the Riccheri Law, see Augusto Da Rocha, ed., *Colección completa de leyes nacionales sancionadas por el honorable congreso durante los años 1852 a 1917*, 14 vols. (Buenos Aires: Libreria La Facultad, 1918): 12, 2nd tome: 519–549.

75. Martínez Pita, *Riccheri*, pp. 161–168.

76. Albert A. Landini, August 24, 1969, personal communication, weapons and ballistics editor of *La Prensa*; Bartolomé Mitre, AM, V: 98–99, 104–105, 110–112, and VI: 272–274, 292–295.

77. Joseph Smith, *Small Arms of the World: A Basic Manual of Small Arms* (Harrisburg, PA: Stackpole Books, 1973), pp. 71–72; James Hamilton Sears and D. W. Wells, United States Navy Department, *The Chilean Revolution of 1891* (Washington, DC: Government Printing Office, 1893), p. 58; Robert W. D. Ball, *Mauser Military Rifles of the World* (Iola, WI: Krause Publications, 1996), pp. 11–13.

78. George von Rauch, "Ejército Argentino," *Armies and Weapons* 6 (1974), pp. 73–75.

79. *Ejército Nacional*, p. 332. After the Paraguayan war, Krupp model 1871 field and mountain pieces in 75 mm caliber were acquired. These were replaced by weapons of the same pattern and caliber in 1880, and these in turn were supplemented by yet another Krupp product, the model 1884 in the same caliber. Buenos Aires's *La Prensa* (October 7, 1880) mentions the arrival of the steamer *La Porteña*, with a cargo of "77 brand-new Krupp cannon, 5,000 sabers, and two-hundred officer's swords." The French 65 mm and Belgian 80 mm mountain guns were observed by the author at the Museo de Armas de La Nación in Buenos Aires during November 1987. Jürgen Schaefer, *Deustche militarhilfe an Südamerika: Militar und Rustunginteressen in Argentinien, Bolivia und Chile von 1914* (Dusseldorf: Bettlesman Universitatsverlag, 1974), pp. 32–33, 73–75. Schaefer erroneously quotes the number of cannon purchased as sixty-six and states this was done in secret. The public notice of the arrival of *La Porteña* and the details of the cargo prove him wrong in both respects. For details of the Argentine transfer of weapons to England during the Boer War, see "Cartas enviadas por Don Carlos Concha, Ministro de Chile en Buenos Aires a Don Rafael Errázuriz, Ministro de Relaciones Exteriores," *Historia* 10 (1971), pp. 345–360. In a letter dated July 6, 1900, for example, Concha states that Argentina had not replaced the 25,000 rifles and 14 batteries of artillery ceded to England. See Roberty W. D. Ball, *Mauser Military Rifles of the World* (Iola, WI: Krause Publications, 1996), pp. 23–24, 173–174; Gerhard Bruh, "Deustche einfluss und Deustche interessen in der professionalisierung einiger Lateinamerikanischer Armeen vor. Dem 1. Weltkrieg (1885–1914)," *JAL* 6 (1969), pp. 278–336. Between 1895 and 1895 Argentina purchased 653 Krupp cannon of various calibers worth over 60 million marks, while during the same period Chile obtained 341 cannon. Neftalí Carranza, *Oratoria argentina*, 5 vols. (Buenos Aires: Sese y Larrañaga Editores, 1905), V: 287–290. The Krupp model 1898 field guns were delivered during 1900–1901.

80. Riccheri's honesty was proverbial. Report No. 7172, December 4, 1941, Colonel John W. Lang to War Department General Staff, Military Intelligence Bureau (RG 165,

National Archives, Washington DC). While Riccheri was minister of war, the Argentine army purchased a number of Krupp artillery pieces. The Krupp agent offered Riccheri a large sum of money saying, "This, according to your custom is your commission." The general used the money to buy 130 mm guns for the army ("Discurso del General Riccheri en la tumba de Roca, 19 de octubre de 1915," *Revista del Círculo Militar* 15, no. 17 (Octubre 1915), pp. 633–642.

81. Humberto F. Burzio, *Armada nacional: Reseña histórica de su origen y desarrollo orgánico* (Buenos Aires: Departamento de Estudios Históricos Navales, serie B, no. 1, 1960), pp. 195–197.

82. Humberto F. Burzio, *Historia de la Escuela Naval Militar*, 3 vols. (Buenos Aires: Departamento de Estudios Históricos Navales, serie B, no. 16, 1972), I: 246–248, 320–321, 353.

83. Ibid., I: 236, 337–338, II: 458–459 for details of other South American students at the ENM; I: 367, II: 767–810 for details of the cruises undertaken by *La Argentina*.

84. Arguindeguy, *Apuntes sobre*, IV: 1315–1317; Burzio, *Armada Nacional*, p. 160.

85. Burzio, *Historia de la Escuela Naval Militar*, I: 337–338.

86. Burzio, *Armada Nacional*, p. 163.

87. Enrique Juan Triadó, *Historia de la Base Naval Puerto Belgrano* (Buenos Aires: Centro Naval, Instituto de Publicaciones Navales, 1992). War Department Report No. 0543, March 24, 1924 (RG 165, U.S. National Archives, Washington DC), "there are five batteries each of 4 Krupp 24cm L.35 mod. 1886–1887 on the coast between Punta Ancla and Punta Tejada. 1st Group includes batteries, 2 and 3, 2nd. Group batteries 4 and 5." Argentine Republic, *Memoria presentada al Congreso de 1899/1900 por el Ministro de Marina* (Buenos Aires, 1900), p. 75; Schaeffer, *Deustche Militarhilfe*, n. 26, p. 234. By 1900 three of the batteries were completed, while the remaining two as well as the armored casemates that housed the range finders were nearing completion. Twelve 280-mm howitzers were in the process of delivery.

88. Martí Garro, *Historia de la artillería argentina*, p. 454 for details of the artillery mounted in 1866. García Enciso, *Historia del Colegio Militar*, p. 143, for details of the Armstrong 150-lb. rifles at Martín García. One of these guns is preserved at the Museo Naval de la Nación, at San Fernando, Buenos Aires. It bears the following inscription: "Armstrong model 1877, 177 mm" (7-inch). Ricardo Piccirilli, Francisco Romay, and Leoncio Gianello, *Diccionario histórico argentino*, 6 vols. (Buenos Aires: Ediciones Históricas Argentinas, 1954) III: 415. Armada Argentina, *Infantería de Marina*; Argentine Republic, *Memoria del Ministerio de Guerra y Marina presentada al honorable Congreso por el Ministro de Guerra y Marina, General de division D. Eduardo Racedo* (Buenos Aires, 1888), pp. 63–67. The gun emplaced at Zárate was test-fired on November 15, 1887, during an official visit by President Miguel Juárez Celman. The first two shots bracketed the target, an old navy hulk anchored at the Globo Channel, some 12,500 meters away. The third round hit the target squarely and sank it.

89. Arguindeguy, *Apuntes sobre*, III: 1122, 1125, 1131, for details of these converted steamers. The armament of the *Brown* consisted of a single 16 pounder, later augmented by a pair of Krupp 75 mm guns.

90. Phelps, *The Tragedy of Paraguay*, pp. 110–112. Some of the Brazilian Monitor-types mounted 7-inch Armstrong guns (150 pounders). Burzio, *Armada*, p. 100; Arguindeguy, *Apuntes sobre*, III: 1221, 1238, 1278, for the characteristics of these ships. *El Plata* and *Los Andes* had a displacement of 1,667 tons, and their main armament consisted of two Armstrong 200-lb. rifled guns in an armored turret. The gunboats *Pil-*

comayo, República, Constitución, and *Bermejo* were armed with a single Armstrong 11-inch rifle and two Krupp 80 mm breech-loaders, while the corvettes *Paraná* and *Uruguay* displaced 550 tons and were initially fitted with Armstrong 7-inch rifles.

91. Armando Braun Menéndez, "Primera presidencia de Roca, 1880–1886," *HAC,* pp. 294–295; Humberto F. Burzio, *Historia del torpedo y sus buques en la Armada Argentina, 1874–1900* (Buenos Aires: Departamento de Estudios Históricos Navales, Serie B No. 12, 1968), pp. 19–20, 23–24, 98–99.

92. Burzio, *Historia del torpedo,* pp. 464–466.

93. Scheina, *Latin American Navies,* pp. 44–46.

94. Burzio, *Armada,* p. 74; Domingo De Mujro, *Discursos y escritos del Dr. Carlos Pellegrini* (Buenos Aires: Martín Garcia Librero-Editor, 1910, 2 vols.), II: 135–139.

95. *Conway's All the World's Warships: 1860–1905* (New York: Mayflower Books, 1979), pp. 351, 403; Arguindeguy, *Apuntes sobre,* IV, 1764–1776.

96. George von Rauch, "Cruisers for Argentina," *Warship International* 15 no. 4 (1978), pp. 297–317; M. G. Mullhall and E. T. Mulhall, *Handbook of the River Plate Republics* (Buenos Aires: M. H. & E. T. Mullhall, 1883), pp. 70–71. For information on naval personnel in 1902, see *The Argentine Yearbook for the Year 1902* (Buenos Aires: John Grand & Sons, 1902), pp. 28–29. For details of the *Garibaldi*-class cruisers, see Arguindeguy, *Apuntes sobre,* IV: 1764, 1778, 1800, 1814. See also Archivo Museo Roca Document No. 97/01 (Manuel Domecq Garcia to General Roca, January 19, 1897). Captain Domecq García was the first commander of the *Garibaldi* and the man who sailed her on her maiden voyage. Domecq García wrote to Roca, praising the sea-going virtues of the ship and informing Roca that the 300 foreign crewmen contracted had performed quite well.

97. Yaben, *Biografías argentinas,* IV: 94–97. Rivadavia was part of a very able group of officers trained in the cutters escadrilles, off the Patagonian coast. Graduated with special distinction from the Military Section of the Escuela de Artes y Oficios in 1869, he was posted to the war steamer *Guardia Nacional* and saw action against the Paraguayans. He left the service in 1870 but was readmitted in 1873. Climbing the naval ladder rung by rung, he served in sailing cutters and gunboats, then commanded steam corvettes, sailed 20,000 miles in twelve months aboard the training ship *La Argentina,* commanded cruisers, supervised the construction of three of the *Garibaldis,* was appointed chief of naval staff, and in October 1898, President Roca entrusted him with the post of minister of marine. Commodore Rivadavia knew the Patagonian coast intimately, having spent the better part of seven years exploring them. He personally piloted the "Belgrano" in 1899, when President Roca sailed to the Straits to meet with his Chilean counterpart. Unfortunately, this brilliant life was cut short by an accident at home. He died at thirty-six, on February 14, 1901,

98. Jaime Eyzaguirre, *Chile durante el gobierno de Errázuriz Echaurren: 1896–1901* (Santiago: Editorial Zig-Zag, 1957), pp. 251–252; Mariano De Vedia, *El General Roca y su tiempo* (Buenos Aires: Ediciones de la Patria Grande, 1962), pp. 137–138. After meeting with Roca at the Straits, Errázuriz conferred with high-ranking Chilean naval officers, vehemently opposed to any sort of agreement with Argentina. Tongue in cheek, Errázuriz shot back, "I trust you gentlemen will have no objections, particularly since you denied, not long ago, that their ships could take that route."

6

The Armed Forces of Chile

Early in the seventeenth century, the Spanish Crown established an army supported by a militia in Chile in order to protect the colonists from the continuous attacks of the Araucanian Indians. Toward the end of the colonial period there were 1,900 men in this army and about 16,000 in the militia. Senior officers were peninsular Spaniards, and Chileans made up the lower ranks. The officer corps of the militia was Chilean in almost its entirety. Most officers lacked administrative experience since the army's primary function was to provide protection against Indian attacks. Most officers lacked professional training, and there were not enough of them to maintain discipline in those units that had been organized. The army was far from being an efficient force.[1]

When news of the uprising of May 1810 at Buenos Aires reached Santiago, a similar process took place in the Chilean capital that culminated with the election of a junta on September 18, the date that signals the beginning of Chilean independence. At first the creoles were able to control the area around Santiago, but the royalists maintained a foothold in southern Chile that enabled them reorganize while awaiting reinforcements from Peru. A small expedition under Brigadier José Antonio Pareja landed at Concepción and began to advance toward the Central Valley. By September 1813, the royalists had regained the initiative, and the military situation of the insurgents was critical. To assist the Chileans in their struggle, the Argentine government dispatched a force of 300 men under Major Santiago Carrera. Attached to a division led by General Juan Mackenna, the Argentine Auxiliaries fought with distinction at an engagement that occurred on February 20 near the junction of the Itata and Nublé rivers and at the battles of Quilo (March 16) and Membrillar (March 20). On May 3, a convention known as the Treaty of Lircay was concluded between the Chilean insurgents and General Gavino Gainza, a royalist commander who had led a second invasion from Peru. The treaty granted Chile autonomy. In return, Chile agreed to remain a dominion of Spain and to abolish its national flag. José Fernando de Abascal, the viceroy of Peru, refused to sanction this treaty and ordered General Mariano Osorio to mount a third expedition against Chile. The royalists were able to defeat the creoles and eventually reconquer Santiago by October 1814. The patriot leaders and their families fled from the capital to the neighboring Argentine province of Cuyo. The governor of that province was José de San Martín, who was forging an army to carry out a plan of his conception, in which a well-organized invasion from Cuyo would free Chile from the royalists and provide him in turn with a base of operations against Peru, the bastion of Spanish power in the southern portion of South America. This was the Army of the Andes, a force that in training, discipline, morale, and equipment was superior to any other hitherto raised in South America. In composition it was preponderantly Argentine; less than one tenth of the troops were Chilean and even these fought under Argentine officers. General Bernardo O'Higgins and Captain Ramón Freire were in fact the only Chileans to hold command.[2]

After crossing the Andes in February 1817, San Martín defeated the royalists at Chacabuco and Maipú and thus secured the independence of Chile. Upon entering Santiago, the citizenry unanimously elected San Martín as head of the new state, but in accordance with instructions from the Argentine government, he declined political office and devoted his energies to the conduct of the war. Bernardo O'Higgins, a Chilean appointed by San Martín to command the Second Division of the Army of the Andes, was then acclaimed as the new Supreme Director of Chile.[3]

The Argentine government had empowered San Martín to enlist Chileans into the Army of the Andes. To replace casualties, he was authorized to form independent companies with Chilean soldiers and to incorporate them into existing army units. These independent companies would be expanded into full-fledged regiments under Chilean officers once a Chilean government was elected. However, once O'Higgins was appointed as head of state, he ordered the formation of a national army. As most units in this force were staffed by Argentine officers, O'Higgins created a military academy that would provide officers for the Chilean army, about half a century before Argentina established her own military academy.[4]

San Martín's strategy called for an invasion of Peru to consolidate Argentine and Chilean independence. The Argentine government up to this time had been thoroughly supportive of this scheme, but the country entered into a period of civil unrest and the head of state resigned. Furthermore, the threat of a Spanish expedition against the Plata forced the Argentine government to withdraw part of the Army of the Andes. As Argentina fell into total anarchy, the Chilean government appointed San Martín commander in chief of the expeditionary force that would liberate Peru. This force was almost 4,000 strong, of whom 2,451 were Argentines and 1,938 Chileans.[5]

The patriot forces first landed at the Bay of Paracas, south of Lima, while agents of San Martín demoralized the royalists by a propaganda campaign. San Martín was well aware that the viceroy of Peru had at his disposal an army of 17,000, which greatly outnumbered his own. Thus he waited, hoping for a bloodless victory. This strategy soon paid off. At first, the garrison at Guayaquil rebelled while units of the royalist army defected and the Chilean navy captured a Spanish warship anchored under the protection of the forts at Callao. Utterly demoralized, the royalists evacuated Lima in July 1821, and the expeditionary force entered the viceregal city in triumph, while San Martín proclaimed the independence of Peru and then assumed the title of Protector.[6]

Chilean political life in the nineteenth century offers a marked contrast to that of other Ibero-American republics. After a brief struggle for peace in the immediate post-independence period, and a civil war between its Conservative and Liberal parties in 1830, the former emerged triumphant. Diego Portales, the acknowledged leader of the Conservative faction, practically became a dictator during the period 1830–1837. Portales developed a highly centralized form of government during his tenure. It is not surprising that, in this atmosphere of relative stability, the military continued to develop as national institutions, while as we have seen, the armed forces of civil war–torn Argentina stagnated.[7]

A law enacted on October 23, 1835, fixed the strength of the Chilean army at 3,000 men. In the 1830s, this force would be most effectively employed against Bolivia. Marshall Andrés de Santa Cruz, the Bolivian dictator, had established an Andean Confederation composed of Bolivia and Peru, with Santa Cruz quite naturally as head of state. Mistrustful of Santa Cruz and his confederation, Chile sought an alliance with Argentina. Aside from geopolitical considerations, there were underlying economic concerns. The ports of Valparaíso and Lima competed for trade. Soon both countries imposed punitive tariffs against each other's products. However, war began as a result of a failed attempt by Chilean exiles in Peru to overthrow Portales. An expeditionary force under Admiral Manuel Blanco Encalada landed at Cobija in September 1837 but was soon encircled and forced to conclude an armistice at Paucarpata on November 17. However, the Chilean government rejected this treaty and organized a new expedition with the assistance of Peruvians opposed to Santa Cruz. In a series of encounters, the Chileans prevailed over the Andeans, until these were decisively defeated at the battle of Yungay, on January 20, 1839, and the Andean Confederation was dissolved.[8]

In the years that followed, limited modernization of army equipment was undertaken. The Escuela Militar (EM) replenished the officer ranks, and in the 1840s promising students were sent to French military schools. The lower ranks were frequently forced into military service, as in Argentina. A decree of 1839 limited the army to 2,200 men, the bulk of whom were stationed along the southern Indian frontier. This small standing force was backed by a national guard that by 1849 numbered 69,982. Financial stringency prevented an increase in manpower, while many breaches of discipline during this period were related to pay considerations. Aside from guarding the Indian frontier, the army was involved in the construction and repair of harbors, forts, and roads as well as in the protection of easily accessible points along the Chilean coast. Army equipment was obsolete and consisted of flintlock rifles and carbines. Chile's long and exposed coastline was devoid of any real protection, as most of the fortifications were in a state of complete disrepair and armed with ancient cannon.[9]

In 1866 Chile joined Bolivia, Ecuador, and Peru in a war against Spain. A Spanish naval squadron sent on a scientific mission prior to the war maintained undisputed control of the waters along the west coast of South America and bombarded Chilean ports with absolute impunity. At the conclusion of the war with Spain, Chilean authorities rapidly began to arm their coastal forts with heavy artillery, ranging from 68- to 600-pound guns. Particular attention was given to the forts around Valparaíso, a port city that had suffered a devastating bombardment from the Spanish fleet. By the late 1860s there were ten batteries protecting Valparaíso, with 87 pieces of artillery, ranging in caliber from 68 to 300 pounds, though it was estimated that at least 150 cannon were required to protect the coast adequately.[10]

A national cannon foundry was established at Limache in 1865 and a few 300-pound iron cannon were produced. These proved unsatisfactory, and it was decided to use bronze in all future gun castings. A few 6- and 12-pounder smoothbore cannon were delivered in 1868; but their cost was judged prohibitive and the end product inferior to models available in the United States and Europe, and production was discontinued. In 1869, breech-loading Minié rifles were acquired for the infantry and Spencer repeating carbines for the cavalry. These weapons were replaced in 1873 by Comblain rifles, but small quantities of other shoulder weapons, such as the Beaumont, Grass, and Chassepot rifles, were acquired, while the older weapons were handed over to the national guard. The government also instituted reforms in the artillery branch, and a commission was sent to Europe to study methods of organization, discipline, and instruction. This commission also sent various samples of artillery pieces to Chile for testing purposes. After tests were completed, two Krupp models (a 60 mm mountain piece and an 87 mm field gun) and the Gatling gun were adopted by the Chilean army.[11]

The Chilean army maintained a sizable portion of its forces along the Indian frontier, which began south of the Bío-Bío River, as in colonial times. Indian unrest increased in the 1850s, following a civil war in Chile. Anxious to settle the region between the Bío-Bío and Tolten rivers, the Chilean government approved a three-stage plan for the pacification of Araucania. In the first stage, the line would be advanced toward the Malleco River, while colonists remained behind the safety of the forts. During the second stage, a subdivision and sale of lands would take place, thus allowing for colonization while containing Indian raids. On the third and final stage, wherever there were easy-to-defend lands of quality, they were to be colonized by Chileans and foreign settlers, thus absorbing the Indians at long last into the Chilean body politic. Little was accomplished until 1861, when the army disobeyed orders, crossed the Bío-Bío and established detachments on the ruins of ancient colonial forts. In the sporadic fighting that ensued, the army deployed 4,000 men supported by 2,000 civilian volunteers. Politics delayed the pacification process when intrigues forced the retirement of the commander of the Frontier Forces, General Cornelio Saavedra, in 1864.[12]

The pacification process was further delayed by the war with Spain in 1865. Saavedra, who was reinstated after the war, proposed the construction of roads to the south as well as the colonization of the frontier. When the line of colonization was extended, the Indians revolted, and the so-called War Without Quarter began. Small Indian war parties raided the fort at Chihauihue in April 1868, and two military expeditions were sent south of the Malleco under Majors Pedro Lagos and Démofilos Fuentes. Lagos detached a force of forty-five men under Captain Juan José de San Martín to set a trap for the Indians, but the reverse occurred, as the Chileans fell foul of a larger Indian force and were decimated. Only San Martín, an Indian scout, and two soldiers were able to escape with their lives.[13]

These actions were characteristic of Indian warfare in the Chilean frontier. Small Indian parties would attack farmhouses, burn crops, and kill settlers. The army in turn undertook punitive strikes against Indian camps with units ranging in size from 40 to 300 men. As punishment, Indian huts, crops, and food reserves were destroyed, while corpses of Indians killed in such raids would be suspended from nearby trees to induce panic. One of the major engagements of the campaign took place in January 1869, when a small force under General José M. Pinto engaged 2,000 Indian warriors under Chief Quilapán. When Pinto was reinforced by the fourth infantry battalion Quilapán retreated. Peace talks between the Chilean government and some of the leading Indian chieftains eventually led to a peace treaty signed at Arauco in September 1869. The Araucanians agreed not to undertake further raids and to respect the new frontier line at Malleco. For its part the Chilean government promised to establish missions in the Indian territories, where young men would be sent to be educated, and to pardon all crimes committed by the Indians during the uprising.[14]

General Pinto judged the treaty to be worthless, a mere tactical delay by the Indians, who were short of supplies. In October, Pinto decided to force the issue and violated the peace agreement by demanding the surrender of "all Indians guilty of crimes." When Chief Quilapán failed to comply, Pinto organized three divisions of 500 men each and began operations in March 1870. After minor encounters, the army reached the Cautín River and began to extend the frontier line further south. This marked the beginning of the end for the Indian frontier, as by the end of the decade, over 100,000 hectares had been wrested from the Indians. The Chilean conquest of Araucania was undertaken at the same time as the Argentines launched their punitive strike, which would culminate in the conquest of Patagonia. As in Argentina, the railroad, the telegraphs, and new armaments played a vital role. A sapper battalion was organized to build roads to link the forts with the southern settlements, but the outbreak of the War of the Pacific put a temporary end to the pacification and occupation of the Indian frontier.[15]

THE WAR OF THE PACIFIC

At the outbreak of the War of the Pacific, in April 1879, the Chilean army numbered 2,440 men (1,500 infantry, 530 cavalry, 410 artillery), including 401 officers. The national guard had been reduced to 6,500 men because of a lack of funds. The allied armies of Bolivia and Peru totaled 10,452 men, while their combined population was at least twice that of Chile, which barely exceeded 1.6 million. Chile, however, had the undisputed advantage of a more homogeneous population, largely of mestizo stock, which was far more integrated into national life than the vast, submerged Indian populations of the allies. The Chileans were also accustomed to military and national discipline and possessed a sense of national identity almost entirely absent among its adversaries. In addition, the Chilean nation was better organized and endowed with an efficient central administration nurtured by decades of political stability. Furthermore, Chile's military equipment, breech-loading rifles, Krupp artillery, and Gatling guns totally outclassed the obsolete park of her enemies, and the Chilean navy soon established supremacy in the waters adjacent to the Pacific coast of South America, an important factor since it prevented the allies from securing military equipment and supplies from Europe and the United States.[16]

The Chilean government decided to invade the Peruvian nitrate fields at Tarapacá in order to exert economic pressure on Peru and to help Chile finance the war. In order to capture the province of Tarapacá, the Chilean army dispatched troops west through the desert, to prevent reinforcements sent from Bolivia from reaching the coastal areas, while landings were effected at Pisagua and Junín to encircle the defenders. At Pisagua, the allies had concentrated the third Bolivian division under General Juan Buendía, 200 Peruvian national guards and some artillery. The Chileans landed on November 2. The fleet overpowered the defenders by an artillery bombardment. The landing was initially checked by small arms fire, while poor handling of the landing barges caused some of them to overturn. Nevertheless, the Chileans won their objective and the allies withdrew, leaving the water deposits and the railway station at Pisagua intact. Both were of considerable value in the sun-baked Tarapacá sands.[17]

Slowly, the Chileans continued their drive inland, southward toward Iquique, clashing with the allies at Dolores on November 19. The Chilean army had a splendid cavalry force and powerful artillery support, thirty-four cannon as well as some Gatling guns. The Chileans had captured the rail head at Pisagua, as we have seen, and the water supplies and thus were regularly provisioned. Not surprisingly, the Andeans were defeated. After a grueling fifty-hour march through the desert, the allied forces reached Tarapacá on November 22. Acting on faulty intelligence that underestimated allied strength at 1,500 men, a Chilean force of 3,900 was moving inland. The exhausted allied forces, about 4,500 strong, launched an attack on November 27. Much to the amazement of the Chileans, who expected a weak defense by a smaller and utterly demoralized force, the Peruvian troops repulsed their assaults and counterattacked. Discouraged, the Chileans retreated, throwing down their rifles and abandoning a battery of Krupp artillery. Elated at their victory, the Peruvians pursued the enemy on foot over a distance of eight kilometers. However, exhaustion, the lack of cavalry, and draught animals forced the allies to retreat, burying the captured Chilean cannon in the sand. Tactically, the battle of Tarapacá was a Peruvian victory, as the Chilean army was routed in the field. Strategically it was a defeat, as the allies, exhausted and poorly supplied, retreated to Arica, leaving Chile in complete control of the province of Tarapacá.[18]

Public opinion in Chile nevertheless demanded another offensive. Defeat, on the other hand, served to destabilize the government of Peru. President Manuel Prado left the country on December 17, reportedly to buy arms in Europe, and left his vice president in charge. The troops of the Lima garrison gave signs of unrest, and mob demonstrations against the government took place. Nicolás Piérola seized the opportunity and proclaimed himself head of state on December 21, with the support of the populace and the military, which loudly demanded a more efficacious conduct of the war. In direct contrast, the authority of Chilean President Anibal Pinto and of his war minister, General Rafael Sotomayor, was reaffirmed. Sotomayor began to reorganize the Chilean army, and after a three-month delay, operations resumed with the invasion of Arica. The allies, who had regrouped, could now field an army of 13,149 men with sixteen cannon, including six ultramodern Krupps, and six machine guns. The Chileans had at their disposal 15,550 men and four batteries of Krupp artillery. On paper, both armies seemed to be equivalent, but Chile enjoyed unity of command, while relations between allied army commanders were strained, thus making cooperation rather difficult. The Chilean rank and file were better trained than their opposite numbers, and their artillery employed Krupp models which had at least twice the range of the guns used by the Andeans.[19]

The attack began on June 6, 1880, after the Chileans had seized Moquehua and Tacna. The guns at the Morro, the imposing hill commanding the Bay of Arica, were all facing west, toward the sea. Their coastal mountings and extreme weight made it impossible to move or depress these guns against the Chilean forces that attacked from the east, while the Arica garrison was outnumbered three to one by the attackers. After furious fighting, Arica fell on June 7, and the road to Lima was wide open. Chile then proceeded to expand her army to 41,981 men, the greater part of whom were deployed near the theater of operations, while 4,400 men guarded the Indian frontier in the South.[20]

Piérola, who had become a virtual dictator of Peru, demonstrated remarkable energies and organizational capabilities by raising an army of 42,837. However, of this impressive total only 20,000 were available for the defense of Lima. The Peruvian capital was protected by a rather primitive and poorly constructed system of trenches that stretched through the surrounding hills. Furthermore, the defending troops were poorly trained. Their artillery was rather numerous but often obsolete, and their light armament was a heterogeneous collection of rifles and ancient muskets, while their cavalry lacked horses. While the United States attempted to mediate in the conflict, both nations continued their preparations. The Chileans, for their part, undertook a series of landings between September and November, forcibly collecting taxes and destroying harbor installations. While the landing force to be employed against Lima embarked at Arica in the early part of November 1880, the Chilean navy blockaded Callao and bombarded Chancay, Ancón, and Chorrillos.[21]

The results were predictable. Chorrillos, near Lima, fell to the Chileans on January 13 and Miraflores two days later. Piérola fled with his staff when the Chileans occupied Lima and was succeeded by Colonel Avelino Pérez, who carried out guerrilla operations against the enemy for another two years, until an armistice was signed at Ancón, a town north of Lima, in November 1883.[22]

Despite the surge of nationalistic feelings and the euphoria that swept Chile in the aftermath of the War of the Pacific, the complaints of the public and press about the shortcomings of the Chilean armed forces were not entirely ignored. Though the populace and some of its leaders were quick to give their nation the title of the Prussia of South America, some farsighted officers pressed for urgent reforms.

TOWARD THE PROFESSIONAL ARMY: 1884–1902

During the war, Sotomayor had established a general staff, surgeon, and chaplain services followed by the Intendencia General del Ejército y Armada, or Army and Navy Supply Branch, as well as the Dirección General de Maestranza y del Parque de Artillería, which dealt with the repair and workshops and artillery depot. Civilian doctors headed the surgeon branch, while a corps of engineers and mechanics was attached to the general staff. To remedy the lack of a scouting element, a Partida de Exploradores, or reconnaissance detachment, was formed. More importantly, the combat branches (infantry, cavalry, artillery), which had hitherto operated as a sort of loose conglomeration of units, were now grouped into four divisions. The annual report presented to Congress by the minister of war and marine indicated that the war had demonstrated the need to update military institutions that were already outmoded and detrimental to the army's overall performance and further demanded the creation of a permanent general staff. Some officers who had studied the campaigns of the Franco-Prussian war felt that mere improvisation in the field and the bravery of the common soldier should give way to the expertise of the officer corps.[23]

There were, however, many other deficiencies to be corrected, especially in the national guard, which would be mobilized in the event of war. The Chilean national guard was of doubtful quality at best. Only the frequent delays that occurred during the invasion of Peru had given Chile the opportunity to update its training. Its strength varied from 53,220 men in 1867 to 6,559 in 1878 and

19,000 in 1884. Recruited by provinces, national guard troops met on Sundays and holidays. Their instruction was deficient, slow, and outmoded. Recruitment was difficult because of the lack of enthusiasm, and by 1890, the strength of the national guard was only half that required. The army of the line also experienced problems in attaining its budgetary strength in the postwar years, largely because of a high rate of desertion. Lack of public enthusiasm also made it difficult for the national guard to secure enlistments. In 1890, only half the required number of men were available. To upgrade the Chilean army, the services of Emil Körner, a German artillery captain, were contracted in 1885. Körner was originally picked as an instructor for the Escuela Militar and entrusted with the organization of the war academy. During the Civil War of 1891, although the bulk of the army remained loyal to the government, Körner and many of the officers he had molded offered their services to the rebel junta at Iquique. Körner drilled the rebel army, which was better armed than the royalist forces, and led it to final victory. As a result, he became an all-powerful figure in the Chilean army and was able to contract additional German officers to help him mold the Chilean army into a miniature replica of its Prussian counterpart. To achieve this end, Körner suggested reforms that called for the establishment of four cantons, with an army division assigned to each. The national guard in each of these cantons would constitute the reserve. Guard registrations totaled 472,688 men.[24]

As in Argentina and in Germany, the national guard was organized by age groups into (1) the active guard, which comprised all males between the ages of eighteen and twenty-one, or 82,318 men; (2) the passive guard in the twenty-two–thirty age group; and (3) the sedentary guard, which included 233,083 men in the forty–fifty year group. In theory, it would have been possible to raise an army of 200,000 men, but the new organization left much to be desired. Its battle effectiveness decreased in relation to its numbers. Nevertheless, by the end of the nineteenth century, Chilean military sources claimed that their trained reserve numbered 150,000 men, who could be mobilized in thirty days in the event of war.[25]

Körner boasted in 1898 that in case of war with Argentina, 87,700 trained soldiers would be immediately available and that these would be in Argentine soil within forty-eight hours. The Argentines, unimpressed, were skeptical about the effectiveness of such a force, and they were not alone, for there were men on the other side of the Andes who had similar misgivings. A number of high-ranking Chilean army officers protested the changes introduced by Körner, among them General Emil Canto, who had previously worked closely with Körner. To remedy deficiencies in her mobilization system, in 1900 Chile enacted the first mandatory universal conscription law in South America. All Chilean males between the ages of twenty and forty-five were required to serve one year, which in practice was reduced to nine months. Unlike the Argentine conscription reforms enacted by Riccheri, there were serious deficiencies with the Chilean mobilization system. Nor were the shortcomings of the Chilean army limited to manpower mobilization schemes, but rather seemed widespread, as they affected the training of officers and noncommissioned officers as well. Prior to the War of the Pacific, the intellectual level of the average Chilean officer was rather low. The Escuela Militar lacked capable instructors, and most cadets had entered that institution because of disciplinary or economic problems. The highlights of training at the EM were close-order drills and parade rehearsals for the national independence day.[26]

Shortly after his arrival in Chile, Körner assumed duties as an instructor at the EM and began planning the organization of a war academy. About a year later, the academy was inaugurated. Its purpose was described in a government decree: "To elevate the level of scientific instruction of army officers, that they may be able, in case of war, to utilize new methods of combat and new armaments."[27]

The three-year curriculum at the academy included tactics, fortifications, cartography, mathematics, world history, general military science, and German. Out of the first fifteen graduates, five were sent to Germany for advanced training. The reduced budget allotted to training led to complaints by Körner, as he lamented the state of the military profession in Chile. To upgrade the level of the noncommissioned officers who had traditionally risen from the ranks, the Escuela de Clases was organized in 1887. The annual reports, or memorias, for the next few years would praise the performance of the army's training institutions, but one must remember that these reports were intended for public consumption and could hardly have reflected any other tone. Körner had been chief of the general staff since the Civil War of 1891, and by 1892 he was again in charge of the war academy. During the next few years he also supervised and directed the acquisitions of armaments in Germany. His power seemed unlimited. In 1895 Körner returned from Germany with the largest mission ever to serve in South America: forty-five officers to serve as instructors in the Chilean army. Another twenty-five German officers arrived in 1897. German missions would in fact guide the Chilean army well into the 1920s. Their performance is open to question. German advisors, as all members of other foreign military missions sent to less developed countries have always done, pretended that no progress could have taken place without their assistance. In fact, German instructors created the myth that German methods and German training had transformed the Chilean army into the best-trained force in South America. By 1898, however, the instruction of the Chilean national guard was still deficient, and the army lacked instructors, equipment, and barracks. Körner himself did not consider the army to be ready for war in the powder-charged atmosphere of 1898, and so informed the president of Chile. Körner envisaged the Chilean army as a cadre force, a skeleton or structure to be completed in the event of war. The structure would be provided by the officers and noncommissioned officers. Conscripts would be called to arms when required, but they would have only a minimal amount of training previous to the conflict. All infantry battalions, cavalry squadrons, and artillery batteries were to consist of four companies, two of which would be at full complement. The other two companies possessed only a skeleton crew of officers and noncommissioned officers. Conscripts would be added to such units in the event of war. However, the funds allowed by the military budgets never permitted the mobilization of sufficient troops or the upgrade of reserve training.[28]

These symptoms, coupled with further reforms after the boundary dispute with Argentina had been resolved, give a hint that the Chilean army left much to be desired as an institution. These were the reforms of 1906, which were intended to mold the Chilean army into a miniature replica of its Prussian original. The reforms were unsuccessful. According to Frederick M. Nunn, the failure of this scheme was largely due to the fact that Chile could not afford to maintain an army as large and complex as that called for and that, furthermore, the new organization called for an intelligent and disciplined soldier class similar to the one that existed in Germany. Nunn tells us that this class of men was lacking in Chile; the lack of funds prevented the mobilization of sufficient conscripts to fulfill the 1906 reforms. In turn the lack of troops to command caused an inordinate growth of the officer and noncommissioned officer corps; it also prevented proper maneuvers and exercises and, hence, the development of a trained officer corps.[29]

This is one of the first indications that Chilean military might and efficiency were greatly exaggerated. Another such indication would come in 1920, when for political reasons the government of Chile, determined to keep Arturo Alessandri from the presidency, leaked false reports of Peruvian concentrations in the north and mobilized its own forces. This mobilization of 1920 revealed a true picture of the Chilean military situation:

It showed the Chilean army as it really was, equipment was lacking, what was available was outdated and in poor condition. Capable leaders, versed in the modern techniques of war, were scarce; well trained troops were in reality poorly prepared as they were equipped and uniformed, the artillery, so necessary in rugged terrain, was not capable of effective performance.[30]

If this was the result, after more than thirty years of cumulative training under German instruction, one cannot but wonder what the real effects of German advisors and methods upon the efficiency of the Chilean army could have really been in 1898, certainly far below the standards that certain Chilean chronicles of the period suggest. Chilean historians are fond of stressing the point that in 1898, because of the greater experience of its officer corps, which included veterans of the War of the Pacific, the Chilean army was an efficient fighting machine. There is no concrete evidence to suggest this or to sustain the claim often made by Chilean writes that their national army was better trained and equipped than the Argentine. In fact, the opposite was true. Argentine intelligence reports at this time indicated that the much-vaunted Chilean war machine was not better and was perhaps much worse than their own.[31]

The perceptions we have regarding Chilean military capabilities come essentially from two sources that as far from impartial on the subject: Chilean government reports and the German instructors. It is highly unlikely that their self-appraisal would contain anything but laudatory tones. German military journals were full of praise for the Chilean army, but praise tinged with the same patronizing, proprietary air the British would take about the Argentine railways, patterned after their own. On the other hand, the German military praise was ambivalent about Argentina. The professionalization of the Argentine army began in the 1880s, under Julio A. Roca. In 1884, the general staff evolved from a simple bureau for the transmission of orders into one of the major institutions for the preparation of war. As we have seen, Riccheri headed the Arms Purchasing Commission in Europe with efficiency and zeal. Not only did he test virtually every rifle, but by shrewd negotiations saved the nation millions of pesos while obtaining a mountain railway and over 100 more cannon than otherwise provided in the budget. Hence, the Argentines did not require a German to lead (or influence) their arms-purchasing process. Similarly, when the government did contract a German mission in 1899, it was to organize the Escuela Superior de Guerra, or war academy, that would be established in the following year. On July 1990 Riccheri was appointed war minister and began to draft law no. 4031, which established obligatory military service, an organizational feat that matched the achievements of Körner. The Argentines were willing to adopt certain features of the German military system but would not allow themselves to be awed by the Germans or slavishly imitate them, as had the Chileans. Rejected, the Germans reacted like spurned lovers.[32]

THE CHILEAN ARMS PARK

At the outbreak of the War of the Pacific, Chile had about 60,000 rifles and carbines of six different patterns and manufacturers. There were eighty-seven pieces of mountain and field artillery, of which fifty-four were old-fashioned muzzle-loaders, as well as six Gatling guns. There were, as we have seen, a large number of heavy caliber pieces in the coastal fortifications, and at the end of the war substantial stocks of small arms and artillery captured from the Allies were brought back to Chile. During the 1891 civil war, the Congressionalist faction purchased 15,000 rifles, 2,000 Winchester carbines, 600 revolvers, 12 Krupp light artillery pieces, and 2,500 cavalry sabers. At the outbreak of hostilities, with the exception of the forts around Valparaíso, coastal defenses were negligible. The forts at Valparaíso mounted nineteen guns, mostly Armstrong and Krupp models, ranging from 8- to 9.2-inch in caliber. Talcahuano, the port of Concepción, was protected by five Armstrong breech-loading rifles and a few old muzzle-loaders. The two small forts at Caldera mounted one gun each, while a single Armstrong 9.2-inch breech-loading rifle was mounted on the island at the harbor of Iquique. By the end of July, a one-gun battery was under construction on the northern end of the harbor. These coastal fortifications were manned by the 1,200 men of the Regimiento de Artillería de Costas.[33]

A Chilean historian, who would have his readers believe that in 1893–1894 the Chilean armed forces were superior to those of Argentina by virtue of their training as well as their arsenal, lists almost 71,000 rifles and carbines of at least fourteen different systems. The list also includes 145 pieces of artillery, both field and mountain models, of which eighty-six were Krupps, most of which dated back to the 1870s, and thirty-eight guns that were considered useless. What this list of armaments really indicates is that the Chilean army in the 1880s and early 1890s was not as ill equipped as its Argentine counterpart. To close the gap, from 1894 onward, Chile ordered over 100,000 Mauser rifles and carbines, 60 Hotchkiss machine guns, and 238 Krupp field and mountain guns in 75 mm caliber, followed by a further 73 pieces of the same caliber on December 23, 1901. Chile had numerous forts along her coast, though the guns installed in these in most cases dated back to the late 1860s. To correct this situation, thirty Krupp 57 mm light cannon in Grusson-armored cupolas and twelve heavy Krupp 280 mm coastal guns were ordered in 1895, although few of the latter were actually emplaced by 1898.[34]

Thus, during the 1890s the Chilean army had received large quantities of equipment from abroad, but it was quite apparent that Chile simply could not afford to equip her army as Argentina did, and what was particularly disturbing to the Chileans was that by the turn of the century, their navy had lost its generation-old supremacy over Argentina.

THE CHILEAN NAVY, 1817–1902

The first Chilean naval squadron was organized in 1817 on the basis of a number of armed merchantmen that were sent to break the Spanish blockade at Valparaíso in April 1818. These improvised men-of-war, supplemented by warships obtained in Europe and the United States, soon gave Chile naval supremacy on the west coast of South America. Command of the Chilean fleet was entrusted in 1819 to Lord Thomas Cochrane, a British naval officer and a veteran of the Napoleonic Wars. Cochrane would eventually command the Chilean naval squadron that transported the joint Argentine-Chilean expedition to Peru in 1820.[35]

The Chilean fleet operated almost with impunity, as Spanish naval forces in the area were considerably weaker. Cochrane caught the imagination of the Chileans when in bold action he led a boarding party that captured the Spanish frigate *Esmeralda* as she lay under anchor, under the protection of the forts at Callao. Cochrane was one of many foreign advisors in the Chilean navy. In fact, virtually all Chilean warships were commanded by foreign officers, despite the establishment of a naval school, or Academia de Guardiamarinas, in 1818. This state of affairs would continue well into the 1830s. When Chile went to war against the Andean Confederation in 1837, her navy soon established an ascendancy over the Peruvian fleet that it maintained throughout the entire conflict. However, the fleet was disbanded at the end of the war for reasons of economy, and the only vessels that remained in operation were two small brigs, the *Colo-Colo* and the *Janequeo*. Their ruinous condition soon forced the Chilean government to embark on a program of naval reequipment.[36]

In May 1840, the Chilean navy took delivery of a powerful new frigate, the 1,100-ton *Chile*, ordered in France. The vessel was impressive on paper, but after a few years it was relegated to the role of pontoon. The Chilean-built *Ancud*, a small brig of around twenty tons, was delivered in 1843, followed a few years later by fourteen whaleboats rated as gunboats and intended for the protection of the port of Valparaíso. The first steam-powered vessel, the 140-ton *Cazador*, was incorporated in 1851, as were the corvette *Constitución* and the brig *Infatigable*. Three other steam-powered vessels, the 800-ton corvette *Esmeralda* and the transports *Maipó* and *María Isabel*, were ordered in 1856, while a second-hand steamer, the 800-ton *Independencia*, was bought in Peru during 1859. By the end of that year the Chilean navy auctioned off its sailing ships and was reduced to three vessels, the *Esmeralda*, the *Maipó*, and the *Independencia*. Fleet strength would remain unchanged for the next six years, until the war with Spain.[37]

As we have seen in chapter 2, a Spanish naval squadron sent to South America soon became involved in a diplomatic incident that eventually led to war. Bolivia, Ecuador, and Peru were joined by Chile in their struggle against the former mother country. The Chilean navy, reduced to a few steamers, was powerless to prevent the Spanish blockade and the bombardment of Valparaíso. Chile nevertheless derived some satisfaction, when the *Esmeralda*, a thirty-two-gun corvette, was able to overpower and capture the Spanish gunboat *Covadonga*, a vessel half its size and armed with a single cannon.[38]

The lessons of the war with Spain were not lost upon Chile. The country was reminded that a well-armed fleet could wreak havoc along her vast and unprotected coastline. In 1869 Chile took delivery of two armored corvettes of 1,690 tons displacement, the *O'Higgins* and the *Chacabuco*. In 1872 the government ordered the construction of two 3,500-ton ocean-going ironclads, which became the *Blanco Encalada* and the *Cochrane*, as well as the gunboat *Magallanes*, the corvette *Abtao*, and the *Tolten*, a paddle steamer intended for fluvial service. In addition, four spar-torpedo boats were purchased in 1878. These vessels constituted the Chilean navy at the outbreak of the War of the Pacific.[39]

The Chilean navy would play a preponderant role in this conflict. It was composed of larger, more powerful vessels; yet it dispatched a weak force, the elderly corvette *Esmeralda* and the gunboat *Covadonga*, to blockade the port of Callao. Its main naval antagonist, Peru, possessed an armored frigate, the *Independencia*, the *Huascar*, a powerful monitor with a good turn of speed built in England, and a pair of older American-built monitors, which in the event could be used only as floating batteries and saw limited action during the conflict.[40]

The first naval engagement of the war occurred on May 12, 1879, when the *Huascar* sank the *Esmeralda* and the Peruvian armored frigate *Independencia* struck a reef while chasing the *Covadonga* and became a total loss. The remaining Peruvian ironclad, the *Huascar*, was slightly faster than the Chilean ironclads, and thus able to escape them. The *Huascar* cruised along the Chilean coast, captured a Chilean transport ship with troops aboard, and paralyzed the movements of the Chilean army until she was trapped at Point Angamos, off the coast of Antofagasta by a Chilean squadron composed of the *Blanco Encalada* and the *Cochrane*. Despite the overwhelming odds in their favor, the Chilean ironclads required an hour and a half to disable and capture the *Huascar*, and only after four succeeding Peruvian commanders and thirty other seamen had been killed. The battle of Angamos left Chile in complete control of the seas. Peru was effectively blocked and thus prevented from receiving munitions from abroad, which eventually led to a Chilean victory.[41]

The uneasy years that followed the armistice at Ancón, which ended the War of the Pacific, and the still-unresolved boundary dispute with Argentina prompted the Chilean government to procure new warships abroad. The exploits of the *Huascar* were fresh in many naval minds. Thanks to a fast turn of speed, the monitor had been able to outrun the Chilean fleet until Angamos. This episode demonstrated the need for fast cruising vessels. Chile in fact ordered the *Capitán Pratt* from the Elswick yard in 1879, but the British government prevented delivery until the end of the conflict. The *Pratt* was rather outdated by then, and Chile was glad when Japan offered 80,000 pounds sterling for it. In its place, the Elswick works began construction of a new protected cruiser that would become the prototype for all others of its type built afterward, a fast and well-armed vessel that became the *Esmeralda*. This was a fateful decision, since as a result of the boundary dispute with Argentina, both countries ordered progressively larger versions of these vessels, until Argentina replied to the Chilean protected cruisers with armored cruisers that totally outclassed them in artillery as well as in armor. High speed in the protected cruisers was obtained at the expense of protection, something apparently overlooked by Chilean naval strategists.[42]

A law enacted on August 20, 1887, that provided for fleet expansion and modernization led to the construction of the battleship *Pratt*, two cruisers and a pair of torpedo-boat destroyers, the *Condell* and the *Lynch*. Only the latter had been delivered when a naval uprising against President José M. Balmaceda led to the civil war of 1891. The Congressionalist, or anti-Balmaceda, faction retained control of most of the navy, while the loyalists could only count on the two newly delivered torpedo boat destroyers and a gunboat. The *Pinto* and the *Errázuriz*, the two protected cruisers provided by the naval program in 1887, were in the final stages of completion at the Forges et Chantiers de la Meditanée, at La Seyne, Toulon. Since warships seemed to be the key to victory, the government pressured the builders to hurry completion, and in the event the vessels sailed without completing their official trials. To man these two warships, loyalist agents hired crews comprised of a most heterogenous mixture that included Frenchmen, Spaniards, Turks, Chinese, and a sampler of virtually all other nationalities. The voyage of the *Pinto* was a veritable odyssey that took her to Genoa, Mahón, Southampton, and Kiel to acquire the necessary fittings and supplies. On August 15, on her way to keel, the luckless crew ran the ship aground. On the return voyage from Kiel to Le Havre, the engine crew mutinied. The cruisers reached Chile in 1892, after the end of the civil war, with their engines seriously damaged. The Congressionalists were able to effectively maintain control of the seas and thus prevented the loyalists from securing military supplies. They also carried out amphibious operations that assured victory for their cause.[43]

New construction would add four more cruisers, a torpedo gunboat, six destroyers and six torpedo boats by 1898. Two destroyers, and three cruisers would follow in 1901. However, Chilean strength vis-à-vis her eastern neighbor was declining, as can be appreciated in Appendix A to this chapter. But in order to properly compare the navies of Argentina and Chile, the quality of Chilean naval personnel as well as its recruiting procedures should be analyzed.

During the war of independence, foreign seamen were contracted to crew Chilean navy vessels. However, in 1818 a levy of 2,000 vagrants was effected in Santiago, and 500 of these were destined to the national squadron. The practice of forced enlistment was maintained in the Chilean navy until the 1880s. Such crews did not inspire much confidence and were quick to desert or create disciplinary problems. In fact, the navy was forced to embark armed troops aboard its warships in order to preserve discipline. At the end of the 1880s, forced enlistment was replaced by voluntary service. However, the low rate of pay resulted in a high rate of desertion. In 1889, for example, out of a naval roster of 815, 41 percent deserted. By 1898, naval personnel were recruited by Enlistment Bureau, or Oficina General de Enganche, in the capitals of maritime provinces. Individual ships could enlist junior petty officers and *grumetes*, or boys, to complete their crews. Enlistment generally lasted a year, but this was judged insufficient to train recruits. When the conscription law of 1900 was enacted, the term of enlistment in the navy was increased to two years.[44]

Foreign technicians, particularly in the engineering branch, had been used as late as the War of the Pacific, and the practice continued until the turn of the century despite the creation of a school for engineers. Efforts to use indigenous personnel often led to rather amusing but expensive episodes. When the cruiser *Esmeralda* was delivered, the ship was in the hands of Chilean engine crews for only six weeks before her machinery required urgent repairs and her boilers were ruined. Similarly, in 1893, when the battleship *Pratt* arrived from the French builders, the foreign engineers were replaced by Chilean crews, which experienced all sorts of difficulties trying to manage the ship's intricate machinery.[45]

Although Chile was reputedly a seafaring nation, from the evidence gathered, the inescapable fact emerges that she experienced considerable trouble not only in crewing her ships but also lacked sufficient seamen to man her merchant fleet. The Chilean merchant marine, which employed vessels of a much simpler technology, employed 1,531 seamen in 1904. Of these, 1,177 were Chilean, 700 of whom were cooks, mess boys, and servants, while only 557 were employed as able-bodied seamen. By comparison, the 354 foreign seamen filled most of the officer and navigator ranks. The number of Chilean naval personnel in service, however, grew in response to new acquisitions made during the arms race with Argentina. In 1883 there were 1,703 naval personnel of all ranks; there were 3,340 in 1894, 4,559 in 1900, 5,260 in 1901, and 5,800 in 1902. There were serious shortages of skilled personnel at all levels. Swedish pilots and navigators as well as English engineers were listed by the naval ministry report for 1899. This publication noted the shortage of junior officers, which averaged over 40 percent in all categories. If the lack of motivation, or perhaps enthusiasm, produced poor results in officer procurement, among the lower ranks the desertion rate was alarmingly high. In 1900 there were 3,374 seamen and 564 deserters, or a rate of 14 percent, an improvement over previous years, when it reached 23 percent.[46]

Colonel Thomas Holdich, the geographer sent by the British Crown to survey the disputed territory in 1902, visited Argentina and Chile. Holdich found the Argentine navy to be superior in terms of ships, armor, and guns but felt that Chile had the indisputable advantage of a seaborne and seafaring people from which to recruit her naval personnel.[47]

This same rationale was bandied about in Chilean naval circles when the Argentine navy surged ahead in the arms race. One of the premises of psychological warfare is that a nation will attempt to demoralize a prospective enemy by exalting its own feat of arms and the efficiency of its armed forces while at the same time undermining the enemy's confidence in its own armed establishment. The unfortunate fact about propaganda is that sometimes the originator believes it himself. The comparisons between the armed forces of Argentina and Chile are inevitable, particularly since both countries were on the brink of war on several occasions during the period 1878–1902. An analysis of the arms available to the potential rivals as well as their comparative naval strength is in order.

THE ARGENTINE AND CHILEAN ARMED FORCES COMPARED

If war had broken out between Argentina and Chile at the turn of the century, the Platine nation would have effected a two-pronged attack through Tierra del

Fuego, thus capturing the Straits of Magellan. Chile would have attacked through the mountain passes at Mendoza and Neuquén. In either hypothesis, mounted infantry and cavalry, mountain, and field artillery would have been the key elements in the field campaign.[48]

There was little to choose between the small arms and artillery used by the first line units of both nations, though Argentina had a greater stock in either case. The Chileans had a bewildering assortment of older weapons that would have been issued to their second line units. The Argentine army, on the other hand, knew well the value of standardization, and most of its Remington rifles had converted military arsenals to the 7.65 mm round utilized by the Mauser. In terms of cavalry, Argentina had the undisputed advantage of being able to provide a horse for virtually every man in the country, whereas Chilean horse reserves were considerably smaller.[49]

In regard to artillery, the Argentines could deploy well in excess of 400 modern field and mountain pieces in 1898, while Chile had only 231, some of which lacked shells until October of that year. By 1901 Argentina had at least 738 Krupp cannon, while Chile hurriedly ordered additional batteries in December, when war seemed imminent.[50] Chile, on the other hand, had an advantage in coastal artillery, a branch that in Argentina was under naval control. These guns were intended only for defensive purposes, and their fixed carriages faced the seaward side. Because of their extreme weight and size, it would have been almost impossible to deploy them in the field. Thus we see that Argentina's armaments were more numerous than Chile's, but what about the soldiers who would employ these weapons in actual combat?

Chilean historians are apt to remind us that their nation had subdued Araucania, that Chilean officers were accustomed to the command of small units, and also that the years of constant struggles against the Indians had turned them into a race of fighters. However, the Chilean army seldom if ever faced Indian hordes 5,000 or 6,000 strong as often as the Argentine army.[51]

The pampas, with their rich bounty of cattle, horses, and grazing lands, attracted Araucanians in large numbers. It was the Argentine who had to face the lances of Calfucurá and his successor and engage them in combat, often hand-to-hand. Hence if we are to accept the premise that the Indian wars turned the Chileans into a race of fighters, it could be justifiably argued that the Indian campaigns similarly molded the Argentines. Description of the gaucho and the roto, who comprised the rank and file of the Argentine and Chilean armies, are almost identical; both are said to be brave, fearless, and indifferent to their own lives as well as the lives of others and endowed with great physical strength.[52]

In Argentina, Chile faced a rival that was considerably stronger and better adapted for warfare than the Andean allies she had vanquished in the War of the Pacific. The Argentine army of 1898 was more than a match for its Chilean counterpart, though few observers were ready to admit this at the time. However, by 1901 even senior Chilean army officers were willing to concede their inferiority of means when compared to the Argentine army. Chilean naval officials expressed similar views when comparing their navy to Argentina's. In both cases, they were quite correct.[53]

Admittedly, the Argentine navy had a late start in developing or, perhaps we should say, in redeveloping its ocean going capabilities. The service, as we have seen, enjoyed prominence during the wars of independence. It cleared the Plate of Spanish warships and blockaded Montevideo, until the last Royalist stronghold capitulated. It raided ports in the Pacific on the coast from Lima to Monterrey and circumnavigated the world. After a brilliant string of victories in the war against Brazil, the service was disbanded, and during the next three decades, the River Plate and its affluents became the focal point in Argentine history. This is where her civil wars were fought, where the war against Paraguay was channeled. During those eventful decades, Argentina turned to her rivers and the inland. She was far too preoccupied with her own vast hinterland to think of the sea until the boundary dispute with Chile forced her to turn her gaze to the Atlantic once again. As we have seen, many Argentine naval officers were molded in the early 1870s, in the cruel waters of the South Atlantic, manning cockle shells that at times only displaced a mere ten tons. Most of these men rose to flag rank and would command the armored cruisers in the 1890s, when the Argentine fleet went through extensive maneuvers that brought their skills to perfection. The extent of these maneuvers can be judged best by the fact that units of the fleet navigated 140,000 miles during 1899 and 200,000 in 1900. By comparison, in 1898, which seems to have been a peak year, Chilean naval units navigated only 87,036 miles.[54]

The task of building a fleet of nearly sixty ships, from armored cruisers to destroyers, from torpedo boats to auxiliaries was enormous, and one that was preceded by the development of service schools, bases, anchorages, and repair stations. Argentine sailors were initially hired from river boats and later on conscripted from the national guard. Personnel recruited from both these sources were quick to learn and possessed mechanical aptitude, something that in the age of steam was as important as seamanship.

The Chileans are fond of noting that the squadron led by Commodore Luis Py in the 1878 expedition to Santa Cruz was composed of ships inadequate for its mission and manned by inexperienced sailors and crews.[55] The appearance of the expertly handled Argentine cruisers through the southern approaches of the Beagle Channel in 1899 must have come as a surprise to these men and a revelation that their once-vaunted superiority over the Argentine navy, not only in the quality and number of its ships, but in training and organization, no longer prevailed.

APPENDIX A
Table 6.1
Argentine and Chilean Navies in 1891

Capital Ships

Argentina		Chile	
A. Brown	4,200 tons	A. Cochrane	3,500 tons
El Plata	1,500 tons	C. Pratt	6,900 tons (2)
Los Andes	1,500 tons (1)	Huascar	1,800 tons (1)
Total	7,250 tons	Total	12,200 tons

Modern Cruisers

Patagonia	1,530 tons (3)	P. Errázuriz	2,080 tons (4)
		P .Pinto	2,080 tons (4)
		Esmeralda	2,950 tons (5)
Total	1,530 tons	Total	7,110 tons

Torpedo Craft

6 small torpedo boats, 240 tons		A. Lynch	750 tons
		A. Condell	750 tons
		6 torpedo boats	420 tons
Total	240 tons	Total	1,920 tons

Auxiliary Vessels

Paraná	550 tons	Abtao	1, 370 tons
Uruguay	550 tons	Magallanes	800 tons
Pilcomayo	416 tons	Pilcomayo	790 tons
República	416 tons		
Bermejo	416 tons		
Constitución	416 tons		
Total	2,764 tons (6)	Total	2,960 tons (7)

Grand Total	11,804 tons		23, 990 tons

[1]Coastal monitor, of limited fighting value in 1891; [2]Not actually delivered until 1893; [3]The cruiser *Patagonia* was too slow (fourteen knots) to be an effective cruiser; [4]Not delivered until 1892; [5]In 1891 this ship was barely capable of fifteen knots; [6]Gunboats built 1874–1875, of limited fighting value; [7]Gunboats built during the 1860s, of limited fighting value.

Source: Bruno Passarelli, "El significado de la creación de la base de Puerto Belgrano," *2o. CNHRA*, III: 75. I have adapted Passarelli's data with some exceptions.

Table 6.2
Argentine and Chilean Navies, 1895–April 1896

Capital Ships

A. Brown	4,200 tons	Huascar	1,800 tons
Libertad	2,300 tons	Cochrane	3.500 tons
Independencia	2,300 tons	C. Pratt	6,900 tons
Total	8,800tons	Total	12, 200 tons

Modern Cruisers

25 de Mayo	3,200 tons	P. Pinto	2,080 tons	
9 de Julio	3,570 tons	P. Errázuriz	2,080 tons	
Buenos Aires	4,740 tons	B. Encalada	4,400 tons	(1)
		Esmeralda	7,500 tons	(1)
		M. Zenteno	3,437 tons	(1)
Total	11,510 tons	Total	19,497 tons	

Torpedo Craft

Espora	520 tons	A. Lynch	750 tons .
Patria	1,050 tons	A. Condell	750 tons
2 torpedo boats	220 tons	Simpson	800 tons
6 torpedo boats	510 tons	3 torpedo boats	330 tons
		4 destroyers	1,200 tons
Total	2,300	Total	3,830 tons (2)

Auxiliary Ships

3	2,630 tons	4	3,430 tons
Grand total	25,240 tons		38, 757 tons

[1]Coastal monitor, of limited fighting value in 1891; [2]Not actually delivered until 1893.

Source: Juan A. Martín, ''Nuestros límites con Chile en la Patagonia austral: El tratado de 1881. Divergencias en su interpretación. Creación de nuestra marina de mar.'' *Boletín del Centro Naval* (76 no. 624), pp. 354–358. Ships delivered after April 1896 are not included in this table.

Table 6.3
Argentine and Chilean Navies, September 1898

Capital Ships

Brown	4,200 tons (1)	Cochrane	3,500 tons (2)
Garibaldi	6,840 tons	Huascar	1,800 tons (2)
San Martín	6,840 tons	Pratt	6,900 tons
Pueyrredón	6,840 tons	O' Higgins	8,500 tons (3)
Libertad	2,300 tons		
Independencia	2,300 tons (4)		
Total	29, 320 tons	Total	20,700 tons

Modern Cruisers (Respective tonnages as shown in Table No. 6.2)

Torpedo Craft

Espora	520 tons	A Lynch	750 tons
Patria	1,050 tons	A. Condell	750 tons
2 torpedo boats	220 tons	A. Simpson	800 tons
6 torpedo boats	510 tons	1 torpedo boat	80 tons
3 destroyers	1,020 tons	6 torpedo boats	840 tons
		4 destroyers	1,200 tons
Total	3,320 tons	Total:	5,220 tons

Auxiliaries

3	2,542 tons	2	1,590 tons
Grand Total	46,692 tons		47,007 tons

[1]The *Brown*, though built in 1881, had been modernized in France during 1897, and her main armament replaced with 10 × 150 mm L.50 Schneider-Cannet quick-firing guns; [2]These ships were of limited fighting value in 1898; [3]The *O'Higgins* was in actuality a large protected cruiser; [4]The *General Belgrano* sailed from Genoa on October 8, 1898 and reached Argentina on November 6.

Source: Juan Martín, "Nuestra marina al iniciarse la segund presidencia del General Julio A. Roca," *Boletín del Centro Naval* (Nov.—Dec. 1957), no. 637, pp. 453–469. As originally published, this table omitted the *Libertad*, which at the time was attached to the Rio de La Plata Division and was rather inaccurate in regard to the numbers and tonnage of the torpedo craft.

Table 6.4
Comparative Naval Strength: Argentina and Chile, 1900

Capital Ships

Garibaldi	6,840 tons	Pratt	6,900 tons
Pueyrredón	6,840 tons	Cochrane	3,500 tons
San Martín	6,840 tons	O'Higgins	8,500 tons
Belgrano	6,840 tons	Huascar	1,800 tons
Libertad	2,300 tons		
Independencia	2,300 tons		
Brown	4,200 tons		
Total	36,160 tons	Total	20,700 tons

Modern Cruisers

Buenos Aires	4,570 tons	Errázuriz	2,080 tons
9 de Julio	3,570 tons	Pinto	2,080 tons
25 de Mayo	3,200 tons	B. Encalada	4,400 tons
		Esmeralda	7,500 tons
		M. Zenteno	3,600 tons
		Chacabuco	4,160 tons
Total	11, 510 tons	Total	22,220 tons

Torpedo Craft and Auxiliaries: As shown in Table No 6. 3

Grand total	55,532 tons		46,690 tons

Table 6.5
Ships Under Construction or on Order, 1901–1902

Maipú	14,850 tons	Libertad	11,800 tons
Chacabuco	14,850 tons	Constitución	11,800 tons
Moreno	7,800 tons		
Rivadavia	7,800 tons		
6 destroyers	1,950 tons	6 destroyers	1,926 tons
Total:	42,250 tons	Total:	25,526 tons

Total Strength Planned : 1903

(Combined tonnage as shown in Tables No. 6.4 and 6.5)

	Argentina	Chile
Grand Total :	100,782 tons	67,545 tons

Table 6.6
Technical Specifications of Argentine and Chilean Battleships Ordered in 1901

	Argentina	Chile
	Maipú- class	Libertad-class
displacement:	14,580 tons	11,800 tons
armament:	4 x 12-inch	4 x 10- inch
	6 x 8- inch	14 x 7,5-inch
	12 x 6-inch	14 x 3-inch
	16 x 3-inch	2 x 8 pdr.
Torpedo Tubes:	4	2
Machinery :	18,500 IHP = 21 knots	12,500IHP= 19 knots

Source: (For Argentine battleships) *Schiffsbau,* Berlin, June 8, 1902, 75; for Chilean battleships, *Conway's All The World's Fighting Ships, 1865–1905* (New York: Mayflower, 1979), p. 39.

Table 6.7
Heavy, Medium Guns (10- to 4.7-inch) and Torpedo Tubes Mounted Aboard Argentine and Chilean Capital Ships and Cruisers, 1900[1]

	Argentina	Chile
10-inch	(6)	(0)
9.4-inch	(4)	(4)
8 or 8.2-inch	(8)	(10)
5.9 or 6-inch	(62)	(55)
4.7-inch	(50)	(28)
T. Tubes	(30)	(29)

Grand Total: 130 guns,   Grand Total : 96 guns,
30 torpedo tubes   29 torpedo tubes

[1]The armaments of the Argentine cruiser *Patria*, the monitors *El Plata* and *Los Andres*, and the Chilean monitor *Huascar*, and the old armored ship *Cochrane* are not included in the above totals.

Source: Frederick T. Jane, *Fighting Ships* (London: 1905): pp. 340–344, 355–356.

Table 6.8

Comparative Military Expenditures, Argentina and Chile, 1890–1902

YEAR	ARGENTINA	BUDGET %	CHILE	BUDGET %
	(In U.S. Dollars)			
1890	7, 335, 351	20	6, 942, 600	18.42
1891	7, 121, 409	22	20, 402, 160	50.89 (*)
1892	12, 955, 857	40	5, 511, 580	19.06
1893	14, 267, 790	39	6, 366, 280	29.52
1894	14, 271, 487	37	5, 007, 760	24.22
1895	14, 924, 899	32	11, 028, 925	33.90
1896	33, 842, 085	45	17, 716, 710	42.26
1897	28, 745, 241	49	8, 403, 610	27.15
1898	37, 326, 510	32	7, 839, 580	43.47
1899	28, 745, 241	40	7, 349 ,800	23.53
1900	17, 145, 059	26	10, 593, 605	18.46
1901	16, 479, 801	26	10, 493, 605	23.54
1902	23, 795, 257	29	19, 219,405	43.49
Grand total	US $ 258, 684, 417		US $ 137, 994, 900	

*The Civil War of 1891 accounts for the heavy military expenditures for that year.

Source: For Argentina, defense expenditures are calculated as a percentage of general expenditures. Expenditures: Ernesto Tornquist and Co., *El desarollo económico de la república argentina durante los ultimos cincuenta años*, p. 271, for the share of general expenditures devoted to national defense; *Reseña Histórica* (1972), II: 500–514. Chilean defense expenditures: S. Hillmon, ''A History of the Armed Forces of Chile from Independence to 1920,'' Unpub. Ph.D. diss., Syracuse University, 1963, p. 324. Hillmon's figures, given in pounds sterling, have been converted into U.S. dollars at the prevailing rate.

APPENDIX B
LIMITATIONS OF ARMAMENTS BETWEEN CHILE AND
ARGENTINA

(Document No. F0.118/25, page 71 (undated but attached to Draft Telegram No. 24,
F.O. 118/57, April 30, 1902)

The idea does not include the establishment of a perfect state of equilibrium between the
number and strength of the ships composing each navy. The limitation of armaments
admits a continuation of the present state of affairs but forbears future increases of
strength on either side. The present state of affairs in this special case would mean: All
war material already constructed and in possession of either country.

A comparison shows that the strength preponderance is well on the Argentine side,
for if we consider what each country can place in the line of battle we find that Chile
has three armored ships, the best of which is the "O'Higgins". This ship, although well
armed and of high speed would be of short endurance in an action against one of the
"Garibaldi" type owing to the very poor distribution and reduced area of her armoured
positions. The "Capitan Pratt" although carrying very thick armour and her belt and
barbettes, is poorly armed and very vulnerable to a Garibaldi's shell fire, which she could
never return.

The "Esmeralda", although well armed, is unfit for the line of battle owing to her
almost absolute want of protection. On the other hand, Argentina has four Garbaldi-types
carrying a more powerful armament than any of the Chilean ships and protected by a
very extensive plating of Terni steel, invulnerable to the Chilean guns at all probable
ranges.

Coming to the cruising types, the only ships worth considering are Argentina's "Buenos Aires," "9 de Julio" and "25 de Mayo" against Chile's "Encalada", "Zenteno"
and "Chacabuco."

Here we find equal forces, and comparing torpedo boat flotillas, Chile surges ahead.
But torpedo armaments are purely defensive and local, and if we compare the populated
coast and numerous exposed ports of Chile with the uninhabited shores and naturally
defended rivers of Argentina, we find that Chile's preponderance in defensive elements
is only apparent.

Last, if we consider auxiliary ships, we find that Argentina can count three useful ships
against one Chilean.

In every way, the balance rests with Argentina; therefore this country would in no
way be a loser if an arrangement were concluded by which Chile would cancel her orders
to England for new ships and in Germany for coast guns and Argentina on her side
cancel orders in Italy for the new ships building or proposed.

The Argentine navy, as it stands, could be worked up to a very high standard of
efficiency. Its materiel is of the highest order and its personnel is considered good. A
slight increase in its budget for expenditure on guns, ammunition, coal, and other elements of training would be much more telling in a war with Chile than hurried and
disproportionate additions to its materiel.

It must be understood that an efficient navy requires experienced crews, and that this
most important of factors can only be attained by the lapse of sufficient time and the
nature of sufficient money. This would be much more stimulating to all those connected

with the navy than the other rather ridiculous policy of buying a fleet of the largest-sized battleships, which would not only be quite out of proportion to the powers of its owner, but which would immediately raise the problem of efficient manning and equipment in case of war.

APPENDIX C
DOCUMENT F.O. 118/258, LOWTHER TO THE MARQUIS OF LANDSDOWNE SANTIAGO, OCTOBER 3, 1902

A report having reached me that an idea had been mooted for Chile to abandon the sale of two battleships now being built in England, and to allow Argentina to acquire the other, while a similar course would be pursued with regard to the cruisers now being built for the Argentine government in Italy. I inquired today of the Minister for Foreign Affairs whether there was any truth in the rumours. Señor Vergara said that a proposition of this nature had been advanced, though it had not been discussed. Chile to her regret and somewhat to her surprise found that there were no purchasers for the two battleships building and that if disposed, it would be at a loss of 500,000 pounds, or about that amount, a sacrifice that this country could ill afford to make. There were vessels of older types, the upkeep of which was as great as that of the new vessels, and these could be disposed of, Colombia being a purchaser, although Congress had declined to sanction such a sale to Colombia as long as the revolution continued and therefore, the acquisition of the new vessels would not entail much extra cost.

I said to Señor Vergara that I was not in a position to examine the economical side of the question, although the view he took seemed to be too sanguine, nor had I any authority from your Lordship to speak on the subject, but I could not conceal from him my opinion that if the proposed arrangement were carried out, it could not fail to produce a bad effect outside the two republics. Although the proposal suggested would have the sanction of the two governments, it could not but appear strange that the very first article of the convention dealing with disarmament should be contravened when the ink on the paper was hardly dry. It had been known all along as the convention for the reduction of armaments. The arrangement proposed would be tantamount to a convention for the increase of armaments and I trusted wiser counsels would prevail, and that in any case, due consideration would be given to the matter from all points of view before a definite decision was taken.

NOTES

1. Tommie Hillmon, Jr., "A History of the Armed Forces of Chile from Independence to 1920," Ph.D. diss., Syracuse University, 1963, pp. 3–5, 13, 14.

2. Stephen Clissold, *Bernardo O'Higgins and the Independence of Chile* (New York: Praeger, 1969), pp. 85–86, 99–100, 140–141; Bartolomé Mitre, *Episodios de la Revolución* (Buenos Aires: *EUDEBA*, 1960), pp. 113–118; Agustín Toro Dávila, *Sintesis histórico militar de Chile* (Santiago: Editorial Universitaria, 1976), pp. 79–100; Simon Collier, *Ideas and Politics of Chilean Independence* (Cambridge, Cambridge University Press, 1979), pp. 98–101, 116–123.

3. Clissold, *Bernardo O'Higgins*, pp. 143–146.

4. Estado Mayor del Ejército, *Historia del Ejército de Chile*, 8 vols. (Santiago: 1982), III: 191–208; Clissold, *Bernardo O'Higgins*, pp. 143–147, 161–163.

5. Carlos Dellepiane, *Historia militar del Perú*, 2 vols. (Buenos Aires: Círculo Militar, 1942), I: 340–347.

6. Clissold, *Bernardo O'Higgins*, pp. 190–192.

7. Collier, *Ideas and Politics*, pp. 7–8; Hillmon, "A History of the Armed Forces," pp. 52–54.

8. Ibid., pp. 144–146; Dellepiane, *Historia militar*, I: 352–356, 392–395.

9. Hillmon, "A History of the Armed Forces," pp. 76–77, 80–82; Jean Pierre Blancpain, *Les Allemands au Chilli, 1816–1945* (Köln and Wien: Bölau Verlag, 1974), pp. 702–703.

10. Blancpain, *Les Allemands*, p. 704; Hillmon, "A History of the Armed Forces," pp. 139–154.

11. Estado Mayor del Ejército, *Historia del Ejército de Chile*, IV: 180–182.

12. Hillmon, "A History of the Armed Forces," pp. 181–187.

13. Ibid., pp. 125–128; Ricardo Ferrando Keun, *Y asi nació la frontera: Conquista, guerra, ocupación, pacificación: 1550–1900* (Santiago: Editorial Antártica, 1986), pp. 398–400.

14. Ferrando Keun, *Y así nació*, pp. 402–406.

15. Ibid., pp. 407–408, 431–437.

16. Robert N. Burr, *By Reason or By Force: Chile and the Balancing of Power in South America, 1830–1905* (Berkeley and Los Angeles: University of California Press, 1967), pp. 141–143; Dellepiane, *Historia militar*, II: 160–164, 181–182, 185–189; William F. Slatter, *Chile and the War of the Pacific* (Lincoln and London: University of Nebraska Press, 1975), pp. 21–22, 37–38; M. Le Leon, *Recuerdo de una misión el ejército chileno: Batallas de chorrillos y Miraflores* (Buenos Aires: Editorial Francisco Aguirre, 1973), pp. 17–19; Dellepiane, *Historia militar* II: 76–77; Diego Barros Arana, *Obras Completas, Vol. XVI, Historia de la Guerra del Pacífico: 1879–1881* (Santiago: Imprenta, Litografía i Encuadernación Barcelona, 1914).

17. Slatter, *Chile and the War*, pp. 20–23.

18. Dellepiane, *Historia militar*, II: 162–164; Slatter, *Chile and the War*, pp. 22–24.

19. Toro Dávila, *Sintesis histórico*, pp. 262–268; Hillmon, "A History of the Armed Forces," pp. 188–193; Slatter, *Chile and the War* p. 21. The army was organized into four divisions; the first with 3,600 men, the second with 4,050, the third with 3,450, and the fourth with 3,400. In addition, there was a 300-man bridging battalion, a total of 14,800 men.

20. Dellepiane, *Historia militar*, II: 76–77, Toro Dávila, *Sintesis histórico*, pp. 273–274; Clements R. Markham, *The War Between Peru and Chile* (London: Sampson, Low Marston, 1892), pp. 208–214.

21. Carlos López Urrutia, *Historia de la Marina de Chile* (Santiago: Editorial Andres Bello, 1969), pp. 278–283; Dellepiane, *Historia militar*, II: 331–336, 356–366; Hillmon, "A History of the Armed Forces," pp. 185–187.

22. Luís Galdames, *A History of Chile* (New York: Russell & Russell, 1941), pp. 344–345.

23. Blancpain, *Les allemands*, pp. 704–705, 713–714.

24. Hillmon, "A History of the Armed Forces," pp. 200–202.

25. Frederick M. Nunn, "Civil-Military Relations in Chile: 1891–1938," Ph.D. diss., University of New Mexico, 1963, pp. 68–70; Hillmon, "A History of the Armed Forces," p. 256; Estado Mayor del Ejército, *Historia del Ejército de Chile* VIII: 26–27; Gonzalo Vial Correa, *Historia de Chile: 1891–1973*, 3 vols. (Santiago: Santillana Editores, 1987) II: 173–174, 292.

26. Hillmon, "A History of the Armed Forces," pp. 244–245; Blancpain, *Les allemands*, p. 710. After Kürner's reforms the "effective militia" (or national guard) would have totaled 87,000 men, including 3,400 officers.

27. Frederick M. Nunn, *Yesterday's Soldiers: European Military Professionalism in South America, 1890–1940* (Lincoln and London: University of Nebraska Press, 1983), pp. 100–101.

28. Nunn, *Yesterday's Soldiers*, pp. 122–130, 143–151; Ronald C. Newton, *German Buenos Aires, 1900–1933: Social Change and Cultural Crisis* (Austin: University of Texas Press, 1977), pp. 22–23; Frederick M. Nunn, "Emil Körner and the Prussianization of the Chilean Army: Origins, Process and Consequences, 1885–1920," *HAHR* 50, no. 2 (May 1970), pp. 300–312. Aside from his other duties, in 1894 Körner supervised the construction and delivery of coastal guns ordered from Krupp. There are many similarities between the Körner mission to Chile and the German mission to Bolivia, headed by General Hans Kundt (1911–1914, 1921–1926, 1929–1930). Under Kundt, the Bolivian army underwent a process of Prussianization not unlike that instituted by Körner in Chile, only to experience a most humiliating defeat in the hands of Paraguay, during the Chaco War. See David H. Zook, Jr., *The Conduct of the Chaco War* (New York: Bookman Associates, 1960); Dionisio Schoo Lastra, *La lanza rota: Estancias, indios, paz en la Cordillerra* (Buenos Aires: Ediciones Peuser, 1953), pp. 201–203. Körner retired from the Chilean army in 1910 and returned to Germany. In 1916, he attempted to purchase a batch of old Remington rifles from the War Arsenal at Buenos Aires, intended for an undisclosed country in the Orient.

29. Vial Correa, *Historia de Chile*, II: 794–798.

30. Nunn, "Civil Military," pp. 88–89; Vial Correa, *Historia de Chile*, II: 797–798.

31. Ernesto Quesada, *La política argentina respecto de Chile, 1895–1898* (Buenos Aires: Arnoldo Moen Editor, 1898), pp. 103–104. "The Chileans' belief in their military superiority derived from the fact that they considered their navy more powerful than Argentina since they took delivery of the cruiser *O'Higgins*, but also because they claimed to have in their arsenals weapons, munitions and supplies for 200,000 men, artillery in greater numbers than Argentina, that their army was in a better war footing, since Körner and his legionaries had imparted military training to the National Guard reserves, which had been mobilized and accustomed to service life, while they held that the Argentines had done precisely the opposite with their National Guard, which was merely a mere agglomeration led by incompetent officers, intended for display at numerous parades." Major Serrato, with Argentine army intelligence, spent seven years in Chile, gathering information. He reported that the Chilean army was far from being the efficient war machine Chileans pretended.

32. Augusto C. Rodríguez, "Ejército Nacional." In *Historia Argentina Contemporánea: 1862–1930*. 7 vols. (Buenos Aires: El Ateneo, 1966), II: 338; Marvin Goldwert, *Democracy, Militarism and Nationalism in Argentina, 1930–1966: An Interpretation* (Austin: University of Texas Press, 1972), pp. 8–9; Nunn, *Yesterday's Soldiers*, pp. 120–126.

33. Details of coastal artillery emplacements and acquisitions can be found in Jürgen Schaefer, *Deutsche militarhilfe en Sudamerika: Militar und Rustunginteressen in Argentinien, Bolivien und Chile von 1914* (Düsseldorf: Bertelsmann Universitätsverlag, 1974), pp. 62–63, 233; Report of the U.S. Military Attache in Santiago de Chile, December 9, 1932; James H. Sears, Lieutenant U.S.N, and Benjamin W. Wells, Ensign U.S.N., *The Chilean Revolution of 1891* (Washington, DC: Government Printing Office, 1893). Details of other arms purchases can be found in Gerhard Brunn, "Deutscher einfluss und Deustche interessen in der professionalisierung einiger Latinamerichet Armeen von der 1. Weltkrieg: 1881–1914," *Jahrbuch für Geschichte von Staat, Wirtschaft und Gesselschaft*, vol. 6 (Köln: Bolau Verlag, 1969), pp. 278–336; Estado Mayor

del Ejército, *Historia del Ejército de Chile,* VII: 220; Chile, *Memoria que el Ministro de estado en del departamento de Guerra ha presentado al Congreso Nacional* (Santiago: 1898), pp. 215–220.

34. Oscar Espinosa Moraga, *La postguerra del Pacífico y la Puna de Atacama: 1884– 1899* (Santiago: Editorial Andres Bello, 1958), pp. 120–121. The type of rifles included (quantities in parenthesis): Manlicher 8 mm (20,059), Manlicher 11 mm (78), Grass (17,269), Grass M.85 (3,844), Comblain (6,146), Lee (1,192), Remington (3,727), Beaumont (3,846), Barmuller (1,686), Snyder (123), Peabody (174), Chassepot (1,596), Minié (7,792), percussion types (1,820), miscellaneous and useless (54), Carbines: Potts (29), Grass (91), Comblain (4), Remington (34), Peabody (54), percussion types (514).

35. Scheina, *Latin America: A Naval History* (Annapolis, MD: Naval Institute Press, 1987), pp. 6–7; Rodrigo Fuenzalida Bade, *La armada de Chile: Desde la alborada al ses-quicentenario, 1813–1968,* 4 vols. (Santiago: 1978), I: 123–131; López Urrutia, *Historia de la Marina de Chile,* pp. 112–133.

36. Fuenzalida Bade, *La armada de Chile,* II: 479–480; Hillmon, "A History of the Armed Forces," pp. 85–86.

37. López Urrutia, *Historia de la Marina de Chile,* pp. 199–200.

38. José Cervera Parry, *Marina y política en la España del siglo XIX* (Madrid: Editorial San Martín, 1979), pp. 88–89.

39. Fuenzalida Bade, *La armada de Chile,* III: 722–723.

40. Scheina, *Latin America,* pp. 31–32; Fuenzalida Bade, *La armada de Chile,* III: 725–727, 913–915, 941–942; *Conway's All The World's Fighting Ships* p. 122. The monitors *Manco Capac,* (ex-U.S.S. *Oneonta*) and *Atahualpa* (ex-U.S.S. *Catawba*), completed in 1864, were sold to Peru in 1868. They were an improved *Passaic*-class monitor, with a displacement of 21,000 tons, and a maximum speed of 8 knots, and were armed with a pair of 15-inch smoothbore guns. Freeboard was only 12 inches and thus unsuitable for sailing on the line. By 1879 their speed was reduced to 3.5 knots, and they were relegated to the role of floating batteries. The *Manco Capac* formed part of the defenses of Arica, and the *Atahualpa* complemented those at Callao. The 15-inch smoothbores, which fired solid-shot balls, lacked the range and penetration of the main armament aboard Chilean warships, which although smaller in diameter fired conical armor piercing shells. The *Manco Capac* was scuttled on June 6, to prevent it from falling into enemy hands when Arica fell. Similarly, the *Atahualpa* was destroyed at Callao on January 15, 1881.

41. Scheina, *Latin America,* pp. 33–36; López Urrutia, *Historia de la Marina de Chile,* pp. 280–282.

42. Fuenzalida Bade, *La armada de Chile,* IV: 1066–1067, 1081–1082; Scheina, *Latin America,* pp. 44–46.

43. López Urrutia, *Historia de la Marina de Chile,* pp. 330–331, Fuenzalida Bade, *La armada de Chile,* IV: 1054–1056, 1060–1061; Scheina, *Latin America,* pp. 61–62.

44. Hillmon, "A History of the Armed Forces," pp. 210–211.

45. Ibid., p. 243; William E. Curtis, *The Capitals of Spanish America* (New York: Harper & Bros., 1888) pp. 480–84.

46. Hillmon, "A History of the Armed Forces," 285–286; Claudio Véliz, *Historia de la marina mercante de Chile* (Santiago: Ediciones de la Universidad de Chile, 1961), pp. 316–317; Chile, *Memoria que el Ministro de Estado en el Departamento de Marina presentó al Congreso Nacional en 1901* (Santiago: 1901), pp. 256–257.

47. Thomas Holdich, *The Countries of the King's Award* (London: Hurst and Blackett, 1904), pp. 108–109. Holdich noted that Argentine sailors were taught the virtues of clean-

liness and discipline and afterward were inculcated in gunnery. Their gun practice, he thought was good, while adding: "The Argentine sailor looks smart enough on deck, but watching him lower a boat over the side revealed that he was not to the manner born. The Argentine sailor was willing, active and showed wonderful aptitude, but that would hardly take the place of the knowledge of the ways of the sea which comes from heredity." Holdich nevertheless commented on Argentine naval maneuvers in which "nearly a hundred ships participated without a single hitch, something which attests to the high degree of efficiency achieved by Argentine navigators in the handling of their ships."

48. Schoo Lastra, *La lanza rota*, pp. 205–206. This source provides accurate details of Argentine military preparations during the 1901 crisis (Ignacio Fotheringham, *Vida de un soldado o reminiscencias de las fronteras*, 2 vols. [Buenos Aires: Círculo Militar, 1970], II: 368–370). Fotheringham commanded the Cuyo division at Mendoza during 1897–1898. In April 1898, a group of Chileans in civilian garb, but obviously military, were intercepted and captured when they proved to be members of the Chilean demarcation team. They left behind detailed maps of strategic border trails. The Cuyo division was on maneuvers at this time and deployed at Punta Vacas, Puente del Inca, and La Cumbre, on the Chilean border. At Fotheringham's suggestion these points were fortified, as the hypothesis of the field maneuvers was precisely an intended Chilean invasion through these passes.

49. Holdich, *The Countries*, pp. 103–104, 174–175.

50. Brun, *Deustcher Einfluss*, p. 329. According to this source, between 1895–1898 Argentina purchased 653 cannon, while Chile obtained a total of 341 pieces during 1872 and 1901. Schaefer, *Deutsche militarhilfe*, pp. 48 (n.18), 62–63, 231. In 1895 Argentina bought 180 quick-firing guns; thus with the purchases made in 1895, it possessed 400 cannon. However, in 1896 an additional 72 quick-firing mountain guns were procured. *Reseña Histórica*, II: 408–409. The latter were designated "model 1896" and were virtually identical to other Krupp mountain guns purchased earlier. The Argentine army assigns model numbers according to the year in which the equipment was purchased (e.g., Mauser modelo 1891). The total number of artillery pieces available in 1898 might be considerably higher than either Brunn or Schaefer reveal. See, for example, a report of the U.S. Military Attache in Buenos Aires dated 25 July 1940 (Document No. 0548, RG 165, U.S. National Archives, Washington DC). The Argentine army assigns its older weapons to reserve status. For example, when the 1909 artillery materiel was introduced, the older guns were placed in reserve, and in turn when the model 1935 field piece came into use in the late 1930s, the model 1909s were placed in storage. The aforementioned document lists 522 model 1896/1898 mountain guns in reserve, along with 12 Krupp 130 mm L.26 siege guns and other types, such as the Krupp model 105 mm mod. 186 cannon, the model 1895, etc. Estado Mayor del Ejército, *História*, VII: 220.

51. See Keun, *Y asi nació*, pp. 398–410, 412–437, for details of the Indian campaigns in Chile,

52. Hillmon, "A History of the Armed Forces," p. 193, for a description of the roto, and pp. 10 and 39 of this work for a similar view of the gaucho.

53. Eyzaguire, *Chile durante el gobierno*, p. 342.

54. Argentine Republic, *Memoria presentada al Congreso Nacional por el Ministro de Marina* (Buenos Aires: Imprenta de La Nación, 1901), pp. 230–232, for the mileage navigated by Argentine ships. See Chile, *Memoria presentada por el Ministro de Estado*

en el Departamento de Marina al Congreso Nacional (Santiago, 1899), pp. 138–176, for the total mileage accumulated by the Chilean fleet.

55. Espinosa Moraga, *El precio*, I: 55–56. For a description of Py's expedition see: Santiago Albarracín, *La escuadra argentina en la Patagonia: Paginas del ayer* (Buenos Aires: Ediciones Marymar, 1976), pp. 10–11, 60–61.

7

Conflict, Arbitration, and Solution

The Fierro-Sarratea Treaty was a formula designed to avoid war between Argentina and Chile and provided for arbitration of their dispute. Until a tribunal settled the controversy, Argentina would exercise jurisdiction over the waters and coasts of the Atlantic and Chile over the water and coasts of the Pacific as well as the Straits of Magellan and adjacent islands. The treaty was ratified by the Chilean Congress in January 1879, but in the Argentine legislature a vocal, anti-Chilean faction opposed ratification. Aside from that, popular sentiment in the Plata had been stirred by news of the War of the Pacific and memories of the *Jeanne Amélie* incident. José Manuel Balmaceda, designated Chilean minister plenipotentiary to Buenos Aires in 1879, was entrusted with the delicate mission of insuring Argentine neutrality in the Pacific conflict. Balmaceda felt relieved, when in a private meeting with Manuel Montes de Oca, the Argentine foreign minister, assured him that his nation would not take advantage of Chile's difficulties and would observe a strict feeling of neutrality.[1]

Chile had been willing to conclude a treaty in order to ensure Argentine neutrality, but when Buenos Aires officially proclaimed such a policy on April 23, the Chilean attitude hardened, and Balmaceda, who once had been willing to make any accommodation to obtain such a promise, insisted that the Fierro-Sarratea Treaty should constitute the basis for any settlement. However, on May 2 Santiago signaled Balmaceda to open negotiations granting control of Patagonia to Argentina while Chile retained its colony at Punta Arenas. The Argentine government was unwilling to submit the treaty for approval. Instead, an agreement to maintain the status quo was concluded on June 3 between Balmaceda and Montes de Oca, along with a protocol that guaranteed free navigation through the Straits of Magellan. No further progress would take place until the North American ministers in Buenos Aires, cousins with almost identical names, offered United States mediation. It was accepted by both countries. A boundary treaty was concluded on July 23, 1880, which established the Andes from north to south, as far as the 52nd Parallel of latitude as the boundary between Argentina and Chile; the boundary line would run over the highest peaks that divided the waters and would pass between the sources of the streams flowing down to either side. It granted Patagonia to Argentina and provided for arbitration, the division of Tierra del Fuego, and the neutralization of the Straits.[2]

The treaty was ratified by both countries on October 22, 1881, but no demarcation was undertaken, as Chile, still involved in the War of the Pacific, delayed matters until Balmaceda was elected to the presidency. A new protocol, signed on August 20, 1889, called for the appointment of demarcation experts, as provided by the treaty of 1881. Both countries ratified this protocol on January 11, 1890. Octavio Pico was chosen as the Argentine expert, while Diego Barros Arana, no newcomer to the boundary controversy, would be his Chilean counterpart. In the first meeting on April 20, both experts exchanged credentials, but Pico insisted that the work of demarcation should begin at the San Francisco Pass, in the province of Atacama. Barros Arana agreed, with the proviso that demarcation should begin simultaneously in the northern and southern sectors of the boundary line, by two separate field commissions. Pico agreed, but both men failed to agree in the larger issue, which was the basic interpretation of the principle of demarcation. A change of government in Argentina postponed further discussions in 1890, while in January 1891 Barros Arana was relieved of his post. He would be reinstated in August 1891 after the overthrow of President Balmaceda. No further meetings between the experts would take place until January 1892.[3]

Pico and Barros Arana met as scheduled, but soon irreconcilable differences in their interpretation of the criteria to be used in the demarcation emerged. Argentina claimed that the line formed by the main range of the Andes was the correct interpretation of article one of the treaty of 1881, since, despite numerous breaks that destroyed their continuity, the Andes massed themselves very conveniently and formed a strong natural barrier, and that these peaks in fact determined the *divortia aquarum*, or watershed water parting. Chile on the other hand claimed that the *divortia aquarum* was of a continental nature and that it affected valleys and plains irrespective of whether this line ran between the highest peaks. Her representatives believed this was a feature so well defined that it required no further mapping. Barros Arana, who often contradicted his own statements and articles, deliberately misinterpreted Pico's statement. The Argentines, he noted, insisted in the "highest peaks," rather than in the line of the water parting established by the treaty of 1881. This refrain was picked up by the Chilean press, which clamored against Argentina's unwillingness to comply with the letter of the treaties and refused arbitration. In point of fact, the text of the treaty, which provided for arbitration by a friendly power, was an indication that the treaty makers wisely regarded neither of the terms "highest peaks" nor "water parting" as a fixed and inalienable principle of the boundary. Thomas Holdich, the geographer entrusted with the demarcation by the British

Crown, dryly observed in a purely abstract sense it was not possible to assume that any general or continental line actually existed and that an elementary knowledge of the history of the world would hardly support that assumption.[4]

What was at stake was a territory of some 94,000 square kilometers, an expanse of fertile lands that stretched from the southern portion of the territories of Neuquén and Río Negro to the Andes, an area larger than the state of Maine. Chile's interest in these lands stemmed from the fact that her cattlemen had utilized valleys in the disputed areas, east of the Andes, to graze and winter their herds. Cattle stolen from the pampas by the Indians were driven to Chile over a trail known as the Camino de los Chilenos, or Road of the Chileans. Many Argentine statesmen, including Roca, had denounced both the illicit trade and the occupation prior to the conquest of the desert. While the power of the Indian in Patagonia remained unchecked, Chilean traders would pay token sums to the various tribes for the use of these grazing lands. This, coupled with the introduction of stolen Argentine herds into Chile, had the effect of lowering the price of Argentine beef in the Chilean market. The Argentine occupation of Patagonia largely ended this situation, but cattle rustling continued, albeit on a smaller scale. Because of the vastness of the territories involved and the nature of the terrain, the problem persisted until a more thorough control could be exercised.[5]

The demarcation process in the northern section of the boundaries stalled in April 1892, after a marker had been placed at the San Francisco Pass, in the province of Atacama. The Argentines objected because they felt the marker lay within Argentine territory. The death of Pico, the Argentine expert, further delayed demarcation, and his successor, Norberto Quirno Costa, did not arrive until January of the following year. In order to break the impasse, Estanislao Zevallos, the Argentine foreign minister, suggested a meeting with his Chilean colleague, Isidoro Errázuriz, in order to settle matters by direct negotiations. Errázuriz declined, ostensibly because of a congested agenda that precluded such a meeting.[6]

To clarify each country's position, an additional protocol was concluded on May 1, 1893. The protocol reaffirmed and clarified the treaty of 1893 and clearly specified that Argentina was to exercise rights over the shores and waters of the Atlantic, while Chile exercised similar rights over the shores and waters of the Pacific Ocean. Little was accomplished on the way of demarcation during the years 1893 and 1894, and no demarcation at all was undertaken in 1895. The solution to the boundary dispute appeared as remote as ever. Relations between Argentina and Chile were further strained at this time, as Bolivia and Peru sought and obtained a rapprochement with Buenos Aires.[7]

ARGENTINE RAPPROCHEMENT WITH BOLIVIA AND PERU: GENESIS OF THE PUNA DE ATACAMA QUESTION

As we have seen earlier, among the factors that dissuaded Argentina from entering into an alliance with Bolivia and Peru was the failure to solve a preexisting border dispute with Bolivia over possession of the former Argentine province of Tarija, which had been annexed by Bolivia when that nation declared its independence in 1825. The issue lay dormant, per force, during the period of the Argentine civil wars. On May 2, 1865, Rufino de Elizalde, the Argentine foreign minister, concluded a series of agreements covering peace and friendship, trade and navigation, and extradition. Article Two of the peace treaty provided an exchange of titles and the appointment of experts from both nations to explore the disputed area in order to establish a line of demarcation and provided for arbitration by a friendly third power. In any event, the treaties were not ratified by the Argentine Congress. Negotiations began anew in 1868, with a treaty under which both nations were to maintain the status quo. On November 27, 1869, the Bolivian government seemed most anxious to settle the border dispute, alleging that Article Sixteen of the Treaty of Triple Alliance granted Argentina the Gran Chaco and the entire Western bank of the Paraguay River up to Bahía Negra. Bolivia demanded a large portion of territory in order to gain access to the Plata system, but the Argentine chancellor refused to broach his subject until the Paraguayan conflict was concluded. An attempt to resolve it years later failed, when the Bolivian congress failed to enact a protocol with Argentina. Discussions were not reopened until 1872. On May 3, Mariano Reyes Cardona, Bolivian minister plenipotentiary to Argentina, Brazil, and Uruguay presented his credentials to President Domingo F. Sarmiento. The Bolivian diplomat was not received by Carlos Tejedor, the Argentine foreign minister, until June. Reyes Cardona attempted to reclaim the Chaco for Bolivia, while avoiding the issue of Tarija. By way of reply, on October 11, the Argentines enacted legislation proclaiming the Chaco an integral part of Argentina. Reyes Cardona angrily protested the actions of the Argentine legislature, but he was silenced by a tongue-lashing reply from Tejedor, which reminded him that the Bolivian congress had passed legislation concerning not only the Chaco, but other territories she had occupied without valid titles. The seeds for the Chaco War of the 1930s had been sown.[8]

Talks were not reopened until 1888, and on May 10, 1889, a protocol known as the Quirno Costa-Vaca Guzmán treaty was concluded. According to the terms of the new agreement, Argentina renounced all claims to Tarija in exchange for control of a Bolivian territory known as the Puna de Atacama. Unbeknownst to Argentina, Chile had occupied a portion of the Puna in 1884. In April 1883 the Chilean government established a commission charged with the exploration of the Atacama desert. When this commission began its appointed tasks, they were informed in a polite though firm manner that they were in Argentine territory. The Chilean foreign ministry cabled Buenos Aires demanding Argentine withdrawal from the Puna as well as recognition of Chilean jurisdiction over the territory.[9]

Thus, the Puna de Atacama question added a new and disturbing element to an otherwise protracted and heated boundary dispute. Bolivia for her part subscribed a supplementary accord with Argentina, under which she categorically asserted that she had never surrendered or renounced previous rights to the Puna to Chile, and in fact recognized all territories south of the 23rd Parallel as Argentine. In Bolivia, there was a strong popular sentiment for a rapprochement with Argentina and an anti-Chilean alliance. The Chilean civil war of 1891 forced a postponement of negotiations, but on October 1, Mariano Baptista, the Bolivian minister in Buenos Aires, concluded a protocol with Zevallos, the Argentine foreign minister, under which Bolivia recognized Argentine sovereignty over the Puna at Jujuy, Salta, and Catamarca up to the line of the highest peak of the Andes. On October 27, a Bolivian newspaper story leaked details of the Matta-Reyes protocol, under which Bolivia granted Chile commercial privileges and more importantly renounced sovereignty over the territories occupied under the terms of the armistice. The notice fell like a bombshell in Buenos Aires. Zevallos held further talks with Baptista, during the course of which the Argentine made it quite clear that if such details were true, the protocol would have an adverse reaction upon Argentinian-Bolivian relations. Baptista assured him that in spite of the armistice, the Bolivian government had never surrendered or renounced previous rights to the Puma to Chile and in fact recognized all territories south of the 23rd parallel as Argentine. Although the Chileans had occupied lands east of the Andes. Zevallos was cognizant of the fact that the Bolivian government had approved the Matta-Reyes treaty in a secret session and regarded Baptista with suspicion. To safeguard Argentine rights to the Puna, he pressed the Bolivian government to postpone ratification of the Matta-Reyes convention and delay definite peace and boundary talks with Chile. On April 26, 1892, a convention known as the Quirno Costa–Vaca Guzmán agreement was ratified by the Bolivian Congress. In Sucre, Matta, the Chilean minister, warned his government that the Quirno Costa–Vacca Guzmán boundary affected the provisions of the armistice.[10]

On June 30, 1894, Argentina and Bolivia signed a new convention that called for the demarcation of the new boundary and provided for the construction of a railway that would link the Argentine province of Jujuy with the Bolivian department of Oruro, thus strengthening commercial relations between Buenos Aires and the Altiplano. Late in 1894, a Bolivian demarcation team arrived at Salta to commence demarcation along with its Argentine counterpart. Matta cabled Santiago, urging his government to press Buenos Aires and Sucre to rescind the treaty of 1889, while noting rising hostility to Chile in the Altiplano. Argentina appeared to have gained the upper hand until March 1895, when the Bolivian government published a statement claiming that Argentina had failed to take material possession of the Puna. The move was calculated to force Argentina to negotiate directly with Chile, relieving Bolivia from further negotiations. On May 18, 1895, after hard bargaining, Bolivia and Chile concluded three separate agreements, the first an armistice that ended the state of war existing since 1879. Chile, furthermore, agreed to assume certain financial obligations of the Bolivian government in return for recognition of Chilean sovereignty over the former Bolivian littoral, while Chile promised to give Bolivia

Tacna and Arica. The May treaties were intended to offset Chile's growing isolation and alter the balance of power by detaching Bolivia from the Argentine orbit and creating a rift between Bolivia and Peru. Argentina, which surprisingly did not maintain a permanent legation at Sucre, was forced to dispatch a diplomatic mission to the Altiplano. Dardo Rocha, former governor of the province of Buenos Aires and founder of the city of La Plata, was chosen for this important post.[11]

The Argentine foreign minister instructed Rocha to ensure Argentine rights over the Atacama, recognized by Bolivia in the convention of 1891, were not affected, to enlist Bolivian assistance to ensure such rights and secure an end to the Chilean occupation of the Puna. Rocha was to safeguard Argentine commercial interests and to counteract with prudence, but firmness, Chile's aggressive policy of invasion and conquest and also to make the Bolivian government aware that Argentina would always lend her moral support to resist such Chilean pressure. Rocha reached Sucre on August 6 and requested an audience with President Mariano Baptista, former Bolivian minister to Buenos Aires, who seemed most anxious to conclude an alliance with Argentina. Outwardly professing friendship, Baptista told Rocha that he would order the Bolivian foreign minister to make available all data pertinent to the agreements with Chile and offered to receive the Argentine diplomat formally on the following week. Baptista appeared to be less than candid and elusive and seemed nervous at the mere mention of Peru. Rocha thanked the Bolivian for his solicitude and refrained from any comments.[12]

During the next few weeks, Rocha displayed considerable energy. In the name of his government, the Peruvian minister to Bolivia solicited Rocha's assistance. The Peruvian had not been formally received by the Bolivian foreign ministry and feared this might lead to a break in relations, which would only benefit Chile. Rocha interceded with Baptista, and conflict was avoided. On August 22 Rocha met with the Bolivian foreign minister, Emeterio Cano, and requested details of the treaties concluded with Chile in May. Rocha then suggested that Bolivia and Chile should conclude a treaty providing for an end to the occupation of the Puna by Chile. Cano for his part suggested a conference among Argentina, Bolivia, and Chile to achieve such ends. Rocha dryly remarked, "In matters pertaining to Bolivia, we should prefer to deal only with Bolivia."[13]

While the May treaties with Chile were the subject of a heated inquiry in the Bolivian congress, Rocha learned that Peru, unwilling to relinquish Tacna and Arica, was preparing to dispatch two divisions to the south to deter Chile from encouraging Bolivia to adopt "aggressive postures." Bolivian public opinion was in favor of delaying the enactment of the May treaties in order to obtain maximum advantages. However, as tensions mounted, signs of strain were soon visible among Bolivian functionaries. Vice president Severo Fernández Alonso met in private with Rocha and inquired whether Bolivia could count on an alliance with the Argentine Republic. Under strict instructions from his government, Rocha declined to answer.[14]

Fernández Alonso met with Rocha once again on October 19 and informed him that the May treaties with Chile would come up before congress any day now and insinuated that Argentine rights to the Puna would be safeguarded, while asking how this could be best accomplished. Rocha replied, "through a protocol and the inclusion of an article which would protect expressly protect these rights." The Chilean legation feverishly tried to hinder such a move. Matta, obviously nervous and out of sorts, visited Rocha in a vain attempt to dissuade him from his course, but Rocha rebuffed him:

Our discussions with Bolivia are an accomplished fact, delayed only by procedural difficulties. If Chile is disposed, as I have heard you state in many occasions, not to venture East of the Andes, and does not turn the Puna into a major issue, or intends to incorporate it to the territories (included) in the armistice, I see no reason why these points should not be cleared up before the (May) treaties win approval.[15]

The May treaties with Chile were ratified on December 9, and a new convention that safeguarded Argentine rights to the Puna concluded three days later. Rocha returned to Buenos Aires by way of the Pacific, after fulfilling the instructions of the Argentine government admirably. Demarcation of the Argentine-Chilean border at the Puna de Atacama region, situated between parallels 26° 52' 45" and 23rd would proceed according to the treaties of 1881 and 1893 and would not be fully resolved until 1899.[16]

By the late 1890s, Argentine public opinion, often indifferent to the boundary dispute issue, became increasingly polarized. Chile was now seen as an aggressor state by the growing and vocal Internationalist faction that was repulsed by the despoliation of Bolivia and Peru at the conclusion of the War of the Pacific and wanted to prevent Chile from embarking upon any future wars of conquest. The Internationalists included distinguished personalities in their ranks, such as Roque Sáenz Peña, who had served with distinction in the Peruvian army during the War of the Pacific; and Indalecio Gómez, Vicente Quesada, and Estanislao Zevallos, all of whom advocated a hard line toward Chile. Another faction, just as vocal, would gather around former presidents Mitre and Pellegrini and other sectors tied to the export-import economy. This faction felt that a war with Chile would be a senseless scandal that would retard Argentina's economic progress and affect her foreign trade. To these men, Argentina's path to greatness was an economic one. They felt that with each passing year Argentina would grow progressively stronger and richer than Chile, until the Transandean nation would no longer constitute a problem.[17]

Across the Andes, Chileans viewed their eastern neighbor with varied emotions. They ran the whole gamut from envy to scorn and from smug complacency to fear.

THE OPPOSING PERCEPTIONS

A smaller country's natural jealousy of the larger was accentuated by the steady growth of Argentina's economic wealth. The Chilean distrust of her more powerful neighbor and its continued existence must be accepted as one of the basic realities of South American international relations. Perhaps this state of affairs began as early as 1817, when the Chileans claimed to have found their Argentine liberators vain and arrogant and continued to develop as Chile found political stability, while Argentina was torn by economic strife and prostrated by economic stagnation. In a letter written to an Argentine friend in 1856, Barros Arana contrasted Chilean progress with the difficult progress of Argentine unification:

Things are better in Chile my friend. [Our] national wealth grows exorbitantly, everyone strives for impossible enterprises and finds willing bankers. In ten years this country will be cris-crossed by railways, and we shall have credit institutions such as England's. We have legal codes, which according to the experts are as good as the French. All industries are prospering, while agriculture, so depressed prior to 1849, produces more wealth than the silver of Copiapó or the gold of Coquimbo.[18]

But as Argentina reached political stability and began to modernize in the 1870s, this same Barros Arana dismissed late developments in the Argentine public school system, particularly the statistics, which he warned should not be taken seriously. Similarly, when in 1881 the Chilean government asked its consul in Buenos Aires to collect data on Argentine immigration procedures and codes, the latter scoffed at Argentine immigration statistics and deemed them "unrealistic." The Argentine school system, which had been given a great impetus under the Sarmiento administration, had outstripped its Chilean counterpart in methods and numbers. Similarly, it is no great secret that Argentina was a country of immigration, while Chile was not. Yet the Chileans dismissed these developments by simply pretending they were not real. After all, could there be anything greater than Chile?[19] These propensities did not escape the attention of the Brazilian Minister in Santiago:

There is much talk and little action here. This is the most boastful nation in the world. For the Chilean there is no other land as rich or flourishing as this, blessed by the very hand of God. To hear [them] sing the praises of this country, its heroism and civilization, one who does not know them, would judge them to be the nation chosen by Providence to serve as an example to all [nations] of the Old and New World. Britain herself, the United States and Belgium must come here to learn the true norms of the representative system. Liberty and democracy are only at home under the tricolor flag of the model republic. When it comes to war, Chile numbers her feats of arms by the thousands. The capture of the *Covadonga* outshines the Battle of Trafalgar, and Nelson himself is a mere pigmy compared to Captain Williams.[20]

This xenophobia had been further accentuated by the outcome of the War of the Pacific. Victory over the Andean nations provoked a spirit of national infatuation, while political firebrands inflamed public opinion with the prospect of new territorial annexations at the expense of their neighbors. Indeed, with a facade of political stability, rapid economic growth and a background of military victory, Chileans came to regard themselves as a sort of Latin American master race. If prior to 1879 their economic progress led them to style themselves the English of South America, their victory over Bolivia and Peru, they believed, had earned them the soubriquet of the Prussia of South America. Many who visualized their nation in the role of Prussia in 1870, wishfully cast Argentina in the role of a South American France, corrupt, divided, and motivated by commercial greed, and one which would be overwhelmed by Chilean military might. There were those in Chile who believed their nation superior in virtue and might to Argentina and were quite willing to go to war to prove it. An American traveler and former commissioner to various Latin American governments noted that the vanity of the Chileans passed all comprehension. When a rumor of war between Britain and Russia reached Chile, officers of the army and navy actually offered their services to England. When an English-language newspaper at Valparaíso published a satire announcing that the Lords of the Admiralty had chosen three-well known Chilean officers to command the Bosporus, Baltic, and North Atlantic squadrons of the Royal Navy, the officers involved took this quite seriously and began to polish their swords and uniforms, until the next issue of the paper revealed the hoax.[21]

Isolated and remote, Chileans believed their nation superior to all neighboring countries. Mayor Juan Serrato, of Argentine Army Intelligence, who spent the years 1895 through 1902 traveling through Chile, dryly commented:

This mirage bewildered and deceived them. While traveling one would hear people ask whether the *cuyanos* [a generic name the Chileans gave all Argentines] could possibly have this or that. The object could be a fruit, a flower, a building. If a provincial newspaper managed a circulation of two hundred [copies], then it was a colossus which the *cuyanos* could never hope to equal. The same (criteria) applied to their men of letters, popular musicians and dancers. Their superiority complex reached ridiculous extremes, and to their mandatory questions, as to whether the *cuyanos* could have this or that, it was an evangelical duty, (in order) to flatter their vanity and win friendships to reply "Of course not!"[22]

This exaggerated sense of self-importance led Chilean diplomats to adopt poses characterized by plaintive and hectoring tones. In their minds, even if unsubstantiated by fact, their army was the finest, after Prussia's, and their navy, "second only to the British Navy," would easily defeat the Argentines.[23]

Unparalleled arrogance, smugness, and a superficially expansive self-confidence colored not only Chilean perceptions of their Argentine neighbors, but their self-assessments as well. The Argentines, for their part, revised their own perceptions of Chile. The admiration for the sister nation and her progress felt in the past gave way to mistrust, particularly after the *Jeanne Amélie* and *Devonshire* incidents, while the connection between Chileans and the Indians caused them to view Chile with ever-growing suspicions. By the late 1890s

Argentina had undergone a very real transformation. This process was but the realization of political ideas formulated by the intellectual elites, at first formulated during the struggles against Rosas, and afterward, during the process of national reconstruction. Institutional stability was a prerequisite for economic development.[24]

There were a number of internal and external problems to overcome (see chapter 2). At the conclusion of the Paraguayan war relations with Brazil, the semi-eternal rivals were severely strained. War seemed imminent. Paraguay, under Brazilian occupation at the time, was another potential enemy, as was Uruguay. There was also the unresolved territorial question with Bolivia, and of course the Patagonian dispute with Chile. Aware of their nation's diplomatic isolation and military inferiority, succeeding Argentine governments during 1862 and 1881 attempted to neutralize the Chilean threat by means of treaties and direct negotiations. But when provoked by Chilean incursions on the Atlantic coast of Patagonia, Argentina could react vigorously, as she did in 1878, by dispatching a naval expedition to the threatened region.[25]

Argentina did not fear Chile militarily, as Chilean historians are fond of stressing. Indeed, they had supreme confidence in their own capabilities and military traditions. Still, the most elemental rules of prudence counseled vigilance over their aggressive Western neighbor. The ancient proverb *si vix pax, para bellum* ("if you wish peace, prepare for war") became an axiom for Argentina, particularly as Chilean "Punic Faith" was blamed for the seemingly never ending succession of protocols.[26]

DIPLOMATIC SPARRING AND THE BOUNDARY DISPUTE, 1895–1898

By mid-1895 tensions between Argentina and Brazil had been relaxed, and relations became progressively more cordial, as the dispute over the Misiones territories was solved through the mediation of Grover Cleveland, the president of the United States. Yet, Chilean diplomats pinned their aspirations, their hopes in a Brazilian alliance and were disappointed when it failed to materialize. Bolivia and Peru, as could be expected, were potential allies of Argentina.

Demarcation along the Andean boundaries between Argentina and Chile proceeded very slowly. In order to stave off a final rupture, an additional protocol was concluded in September 1895. Further negotiations would result in the Guerrero–Quirno Costa protocol of April 17, 1896, which extended the demarcation northward into areas Chile had seized from Bolivia and made specific provisions for demarcation. Should differences occur between the experts regarding boundary markers, the matter would be turned over to Her Britannic Majesty's government, which would act as an arbiter in the dispute, thus allowing the Chilean government to save face while providing for Bolivian participation in the talks regarding the Puna de Atacama question.[27]

Norberto Quirno Costa, who doubled as Argentine minister plenipotentiary to

Chile and boundary expert, resigned. To replace him in the latter capacity, on September 21, the Argentine government designated Francisco P. Moreno. Moreno was a distinguished Patagonian explorer and savant, as well as a member of the Public Museum at La Plata. His mission was interrupted by the death of his wife in June 1897, which forced him to return to Buenos Aires. During his prolonged absence Moreno published a preparatory study of the territories in dispute entitled *Reconocimiento de la Región Andina de la República Argentina*, where he questioned the validity of the divortia aquarum theory as formulated by the Chileans. Moreno's point of contention was that in a mountainous region, fallen rocks or uprooted tree trunks could easily deflect the course of a river, something he clearly demonstrated by deflecting the Fenix River to its original course. This was misinterpreted in Chile by sectors that favored war with Argentina, and Moreno's book was received with anger by the Chileans. The newspaper *La Tarde*, which advocated a hard line toward Argentina, charged that Moreno attempted to distort the theory of divortia aquarum in order to grant Argentina ports in the Pacific.[28]

Moreno returned to Chile on January 8, 1898, but departed again three weeks later in order to study the Santa Cruz region; he would not return to Chile until May. His arrival was preceded by angry editorials in the Chilean press. Typical of these was a commentary in the May 2 edition of *La Tarde*: "The functionary which has just arrived is an implacable enemy of Chile (but) it is not our intention to incite the people to receive that deflector of rivers in a violent but otherwise thoroughly deserved fashion."[29]

The press campaign had its desired effect. On May 7 Moreno arrived at Santiago's Mapocho railway, where he was greeted by Norberto Piñeiro, the new Argentine minister to Santiago. Both Argentines were met by an angry mob that proffered threats and jeered at them. Argentina registered a stern note of diplomatic protest and received an apologetic explanation from the Chilean government, which professed to be surprised by the turn of events. In order to expedite a solution to the vexing demarcation process, on May 14, a meeting took place in the office of the Chilean president with Moreno, Barros Arana, Piñeiro, and the Chilean foreign minister present. It was agreed that the experts would submit maps of the demarcation area showing their respective lines, and afterward, irrespective of the progress in the negotiation, the role of the experts would give way to government initiatives aimed at bringing the dispute to an end.[30]

A Chilean historian describes Norberto Piñeiro as

A man gifted with clear intelligence, but not gifted as a diplomat. His frank character often won him the enmity of those who came in contact with him, because of his rare if somewhat exaggerated habit of telling the truth, a profoundly well inspired man, incapable of distorting matters or employing devious methods. One could have absolute certainty of being in the presence of a man of honor by natural inclinations.[31]

Piñeiro arrived at Santiago on February 9, 1897; he was officially received on February 17. His first ministerial task involved the Puna de Atacama. A

Chilean government decree dated February 29 instructed surveyors that the map of Chile was to include the entire Puna de Atacama region. Piñeiro addressed a formal note to the Chilean foreign minister protesting this action. The Chilean foreign ministry in turn apologized for a "poorly redacted letter," stating that the Chilean government did not presume to establish sovereignty or jurisdiction in a territory submitted to demarcation and would instruct the map makers to include a note stating that the line of demarcation of that territory would be drawn according to the treaties subscribed by the Argentine and Chilean governments in 1881 and 1896. The Argentine government approved Piñeiro's conduct and his handling of the incident, which was now considered closed. A Chilean parliamentarian approached Piñeiro on his own initiative and made him aware of rumors circulating in Chilean government circles about a secret alliance among Argentina, Bolivia, and Peru. In a dispatch to the Argentine foreign ministry dated September 29, Piñeiro traced the rumors to the Chilean foreign minister, who had not broached the subject, who had failed to expedite matters, and who had further demonstrated a lack of conviction and distrust when confronted. Later on, Piñeiro learned that Joaquín Walker Martínez, the Chilean minister in Buenos Aires, had urged the Chilean government to beware and to arm the nation because Argentine intentions were not at all peaceful, as the alliance with Bolivia demonstrated.[32]

Earlier in the year, Joaquín Walker Martínez had begun talks with the Argentine minister, Amancio Alcorta. The latter, aware that the Chilean diplomat had advocated a preventive war against Argentina, regarded him with natural suspicion. Nevertheless, Alcorta agreed to Walker Martínez's suggestion to consider ways and means to end the disquietude and suspicions that disturbed relations between both countries as well as reaching definite means of finalizing the remaining operations in the process of demarcation. Yet another issue emerged during the talks between Alcorta and Walker Martínez. The Chilean inquired about the presence of Argentine troops in the Lake Lacar region, in the territory of Río Negro. Alcorta expressed his surprise and sternly reminded Walker Martínez that a fort had been established in the area by Argentine troops during the Andean campaign of 1881–1883 and that more recently a village had been founded. Both village and outpost were situated east of the Andes, and the latter dated back to 1881. Chile, at any rate, had never contested the area. Rebuffed, Walker Martínez concluded the session.[33]

The Chilean president, Federico Errázuriz Echaurren, felt that peaceful negotiations would prevent an immediate war and spare both countries from future hatreds and a war of revenge in the future. There were many across the Andes who shared such sentiments, including the Argentine president, José Evaristo Uriburu, former President Roca, who had been reelected for a second term, and Bartolomé Mitre, the aged patriarch of the republic. All that remained was to give the Argentine government assurances on the question of the Puna de Atacama. Accordingly, on July 7, the Chilean foreign minister cabled Walker Martínez, instructing him that the experts would meet during August to discuss their respective lines for the territories between parallel 26° 52' 45" down to the 52nd Parallel of latitude south, thus leaving the Puna, which Chile recognized as Argentine territory, out of the hands of the experts and providing for British arbitration in those sections of the boundary line upon which the experts failed to agree. Embittered, Walker Martínez tendered his resignation.[34]

Joaquín Walker Martínez was a curious diplomat. From his post in Buenos Aires, he sent his government obviously false information that purported Argentina's "unpreparedness" for war and urged his government to begin hostilities immediately, while Chile "still retained some advantages." In a dispatch sent in August to the Chilean foreign minister, Walker Martínez urged immediate action, arguing that at the present time a Chilean victory was assured and that a naval campaign would end the struggle. In another three months, he added, the naval balance of power would be unfavorable for Chile. The country would be forced to protect its territory, presently safeguarded by the snows. Meanwhile, General Emil Körner informed President Errázuriz that the Chilean army would not be ready for war for several months.[35]

Moved by his desire to put an end to the frontier dispute and pave the way for improved relations with Argentina, Errázuriz invited Norberto Piñeiro to meet with him on September 18, during the Chilean independence celebrations, for frank and intimate talks. Piñeiro met with the Chilean foreign minister, José Latorre, and signed three parts of the protocol agreed by the Argentine government, one on September 15 and two on September 17. On their next meeting, on September 19, Latorre requested a joint statement in which each nation delineated its position regarding arbitration. Chile, he added, felt arbitration should be ample, unrestricted, and unlimited. Piñeiro replied that such a statement would actually hinder and delay the solution of the boundary dispute. He also reminded Latorre that the Argentine government had not requested a similar declaration from Chile, suggested a joint meeting with President Errázuriz, and rejected Latorre's arguments. That same afternoon, Pedro Montt, advisor to Errázuriz, met with Piñeiro. Montt characterized Latorre as a man who was misguided and incompetent, one who wanted to provoke a war and was totally unsuited to deal with matters of such importance. Thus, Latorre was left out of the negotiations and no further meetings between him and Piñeiro occurred until September 22. Much to his surprise, Piñeiro would later learn that Latorre claimed to have presented him with an ultimatum![36]

A search of the diplomatic files in the Public Records Office in London as well as in the National Archives in Washington has failed to produce evidence of the pretended Chilean ultimatum. This author is firmly convinced that it existed only in the imagination of some Chileans. North American studies on the subject, largely based upon Chilean sources, err in lending credence to this story. Furthermore, recent Chilean research on the boundary question omits the mythical episode and takes to task older Chilean works on the matter, as they are capricious and cast a different light upon the true course of events. Piñeiro, in fact, faithfully carried out the instructions received from his government in a polite but otherwise official manner. In a meeting with Errázuriz on September 20, when the former tried to reintroduce the matter of the Puna into the agenda, Piñeiro wired Buenos Aires, which curtly informed him that the Puna was to be excluded from all possible negotiations. Thus only the disputed areas in the south were submitted to British arbitration.[37]

By the spring of 1898, the press of both nations had given wide coverage to events relating to the boundary dispute issue as these developed, and a more bellicose tone was discernible on both sides of the Andes. Despite negotiations, both nations had mobilized part of their reserves. Argentina, in fact, called 30,000 men to arms and shipped arms and equipment for 60,000 national guardsmen to areas of initial concentration. Tensions soon relaxed after the September protocols, and new figures appeared on the stage. Julio A. Roca, reelected to the presidency of Argentina in April, assumed office on October 12. Much to his surprise, Piñeiro, who had so staunchly kept the Puna out all negotiations, learned that Roca and Errázuriz had been dealing privately as early as June through the person of Francisco P. Moreno, the Argentine boundary expert. Enraged, he resigned. Latorre and Joaquín Walker Martínez tendered their resignations, although for an entirely different reason. They were angered at their government's refusal to go to war with Argentina.[38]

Roca and Errázuriz had apparently agreed to resolve the question of the Puna secretly. By an agreement signed on November 2, an international conference would take place in which ten delegates, five from each country, would try to arrive at an understanding on the Puna question through direct negotiation, as Argentina had always intended. If the delegates failed to come to terms with each other, the matter would be turned over to a commission composed of an Argentine, a Chilean, and William I. Buchanan, the U.S. minister to Argentina. To signal an improvement in their relations, the presidents of Argentina and Chile agreed to meet at the Straits on February 12, 1899.[39]

The international conference at Buenos Aires began work on March 1; by March 9 two separate proposals for a demarcation line, one Argentine, the other Chilean, were rejected. José E. Uriburu of Argentina and Enrique McIver of Chile acted as their countries' representatives. This commission met from March 21 through 24 but remained deadlocked, as each Argentine proposal was rejected by the Chilean, and the converse was also true. Finally Buchanan drew a line of his own and divided it into seven sections. Four times Buchanan voted with the Argentine delegate, twice with the Chilean, and in the remaining sector, the vote was unanimous. Thus was the Puna de Atacama question resolved. Of the 75,000 square kilometers of disputed territory, 64,000, or 85 percent, went to Argentina and 11,000, or 15 percent, to Chile.[40]

Several more years were to elapse before the Patagonian issue was resolved, but before an agreement was reached, both countries were on the verge of war once again. The treaty of 1896 had offered Queen Victoria the position of arbiter in case the experts of Argentina and Chile failed to agree on a line of demarcation. On November 23, 1898, both countries took steps to submit the dispute.

Argentina presented her case on January 17 and Chile shortly afterward. Queen Victoria appointed a commission to settle the dispute, but she died, on January 22, 1901, before it had reached a decision.[41]

ARGENTINE-CHILEAN RELATIONS, 1900–1902

Several issues were to disturb the fragile truce between Argentina and Chile. Santiago learned in May 1900 that a detachment of Argentine soldiers had entered into the Lake Lacar area, which Chile considered hers, and set up camp at Pirehuico. On May 25, a member of the Chilean demarcation commission sent a report in which he indicated that troopers of the Argentine third cavalry at San Martín de Los Andes had occupied an area forty kilometers to the west of that village. Although outcries were raised against this Argentine "invasion," the Chilean minister of the interior did not attach importance to the incident, as he felt that the word *invasion* was a rather exaggerated term to describe "the wanderings of three or four armed men in a deserted area." The matter might have ended after a note of protest, but Joaquín Walker Martínez, from his newly elected seat in the Chilean Chamber of Deputies, took every opportunity to harass and importune the Chilean president. While on June 2 the Chilean foreign ministry sent a letter of protest to Argentina regarding these "invasions" of the Lake Lacar area, Walker Martínez requested a congressional inquiry into the matter. To gain political capital, he blew the Lake Lacar affair out of all proportion to its true importance, and the Chilean press seized upon it eagerly. Although the Chilean government was preoccupied with the incident, it hesitated to make a major issue out of it at a time when it was trying to improve relations with Bolivia and Peru. A major incident could drive the Andean nations into the arms of Argentina, and the nightmare Chile had always dreaded, an effective alliance of Argentina, Bolivia, and Peru, could well become a threatening reality.[42]

The Walker Martínez inquiry dragged on until July 17, when the foreign minister received a vote of confidence. Walker Martínez acted out of spite. After all, he believed that war with Argentina was unavoidable, and yet war was avoided. He believed Argentina would not accept arbitration, and arbitration was accepted. The Argentine press, with the exception of *La Prensa*, was indifferent to the entire affair. Walker Martínez had only succeeded in hardening Roca's attitude toward Chile.[43]

Shortly after the so-called Lake Lacar invasions, another incident brought anti-Chilean sentiments in Buenos Aires to a high pitch. While it appeared that tensions with Argentina had slackened, Santiago believed it could take a harder stand toward Bolivia. The Altiplano nation never ceased to hope for the return of her lost seacoast, but these hopes were to be dashed abruptly by the arrival of Abraham Konig, the new Chilean minister to Sucre. Konig's initial contacts with President José Manuel Pando and his foreign minister, Heliodoro Villazón, had been promising. Konig had suggested that instead of the port, which his nation was no longer prepared to grant, Chile would undertake the construction of a railway linking Bolivia with the Pacific coast, grant free transit to Bolivia's foreign trade, and assume certain debts incurred by the Andean nation. Villazón accepted the offer but insisted on the port issue. Rather undiplomatically, Konig replied in a caustic note dated July 13, warning the Bolivian that his nation should not entertain thoughts of a war of revenge against Chile. Furthermore, the Bolivian public and press were wrong to assume that their nation had any right to expect a port in the littoral and even if such a port was granted, Chile would retake it in case of war, adding: "Chile has occupied and seized the littoral with the same rights with which Germany seized Alsace-Lorraine, and the same rights with which the United States seized Puerto Rico. Our rights stem from the victory, the supreme law of nations."[44]

Once the import of the Konig note became publicly known in Argentina, it sparked deep feelings of revulsion against Chile. Throughout the rest of the year, there occurred a series of demonstrations in Buenos Aires and in many cities of the interior in which the people of Argentina manifested their support of Bolivia and Peru and their antipathy to Chile. Relations with Santiago grew noticeably colder when it became known that Chilean engineers had begun to construct roads and trails in Argentine territory, ostensibly to facilitate demarcation, but in reality as a prelude to Chilean colonization of lands east of the Andes. Chilean agents were offering these lands for sale in Europe with the hope of attracting new immigrants. The Argentine foreign ministry sent a letter of protest in April 1901, but Chile replied evasively, while protesting the "innocence" of trails built in Argentine territory, and blamed the exasperating delays in replying to the Argentine protest on the illness of President Errázuriz. At the same time, the tenacious Joaquín Walker Martínez, whose hatred of Argentina was well known, received details of another Argentine "invasion" at Última Esperanza, a spot on the Pacific coast of Patagonia, about three degrees north of Punta Arenas. Walker Martínez, ever on the offensive, requested an official explanation from the Chilean executive on the "Argentine invasion" and seemed satisfied when he learned that a patrol vessel and a detachment of troops had been sent to the area. For its part, the Argentine government interpreted the whole affair as another stratagem in which Chile became the accuser rather than the accused and dispatched a cruiser to Río Gallegos.[45]

Mobs in Santiago demonstrated against Argentina as the atmosphere grew even more rarified. Chile diverted 3 millions pounds sterling, originally borrowed abroad to improve Santiago's sewage system, and ordered two light battleships, while Argentina replied with an order for two larger and more powerful vessels and called up the 1878 and 1879 contingents of the national guard to active duty on January 5, 1902. The Argentine public, normally aloof to the boundary dispute, began to take a more active part. Rifle associations in recess since 1898 were activated. Private citizens offered donations in cash and horses, while the more affluent volunteered to equip regiments, and public demonstrations against Chile took place throughout Argentina. More than 100,000 troops were reported to be armed and ready for action.[46]

A deadlock in the trails building incident occurred when Eliodoro Yáñez, the Chilean foreign minister, insisted that both countries evacuate those areas in dispute or police them jointly. Alcorta cabled Epifanio Portela, the Argentine minister to Santiago, on December 21 and instructed him to request an audience with Yáñez. Portela was to inform him that the Argentine government rejected the Chilean suggestion and desired to know whether this was, in fact, the definite proposal of the Chilean government on the matter. If the Chilean government replied in the affirmative, Portela was to inform them that further negotiations would be useless and then withdraw. Chile would have until midnight on December 24 to reply. If a favorable reply was not received, relations would be broken off. Pablo Riccheri, the Argentine war minister, had drawn plans for an invasion of Chile that would begin with the seizure of Punta Arenas. A few minutes after the deadline expired, Concha Subercaseaux, the Chilean minister to Buenos Aires, arrived at the Casa Rosada, the Argentine executive mansion, raced through the marble corridors, and announced his government's compliance.[47]

While Portela was taking his leave of President German Riesco, he was appraised of the Chilean's desire for further negotiations. Portela agreed to relay the information privately, as his official mission had already concluded. Riesco suggested that both nations should revert to the status quo of 1898, and this was the information that Concha Subercaseaux rushed breathlessly to President Roca on that fateful Christmas eve. The Argentine government accepted and cabled the governor of Santa Cruz to withdraw his forces from Última Esperanza. Portela met again with Riesco and Yáñez on December 25, and two acts were composed. The first provided for mutual withdrawal of forces in the Última Esperanza area, while in the second Chile affirmed that the trails she had constructed did not constitute an act of occupation. Apparently, the matter had been solved, but once the acts were signed, Portela became aware that an additional paragraph, not previously agreed to, had been inserted. Whereas Portela had approved a paragraph by which both nations agreed to continue relations and to regulate police service in some regions of the territory enclosed between the lines of the two boundary commissions, the additional paragraph extended such policing tasks over all disputed territories. When the acts were published, Portela realized that the wording had been altered. The revelation angered the Argentine government, which demanded an amendment in the wording of the acts. Reflecting this mood, Alcorta informed Concha Subercaseaux that if a satisfactory answer to his demand was not forthcoming in forty-eight hours, diplomatic relations would be severed. At that, Chile anxiously sent word through its minister in Buenos Aires that it was willing to comply with the Argentine demands, while requesting that details of this agreement should not be released to the press for eight days.[48]

While only a minority on either side of the Andes favored a solution of the boundary dispute by force of arms, the incidents and misunderstandings that occurred in the final days of 1901 had brought the controversy to its most dangerous boiling point. Twice Chile had attempted to drive a coach-and-four through established procedure, and twice the Chilean government had been given an ultimatum. Twice Chile had backed off short of war. Chilean government circles feared Argentine intervention in the solution of pending problems with Bolivia and Peru. Alcorta had warned Lord William Barrington, the British Ambassador to Buenos Aires, that Argentina would not tolerate further Chilean expansion in the Pacific. While private citizens of Argentina and Chile had attempted to accelerate the peace process, it was not until the arrival of Gerald Lowther, the new British minister in Santiago, that the search for a permanent solution began. The naval arms race was a severe strain on the economies of both nations. Therefore, shortly after his arrival in Santiago, Lowther sought to bring this costly arms competition to an end.[49]

THE NAVAL ARMS RACE

The naval arms competition, a by-product of the boundary dispute, began slowly in the late 1880s and gained momentum by the mid-1890s. As seen in chapter 5, Argentina first achieved qualitative and then quantitative superiority with the purchase of the *Garibaldi*-class cruisers. Painfully aware that the possession of these four homogeneous units would alter the balance of power in Argentina's favor, the Chilean foreign minister ordered Ramón Subercasseaux, Chile's minister plenipotentiary to Berlin and Rome, to pressure the Italian government to block delivery of these ships to Argentina. Subercasseaux was rebuffed by the Italians, who informed him that vessels of that class were available to all nations. Subercasseaux relayed this offer to his government, which turned it down. Bitterly, the diplomat would later write in his memoirs that "The rejection came after the government consulted the navy. [Apparently] the navy did not consider a ship to be a ship unless it came from England. The Japanese, who are well-versed in naval matters thought differently, [hence] Italian ships of this type fought brilliantly at Tsu-Shima.''[50]

The Chilean diplomats' efforts to halt delivery of the *Garibaldi*-class armored cruisers merely served to emphasize the fact that their government realized that Chile had lost naval supremacy in the Southern Cone. Roca had warned the Chilean ambassador that Argentina would simply counteract all Chilean naval acquisitions by ordering twice as many ships. What Roca did not state, though in view of the circumstances, it was quite logical to assume, was that every subsequent Argentine purchase would not only involve a larger number of ships, but that these units would be invariably larger and more powerful than the previous Chilean order. Thus, when Chile purchased the 4,500-ton protected cruiser *Chacabuco*, three destroyers, and a pair of transports, the Argentine reply was immediate: two additional *Garibaldi*-class armored cruisers, larger and faster than the previous four. These ships became the *Rivadavia* and *Moreno*.[51]

Conscious of the ever wider disparity between the Argentine and Chilean navies, Carlos Mora Vicuña, Chile's minister in Washington, approached Lieutenant Thomas Snowden, the Chief of Intelligence of the U.S. Navy, and inquired whether the U.S. government would be willing to sell Chile two battleships of 10,000 tons displacement and then made an offer for two *Indiana*-class battleships, which far exceeded the actual cost of these ships. The *Indiana* class had revealed glaring deficiencies in design and construction that were widely commented on by the world's naval press; yet this particular offer showed the heights of desperation reached by Chile. When the United States government rejected the offer, Chile utilized funds from its gold conversion reserves and ordered a pair of 12,000-ton "light battleships." Not to be outdone, Argentina ordered two 15,000-ton battleships from Italian yards, and for good measure, six destroyers of the *Nembo* class, originally laid down for the Italian navy. Thus Argentina reaffirmed her naval superiority. It was apparent to many that the naval arms race and indeed the boundary question were minor incidents, and what really lay behind them was the question of South American supremacy.[52]

The intervention of British diplomacy at this stage was understandable, for that country not only had considerable investments in Argentina and Chile but was the largest trading partner as well as the principal creditor to both nations. The period of "armed peace" was severely straining the economies of Argentina and Chile. Jorge Hunneus, a Chilean businessman, quietly approached Britain, in search of a solution. At a later date, in an unconnected move, Ernesto Tornquist, a leading Argentine banker, made a similar request. The arrival of Lord Lowther marked a new chapter in the Argentine-Chilean controversy. Lowther and Barrington, his colleague in Buenos Aires, had been authorized by Lord Gerard Landsdowne, the British foreign secretary, to offer the good services of His Majesty's government to Argentina and Chile. In his initial interview with Lowther, Yáñez manifested concern over possible Argentine interference in Pacific matters and protested Chile's peaceful intentions. Lowther rebuked him by reminding him that it was hard to reconcile a peaceful spirit with the acquisition of warships, something Yáñez tried to dismiss as an attempt by Chile to regain its naval superiority. Barrington had similarly approached the Argentine government and signaled that Buenos Aires would be willing to cancel its recent orders for warships if she could be assured that Chile would agree to do likewise. On April 8, Lowther met with the foreign minister of the interior, who expressed similar views to Yáñez, but also added that "Chile was much richer than Argentina, that its financial resources were intact, and thus better prepared to deal with an arms race." This was pure fantasy, since Chile had to divert money from its gold conversion box as well as funds destined for the sewage system of Santiago in order to finance her last naval purchases.[53]

Naval superiority was an important point that neither country was prepared to grant. In 1902, even without the ships under construction in Europe, the Argentine fleet was twice as strong as Chile's. The arrival of the 12,000 tonners would have given Chile the naval superiority she had lost years before. Of course, the 15,000-ton Argentine vessels, which were to have been delivered at the same time as the Chilean battleships, and the two 8,000-ton cruisers of an improved *Garibaldi* would have heavily tilted the strategic balance in Argentina's favor. When British diplomacy suggested a halt in naval construction, Chile made desperate efforts to retain at least some of the vessels and even offered an alternate solution. If Argentina agreed to halt delivery of her 15,000 tonners, Chile would be willing to divide the 12,000 tonners as well as the 8,000-ton armored cruisers with Argentina, but this initiative was rejected by the British diplomat. There is ample evidence in Argentine, British, and U.S. archives to support the fact that the contract for the 15,000-ton battleships was indeed finalized. This fact seems to have been largely ignored by most Chilean works on the subject. Others simply dismiss it as a bluff on the part of Argentina, following a well-established Chilean characteristic we have seen repeatedly in these pages: ignoring unpleasant truths.[54]

Further negotiation finally resulted in mutual agreement to dispose of all pending naval construction and to effect naval reductions that in fact would allow both countries to achieve parity. In practice, these reductions were confined to deactivating three vessels, two Argentine armored cruisers and an older Chilean battleship, the *Pratt*. This left Argentina in the position of naval supremacy she had enjoyed since 1898.[55]

Once British diplomats were able to put a halt to the arms race, the matter of Argentine intervention in the affairs of the Pacific still posed problems. The Argentines felt themselves compelled to safeguard their own security as well as the peace the continent against the expansionist policies of Chile, which sought to gain territory by force, and whenever it could, pursue a policy of intimidation against her weaker neighbors, but a compromise was reached. Chile announced she had no further territorial ambitions in the area. For its part, Buenos Aires vowed it would not interfere in the solution of pending matters relating to the War of the Pacific and would intervene only if Chile tried to reduce Bolivia and Peru to the level of vassal states.[56]

While some of these negotiations were underway, some of the leading figures involved in the process were removed by various circumstances. Epifanio Portela, a tenacious defender of Argentine interests and an advocate of a hard line toward Chile, was replaced by Antonio Terry. Alcorta, who was of a similar mind, died on May 6, while Yáñez left the Chilean foreign ministry during March. A series of protocols was concluded in Santiago on May 28 between Antonio Terry and José Antonio Donoso, the new Chilean foreign minister. Known as the Pacts of May, these protocols included a general treaty of arbitration, a naval armaments agreement, and an act requesting the appointment of a demarcation commission by the arbitrating power. The demarcation commission, headed by Colonel Holdich, had in fact arrived in South America during January of that year and would complete its tasks in June, returning to England in the following month, while both countries would await the verdict of the British Crown. When the Pacts of May were submitted to the Argentine Congress in July, hard-liners, led by Estanislao Zevallos, lamented "the triumph of Chilean diplomacy," which had secured carte blanche on the Pacific, while Chilean opponents of the treaties denounced them because they relegated their nation to a position of naval inferiority. Nevertheless, the legislatures of both countries approved the Pacts of May by wide majorities. On November 20, King Edward VII handed down his boundary award, granting Argentina 40,000 of the 94,000 square kilometers in dispute and Chile the remaining 54,000. The award produced waves of popular discontent in both Argentina and Chile. Nevertheless, both concluded an agreement on January 9, 1903, requesting the British government to proceed with the boundary demarcation. Though nationalist elements on both sides of the Andes sorely opposed the new treaties, old suspicions could at least temporarily be put aside.[57]

NOTES

1. Geoffery S. Smith, "The Role of José M. Balmaceda in Preserving Argentine Neutrality in the War of the Pacific," *HAHR* 49, no. 2 (May 1968), pp. 254–255.

2. Ibid., pp. 256–262; Isidoro Ruíz Moreno, *Historia de las relaciones exteriores argentinas* (Buenos Aires: Editorial Perrot, 1961), p. 226–228; Robert Talbott, *A History of the Chilean Boundaries* (Ames: Iowa State University Press, 1974), pp. 96–99.

3. Ruíz Moreno, *Historia de las relaciones*, pp. 232–233; Talbott, *A History of the Chilean Boundaries*, p. 102.

4. Holdich, *The Countries of the King's Award* (London: Hurst and Blackett, 1904), pp. 53–55; Vicente Quesada, *La política chilena en el Plata* (Buenos Aires: Arnoldo Moen, 1895), pp. 184–190; Raul C. Rey Balmaceda, *Límites y fronteras de la República Argentina* (Buenos Aires: OIKOS, 1979), pp. 105–106.

5. Félix Best, *Historia de las guerras argentinas: De la independencia, internacionales, civiles y con el indio*, 2 vols. (Buenos Aires: Ediciones Peuser, 1960), II: 397–398.

6. Ruíz Moreno, *Historia de las relaciones*, pp. 206–207.

7. Talbott, *A History of the Chilean Boundaries*, p. 105.

8. Ricardo Marcó del Pont, "Cuestión de límites entre la República Argentina y Bolivia," *Revista Argentina de Ciencias Políticas* 26 (abril–septiembre 1923), pp. 39–104; Harris Gaylord Warren, *Paraguay: An Informal History* (Norman: University of Oklahoma Press, 1949), pp. 290–291; David H. Zook, *The Conduct of the Chaco War*, (New York: Bookman Associates, 1960), pp. 25–26. After the defeat of Paraguay in the War of the Triple Alliance, Bolivia attempted to secure allied recognition of her claims to the Chaco, but Argentina and Brazil turned her away, empty handed. Alberto D. H. Scunio, *La Conquista del Chaco* (Buenos Aires: Círculo Militar, 1972), pp. 167–169. Bolivia tried to infiltrate the Argentine Chaco. Following several border violations by small detachments of Bolivian troops, the Argentine army detached the twelfth cavalry to stand watch on the border between Salta and the Chaco. In 1871, a Bolivian detach-

ment of fifty men under Major Teran was captured by an Argentine patrol, disarmed, imprisoned, and escorted to the Bolivian border, thirty-one leagues away.

9. Mario Barros, _Historia diplomática de Chile_ (Barcelona: Ediciones Ariel, 1971), pp. 472–474; Robert N. Burr, _By Reason or by Force: Chile and the Balancing of Power in South America, 1830–1905_ (Berkeley and Los Angeles: University of California Press, 1967), p. 184.

10. Valentín Abecia Valdevieso, _Las Relacciones Internacionales en la Historia de Bolivia_ (Cochabamba: Editorial Los Amigos del Libro, 1979), pp. 995–996; Marco del Pont, "Cuestión de límites," pp. 53–54.

11. Ricardo T. Caillet-Bois, "La misión Rocha a Bolivia en 1895," _Boletín del Instituto de Historia Argentina "Doctor Emilio Ravignani"_ Vol. 11, no. 18–19 (1969), pp. 202–256; Burr, _By Reason or by Force: Chile and the Balancing of Power in South America, 1830–1905_ (Berkeley and Los Angeles: University of California Press, 1967), pp. 204–215.

12. Caillet-Bois, "La misión Rocha," p. 225.

13. Ibid., p. 226.

14. Ibid., p. 233.

15. Ibid., p. 228.

16. Rey Balmaceda, _Límites y fronteras_, pp. 85.

17. Gustavo Ferrari _Conflicto y paz con Chile, 1898–1903_. Buenos Aires: Editorial Universitaria de Buenos Aires, 1968, pp. 29–30, 46–47.

18. Domingo Amunátegui Solar, "Veintiuna cartas inéditas de Barros Arana," RCHG 86 no. 34 (enero-junio de 1939), p. 18.

19. Domingo Amunátegui Solar, "Epistolario: Cartas de Don Diego Barros Arana a Don Luis Amunátegui," RCHG 86, no. 70 (enero-junio 1930), p. 89; George Calafut, "An Analysis of Italian Emigration Statistics: 1876–1914," JAL 19 (1977), pp. 310–331. Such statements were caused by envy. Calafut's study shows that the margin of error in Argentine statistics on the arrival of Italians, which made up the largest group of immigrants to Argentina, is remarkably small and approximates American figures.

20. Juan José Fernández, _La República de Chile y el imperio del Brasil: Historia de sus relaciones diplomáticas_ (Santiago: Editorial Andres Bello, 1959), p. 56.

21. William E. Curtiss, _The Capitals of South America_ (New York: Harper and Bros., 1888), p. 476; Frederick B. Pike, _Chile and the United States, 1880–1962: The Emergence of Chile's Social Crisis and the Challenge to United States Diplomacy_ (South Bend, IN: University of Notre Dame Press, 1963), p. 34.

22. Ferrari, _Conflicto y paz_, pp. 65–66.

23. Vicente Quesada, _La política argentina respecto de Chile_ (Buenos Aires: Arnoldo Moen, Editor, 1898), pp. 72–73.

24. Oscar E. Cornblitt, Ezequiel Gallo, and Alfredo A. O'Connell, "La generación del 80 y su proyecto antecedentes y consecuencias," in Torcuato A. Di Tella, ed., _Argentina, sociedad de masas_ (Buenos Aires: EUDEBA, 1965), pp. 48–49.

25. Ricardo Alberto Paz, _El conflicto pendiente_, 2 vols. (Buenos Aires: Editorial Universitaria de Buenos Aires, 1980), II:26–27.

26. For typical Chilean views on Argentine capabilities and courage see Barros, _Historia diplomática de Chile_, pp. 322–323, 353–355; Oscar Espinosa Moraga, _La postgeurra del Pacífico y la Puna de Atacama_ (Santiago: Editorial Andres Bello, 1958), pp. 232–233. Quesada, _La política chilena_, pp. 65–66. Quesada considered Chilean mobilization and threats so much braggadocio and wrote, prophetically, "The Chileans

have cried wolf once too many times, and as a result, they've spoilt the trick, and their outcries worry no one. . . . There will be no war.''

27. Burr, *By Reason or by Force*, p. 220.

28. Espinosa Moraga, *La postguerra del Pacífico*, pp. 212–21; Exequiel González Madariaga, *Nuestras Relacciones con Argentina: una historia deprimente* (Vols. 1–2, Santiago: Editorial Andres Bello, 1974; Vol. 3, Santiago: Editorial Neupert, 1974), II: 239–240 for a very jaundiced description of Moreno. Holdich, *The Countries of the King's Award*, p. 249, on the other hand, states that the river Fénix, which supplied a nearby lake from the north, had hardly parted with its ancient Atlantic connection. This vindicates Moreno's theories. For a biography of Moreno, see Aquiles D. Ygobone, *Francisco P. Moreno: Arquetipo de argentinidad* (Buenos Aires: Editorial Plus Ultra, 1979).

29. Espinosa Moraga, *La postguerra del Pacífico*, p. 181.

30. Ricardo Donoso, *Diego Barros Arana* (Mexico DF: Instituto Panamericano de Geografía e Historia, Comisión de Historia, 1967), pp. 226–227.

31. Espinosa Moraga, *La postguerra del Pacífico*, p. 155.

32. Norberto Piñero, *En Chile: La cuestión de límites. El arbitraje. La Puna de Atacama, 1897–1898* (Buenos Aires: Librería y Casa Editora de Jesús Menéndez, 1937), pp. 7–9, 12–17, 25–28.

33. Luís V. Varela, *La República Argentina y Chile: Historia de la demarcación de sus fronteras desde 1843 hasta 1899*, 2 vols. (Buenos Aires: Imprenta de M. Biedma e hijos, 1899), I:447–448, Ricardo Alberto Paz, *El Conflicto Pendiente*, 2 vols. (Buenos Aires: *EUDEBA*, 1980), II: 100. Rather impertinently, Walker Martínez remarked that the process of demarcation should be hastened ''for the sake of the foreign creditor of both nations.'' Visibly annoyed, Alcorta dismissed the Chilean with a brief but terse note.

34. Donoso, *Diego Barros Arana*, p. 228.

35. Jaime Eyzaguirre, *Chile durante el gobierno de Errázuriz-Echaurren, 1896–1901* (Santiago: Editorial Zig-Zag, 1957), pp. 183–184, 196–197, 208–209. Among the obviously false reports or purposely distorted dispatches were those dated February 25 and 28, March 23 and 26, highlighting the ''failure'' of the Argentine army maneuvers held at Uspallata because of the lack of a proper supply system. Admittedly the mobilization of the national guard disclosed some shortcomings in organization of the commissariat service, which is exactly what such field problems are intended to do. For an accurate picture of the Uspallata maneuvers see Ignacio H. Fotheringham, *La vida de un soldado o reminiscencias de las fronteras*, 2 vols. (Buenos Aires: Círculo Militar, 1970), II: 347–377. Fotheringham was in command of the Cuyo division, which carried out the maneuvers at Uspallata. He recalls the enthusiasm and patriotism demonstrated by all ranks, whether army of the line or national guard, and their readiness for war. Local ranchers willingly offered their cattle herds to the army. On another dispatch dated June 2, Walker indicates that Argentina was urgently seeking to purchase a 10,000-ton battleship known as the *Don Juan de Austria*. *Conway's All the World's Fighting Ships: 1865–1905* (New York: Mayflower Books, 1979), pp. 270–271, 383. There were two warships bearing that name at the time. One was a barquentine-rigged frigate of 3,548 tons launched for the Austro-Hungarian navy in 1875 and hopelessly outdated by 1898. The other was a 1,152-ton Spanish gunboat that in fact had been sunk at the battle of Cavite Bay in the Philippines on May 1.

36. Piñero, *En Chile*, pp. 171–174, 176–177; Varela, *La República Argentina y Chile*, I: 463. ''After a sharp disagreement between the demarcation experts, the Chileans con-

vinced several foreign diplomats that Admiral Latorre had in fact sent an ultimatum to the Argentine government. Latorre leaked this canard to the Buenos Aires daily *El Tiempo*. This prompted questions from several of the ministers from the leading powers, who were astonished when they realized they had been duped, since the ultimatum never in fact existed.'' ''A Buenos Aires newspaper, misinformed, gave the sensational 'bombshell' that Chile had given Argentina five days to accept or reject arbitration The game is afoot! An ultimatum is synonymous with a declaration of war. The stupendous (and horrendous) news spread like wildfire, and instead of striking funeral marches, the bands loudly played reveille in the midst of frenzied cheering. The news turned out to be false.'' (See Ignacio Fotheringham, *La Vida de un soldado* (Buenos Aires: Círculo Militar, 1970), II: 389.)

37. Talbott, *A History of the Chilean Boundaries*, pp. 106–107; Piñero, *En Chile*, pp. 117–119, 129–135.

38. *Reseña Política*, II: 384; Ferrari, *Conflicto y paz*, pp. 20–21.

39. Gordon Ireland, *Boundaries, Possessions and Conflicts in South America* (New York: Octagon Books, 1971), pp. 16–20; Eyzaguirre, *Chile durante el gobierno de Errázuriz-Echaurren* pp. 257–261; Rey Balmaceda, *Límitas y fronteras*, pp. 84–86.

40. Ibid., pp. 88–89; Espinosa Moraga, *El precio de la paz*, pp. 305–307.

41. Eyzaguirre, *Chile durante el gobierno de Errázuriz-Echaurren*, pp. 327–328; Ferrari, *Conflicto y paz*, pp. 28–29, ''Cartas Enviadas por Don Carlos Concha, Ministro de Chile en Buenos Aires a Don Rafael Errázuriz, Ministro de Relacciones Exteriores, sobre problemas limítrofes,'' *Historia* 10 (1971), pp. 350–351.

42. Burr, *By Reason or by Force*, pp. 231–233; Mateo Martinic Beros, *Última esperanza en el tiempo* (Santiago Ediciones de la Universidad de Magallanes, 1985), pp. 90–93.

43. Eyzaguirre, *Chile durante el gobierno de Errázuriz-Echaurren*, pp. 334–336; Ferrari, *Conflicto y paz*, pp. 29–30.

44. Burr, *By Reason or by Force*, pp. 233–235.

45. Ferrari, *Conflicto y paz*, p. 32; *The Economist* (January 4, 1902), p. 7. This journal found the roads built by Chile to be of ''a suspiciously strategic kind.'' The article also pointed out that Barros Arana and a majority in the Chilean Chamber of Deputies favored war. The situation would have been serious, it adds, if Chile had been ready for war, which she was not. Eyzaguirre, *Chile durante el gobierno de Errázuriz-Echaurren*, pp. 332–334; Dispatch No. 215, Wilson to Secretary of State John Day, November 26, 1901. Wilson describes the road building and troop mobilization. He also noted that a rather truculent diplomacy on the part of the Argentine minister contributed to turn a comparatively insignificant issue into a dangerous situation (RG 59, U.S. National Archives, Washington DC); Martinic Beros, *Última Esperanza*, pp. 94–95.

46. *The Economist* (February 8, 1902), p. 8; Martinic Beros, *Última Esperanza*, pp. 95–96; *American Review of Reviews* (January–June 1902), p. 10; Ferrari, *Conflicto y paz*, pp. 42–44. Appearing before the Senate, War Minister Riccheri revealed that Argentina had sufficient arms and equipment to equip 300,000 men.

47. Ferrari, *Conflicto y paz*, pp. 48–49; Dionosio Schoo Lastra, *La lanza rota: Estancias, Indios, paz en la Cordillera* (Buenos Aires: Ediciones Peuser, 1953), pp. 198–210. The great railway companies prepared 4,000 railway cars and 600 locomotives, which were ready to transport 80,000 men and their equipment in forty-eight hours wherever required. In the event of war, the main body of the army, under General Lorenzo Vintter, would cross the Andes and invade the Chilean province of Tarapacá, while a battalion of the first infantry would capture Punta Arenas.

48. Ferrari, *Conflicto y paz*, pp. 50–51; German Riesco, *Presidencia de Riesco, 1901–1906* (Santiago: Imprenta Nascimento, 1950), pp. 193–195; Dispatch No. 162 from Henry L. Wilson, U.S. Minister in Chile, to John Hay, Secretary of State, January 8, 1902 (RG 59, U.S. National Archives, Washington, DC).

49. *The Economist* (February 8, 1902), pp. 208–209; Juan José Fernández, "Los Pactos de Mayo y la diplomacia Británica," *Boletín de la Academia Chilena de la Historia* 32, no. 73), pp. 99–131.

50. Ramón Subercaseaux, *Memorias de ochenta años: Recuerdos personales, reminescencias, historias, viajes y anecdotas*, 2 vols. (Santiago: Ediorial Nascimento, 1936), I: 158–160. The obvious failure of his mission did not prevent Subercaseaux from recording a highly imaginative, but totally fictitious version of what transpired in the Italian Parliament during an inquiry instigated by a deputy named Santini. According to Subercaseaux, Santini had proof of irregularities and lashed out against the navy minister, Beneddeto Brin. The latter, or so would Subercaseaux have us believe, was unable to present a coherent defense against Santini's allegations and raved on until he suffered a mild stroke. A house vote decided against the sale of warships to Argentina. However, a glance at the Italian parliamentary records reveals otherwise. See *Documenti della Camera dei Diputati: Atti Parlamentari della Camera dei Deputati*, Vol. 567, (Rome, 1898) pp. 5646–5648. While it is true that Santini raised some questions, Brin calmly reviewed the progress made by the Italian shipbuilding industry in the past decades. He pointed out that ships once imported were now entirely built in Italian yards and exported to Argentina and Spain. These sales had earned firms such as Tossi, Terni, and Pozzuoli 54 million lire. If the sale was blocked, he argued, nothing would prevent Argentina from buying warships elsewhere. A vote was taken and the resolution was favorable to Brin. Hence, the ships were delivered as scheduled. See also Eyzaguirre, *Chile durante el gobierno de Errázuriz-Echaurren*, p. 194. This source admits that Subercaseaux's efforts to halt delivery of the cruisers failed. *La Nación*'s edition of September 18, 1898, contains the following news item: "Rome, September 17: I have been informed that the urgency to hasten the departure of the armored ship *General Belgrano*, once last-minute details were completed, no longer exists. It has been decided, therefore, that the cruiser shall undergo speed trials at La Spezia early next week."

51. George von Rauch, "Cruisers for Argentina," *Warship International* 15, no. 4, (1978), p. 304.

52. Dispatch No. 201, Henry I. Wilson to Secretary of State, July 1, 1901 (RG 59, U.S. National Archives, Washington, DC). President Riesco approached Wilson, the U.S. minister in Santiago, during a private dinner. Riesco took Wilson aside and inquired whether the United States would be prepared to make imminent delivery of two first-class battleships which, Riesco added, were necessary to match the strength of the Argentine navy. Robert L. Scheina, *Latin America: A Naval History* (Annapolis, MD: Naval Institute Press, 1987), p. 50.

53. Burr, *By Reason or by Force*, p. 27; von Rauch, "Cruisers for Argentina," p. 304.

54. Barington to Foreign Office, May 5, 1902; Fernández, "Los Pactos de Mayo," pp. 111–115.

55. González Madariaga, *Nuestras relaciones con Argentina*, III: 192, prefers to believe that the Argentine 15,000-ton battleships were a bluff. Von Rauch, "Cruisers for Argentina," p. 304, states that not only were these ships ordered, but that six destroyers as well were to have been delivered to Argentina. Scheina, *Latin America*, p. 33, is

uncertain how far Argentina went toward purchasing these ships, and he adds that according to a Chilean source, the negotiations for these ships failed in May 1902. This is very unlikely, to say the least. Dispatch No. 18, U.S. Legation (Buenos Aires) to Secretary of State, May 1902 (RG 59, U.S. National Archives, Washington, DC) cites President Roca's message to the Argentine Congress in which he clearly states that Chile had contracted for two formidable warships at a heavy price to place her navy on an equal footing with Argentina's, whereas Argentina responded by ordering two warships larger in size and more formidable at an equal cost in order to maintain naval superiority. The Argentine purchase of four ships is also mentioned in Barrington's dispatch to the Foreign Office (May 2, 1902, Public Records Office, London). *The Economist* (May 17, 1902), p. 777, confirms the ratification of a contract with an Italian shipbuilder for two battleships of 15,000 tons.

56. Confidential Dispatch no. 24, April 24, 1902. Barrington to Foreign Office, Dispatch No. 25, May 5, 1902,

57. Burr, *By Reason or by Force*, pp. 246, 255; Germán Carrasco Dominguéz, *El Arbitraje Británico de 1899–1903* (Santiago: Editorial Andres Bello, 1968), pp. 191–192, 225–227; Ferrari, *Conflicto y paz*, pp. 91–102.

8

Conclusions

Estanislao Zevallos, a figure often mentioned in these pages, published the text of *Diplomacia desarmada* in the *Revista de Derecho, Historia y Letras* during September 1908 and May 1920. Its main theme was the interplay between military power and diplomacy. Throughout its pages, Zevallos related the vissicitudes encountered by Argentina during the years which followed the Paraguayan war, when it was faced by the Empire of Brazil. Argentine unity was rather precarious at the time—not only did she lack cohesion, but the financial ability to maintain a sophisticated defense apparatus. By the 1870s, Brazil had surged ahead at a time when competition with Argentina over spheres of influence in the Plata and control of the prostrated Paraguayan nation were acute.[1]

Under Mitre, Zevallos argued, the nation was disarmed; Brazilian influence in the Plata was, hence, on the rise; and thanks to the defense preparations made by Sarmiento in the years that followed, Brazilian moves were checkmated. By the late 1870s, Argentine-Brazilian relations were distinctly chilly but showed some signs of a thaw. The process of Argentine reunification had been solidified by the defeat of the last provincial caudillos during the years 1862–1876. The Indian tribes in Patagonia had suffered severe reverses at the hand of the national forces, and at last the nation was able to focus on the Patagonian question. Chile, on the other hand, had emerged in the 1830s as a small but homogeneous nation state, largely because of the fact that it was able to avoid the balkanization and civil wars that afflicted Argentina. By the mid-1840s, Chile, hemmed in by the Andes and the Pacific Ocean, was beginning to project southward. Torn by internal strife, Argentina could not respond at first. Chilean influence on Patagonia grew through alliances with the Indians, who fattened cattle herds stolen in the pampas prior to selling them across the Andes. These cattle were taken from the pampas to Chile over the *camino de los chilenos*, the road of the Chileans.[2]

The Chilean boundary dispute was undoubtedly the most important and enduring challenge the Argentine nation faced since the wars of independence. The dispute stemmed from confusing, contradictory, and overlapping colonial titles. Both nations signed a convention in 1856, under the terms of which they agreed to recognize their boundaries as "those which existed in the era of the Viceroyalties in 1810." This ambiguous wording would lead into further controversy, since Argentina plainly considered the Andes as the boundary and, therefore, the whole of Patagonia and the straits as her own. Chilean ambitions grew with the passing of time. Initially Chile claimed the straits, then a narrow strip of territory along the southern portion of Santa Cruz, and finally all of Patagonia.[3]

After the seizure of the Straits in 1843, Chile did not establish any more colonies in the disputed area. Her own Indian frontier had to be subdued. During the Paraguayan war, Chile remained neutral, but her territory was used by the Argentine caudillo Felipe Varela as a springboard for his invasions of Argentina, and there are indications that Chile might have played a more active role in these episodes. The cold war between Argentina and Brazil coincided with the high point of Chilean exploration of Atlantic Patagonia, as well as her attempts to establish permanent outposts in Santa Cruz. When Argentina was free of her northern entanglements, she decided to make her occupation of the disputed area effective. To counteract the Argentine rapprochement with Bolivia and Peru, Chile tried to develop an alliance with Brazil, which did not materialize. Argentina remained neutral during the War of the Pacific. The Argentine conquest of the desert began days after the Chilean declaration of war against the Andean nations. The Treaty of 1881 left Argentina in possession of Patagonia and Chile, her colony in the straits. There were those in Chile who considered this a necessary evil, designed to appease Argentina and prevent a stab in the back while Chilean forces were committed elsewhere. Yet, in the immediate period following the War of the Pacific, Chile made no overt efforts to regain control of Patagonia. Indeed, the issue lay dormant at a time when Chilean naval superiority was unquestionable. There were no voices clamoring for a preventive war against Argentina, as there would be in 1898. In 1878 Chile had to opt for either Patagonia or the nitrate fields of Tarapacá. She chose the latter. When the nitrate-based prosperity proved fleeting, there were voices in Chile that lamented the loss of Patagonia and the fertile valleys of Neuquén.[4]

Chile had been an aggressive state that overthrew alliances and seized the territories of its adversaries by force when it suited her interests. Yet, in the case of Argentina, in direct contradiction to her previous policies, and despite all of her bellicose posturing, Chile became an advocate of arbitration. "Misplaced Pan-Americanism!" claim Chilean revisionist historians who level the charge that their governments at the turn of the century were drugged with dreams of inter-American brotherhood.[5]

Let the history of Bolivia and Peru relate Chilean ideals of brotherhood. The growth and development of the Argentine armed forces seems a rather more likely motivation for the amicable settlement of the Argentine-Chilean boundary dispute. Were it not for Argentina's continued military growth, Patagonia might have suffered the same fate as the nitrate fields of Bolivia and Peru. The demarcation team sent by the British Crown in 1902 traced a line along what were generally clearly defined geographical features. In many cases, it merely observed de facto occupation, and the Crown confirmed this by its award. Such were the cases with the much contested Lake Lacar and Última Esperanza regions along the Andean slopes. Military force had been used by both litigants in the exploration and occupation of the disputed territory. The armed forces were also indispensable in preserving the territorial integrity of each nation and would have undoubtedly been used to back their respective claims by force if necessary.

While there was little to choose between the élan and valor of the opposing forces, it was quite apparent to each of the rivals that modern arsenals and modern warships would decide the eventual outcome if a conflict materialized. One lesson that emerged out of the border dispute was that a nation's armed forces, its institutions and equipment are generally commensurate with its wealth. It is hard to envision the expansion of the Argentine armed forces without solid economic growth and solid institutional development. This lesson was not wasted on the Argentines of the Generation of 1880, who sought to consolidate their nation and embarked upon a program of modernization that naturally extended to the armed forces. Stable government provided a climate in which immigrants would come to settle in the vast hinterlands of the underpopulated Platine nation. Foreign capital would play a vital role in further integrating Argentina into the world's economy. The growth of the Argentine economy and most particularly its foreign trade sector helped Argentina to develop her infrastructure, equip her armed forces, and overcome a position of naval inferiority vis-à-vis Chile. Both nations depended upon their foreign trade for government revenues. Neither Argentina nor Chile could produce the weapons systems required by their armed forces; nor could they successfully meet the everyday needs of the armed services. Thus not only were major items such as warships, artillery, and small arms imported, but uniforms, ammunition tents, blankets, and medical supplies.

Argentine government revenues were about the same as Chile's during the 1870s, but substantial sums were diverted to the upkeep of the frontier forces and to quell provincial insurrections. This left precious little for modern equipment. Once the Indian frontier had been closed, and the last of the caudillos defeated, a greater share of the military budget was devoted to arms purchases and less to internal pacification needs. The economy boomed after the conquest of the desert, and government revenues continued to increase until that had almost tripled by the turn of the century. When these revenues proved insufficient to meet expenditures, the nation borrowed freely from European creditors.

Save for relatively short depressions, such as that of 1890, its credit and currency inspired confidence. When in 1900, in a monumental example of fiscal responsibility the Argentine government floated bonds that exceeded its national debt, foreign bankers readily agreed. The arms purchases made in the 1890s gave Argentina military and naval superiority over its adversary. The period of armed peace (1890–1902) required a cash outlay by Buenos Aires of U.S. $258 million, a stupendous sum that Chile could not hope to match.

As the balance of power tilted, slowly at first and more dramatically by the turn of the century, Chile had a choice: compromise or war. Much has been said about the Chilean "ultimatum that never was." The demands made by the Argentine government in December 1901 and the subsequent withdrawal of its representative from Santiago was in fact an "ultimatum that was," and Chile had to comply. It is hard to visualize such a result without adequate military power to enforce it, and that, this author claims, was brought about by a continuous program that at the turn of the century made the Argentine armed forces second to none in South America.

The reconstitution of the Argentine state in 1862 brought about a change in the role of the armed forces. By the 1890s they were no longer a political instrument in the hands of provincial caudillos, but rather instruments of national policy, first by their growing fidelity to the constitutional order and then becoming an instrument of national policy. Argentina never abandoned her traditional policy of pacifism, but when the nation entered into the period of armed peace, the strength of its armed forces was effective in deterring the potential enemy.

Nations have a foreign policy dictated more often than not by their military strength and their economic capacity. The foreign policy of Argentina with respect to Chile was no exception. In the 1860s, the Argentine armed forces had emerged victorious from a long series of civil wars that produced national reunification. But like most armed forces that result from such conflicts, they were primarily concerned with policing tasks, able to prevail internally, but not equipped or trained to fight a modern war. The Argentine army of 1879 was greatly superior in firepower, training, and organization than it had been in 1862. The Indian campaigns developed a remarkable group of officers and a body of men with discipline and esprit de corps.

The Argentine navy was likewise transformed into a modern force by the acquisition of its first modern warships in the 1870s. Twenty years of methodical work would mold these institutions into proper instruments of national policy. While the mobility of land armies had remained unchanged since the end of the civil war in the United States, the principal navies of the world were improving the speed, range, efficiency, firepower, and tactical applications of their capital ships at an incredibly fast pace. The greatest accomplishment of the Argentine navy, reborn in the last quarter of the nineteenth century, was its rapid adaptation to modern technology. In that relatively short period it grew from a force of a few river boats, armed with slow-firing guns and spar torpedoes, into a fleet of more than sixty vessels of all types, which could be deployed at will.[6]

The contributions made by the armed forces of Argentina in the period studied were many: exploration and development of the newly conquered territories, the maintenance of constitutional order, and most important of all, the preservation of the Patagonian lands Argentina considered hers by right. The Argentine-Chilean boundary dispute had been solved, though in decades to come differences of interpretation over the boundary line in certain sections of territory would result in new disagreements, clashes, and renewed appeals for arbitration.

While it is certain that a nation's preparedness or unpreparedness for war does not constitute a guarantee for peace, the war party in Chile, though small, had ample following. An awareness of their nation's limitations in territorial expanse and wealth provoked the wars of 1837 and 1870 against the Andean allies in order to overcome these advantages. The rapid growth of the Argentine economy surprised and demoralized the Chilean ruling classes, which watched their eastern neighbor with jealousy, fear, and envy. Francisco A. Encina echoed these sentiments:

Our proximity to Argentina must be counted among the factors [responsible] for our economic inferiority. This is not a permanent cause of inferiority. In the past, its influence, though it impeded the cultivation of [those of] our lands suitable for cattle raising, triggered, instead, industrial and commercial activities throughout most of our territory. In the near future it might become a favorable factor. But during 1860 and 1911, this proximity has been simultaneously a bloodletting which has weakened us and a tree which has cast its shadow over us.[7]

This author maintains that without a proper military establishment, Argentina would not have been able to apply military pressure on Chile and force her to accept compromises that even Chilean historians consider were more beneficial to Argentina.[8]

This should not signify that the Argentine-Chilean boundary dispute is a dead issue or one that has been relegated to the minds and shelves of antiquarians. An often-quoted Chilean study by José Irarrázaval Larraín corroborates this feeling:

However, since the lives of nations are subject to even greater contrasts than the lives of individuals, it is necessary that future generations should not lose sight of the fact that, in the light of integrity, which governs relations between peoples, the Treaty of 1881 which delivered Patagonia to Argentina is void. . . . There was, as we have demonstrated, ignorance, culpable perhaps, on the part of Chile. On the other hand, Argentina had sufficiently exact knowledge of the true nature of the disputed territories to use force, if not to impose the signing of treaties, to take possession of the land. Chile should not forget that, by decrees of nature which overshadow treaties, she owns at least the valleys and mountains West of the Andes, lands which aside from being proverbially fertile and rich, add up to a considerable area of which Chile has been despoiled by the award of 1902.[9]

During the years 1960–1998, a wealth of official publications regarding the boundary dispute have appeared in Chile, more often than not with the approval and support of the Chilean government, and the above sentiment is echoed by the overwhelming majority of these publications. If the trend exemplifies Chilean thought and policy in the frontier dispute with Argentina, it would reinforce the contention that if not for the growth and development of the Argentine armed fores in the latter half of the nineteenth century, the map of South America might present considerable variations.

NOTES

1. Estanislao S. Zevallos, *Diplomacia desarmada* (Buenos Aires: Editorial Universitaria de Buenos Aires, 1974), pp. 22–40.

2. Carlos Escudé, *La Argentina vs. las grandes potencias: El precio del desafío* (Buenos Aires: Editorial de Belgrano, 1986), pp. 208–210, 222–224.

3. Ricardo Alberto Paz, *El Conflicto Pendiente* (Buenos Aires: *EUDEBA*, 1980); II: 6–13.

4. Ricardo Caillet-Bois, *Cuestionas Internacionales, 1852–1966* (Buenos Aires: Editorial Universitaria de Buenos Aires, 1970), p. 33; D. Richard Perry, ''Argentina and Chile: The Struggle for Patagonia, 1843–1881,'' *TAM* 26, no. 3 (January 1980), p. 363.

5. See, for example, Oscar Espinosa Moraga, *El Precio de la paz chileno-argentina*, 3 vols. (Santiago: Editorial Nascimento, 1969).

6. Humberto F. Burzio, *Historia del torpedo y sus buques en la Armada Argentina* (Buenos Aires: Departamento de Estudias Históricas Navales, serie B, no. 12, 1968), pp. 12–14.

7. Francisco A. Encina, *Nuestra inferioridad económica* (Santiago: Editorial Universitaria, 1986), p. 107.

8. For examples of this trend, see Espinosa Moraga, *El Precio*; Manuel Hormazabal Gonzalez, *Dialogando con Argentina! Sintesís Histórica de las Desmembraciones Territoriales de Chile* (Santiago: Biblioteca del Oficial, Estado Mayor del Ejército, Departamento de Relaciones Internas del Ejército, Sección Publicaciones Militares, 1979); José Irarrázaval Larraín, *La Patagonia: Errores geográficos y diplomáticos* (Santiago: Editorial Andres Bello, 1966).

9. Ibid., pp. 205–206.

Glossary

adelantado (or *adelantado de mar*): title given to the leader of a maritime expedition who would also become governor of all territories he discovered or conquered.

bolas (or *boleadoras*): stone or lead balls wrapped in leather and attached to thongs of the same material.

cabildo: city council, central authority in Spanish colonial cities.

capitulaciones: from the Latin *capitulatio*, meaning a contract between the Spanish Crown and other royal officials.

caudillo: (''leader'') nineteenth-century political chieftain.

cédula: written order or directive.

comercio libre: neomercantilist Spanish trade system.

Consulado: eighteenth-century Chamber of Commerce.

corregidor: mayor of a township or village.

criollos: a term applied to the offspring of Europeans born overseas; in the Argentine context, the sons of Spaniards born in Argentina.

destinado: term used to denote petty criminals, vagrants, and others who were sentenced to serve in the army.

enganchado: a volunteer for military service.

enganche: voluntary system of military enlistment used throughout the Spanish Empire.

estancia: a cattle ranch.

estanciero: cattle ranch owner.

facón: a long, triangularly bladed knife. The term comes from the Spanish term *faca*, which in turn is derived from the Arabic *farja*, meaning a long pointed knife.

frigorífico: packing house; the Latin *frigus* (cold) and *oris* (to make). The term entered common usage after the arrival of the French steamer *Le Frigorifique*, the first vessel equipped with a mechanically produced refrigeration system, to Buenos Aires in 1876.

gaucho: nomadic horsemen who inhabited the plains of Argentina. Uruguay, and the Brazilian state of Rio Grande do Sul. Untamed, they became armed retainers of the *estancieros*.

leva: forcible draft.

pastos fuertes: the tough grasses of the *pampas*.

personero: a substitute for military service purchased by a few hundred pesos.

porteño: "port dweller"; a term given to the inhabitants of Buenos Aires.

reducciones: under Spanish colonial rule, by law Indians were grouped into villages administered by a *corregidor* and a *cabildo* composed of Indian officials. Between the ages of 18 and 50, Indians living in *reducciones* paid a tribute in kind (e.g., wheat, corn, fish).

sorteo: lottery or raffle.

utis possidetis: a Latin term meaning "as you possess"; a term used in the language of diplomacy regarding the actual possession of territories.

Selected Bibliography

UNPUBLISHED MATERIALS

Archivo del Museo Roca, Buenos Aires. Record Group 97.98.
Public Records Office, London. Diplomatic Series F, Records Group FO.118.
United States National Archives, Washington, DC. Record Groups RG59, RG94, RG165.

OTHER UNPUBLISHED SOURCES

Ferrer, José. "The Armed Forces in Argentine Politics to 1930." Ph.D. diss., University of New Mexico, 1966.
Hillmon, Tommie, Jr. "A History of the Armed Forces of Chile from Independence to 1920." Ph.D. diss., Syracuse University, 1963.
Nunn, Frederick McKinley. "Civil-Military Relations in Chile, 1891–1938." Ph.D. diss., University of New Mexico, 1963.
Winson, Curtin, Jr. "The National Security and Armament Policies of Argentina." Ph.D. diss., American University, 1971.

OFFICIAL PRINTED SOURCES

Argentina

Argentine Republic. *El comercio exterior argentino en 1940 y 1941 y estadísticas económicas retrospectivas.* Buenos Aires, 1942.
———. *Segundo censo de la República Argentina.* 3 vols. Buenos Aires, 10 de mayo de 1895.
———. *Tercer censo nacional, levantado el 1o. de junio de 1914.* 10 vols. Buenos Aires, 1916–1917.

————. Ministerio de Guerra, *Memoria presentada al Honorable Congreso.* Buenos Aires, 1898, 1899, 1900, 1901. Titles may vary slightly.

————. Ministerio de Marina, *Memoria presentada al Honorable Congreso.* Buenos Aires, 1887, 1888–1889, 1899–1900, 1900–1901, 1901–1902. Titles may vary slightly.

————. Ministerio de Relaciones y Culto, *Memoria presentada al Honorable Congreso Nacional.* Buenos Aires, Talleres de la Penitenciería Nacional, 1901.

Chile

Ministerio de Guerra. *Memoria que el Ministro de Estado en el Departamento de Guerra presenta al Congreso Nacional.* Santiago: 1887–1904. Titles may vary slightly.

Ministerio de Marina. *Memoria que el Ministro de Estado en el Departmento de Marian presenta al Congreso Nacional.* Santiago: 1894–1906. Titles may vary slightly.

Italy

Documenti della Camera dei Diputati. *Atti Generalle della Camera dei Diputati.* Rome, 1898: Vol. 567.

United States

Navy Department. *Notes on the Year's Naval Progress. Annual of the Office of Naval Intelligence Compiled for the Use of Naval Officers and Others.* ONI General Information Series. Washington DC: Government Printing Office, 1890–1902.

————. *The Chilean Revolution of 1891.* By Lieutenant James Hamilton Sears and Ensign B. W. Wells Jr., Office of Naval Intelligence, Information from Abroad War Series No. IV. Washington DC, U.S. Government Printing Office, 1893.

SECONDARY SOURCES

Books

Abad de Santillan, Diego. *Historia agentina.* 5 vols. Buenos Aires: Tipográfica Argentina, 1965–1971.

Abecia Valdivieso, Valentin. *Las relacciones internacionales en la historia de Bolivia.* 2 vols. Cochabamba: Los Amigos del Libro, 1979.

Academia Nacional de la Historia. *Congreso nacional sobre la conquista del desierto.* 4 vols. Buenos Aires: 1977.

————. *Historia Argentina Contemporánea.* 8 vols. Buenos Aires: El Atenéo, 1963–1966.

————. *Cuarto congreso nacional y regional de historia argentina.* 4 vols. Buenos Aires: 1983.

————. *VI congreso internacional de historia de America.* 4 vols. Buenos Aires: 1983.

————. *Segundo congreso nacional y regional de historia argentina.* 4 vols. Buenos Aires: 1973.

Aguilera, Alfredo, and Vicente Elias. *Buques de guerra españoles, 1885–1971.* Madrid: Editorial San Martin, 1980.

Akers, Charles Edmond. *A History of South America.* London: John Murray, 1930.

Albarracín, Santiago. *La escuadra argentina en Patagonia: Paginas del ayer.* Buenos Aires: Ediciones Marymar, 1976.

Alhub, Leopoldo. *Origines del autoritanismo en America latina.* Mexico, DF: Editorial Katun, 1983.

Amunátegui, Miguel L. *Títulos de la República de Chile a la soberanía y domínio de la estremidad austral del continente.* (Santiago: Imprenta de Julio Belin, 1853.

Arana, Felipe. *Historia económica y social argentina.* Buenos Aires: Editorial El Coloquio, 1969.

Arenas Aguirre, L. Alfredo. *Encina contra Encina: Restablecimiento de la verdad histórica sobre la Guerra del* Pacífico. Santiago: 1958.

Arendt, Alfred. *Argentinien ein land der zukunft! Jubilaüschrift der Begrüdung Republik Argentinien.* Leipzig: Verlag von Bruno Schönfelder, 1910.

Argentina: La otra patria de los italianos. Buenos Aires: Manrique Ediciones, 1984.

The Argentine Yearbook. Buenos Aires: John Grant & Son, 1902.

Arguindeguy, Pablo E. *Apuntes sobre los buques de la armada argentina.* 7 vols. Buenos Aires: Departamento de Estudios Históricos Navales, 1972.

Armada Argentina. *Infanteria de Marina: Tres siglos de historia y cien años de vida orgánica.* Buenos Aires: 1979.

Armaignac, H. *Viaje por las pampas argentinas: Cacerías en el quequen grande y otras andanzas.* Buenos Aires: Editorial Universitaria de Buenos Aires, 1974.

Baillinou, Juan Bautista. *Centenario de Rio Gallegos.* Municipalidad de Río Gallegos, 1985.

Baldrich, Amadeo J. *Historia de la guerra del Brasil: Contribución al estudio razonado de la historia militar argentina.* Buenos Aires: Imprenta La Harlem, 1905.

Ball, Robert W. D. *Mauser Military Rifles of the World.* Iola, WI: Krause Publications, 1996.

Barclay, W. C. *The Land of Magellan.* New York: Brentano, n.d.

Barros Arana, Diego. *Historia de América.* 2 vols. Santiago: Imprenta Cervantes, 1908.

———. *Obras completas de Diego Barros Arana, Vol. XVI. Historia de la Guerra del Pacífico: 1879–1881.* Santiago: Imprenta, Litografía i Encuadernación Barcelona, 1914.

Barros, Álvaro. *Indios, fronteras y seguridad interior.* Buenos Aires: Solar/Hachette, 1975.

Barros, Mario. *Historia diplomática de Chile.* Barcelona: Ediciones Ariel, 1971.

Bealer, Lewis Winkler. *Los corsarios de Buenos Aires: Sus activadades en las guerras hispano-americanas de independencia, 1815–1821.* Buenos Aires: Coni, 1937.

Benavídez Santos, Arturo. *Historia compendiada de la Guerra del Pacífico.* Buenos Aires: Editorial Francisco de Aguirre, 1972.

Bermúdez Miral, Oscar. *Historia del Salitre: Desde des origenes hasta la Guerra del Pacífico.* Ediciones de la Universidad de Chile, 1963.

Best, Félix. *Historia de las guerras argentinas: De la independencia, internacionales, civiles y con el indio.* 2 vols. Buenos Aires: Ediciones Peuser, 1960.

Beverina, Juan. *El virreinato de las provincias del Río de la Plata: Su organización militar, contribución a la historia del Ejército Argentino.* Buenos Aires: Círculo Militar, 1935.

————. *La guerra del Paraguay, 1865–1870, resumén histórico.* Buenos Aires: Círculo Militar, 1973.

Bidondo, Emilio A. *La guerra de la independencia en el norte argentino.* Buenos Aires: Editorial Universitaria de Buenos Aires, 1978.

Blakemore, Harold. *British Nitrates and Chilean Politics, 1885–1896: Balmaceda and North.* London: University of London, 1985.

Blanco Acevedo, Pablo. *Historia de la República Oriental del Uruguay.* Montevideo: A. Barreiuro y Ramos, 1910.

Blancpain, Jean Pierre. *Les Allemands au Chili, 1818–1945.* Köln and Wien: Bölau Verlag, 1974.

Bosch, Beatríz. *Benjamín Victorica: Doctor y general, 1831–1913.* Buenos Aires: Emecé Editores, 1994.

Bosch, Felipe. *Historia Naval Argentina.* Buenos Aires: Editorial Alborada, 1962.

Botana, Natalio. *El orden conservador: La política argentina entre 1880 y 1916.* Buenos Aires: Editorial Sudamericana, 1994.

Brady, George S. *Railways of South America, Part I: Argentina.* Bureau of Foreign Commerce, Trade Promotion Series No. 30. Washington DC: Government Printing Office, 1926.

Braun Menéndez, Armando. *El motin de los artilleros.* Buenos Aires: Editorial Francisco de Aguirre, 1973.

————. "Primera presidencia de Roca." (1880–1886)." *HAC* I, Ia. Sección, 269–330.

————. "La segunda presidencia de Roca." 1889–1904. *HAC* I, IIa. Sección, pp. 7–76.

Bray, Arturo. *Solano López: Soldado de la gloria y del infortunio.* Buenos Aires: Guillermo Kraft, 1945.

Brown, Jonathan. *A Socioeconomic History of Argentina, 1776–1960.* London, New York, Melbourne: Cambridge University Press, 1979.

Bueno, Clodoaldo. *A República e sua Política Exterior: 1889 a 1902.* Rio de Janeiro: Editora Unesp, 1950.

Bulnes, Gonzalo. *Chile and Peru: The Causes of the War of the Pacific.* Santiago: Imprenta Universitaria, 1920.

————. *La Guerra del Pacífico.* 3 vols. Santiago: Editorial del Pacífico, 1962.

Burgin, Miron. *The Economic Aspects of Argentine Federalism, 1820–1852.* Cambridge, MA: Harvard University Press, 1946.

Burr, Robert N. *By Reason or by Force: Chile and the Balancing of Power in South America, 1830–1905.* Berkeley and Los Angeles: University of California Press, 1967.

Bustos Dávila, Nicolás. "Coronel Manuel José Olascoaga, precursor de la Patagonia." In *2o.CNRHA*, IV: 63–77.

Burzio, Humberto F. *Armada nacional: Reseña histórica de su origen y desarrollo orgánico.* Buenos Aires: Departamento de Estudios Históricos Navales, ser. B, no. 1, 1960.

————. *Historia de la Escuela Naval Militar.* 3 vols. Buenos Aires: Departamento de Estudios Históricos Navales, ser. B, no. 16, 1972.

————. *Historia del torpedo y sus buques en la Armada Argentina.* Buenos Aires: Departamento de Estudios Históricos Navales, ser. B, no. 12, 1968.

Caillet-Bois, Ricardo. *Cuestiones Internacionales, 1852–1966.* Buenos Aires: Editorial Universitaria de Buenos Aires, 1970.

————. "Presidencia de Miguel Juárez Celman." *HAC* I: 331–394.

Cambras, Aníbal. "El proceso de la colonización en Misiones." *3o. CNRHA*, III: 107–121.

Cardozo, Efraím. *El Imperio del Brasil y el Río de la Plata: Antecedentes y estallido de la guerra del Paraguay.* Buenos Aires: Libreria del Plata, 1961.

Cariola Sutter, Carmen, and Osvaldo Sunkel. *Un siglo de historia económica de Chile: 1830–1930, dos ensayos y una bibliografía.* Madrid, Ediciones Cultura Hispánica del Instituto de Cooperación Iberoamericana, 1982.

Carman, W. Y. *A History of Firearms: From Earliest Times to 1914.* London: Routledge & Kegan, 1955.

Carranza, Neftalí. *Oratoria argentina.* 5 vols. Buenos Aires: Sese y Larrañaga, 1905.

Carrasco, Angel. *Lo que yo ví desde el Ochenta: Hombres y Episodios de la transformación nacional.* (Buenos Aires: 1947).

Carrasco, Gabriel. *Intereses nacionales de la República Argentina* Buenos Aires: J. Peuser, 1895.

Carretero, Juan. *La Santa Federación: 1840–1850.* Buenos Aires: Ediciones La Bastilla, 1975.

Castro Magalhâes Marques, Maria Eduarda, *A Guerra do Paraguai: 130 anos depois.* Rio de Janeiro: Reume Dumará, 1995.

Cervera Perry, José. *Marina y política en la España del siglo XIX.* Madrid: Editorial San Martín, 1979.

Chaves, Julio César. *Descubrimiento y conquista del Río de la Plata y el Paraguay.* Asunción: Editorial Niza, 1958.

Chiaramonte, José C. *Mercaderes del Litoral: Económia y sociedad en la Provincia de Corrientesen la primera mitad del siglo XIX* (Buenos Aires: Fondo de Cultura Económica, Mexico, 1991).

Collier, Simon. *Ideas and Politics of Chilean Independence: 1808–1833.* Cambridge: Cambridge University Press, 1979.

Comando General del Ejército, Dirección de Estudios Históricos. *Politica seguida con el aborigen, 1750–1810.* 3 vols. Buenos Aires: Círculo Militar, 1973.

Comando en Jefe del Ejército. *Reseña Histórica y orgánica del Ejército Argentino.* 3 vols. Buenos Aires: Cículo Militar, 1971.

Coni, Emilo. *El gaucho: Argentina, Brasil, Uruguay.* Buenos Aires, Ediciones Solar/Hachette, 1969.

Contreras Polgatti. *Chile: Proceso político y Rol Militar, Siglo XIX.* Santiago, Biblioteca del Oficial, 1990.

Contribuçoes para a historia da guerra entre Brasil e Buenos Aires: Una testemunha ocular. Editorial da Universidad de Sao Paulo, 1975.

Conway's All the World's Fighting Ships: 1865–1905. New York: Mayflower Books, 1979.

Corporación de Fomento de la Producción Agrícola. *Geografía económica de Chile.* 2 vols. Santiago, 1950.

Cortés Conde, Roberto. *El progreso argentino, 1880–1914, la formación del mercado nacional.* Buenos Aires: Editorial Sudamericana, 1983.

———, and Ezequiel Gallo. *La formación de la Argentina moderna.* Buenos Aires: Editorial Paidós, 1974.

———. "The Growth of the Argentine Economy 1870–1914." In *The Cambridge History of Latin America.* 5 vols. London, Cambridge University Press, 1985, V: 327–358.

Crespo, Alfonso. *Santa Cruz, El condor indio.* Mexico, DF: Fondo de Cultura Económica, 1944.

Cronología Militar Argentina. Buenos Aires: Ediciones Clio, 1983.

Cuccorese, Horacio Juan. *Historia económica financiera Argentina, 1862–1930.* Buenos Aires: El Ateneo, 1962.

———. *Historia de los ferrocarriles argentinos.* Buenos Aires: Ediciones Macchi, 1969.

———. *En tiempo histórico de Carlos Pellegrini.* 2 vols. Buenos Aires: Fundación para la educación, la ciencia y la cultura, 1985.

Cunninghame Graham, R. B. *Portrait of a Dictator, Francisco Solano Lopez: Paraguay, 1865–1870* (London: William Heineman, 1933).

Curruhuinca-Roux. *Las Matanzas del Neuquén.* Buenos Aires: Editorial Plus Ultra, 1984.

Curtiss, William E. *The Capitals of Spanish America.* New York: Harper and Bros., 1888.

Da Rocha, Augusto. *Colección completa de leyes nacionales sancionadas por el honorable congreso durante los años 1852 a 1917.* 14 vols. Buenos Aires: Libreria La Facultad, 1918.

De Angelis, Pedro. *Memoria histórica sobre los derechos de soberanía y dominio de la Confederación Argentina a la parte austral del continente.* Buenos Aires: 1852.

De Gandía, Enrique. *Historia Política Argentina: Rivadavia y su tiempo.* 2 vols. Buenos Aires: Editorial Claridad, 1990.

De Marco, Angel. *La guerra del Paraguay.* Buenos Aires: Editorial Planeta, 1995.

De Paula, Alberto, S. J. Martín, Maria Haydeé, and Ramón Gutiérrez. *Los ingenieros militares y sus precursores en el desarrollo argentino.* 2 vols. Buenos Aires: Dirección General de Fabricaciones Militares, 1980.

Destéfani, Laurio H. *Famosos veleros argentinos.* Buenos Aires: 1967.

Díaz Alejandro, C. F. *Essays on the Economic History of the Argentine Republic.* New Haven, CT: Yale University Press, 1970.

Di Tella, Guido, and Manuel Zymelman. *Las etapas del desarrollo argentino.* Buenos Aires: Editorial Universitaria de Buenos Aires, 1967.

Di Tella, Torcuato S., ed. *Argentina, sociedad de masas.* Buenos Aires: Editorial Universitaria de Buenos Aires, 1965.

Donoso, Ricardo. *Diego Barros Arana.* Mexico, DF: Instituto Panamericano de Geografía e Historia, Comisión de Historia, 1967.

Dupuoy y Grez, Jorge. *Las relaciones chileno-argentinas durante el gobierno de Don Jorge Montt, 1891–1896.* Santiago: Editorial Andres Bello, 1968.

Dupuy, Ernest R., and Trevor N. Dupuy. *The Compact History of the Revolutionary War: The Story of the American Revolution.* New York: Harper & Row, 1966.

Earl Church, George. *Aborigines of South America.* London: Chapman & Hall, 1912.

Ébélot, Alfred. *Relatos de la frontera.* Buenos Aires: Solar/Hachette, 1968.

Encina, Francisco A. *Historia de Chile: Desde la prehistoria hasta 1891.* 20 vols. Santiago: Imprenta Nascimento, 1940–1952.

———. *La cuestión de limites entre Chile y la Argentina: Desde la independencia hasta el tratado de 1881.* Santiago: Editorial Nascimento, 1969.

———. *Nuestra inferioridad económica.* Santiago: Editorial Universitaria, 1986.

Ensick, Oscar L. *Historia económica de la Provincia de Santa Fé.* Universidad Nacional de Rosario, 1985.

Espinosa Moraga, Oscar. *El precio de la paz chileno-argentina.* 3 vols. Santiago: Editorial Nascimento, 1969.

―――. *La postguerra del Pacífico y la Puna de Atacama.* Santiago: Editorial Andres Bello, 1958.

Estado Mayor del Ejército. *Historia del Ejército de Chile.* 8 vols. Santiago: 1982.

Etchepaborda, Roberto. *Zeballos y la política exterior argentina.* Buenos Aires: Editorial Pleamar, 1982.

Eyzaguirre, Jaime. *Chile durante el gobierno de Errázuriz-Echaurren, 1896–1901.* Santiago: Editorial Zig-Zag, 1957.

Fernández, Isabel. *Los Indios de Argentina.* Madrid: Editorial Mapfre, 1992.

Fernández, Juan José. *La República de Chile y el Imperio del Brasil: Historia de sus relaciones diplomáticas.* Santiago: Editorial Andres Bello, 1959.

Ferns, H. S. *Britain and Argentina in the Nineteenth Century.* London: Oxford University Press, 1960.

Ferrando Keun, Ricardo. *Y asi nació la frontera: Conquista, guerra, ocupación, pacifación: 1550–1900.* Santiago: Editorial Antartida, 1986.

Ferrari, Gustavo. *Conflicto y paz con Chile: 1898–1903.* Buenos Aires: Editorial Universitaria de Buenos Aires, 1968.

―――, and Ezequiel Gallo. *La Argentina desde el Ochenta al Centenario.* Buenos Aires: Editorial Sudamericana, 1980.

Ferrer, Aldo. *The Argentine Economy: An Economic History of Argentina.* Berkeley and Los Angeles: University of California Press, 1967.

Fitte, Ernesto J. *Los límites con Chile.* Buenos Aires: Editorial Plus Ultra, 1967.

―――. *Martín García: Historia de una isla argentina.* Buenos Aires: Emecé Editores, 1971.

Ford, A. G. *El patron oro: 1880–1914, Inglaterra y Argentina.* Buenos Aires: Editorial del Instituto, 1968.

Fotheringham, Ignacio H. *La vida de un soldado o reminescencias de las fronteras.* 2 vols. Buenos Aires: Círculo Militar, 1970.

Fuentes, Gabriel A. *Don Francisco Javier de Elió en El Río de la Plata.* Buenos Aires: Ediciones Espano, 1966.

Fuenzalida Bade, Rodrigo. *La armada de Chile: Desde la alborada al sesquicentenario, 1813–1968.* 4 vols. Santiago: 1978,

Gaignard, Roman. *La Pampa Argentina: Ocupación, poblamiento, Explotación, de la Conquista a la crisis mundial, 1550–1930.* Buenos Aires: Ediciones Solar, 1989.

Gallo, Ezequiel. *La Pampa Gringa: La colonización agrícola en Santa Fé, 1875–1895.* Buenos Aires: Editorial Sudamericana, 1984.

Galvez, Manuel. *Humaitá.* Buenos Aires: Editorial Losada S. A., 1959.

Garcia, Rigoberto. *Incipient Industrialization in an "Underdeveloped" Country: The Case of Chile, 1845–1879.* Stockholm: Institute of Latin American Studies, Monograph no. 17, 1989.

García Enciso, J. *Historia del Colegio Militar de la Nación.* Buenos Aires: Círculo Militar, 1970.

García Molina, Fernando, and Carlos A. Mayo. *Archivo del General Uriburu: Autoritarismo y ejército.* 2 vols. Buenos Aires: Centro Editor de la América Latina, 1985.

Garra, Lobodon. *A sangre y lanza.* Buenos Aires: Ediciones Anaconda, 1969.

Gianello, Leoncio. *Estanislao López: Vida y obra del patriarca de la confederación.* Santa Fé: El Litoral, 1958.

González Climent, Aurelio, and Anselmo González Climent. *Historia de la marina mercante argentina.* 20 vols. Buenos Aires: 1972.

González Lonzieme, Enrique. *La armada en la conquista del desierto.* Buenos Aires: Instituto de Publicaciones Navales, 1973.

González Madariaga, Exequiel. *Nuestras relaciones con Argentina: Una historia deprimente.* 3 vols. Santiago: Editorial Andres Bello and Neupert, 1974.

Gravil, Roger. *The Anglo-Argentine Connection, 1900–1939.* Boulder: Westview Press, 1985.

Grela, Plácido. *Fuerzas armadas y soberanía nacional: Vida y obra del teniente general Pablo Riccheri, forjador del moderno ejército argentino.* Rosario, Argentina: Litoral Ediciones, 1973.

Güenaga, Rosario. *Santa Cruz y Magallanes historia socioeconómica de los territorios de la Paragonia Austral Argentina y Chilena.* Mexico, D.F.: Instituto Panamericano de Geografia e Historia, 1994.

Halperin Donghi, Julio. *Guerra y finanzas en los orígenes del estado argentino, 1791–1850.* Buenos Aires: Editorial de Belgrano, 1982.

———. *Politics, Economics and Society in Argentina During the Revolutionary Period.* London, New York and Melbourne: Cambridge University Press, 1975.

Hanson, Simon G. *The Argentine Meat Trade and the British Market: Chapters in the History of the Argentine Meat Industry.* Stanford, CA: Stanford University Press, 1938.

Held, Robert. *The Age of Firearms: A Pictorial History.* New York: Harper & Row, 1957.

Hennesey, Alistair. *The Frontier in Latin American History.* London: Edward Arnold, 1978.

Heras, Carlos. "Presidencia de Avellaneda." In *HAC*, I: 149–268.

Holdich, Thomas H. *The Countries of the King's Award.* London: Hurst & Blackett, 1904.

International Bureau of the American Republics. *Argentine Republic, a Geographic Sketch with Special Reference to Economic Conditions, Actual Development and Prospects of Future Growth.* Washington, DC: U.S. Government Printing Office, 1903.

Ireland, Gordon. *Boundaries, Possessions and Conflicts in South America.* New York: Octagon Books, 1971.

Justo Guedes, Max. "A Guerra: Uma análise." *GP*, pp. 53–62.

Kolinski, Charles J. *Independence or Death! The Story of the Paraguayan War.* Gainesville, University of Florida Press, 1965.

Kroeber, Clifton K. *The Growth of the Shipping Industry on the Rio de la Plata Region, 1794–1860.* Madison: University of Wisconsin Press, 1957.

Larriqueta, Daniel. *La Argentina Imperial.* Buenos Aires: Editorial Sudamericana, 1996.

Le Leon, M. *Recuerdo de una misión en el ejército chileno: Batallas de Chorillos y Miraflores.* Buenos Aires: Editorial Francisco de Aguirre, 1973.

Levene, Ricardo. "Presidencia de Mitre." *HAC*, I, Ia. Sección, pp. 5–64.

Levillier, Roberto. "Presidencia del Doctor José Evaristo Uriburu: 28 enero 1895–12 octubre 1898." *HAC*: I, Ia. Sección, 433–468.

Lista, Ramón N. *Mis exploraciones y descubrimientos en la Patagonia, 1877–1880.* Buenos Aires: Marymar, 1975.

Lopez, Vicente Fidel. *Historia de la República Argentina: Su origén, su revolución y su desarrollo político hasta 1852.* 8 vols. Buenos Aires: Editorial Sopena Argentina, 1949.

López Urrutia, Carlos. *Historia de la Marina de Chile*. Santiago: Editorial Andres Bello, 1969.

Loveman, Brian. *Chile: The Legacy of Spanish Capitalism*. New York: Oxford University Press, 1979.

Lynch, John. *Argentine Dictator: Juan Manuel de Rosas, 1829–1852*. New York: Oxford University Press, 1981.

———. *Spanish Colonial Administration, 1782–1810: The Intendant System in the Viceroyalty of the Río de la Plata*. London: Athlone Press, 1958.

Mackesy, Piers. *The War for America*. Cambridge, MA: Harvard University Press, 1964.

Mackinon, L. B. *La Escuadra-Anglo-Francesa en el Paraná: 1846*. Buenos Aires: Librería Hachette, 1957.

Magnet, Alejandro. *Nuestros vecinos argentinos*. Santiago: Editorial del Pacífico, 1958.

Mamalakis, Markos. *The Growth and Structure of the Chilean Economy from Independence to Allende*. New Haven, CT: Yale University Press, 1978.

Mansilla, Luico V. *Una excursion a los Indios Ranqueles*. Caracas: Editorial Ayacucho, 1985.

Markham, Clement Roberts. *The War Between Chile and Peru*. London: Sampson, Low, Marston & Co., 1882.

Marti Garro, Pedro E. *Historia de la artillería argentina*. Buenos Aires: Comisión del arma de artillería "Santa Barbara," 1984.

Martínez, Alberto, and Maurice Lewandoski. *The Argentine in the twentieth Century*. London: T. Fisher Unwin, 1911.

Martínez Pita, Rodolfo. *Riccheri*. Buenos Aires: Círculo Militar, 1952.

Martinic Beros, Mateo. *Presencia de Chile en la Patagonia Austral, 1843–1879*. Santiago: Editorial Andres Bello, 1963.

———. *Última esperanza en el tiempo*. Ediciones de la Universidad de Magallanes, 1985.

Martner, Daniel. *Estudio de la política comercial chilena e historia económica nacional*. Santiago: Imprenta Universitaria, 1923.

Matyoka Yeager, Gertrude. *Barros Arana's "Historia Jeneral de Chile": Politics and National Identity*. Fort Worth: Texas Christian University, 1981.

Mayo, Carlos. "La revolución de 1874 a traves del testimonio de Thomas O. Osborn, Ministro residente de los E.E.U.U. en nuestro país." *3.CNRHA*, III: 301–311.

Meister, Jürg. *Francisco Solano Lopez: Nationalheld oder Kriegsverbrecher?: Der Krieg Paraguays genen die Triple Allianz 1864–1870*. Osnabrück: Biblio Verlag, 1987.

Meller, Patricio. *Un siglo de económia política chilena*. Santiago: Editorial Andres Bello, 1996.

Memorias del General Gregorio Aráoz de la Madrid. 2 vols. Buenos Aires: Editorial Universitaria de Buenos Aires, 1968.

Menéndez, Rómulo Félix. *Las conquistas territoriales argentinas*. Buenos Aires: Círculo Militar, 1982.

Merrill, Andrea T., and Thomas E. Weil, *Chile: A Country Study*. Washington, DC: American University Press, 1982.

Miller, John. *Memorias del General Miller*. Buenos Aires: Emecé, 1997.

Mitre, Bartolomé. *Archivo del General Mitre*. 26 vols. Buenos Aires: 1911–1912.

———. *Episodios de la revolución*. Buenos Aires: Editorial Universitaria de Buenos Aires, 1960.

———. *Guerra del Paraguay: Memoria militar*. Buenos Aires: Imprenta de la Nación, 1903.

————. *Historia de San Martín y de la emancipación nacional.* 3 vols. Buenos Aires: Libreria El Ateneo, 1950.

Monteón, Michael. *Chile in the Nitrate Era: The Evolution of Economic Dependence.* Madison: University of Wisconsin Press, 1983.

Mulhall M. G., and E. T. Mulhall. *Handbook of the River Plate.* London: Trubner and Co., 1883.

————. *Manual de las Repúblicas del Plata.* Buenos Aires: 1876.

Musters, George Chaworth. *At Home with the Patagonians: A Years's Wandering over Untrodden Ground from the Straits of Magellan to the Rio Negro.* London: John Murray, 1871.

Newton, Ronald C. *German Buenos Aires, 1900–1933, Social Change and Cultural Crisis.* Austin & London: University of Texas Press, 1977.

Nunn, Frederick M. *Chilean Politics: 1920–1931.* Albuquerque: University of New Mexico Press, 1970.

————. *The Military in Chilean History, Essays on Civil-Military Relations, 1810–1973.* Albuquerque: University of New Mexico Press, 1976.

————. *Yesterday's Soldiers: European Military Professionalism in South America, 1890–1940.* Lincoln & London: University of Nebraska Press, 1983.

Olascoaga, Manuel J. *Estudio topográfico de La Pampa y Río Negro.* Buenos Aires: Editorial Universitaria de Buenos Aires, 1974.

Orsolini, Mario Horacio. *Ejército argentino y crecimeinto nacional.* Buenos Aires: Ediciones Arayú, 1965.

Ortega Peña, Adolfy, and Eduardo L. Duhalde. *Mariscal Francisco Solano López: Pensamiento político.* Buenos Aires: Editorial Sudestada, 1969.

Ortíz, Ricardo M. *Historia económica de la Argentina, 1830–1930.* Buenos Aires: Editorial Plus Ultra, 1987.

————. *El ferrocarril en la economía Argentina.* Buenos Aires: Editorial Problemas, 1958.

Ozlak, Oscar. *La conquista del orden político y la formación del estado argentino.* Buenos Aires: Centro de Estado y Sociedad, 1982.

Palacio, Ernesto. *Historia de la Argentina, 1515–1943.* 2 vols. Buenos Aires: A. Peña Lillo Editor, 1965.

Palacios, Nicolás. *Raza Chilena: Libro escrito por un chileno y para chilenos.* 2 vols. Santiago: Editorial Chilena, 1918.

Palcos, Alberto. "Presidencia de Sarmiento." In *HAC,* Ia. Sección, pp. 89–148.

Palleja, Leon de. *Diario de la campaña de las fuerzas aliadas contra el Paraguay.* 2 vols. Montevideo: Ministerio de Instrucción Pública y Previsión Social, 1960.

Panetieri, José. *Inmigración en la Argentina.* Buenos Aires: Ediciones Macchi, 1970.

Passarelli, Bruno. "El significado de la creación de la base de Puerto Belgrano." In *2o. CNRHA,* 2: pp. 68–75.

Paz, José Maria. *Memorias.* Buenos Aires: Editorial Schapire, 1968.

Paz, Ricardo Alberto. *El conflicto pendiente.* 2 vols. Buenos Aires: Editorial Universitaria de Buenos Aires, 1980.

Pechman, Guillermo. *El Campamento 1878: Algunos cuentos históricos de fronteras y campañas.* Buenos Aires: *EUDEBA,* 1980.

Pelliza, Mariano A. *La cuestión del Estrecho de Magallanes.* Buenos Aires: Editorial Universitaria de Buenos Aires, 1969.

Peñaloza, Luis C. *Historia del movimiento nacionalista revolucionario, 1943–1952*. La Paz: Editorial La Paz Juventud, 1965.

Perez, Domingo T. *Discursos parlamentarios de los pactos con Chile*. Buenos Aires: Imp. Lit. Y Ex. De F. Doblan, 1908.

Perren, Richard. *The Meat Trade in Britain, 1840–1914*. London, Henley and Boston: Routledge & Kegan Paul, 1978.

Peterson, Harold. *Argentina and the United States, 1810–1960*. Albany: State University of New York Press, 1964.

Phelps, Gilbert. *The Tragedy of Paraguay*. New York: St. Martin's Press, 1975.

Piccinali, Héctor J. *Vida del teniente general Nicolás Lavalle*. Buenos Aires: Círculo Militar, 1981.

Piccirilli, Ricardo, Francisco L. Romay, and Leoncio Gianello. *Diccionario histórico argentino*. 6 vols. Buenos Aires: Ediciones Históricas Argentinas, 1954.

Plá, Josefina. *The British in Paraguay*. Richmond Publishing Co., 1976.

Platt D. C. M. *Latin America and British Trade, 1806–1914*. London, Adams and Charles Black, 1977.

Polloni, Albert R. *Las fuerzas armadas en Chile en la vida nacional: Compendio cívico-militar*. Santiago: Editorial Andres Bello, 1972.

Pomer, Léon. "A guerra do Pareaguai e a formaçao do estado na Argentina." *GP*, pp. 115–120.

Potash, Robert A. *The Army in Politics in Argentina, 1928–1945: Yrigoyen to Peron*. Stanford, CA: Stanford University Press, 1964.

Prado, Manuel. *La conquista de la Pampa*. Buenos Aires: Libreria Hachette S. A., 1960.

———. *La Guerra al malón*. Buenos Aires: Editorial Universitaria de Buenos Aires, 1960.

Quesada, Vicente. *La política argentina respecto de Chile, 1895–1898*. Buenos Aires: Arnoldo Moen, Editor, 1898.

———. *La política chilena en el Plata*. Buenos Aires: Arnoldo Moen, Editor, 1895.

Randall, Laura. *A Comparative Economic History of Latin America. Volume 2: Argentina*. New York: Columbia University Press, 1977.

Rangel, Alberto. *Gastâo de Orleans: O ultimo Conde d'Eu*. Sao Paulo: companhia Editora Nacional, 1935.

Ramayón, Eduardo E. *Ejército guerrero, poblador y civilizador*. Buenos Aires: *EUDEBA*, 1975.

———. *Las caballadas en la guerra del Indio: Adhesión de remonta y veterinaria del ejército en el centenario de la conquista del desierto*. Buenos Aires: Editorial Universitaria de Buenos Aires, 1975.

Ratto, Héctor F. *Historia de Brown*. 2 vols. Buenos Aires: Libreria y Editorial La Facultad, 1939.

Rennie, Ysabel F. *The Argentine Republic*. New York: Macmillan, 1945.

Rey Balmaceda, Raúl C. "La supuesta frontera interior pampeana." In *CHNCD*, 4: 573–581.

———. *Límites y fronteras de la República Argentina: Epitome geográfico*. Buenos Aires: OIKOS, 1979.

Riesco, German. *Presidencia de Riesco, 1901–1906*. Santiago: Imprenta Nascimento, 1950.

Rock, David, ed. *Argentina in the Twentieth Century*. London and Pittsburgh: Duckworth University of Pittsburgh Press, 1977.

————. *Argentina, 1516–1982: From Spanish Colonization to the Falklands War.* Berkeley and Los Angeles: University of California Press, 1985.

————. *Politics in Argentina, 1890–1930: The Rise and Fall of Radicalism.* Cambridge: Cambridge University Press, 1975.

Rodríguez, Augusto C. "Ejéricito Nacional." In *Historia argentina contemporánea: 1862–1930.* 7 vols. Buenos Aires: El Ateneo, 1966, 2: 267–372.

————. "Guerra del Paraguay." *HAC* I (1966), Ia. Sección, pp. 65–88.

Rodríguez, Bernardo N. "El factor naval en la Revolución de 1874." In *3o. CNRHA,* III: 451–463.

Rodríguez Mola, Ricardo. *Historia social del gaucho.* Buenos Aires: Ediciones Maru, 1968.

Rouquié, Alain. *Poder militar y sociedad política en la Argentina.* 2 vols. Buenos Aires: Emercé, 1978.

Rube, Horacio. *Hacia Caseros.* Buenos Aires: Ediciones La Bastilla, 1975.

Ruíz Moreno, Isidoro J. *La federalización de Buenos Aires.* Buenos Aires: Hyspamerica, 1980.

Saldías, Adolfo. *Porqué se produjo el Bloqueo Anglo-Francés.* Buenos Aires: Editorial Plus Ultra, 1974.

Sánchez-Albornoz, Nicolás. *The Population of Latin America: A History.* Berkeley, Los Angeles: University of California Press, 1974.

Sarmiento, Domingo F. *Civilización y barbarie: Trilogía de Quiroga, Aldao, El Chacho.* Buenos Aires: Editorial El Ateneo, 1957.

Sayago, Carlos M. *Historia de Copiapó.* Buenos Aires: Editorial Francisco de Aguirre, 1973.

Scalabrini Ortíz, Raul. *Historia de los ferrocarriles argentinos.* Buenos Aires: Editorial Devenir, 1958.

Scenna, Miguel Angel. *Argentina-Chile: Una frontera caliente.* Buenos Aires: Editorial de Belgrano, 1981.

Schaefer, Jürgen. *Deustche militarhilfe an Sudamerika: Militar und Rustunginteressen in Argentinien, Bolivien und Chile von 1914.* Düsseldorf: Bertelsmann Universitäts-verlag, 1974.

Scheina, Robert L. *Latin America: A Naval History, 1810–1987.* Annapolis, MD, Naval Institute Press, 1987.

Scobie, James R. *Argentina: A City and a Nation.* New York: Oxford University Press, 1974.

————. *La lucha por la consolidación de la nacionalidad argentina.* Buenos Aires: Librería Hachette, 1964.

————. *Revolution in the Pampas: A Social History of Argentine Wheat, 1860–1910* (Austin: University of Texas Press, 1964).

Secretaría General del Ejército. *Semblanza histórica del ejército argentino.* Buenos Aires: 1981.

Segretti, Carlos S. A. *Limites con Chile.* Buenos Aires: Editorial Era, 1981.

Sergi, Jorge F. *Historia de los italianos en la Argentina.* Buenos Aires: Editora Italo-Argentina, 1940.

Serres Güiraldes, Alfredo M. *La estrategia del General Roca.* Buenos Aires: Editorial Pleamar, 1979.

Séve, Edouard. *La patria chilena: Le Chili tel qu'il est.* Vol. 1. Valparaíso, Chile: Imprenta del Mercurio, 1876.

Shipton, Eric. *Tierra del Fuego: The Fatal Loadstone*. London: Charles Knight & Co., 1973.

Slatta, Richard. *Gauchos and the Vanishing Frontier*. Lincoln and London: University of Nebraska Press, 1983.

Slatter, William F. *Chile and the War of the Pacific*. Lincoln and London: University of Nebraska Press, 1975.

————. *The Heroic Image in Chile: Arturo Pratt, Secular Saint*. Berkeley and Los Angeles: University of California Press, 1975.

Smith, Joseph. *Small Arms of the World: A Basic Manual of Small Arms*. Harrisburg, PA: Stackpole Books, 1973.

Solberg, Carl E. *Immigration and Nationalism: Argentina and Chile, 1890–1914*. Austin and London: University of Texas Press, 1970.

————. *The Prairies and the Pampas: Agrarian Policy in Canada and Argentina, 1880–1930*. Stanford, CA: Stanford University Press, 1987.

Street, John. *Artigas and the Emancipation of Uruguay*. Cambridge: Cambridge University Press, 1959.

Subercaseaux, Guillermo. *Monetary and Banking Policy of Chile*. Oxford: Clarendon Press, 1922.

Subercaseaux, Ramón. *Memorias de ochenta años: Recuerdos personales, reminescencias, historias, viajes y ancedotas*. 2 vols. Santiago: Imprenta Nascimento, 1936.

Talbott, Robert D. *A History of the Chilean Boundaries*. Ames: Iowa State University Press, 1974.

Tau Anzoátegui, Victor, and Eduardo Martire. *Manual de historia de las instituciones argentinas*. Buenos Aires: La Ley, 1968.

Thompson, George. *The War in Paraguay*. London: Longmans Green & Co., 1869.

Tornquist, Ernesto, and Co. *El desarollo économico de la República Argentina en los últimos cincuenta años* (Buenos Aires: 1919).

Toro Dávila, Agustín. *Sintesis histórico-militar de Chile*. Santiago: Editorial Universitaria, 1975.

Triadó, Enrique Juan. *Historia de la Base Naval de Puerto Belgrano*. Buenos Aires: Instituto de Publicaciones Navales, 1992.

Twentieth International Conference of Agricultural Economists. *The Argentine Agricultural Economy: An Analysis of Its Evolution and Present Situation*. Buenos Aires: Asociación Argentina de Económia Agraria, 1988.

Vapñarsky, César A. *Los Pueblos del Norte de la Patagonia, 1779–1957*. Fuerte General Roca: Editorial de la Patagonia, 1979.

Varela, Luis V. *La República Argentina y Chile: Historia de la demarcación de sus fronteras*. 2 vols. Buenos Aires: Imprenta de M. Biedma e Hijos, 1899.

Vázquez Presedo, Vicente. *El caso argentino: Migración de factores, comercio exterior y desarrollo, 1875–1914*. Buenos Aires: Editorial Universitaria de Buenos Aires, 1975.

————. *Estadísticas históricas argentinas comparadas*. 2 vols. Buenos Aires: Ediciones Macchi, 1971.

Vedoya, Juan C. *La campaña del desierto y la tecnificación ganadera*. Buenos Aires: Editorial Universitaria de Buenos Aires, 1979.

Véliz, Claudio. *Historia de la marina mercante de Chile*. Santiago: Ediciones de la Universidad de Chile, 1961.

Vera de Flachs, María C. *El ferrocarril Andino y el desarrollo socioeconómico del Sur de Córdoba*. Buenos Aires: Fundación para la Ciencia y la Cultura, 1982.

Vial Correa, Gonzalo. *Historia de Chile, 1891–1973.* 3 vols. Santiago: Editorial Santillana, 1987.

Villalobos, R. Sergio. *La vida fronteriza en Chile.* Madrid: Editorial Mapfre, 1992.

Villegas, Conrado. *Expedición al Gran Lago Nahuel Huapi en el año 1881.* Buenos Aires: Editorial Universitaria de Buenos Aires, 1974.

Walker, John, ed. *The South American Sketches of R. B. Cunningham Graham.* Norman: University of Oklahoma Press, 1978.

Walther, Juan C. *La conquista del desierto.* Buenos Aires: Editorial Universitaria de Buenos Aires, 1970.

Ward, Christopher. *The War of the Revolution.* 2 vols. New York: Macmillan, 1952.

Warren, Harris Gaylord. *Paraguay: An Informal History.* Norman: University of Oklahoma Press, 1949.

———. *Paraguay and the Triple Alliance: The Post-war Decade, 1869–1878.* Austin: University of Texas Press, 1978.

———. *Rebirth of the Paraguayan Republic, the First Colorado Era, 1878–1904.* Pittsburgh, PA, University of Pittsburgh Press, 1985.

Whitson Fetter, Frank. *Monetary Inflation in Chile.* Princeton, NJ: Princeton University Press, 1931.

Williams, John H. *Argentine International Trade Under Inconvertible Paper Money.* Cambridge, MA: Harvard University Press, 1920.

Wright, Winthrop A. *British-owned Railways in Argentina: Their Effects on Economic Nationalism, 1864–1948.* Austin and London: University of Texas Press, 1974.

Yaben, Jacinto R. *Biografías argentinas y sudamericanas.* 5 vols. Buenos Aires: Editorial Metropolis, 1938.

Ygobone, Aquiles D. "Algunos resultados de la conquista del ejército en el Desierto." In *CHNCD*, III: 215–229.

Zaefferer de Goyeneche, Ana. *La Navegación mercante en el Río de la Plata.* Buenos Aires: Emecé, 1987.

Zalduendo, Eduardo A. *Libras y rieles: Las inversiones británicas para el desarrollo de los ferrocarriles en la Argentina, Brasil, Canada e India durante el Siglo XIX.* Buenos Aires: Editorial El Coloquio, 1979.

———. "Aspectos económicos del sistema de transportes en la Argentina." In *AOC*, pp. 439–446.

Zevallos, Estanislao S. *Descripción Amena de la República Argentina: Vol. 1, Viaje al país de los Araucanos.* Buenos Aires: Jacobo Peuser, 1988.

———. *Diplomacia desarmada.* Buenos Aires: Editorial Universitaria de Buenos Aires, 1974.

———. *La conquista de 15,000 leguas.* Buenos Aires: Libreria Hachette, 1958.

Zeitlin, Maurice. *The Civil Wars in Chile or the Bourgeois Revolutions That Never Were.* Princeton, NJ: Princeton University Press, 1984.

Periodicals, Newspapers, and Other Publications

Allende, Andrés R. "La presidencia de Luís Sáenz Peña." *HAC* I, Ia. Sección, 395–432.

Almedia, Juan Lucio. "La armada argentina en la primera presidencia de Roca: 1880–1886." ANH, 4o. CAR. 4 vols. Buenos Aires: 1983, IV: 91–103.

Amunátegui Solar, Domingo. "Veintiuna cartas inéditas de Barros Arana." *RCHG* 34, 94 (enero-julio 1939): pp. 5–59.

Arriaga, Eduardo E., and Kingsley Davis. "The Patterns of Mortality Change in Latin America," *Demography* 6, 3 (August 1969): pp. 223–242.

Bazán, Armando Raúl. "La guerra de la independencia en el norte: Consecuencias geopolíticas." *IE* 36 (julio-diciembre 1980): pp. 343–363.

Benencia, Arturo J. "La larga carta del teniente de navio Don Juan Latre y la rendición de Montevideo." *Historia* 9, no. 36 (julio-septiembre 1964), pp. 75–92.

Bethell, Leslie. "A Guerra do Paraguai: História e historiografía." *GP* (1995), pp. 11–26.

———. "O Imperialismo Britânico e a Guerra do Paraguai." *GP* (1995), pp. 39–52.

Bidondo, Emilio A. "Los ejércitos de la revolución: 25 de mayo de 1810–9 de julio de 1818." *IE*, no. 37, (enero-junio 1988), pp. 337–377.

———. "Un episodio de la guerra contra el Mariscal Santa Cruz: El combate de Santa Barbara (Humahuaca, Provincia de Jujuy) 13 de septiembre de 1837." *IE* 33 (julio-diciembre 1982), pp. 277–312.

———. "La preparación de las tropas de Jujuy para la guerra contra el Mariscal Santa Cruz." *IE*, no. 26 (enero-junio 1975), pp. 367–388.

Blancpain, Jean Pierre. "Intelligentsia nationale et immigration européenne au Chili de l'independence à 1914." *JAL* 19 (1982), pp. 249–289.

Blinn Reber, Vera. "The Demographics of Paraguay: A Reinterpretation of the Great War, 1864–1870." *HAHR*, 68, no. 2 (May 1988), pp. 289–319.

Bosch, Brian J. "Army of the Andes." *Military Review* 47, no. 2 (February 1967), pp. 9–14.

Bowman, John, and Michael Wallerstein. "The Fall of Balmaceda and Public Finance in Chile: New Data for an Old Debate." *JISWA* 24, no. 4 (November 1982), pp. 421–460.

Brezo, Liliana María. "Armas norteamericanas para la Guerra del Paraguay." *Todo es Historia*, no. 326 (septiembre 1994), pp. 28–41.

Bruno, Cayetano. "Leon XIII y el conflicto argentino-chileno en 1896." *IE*, no. 26 (enero-junio 1975), pp. 491–516.

Caillet-Bois, Teodoro. "El combate de Martín García: 18 de Abril de 1853." *Sociedad de Historia Argentina, Anuario: 1943–1945*. Buenos Aires: 1947, pp. 57–70.

Calafut, George. "An Analysis of Italian Emigration Statistics, 1876–1914." *JAL* 14 (1977), pp. 310–331.

Canclini, Arnoldo. "La cuestión del *Beagle* y los avances chilenos en el sur argentino." *Historia* 1, no. 3, (septiembre-noviembre 1981), pp. 62–85.

"Cartas enviadas por Don Carlos Concha, Ministro de Chile en Buenos Aires a Don Rafael Errázuriz, Ministro de Relaciones Exteriores sobre problemas limítrofes." *Historia* 10 (1971), pp. 345–360.

Chejter, Silvia. "Panorama demográfico argentino." *EST* 6, no. 24 (enero-marzo 1967), pp. 65–95.

Cornblitt, Oscar. "Inmigrantes y empresarios en la política argentina." *DE* 6, no. 24 (enero-marzo 1967), pp. 641–691.

Destéfani, Laurio H. "Un marino estraordinario: Vice Almirante Juan Pablo Saénz Valiente, su actuación en el *Beagle*." *IE* 28 (enero–junio 1980), pp. 103–122.

———. "Piedrabuena: Nuestro maximo heroe Patagónico." *Boletín de la Academia Nacional de la Historia* 56–57 (1983–1984), pp. 141–147.

Dieguez, Héctor L. "Crecimiento e inestabilidad del valor y el volumen físico de las exportaciones argentinas en el periodo 1864–1963." *DE* 12, no. 46, (julio-septiembre 1972), pp. 333–349.

Donoso, Ricardo. "Una amistad para toda la vida: Vicuña Mackenna y Mitre." *RCHG* (50, no. 34, 1926), pp. 67–108.

Dublé Almeida, Diego. "Diario del viaje al Río Santa Cruz, Patagonia." *RCHG* 94, no. 92 (enero-junio 1938), pp. 208–231.

Edwards, Alberto. "Apuntes para el estudio de la organización política de Chile." *RCHG*, 5, no. 9 (1913), pp. 248–293.

Endrek, Emiliano S. "La conquista del desierto durante el segundo gobierno de Rosas, 1835–1852." *Historia* 1, no. 4 (diciembre 1980–Febrero 1981), pp. 44–57.

Farinaccio, Francisco A. "San Martín at Chacabuco." *Military Review* 47, no. 2 (February 1967), pp. 15–21.

Fernández, Juan José. "Los Pactos de Mayo y la diplomacia británica." *Boletín de la Academia Chilena de la Historia* 32, no. 73 (1965), pp. 99–131.

Fitte, Ernesto J. "La Escuadra de la Confederación Argentina y el bloqueo de Buenos Aires en 1853." *Historia* 5 no. 17 (julio-septiembre 1959), pp. 55–73.

Ford, A. G. "British Investments in Argentina and Long Term Swings." *JEH* 31, no. 3 pp. 650–663.

Gajardo, R. Ismael. "Investigación histórica sobre el combate de Abtao." *RCHG* 2, no. 8, (1912), pp. 108–136.

Garavaglia, Juan Carlos. "Economic Growth and Regional Differentiations: The River Plate Region at the end of the Eighteenth Century." *HAHR* 65, no. 1 (1989), pp. 51–89.

Gelman, Jorge. "New Perspectives on an Old Problem and the Same Source: The Gaucho and the Rural History of the Colonial Río de la Plata." *HAHR* 69, no. 4 (1989), pp. 715–745.

Girbal de Blacha, Noemí. "Comercio exterior y producción agrícola en la República Argentina." *IE* 21 (julio-diciembre 1976), pp. 343–366.

González Lonzieme, Enrique. "Como nació nuestra armada moderna." *Boletín del Centro Naval* 105, no. 749 (abril-junio 1987), pp. 287–333.

Guedes, Max Justo. *A Guerra uma analise. GP* (1995), pp. 53–65.

Halperin Donghi, Julio. "Canción de otoño en primavera: Previsiones sobre la crisis de la agricultura cerealera argentina, 1894–1930." *DE* 24, no. 96 (octubre-diciembre 1984), pp. 367–386.

———. "La expansión ganadera en la campaña de Buenos Aires, 1810–1853." *DE* 3, nos. 1/2 Septiembre 1963), pp. 57–110.

———. "Gastos militares y economía regional : El ejército del norte, 1810–1817." *DE* 11, no. 41 (abril-junio 1971), pp. 87–100.

———. "¿Para que la inmigración? Ideología y política inmigratoria y acelareción del proceso modernizador argentino: 1810–1914." *JAL* 13 (1976), pp. 437–489.

Hasbrouck, Alfred. "The Conquest of the Desert." *HAHR* 15 (1935), pp. 195–228.

Hodge, John E. "Carlos Pellegrini and the Financial Crisis of 1890." *HAHR* 50, no. 3 (August 1970), pp. 499–523.

———. "Julio Roca and Carlos Pellegrini: An Expedient Partnership." *TAM* 32, no. 3 (January 1976), pp. 327–347.

———. "The Role of the Telegraph in the Consolidation and Expansion of the Argentine Republic." *TAM* 21, no. 1 (July 1964), pp. 59–80.

Holdich, Thomas H. "The Patagonian Andes." *The Geographical Journal* 13, no. 2 (February 1904), pp. 153–176.

Iñigo Carrera, Héctor J. "El espíritu solidarista en la vida militar del desierto: 1867–1885." *CNHCD*, III: 423–440.

Jones, Charles. "Business Imperialism and Argentina, 1875–1909: A Theoretical Note." *JLAS* 12, pt. 2 (November 1980), pp. 437–449.

Kellebenz, Herman, and Jürgen Schneider. "La emigración alemana a America Latina desde 1821 hasta 1930." *JAL* 13 (1976), pp. 386–403.

Lattes, Alfredo. "Las migraciones en la Argentina entre mediados del Siglo XIX y 1960." *DE* 12, no. 48 (enero-marzo 1973), pp. 849–866.

Martín, Juan Alte. "Nuestra marina al iniciarse la segunda presidencia del General Julio A. Roca." *BCN* 76, no. 637 (noviembre-diciembre 1957), pp. 453–469.

———. "Nuestros límites con Chile en la Patagonia Austral. El Tratado de 1881. Divergencias en su interpretación, Creación de nuestra marina de mar." *BCN* 76, no. 634 (septiembre-octubre 1955), pp. 345–358.

Martínez de Gorla, Dora Noemí. "Antecedentes de la colonización y explotación de la Patagonia y su relación con la cuestión de límites con Chile." *Revista de Historia de America* no. 115 (enero-junio 1993): pp. 94–134.

Martire, Eduardo. "La crisis argentina de 1873–1876." *Historia* 10, no. 39 (abril-junio 1964), pp. 33–66.

McLynn, Francis James. "Economic Trends and Policies in Argentina During the Mitre Presidency." *JAL* 19 (1982), pp. 254–284.

Molina, Horacio E. "La crisis argentino-chilena de 1878–1879: Algunos entretelones del Pacto Fierro-Sarratea." *RH* 4, no. 12 (1983): pp. 67–109.

Molina, Raúl A. "Los conflictos de límites y las primeras misiones diplomáticas en archivos nacionales y extranjeros." *Historia* 8, no. 29 (1962), pp. 20–53.

Monteón, Michael. "The British in the Atacama Desert: The Cultural Bases of Economic Imperialism." *JEH* 25, no. 1 (March 1975), pp. 117–133.

Monthly Bulletin of the Bureau of American Republics. Washington, DC: International Union of American Republics, 1894–1904.

Nellar Fuad, Gabriel. "Aspectes salientes de la institución ejército durante la primera presidensia del General Roca." In *4o. CNRHA*, IV: 71–75.

Oberacker, Carlos H. Jr. "O Marechal de Campo Henrique von Braun: Chefe do primeiro estado maior do Exercito Brasilero." *JAL* 21 (1984), pp. 211–263.

Orsí, René. "1822: Disolución del ejército y marina nacionales." *EST* 3, no. 18 (septiembre/octubre 1972), pp. 112–119.

Panettieri, José. "La ley de conversión monetaria de 1899 en el marco de la formación de la Argentina moderna." *DE* 21, no. 82 (Julio-septiembre 1987), pp. 231–252.

Passarelli, Bruno. "La omisión Patagónica de la generación del ochenta." *EST* 3, no. 16 (Mayo-Junio 1972), pp. 109–115.

Percy, Alvin Matin. "Artigas, the Founder of Uruguayan Nationality." *HAHR* 19, 1 (February 1939); pp. 2–15.

Perry, Richard D. "Argentina and Chile: The Struggle for Patagonia, 1843–1881." *TAM* 26, no. 3 (January 1980), pp. 347–364.

Peterson, Harold F. "Mariano Moreno: The Making of an Insurgent." *HAHR* 14 (1934), pp. 450–476.

Pianetto, Ofelia. "Mercado de trabajo y acción sindical en la Argentina, 1890–1922." *DE* 24, no. 94 (julio-septiembre 1974), pp. 297–307.

Pope Atkins, George, and Larry V. Thompson. "German Military Influence in Argentina." *JLAS* 4, pt. 2 (November 1972), pp. 252–274.

Revista del Círculo Militar. 15, no. 177, pp. 633–642.

Rippy, Fred J. "Latin America and the British Investment boom of the 1820s." *Journal of Modern History* 19, no. 2 (June 1947), pp. 122–129.

———. "The British Investment Boom of the 1880s in Latin America." *HAHR* 30, no. 1 (February 1950), pp. 281–286.

Riquelme de Lobos, Norma, and Vera de Flachs, María C. "Cincuenta años de industria molinera en Córdoba: Su repercusión en la actividad nacional, 1860–1914." *IE*, no. 26 (enero-junio 1976).

Rodríguez Mola, Ricardo. "Aspectos econímicos y sociales de la Decada del 80." *Boletín de la Academia Nacional de la Historia* 28, no. 22 (1961), pp. 387–416.

Rothman, Ana María. "La fecundidad en la Argentina entre mediados del Siglo XIX y 1970." *DE* 12, no. 48 (enero-marzo 1973), pp. 829–848.

Ruíz Moreno, Isidoro. "Félix Frias y la defensa de los derechos argentios: Cuestión de límites con Chile." *Historia* 8, no. 29 (1962), pp. 54–73.

Sánchez Albornoz, Nicolás. "La saca de mulas de Salta al Perú: 1778–1808." In *America Colonial, población y económia* (Rosario: Universidad del Litoral, 1965), pp. 262–265.

Schiff, Warren. "The Influence of the German Armed Forces and War Industry on Argentina." *HAHR* 52, no. 3 (August 1972), pp. 436–455.

Segretti, Carlos A. "La repercusión en Mendoza de la política comercial porteña el la primera decada revolucionaria." *JAL* 19 (1982), pp. 183–222.

Serres Güiraldes, Alfredo. "Usurpación del Puerto de Santa Cruz." *IE* (enero-febrero 1977): pp. 393–400.

Smith, Geoffrey S. "The Role of José M. Balmaceda in Preserving Argentine Neutrality in the War of the Pacific." *HAHR* 49, no. 2 (May 1969), pp. 252–267.

Solberg, Carl. "A Discriminatory Frontier Land Policy: Chile, 1870–1914." *TAM* 26, no. 2 (October 1969), pp. 134–151.

———. "Farm Workers and the Myth of the Export-led Development of Argentina." *TAM* 31, no. 2 (October 1974), pp. 121–138.

Stabili, María R. "Las políticas inmigratorias de los gobiernos chilenos desde la segunda mitad del siglo pasado hasta la decada de 1920." *Estudios Migratorios Latinoamericanos* 1, no. 2 (abril 1986), pp. 181–202.

Sternberg, Rolf. "Occupance of the Humid Pampa, 1856–1914." *Revista Geográfica* 76 (junio 1976), pp. 61–102.

Stone, Irving. "British Direct and Portfolio Investment in Latin America." *JEH* 37, no. 3 (September 1977), pp. 690–722.

Vidaurreta, Alicia. "Los Farrapos y el Río de la Plata." *JAL* 24 (1987), pp. 417–454.

Vicuña Mackena, Carlos. "El territorio de Chile: El 'Utis Possidetis' de 1810." *RCHG* 14, no. 18 (1915), pp. 148–158.

Von Rauch, Georg. "Ejército Argentino." *Armies and Weapons* 7 (1973), pp. 39–42.

———. "Cruisers for Argentina." *Warship International* 15, no. 4 (1978), pp. 296–317.

Wright, Thomas C. "Agriculture and Protectionism in Chile." *Journal of Latin American Studies* 7, part 1, (May 1975), pp. 45–58.

———. "Origins and Politics of Inflation in Chile, 1880–1918." *HAHR* 53, no. 2 (May 1973), pp. 239–259.

Zamudio, José. "Isidoro Errázuriz, Ministro en Brasil, 1897–1898." *RCHG*, no. 113 (enero-junio 1949), pp. 5–40.

Index

About the Author

GEORGE v. RAUCH is an editor and correspondent for various magazines, including *Avions*, *Jets*, and *Soldiers and Raids*. Dr. Rauch has been an officer in the U.S. military.

ISBN 0-275-96347-0

HARDCOVER BAR CODE